D1130907

Morningstar®
Complete Investor

Morningstar®
Complete Investor

Practical, authoritative,
and proven strategies
for building wealth and
winning in the market

Christine Benz
Pat Dorsey

WILEY
John Wiley & Sons, Inc.

Contents

Morningstar®
Complete Investor

Introduction

WE ARE FIVE YEARS into the new millennium—and you couldn't blame most investors for wanting to go back to the old one.

First, many stocks and mutual funds that had been riding high during the glory days of the late 1990s' stock market rally came crashing down with the brutal collapse of the technology-stock boom. But as the bear market broadened beyond the tech sector, investors endured the worst market downturn since the Great Depression, and few portfolios escaped unscathed.

Around the same time, many individual investors began to question whether the playing field was hopelessly tilted toward the biggest players. Although it had long been an open secret that the brokerage divisions of big financial conglomerates often touted the stocks of their investment-banking clients, the practice reached a fever pitch during the late 1990s. As scores of dotcoms with worthless business models came public, brokerage firms did their part to peddle the merchandise, helping vaporize billion of dollars of shareholder capital almost overnight. (Unfortunately, many investors were all-too-willing accomplices.) At the same time, the well-publicized blowups of

Worldcom and Enron amply illustrated the ease with which publicly traded corporations—even giant ones—could fudge their financial statements.

Meanwhile, a scandal was unfolding in the mutual fund world, once thought to be a squeaky-clean pocket of the investment landscape. In late 2003, New York Attorney General Eliot Spitzer accused a host of large mutual fund companies of allowing favored clients—often hedge funds geared toward the well-heeled—to make improper trades at the expense of small mutual fund investors. Before it was all over, a number of top fund executives and portfolio managers were implicated in the wrongdoing.

Thus, as we set out to produce this book in early 2005, we realized that a new and important question had emerged: Can small investors possibly get a fair shake in the market?

At Morningstar, we believe the answer to that question is a resounding "yes." Although the events of the past five years have been harrowing, they prompted a host of reforms that have helped make the investment playing field cleaner and better-lit than ever before.

Regulation Fair Disclosure, enacted in 2000, requires that publicly traded companies share material information with all interested parties. And owing to a series of costly settlements with New York Attorney General Spitzer, investment conglomerates now have a powerful motivation to keep their brokerage units distinct from their investment-banking arms, greatly reducing what had been a blatant conflict of interest.

Perhaps even more significantly, the misdeeds that brought down Enron and Worldcom resulted in the passage of the Sarbanes-Oxley Act of 2002, which requires public companies to annually assess their internal financial controls. Although "Sarbox" has elicited groans among corporate managers due to the cost of implementation, we think there's little question that it has made financial statements about as trustworthy as they've ever been.

The mutual fund industry, for its part, has also adopted some notable reforms. In an effort to eliminate the improper trading that set the fund scandal into motion, fund firms are now required to hire chief compliance officers. Meanwhile, a ban of so-called "directed brokerage" arrangements, whereby fund shops steer trades to certain brokerage firms in exchange for having the broker peddle their funds, should serve to lower fund investors' overall costs and help ensure that brokers select the right funds for their clients' needs. Finally, a new requirement that funds disclose how they're compensating portfolio managers and whether the portfolio manager "eats his own cooking" by investing in the fund should help investors identify funds whose managers' interests are aligned with their own.

At Morningstar, we've been in the business of leveling the playing field for individual investors for more than 20 years, and the impetus behind this book was to extend our research to the broadest possible audience.

The first part of this book introduces readers to Morningstar's approach to analyzing mutual funds and building fund portfolios, a field in which our firm has emerged as the undisputed leader. You'll find that our approach to fund investing, as with our stock research, relies entirely on fundamental analysis: knowing a fund's strategy, getting familiar with the manager and evaluating the quality his or her firm, and, perhaps most importantly, identifying your own goals and what you're trying to achieve. We also address other fund-related questions you might have, such as: What do you do if the fund manager leaves? Should you buy index funds? What role should bond and international funds play? What about exchange-traded funds? And much more.

The second part of this book focuses on Morningstar's stock-investing philosophy, which centers on thinking like the part owner of a business. Not only do we show you how to identify great companies—truly profitable firms with strong management teams and competitive advantages that should serve them well in the years ahead—but we also help you determine the correct price to pay for those great businesses. If you can build a portfolio of wonderful companies purchased at fair prices, you'll do well in the market.

We hope that the following pages makes the knowledge we've built up over these years available to you in a detailed yet easily accessible form, and serve as a guide to help you to navigate the thorny financial landscape over the years ahead.

PART ONE

Mutual Funds

I

Know What Your Fund Owns

MOST OF US wouldn't buy a new home just because it looked good from the outside. We would do a thorough walk-through first. We'd examine the furnace, check for a leaky roof, and look for cracks in the foundation.

Mutual fund investing requires the same careful investigation. You need to give a fund more than a surface-level once-over before investing in it. Knowing that the fund has been a good performer in the past isn't enough to warrant risking your money. You need to understand what's inside its portfolio—or how it invests. You must find out what a fund owns to know if it's right for you.

The stocks and bonds in a fund's portfolio are so important that Morningstar analysts spend a lot of their time on the subject; news about what high-profile fund managers are buying is a constant source of e-mail chatter in the office. Our analysts examine fund portfolios of stocks or bonds, talk with the managers about their strategies in picking those holdings, and check on recent changes to the portfolio. Knowing what a fund owns helps you understand its past behavior, set realistic expectations for what it might do in the future, and figure out how it will work with the other investments you might own.

At the most basic level, a fund can own stocks, bonds, cash (usually money market securities), or a combination of the three. (Funds might also own other securities, including other funds and stock/bond hybrid securities, but let's stick with the basics for now.) If it invests in stocks, it could focus on U.S. companies or venture abroad. If the fund owns U.S. companies, it might invest in giants such as General Electric or Microsoft or seek out tiny companies that most of us have never heard of. If a fund invests in bonds, it could focus only on those issued by companies with rock-solid finances and a high probability that they'll make good on their debts or it could venture into higher-yielding bonds issued by firms with shaky future prospects. How a manager chooses to invest your money has a big impact on performance. For example, if your manager devotes much of the portfolio to a single volatile area such as technology stocks, your fund may generate high returns at times, but there's also a greater likelihood that you'll lose money at other times. Stocks have historically generated higher returns than cash or bonds. Because you take the least risk when you invest in cash, those securities also tend to generate lower returns than you'd get with stocks or bonds.

A fund's name doesn't always reveal what a fund owns because funds often have generic handles. Take the intriguingly named Janus Olympus and American Century Veedot funds. If you were to skim over only their names, you would be hard-pressed to glean that the former focuses on mid- and large-sized companies that are growing quickly (think Yahoo! and eBay), whereas the latter is a fund that uses computer models to help direct investments to whatever type of stocks look like they could be strong performers in the future.

Nor will a fund's prospectus—a legal document filed with the Securities and Exchange Commission (SEC) that lays out the basics of an investment— necessarily be of much help in determining what a given fund is up to. While fund prospectuses do include information about who's running a fund and its basic investment parameters, prospectuses are typically written in very broad terms to give managers the latitude to invest as they see fit.

In their prospectuses, funds are also required to state their objectives—a one- or two-word description of their basic goals, such as "Growth," "Equity-Income," "Growth & Income," and so on. You'd think these so-called prospectus objectives might help you sort out who's doing what, but in reality funds with the same prospectus objectives can be pursuing radically different investment approaches and end up with very different returns. For example, both Aegis Value Fund and AllianceBernstein Large Cap Growth have prospectus objectives of "Growth." But the former focuses on tiny, budget-priced stocks, whereas the Alliance fund focuses on fast-growing stocks of large companies. When the bear market struck between 2000 and 2002, the Aegis fund returned 18% annually, whereas the Alliance fund lost 26% over that stretch.

Understanding The Morningstar® Style Box™

A desire to help investors choose funds based on what they really own—instead of on what funds call themselves, how they classify themselves, or how they've performed recently—was precisely what inspired Morningstar to develop its investment style box in the early 1990s. The style box provides a quick visual summary of a given fund's portfolio, showing you, using a nine-box investment-style grid, where most of your fund's portfolio is invested. (To check out a fund's current style box, go to Morningstar's Web site, www.morningstar.com, and type in a fund's name or ticker.) While investors needn't own a fund from each and every square of the style box, the tool can help you know whether your portfolio is diversified. If all of your funds are huddled in a single corner of the style box, that's a tip-off that you'll probably want to spread your bets around more. The style box also helps investors keep track of whether a fund has changed its approach, because we update each fund's style-box placement every time we receive a new portfolio. If a fund that you bought to bring your portfolio exposure to the fast-moving technology and telecom industries is suddenly delving into the securities of small manufacturing firms, you'll see that change reflected in your fund's style-box placement.

For stock funds, the style box isolates two key factors that drive its performance: the size of the stocks the fund invests in and the type of companies it buys—rapidly growing companies for which investors are willing to pay a pretty penny, slower growers that trade at lower prices, or a combination of the two (see Figure 1.1). Those two factors—company size and investment style—form the two axes of the stock, or equity, style box. For bond funds, the style box focuses on the two key determinants of bond-fund behavior: a fund's sensitivity to changes in interest rates and the credit quality of the bonds in which it invests. Those two factors form the axes of the bond-fund

Level of Risk		Investment Style			Average Market Capitalization
		Value	*Blend*	*Growth*	
Low	○	Large-Cap Value	Large-Cap Blend	Large-Cap Growth	Large
Moderate	○	Mid-Cap Value	Mid-Cap Blend	Mid-Cap Growth	Medium
High	●	Small-Cap Value	Small-Cap Blend	Small-Cap Growth	Small

Figure 1.1   The Morningstar stock style box is a nine-square grid that provides a quick and clear picture of a stock fund's investment style.

style box (see Figure 1.2). Once we have determined the size and investment-style coordinates for a stock fund and the interest-rate sensitivity and credit-quality coordinates for a bond fund, we can use our nine-square style box grid to show investors—visually—where their fund lands.

Using the Stock-Fund Style Box

To figure out which square of our stock style box a fund portfolio lands in, we first analyze each and every stock in that portfolio. We begin by grouping each stock in a portfolio into one of seven regions: the United States, Latin America, Canada, Europe, Japan, Asia ex-Japan, and Australia/New Zealand.

Once we've placed a stock within one of our regional zones, we then go on to evaluate how it stacks up relative to other firms within that same zone. We start that process by determining whether a security is small, medium, or large within its region. In investing parlance, stock size is often called market capitalization, or market cap. Market cap sounds like a technical term, but it's not particularly hard to understand—essentially, it's the current dollar value of all of a given company's stock shares. So if a stock is selling for $30 and there are

Level of Risk		Duration			Credit Quality
---	---	Short	Intermediate	Long	---
Low	◯	High Short	High Interm.	High Long	High
Moderate	◯	Med Short	Med. Interm.	Med Long	Medium
High	⬤	Low Short	Low Interm.	Low Long	Low

Figure 1.2   The Morningstar bond style box is a nine-square grid that provides a quick and clear picture of a bond fund's investment style.

a million shares of it floating around in the market, the company has a mar-ket cap of $30 million. We consider companies whose market caps land within the largest 70% of their region to be large cap; the next 20% are midcap; and the smallest 10% are small caps. Although small-cap stocks only account for 10% of each region's market, there are actually many more of them than there are large-cap companies.

Having determined a security's regional and size classification, we turn our attention to its investment style. Investing aficionados typically group stocks into one of two major buckets—growth stocks or value stocks—and often identify themselves as growth investors or value investors. Understanding the difference between the two styles is critical to understanding what makes a fund tick.

Growth stocks typically enjoy strong growth in earnings or revenues be-cause they've got a hot new product or service. Because the market expects good things from these fast growers, and earnings growth usually drives a higher share price, investors are willing to pay more for the shares than they will pay for slower growers.

Value stocks, conversely, look like growth stocks' less successful cousins. These companies' earnings are usually growing slowly, if at all, and they often operate in industries that are prone to boom-and-bust cycles. So why does anyone bother with these underachievers? The answer is, because they're cheap. Fund managers who focus on value stocks are willing to put up with lackluster earnings growth because they think the market is being overly pessimistic about the company's future. Should things turn out better than the market thinks, the bargain-hunting fund stands to profit.

Some companies display a mixture of both growth and value characteristics—we call these *core stocks*. Many pharmaceuticals stocks currently fit the core designation. Historically, these firms have been terrific growers, as new drug launches and stepped-up demand from aging baby boomers have driven high profits and, in turn, high stock prices. But lately, problems with a few high-profile drugs as well as chatter about lackluster new products and drug-price controls have depressed the prices for drug stocks.

To help classify a stock as growth, value, or core, we look at 10 separate factors, including dividend yields, price/earnings ratios (a company's current share price divided by its earnings), and historical and projected earnings growth.

Once we have classified each stock's investment style, we then classify the entire portfolio, based on which square of our style box most of its stocks land in. Securities that the manager has weighted the most heavily will play a bigger role in determining a fund's investment style than will smaller positions. For example, a stock that takes up 10% of a portfolio will be a much bigger determinant of a fund's style-box positioning than will a stock that takes up 2%.

Funds that devote most of their assets to stocks with strong growth characteristics will land in the growth column of our style box, while those with a higher concentration of value stocks will land in our value column. Funds that hold both growth and value stocks, or those that focus mainly on so-called core stocks, will land in the blend column of our style box.

Using the Bond-Fund Style Box

The bond-fund style box, like the stock style box, is also a nine-square grid. Whereas the stock style box has a growth/value axis and a small/large axis, however, the two axes of the bond style box are interest-rate sensitivity (or duration, which we define in the following discussion) and credit quality. Unlike the equity style box, we arrive at a bond portfolio's style box not by drilling into each and every security, but instead by measuring the average weighted characteristics of the portfolio. (Average weighted means that our calculation gives greater weight to a portfolio's big positions than its small ones.)

Knowing a bond fund's interest-rate sensitivity helps you determine how much it will react when interest rates go up or down. When interest rates go up, that typically depresses the price of already-existing bonds, particularly those with longer maturities, because investors would rather buy a newer bond with a higher interest payment, or yield, than get locked into a long-term bond that happens to have a lower yield. The reverse happens when interest rates go down. Investors would rather buy an existing bond with a higher yield than they would opt for a new, lower-yielding bond. That demand drives up the price of existing bonds.

To help measure a bond fund's interest-rate sensitivity, we rely on a figure called *duration*. Duration is a pretty knotty concept; it's defined as the average time it takes a bondholder to receive the interest and the principal payments from a bond. Because it's a measure of time, duration is expressed in years. As a general rule of thumb, every one-percentage-point change in interest rates will cause a fund to gain or lose the amount of its duration. For example, a bond fund with a duration of 8 years is apt to lose 8% of its value if interest rates go up by one percentage point. For the purpose of our fixed-income style box, we classify bond funds with average durations of less than 3.5 years as short term, those with durations between 3.5 and 6 years as intermediate term, and those with durations of 6 years or more as long term. (We use a slightly different framework for classifying municipal-bond funds' interest-rate sensitivity. Municipal bond funds with durations of less than 4.5 years are short; those with durations between 4.5 and 7 years are intermediate term; and those with durations of 7 years or more are long.)

A bond portfolio's average duration helps us plot a fund on the horizontal axis of the style box. To determine its placement on the vertical axis, we examine the average credit quality of the bonds in the portfolio. Third parties such as Moody's and Standard & Poor's assign credit qualities to bonds. By looking at a bond's credit quality, you can get a sense of how likely it is that a bond's issuer will be able to continue making its interest payments to bondholders—an important consideration if you're looking for regular income, as many bond investors are. Morningstar considers bond funds with average credit qualities of AAA or AA to be high quality, those with credit qualities that are lower than AA but greater than or equal to BBB to be of medium quality, and those with average credit qualities below BBB to be low quality.

Armed with both a portfolio's interest-rate sensitivity and its average credit quality, we can plot that fund in our style box.

Using Morningstar's Category System

Despite the usefulness of the Morningstar style box, it's just a snapshot of the fund's most recent portfolio. When you are selecting a fund to play a particular role, such as adding a high-quality bond fund because you want stability and regular income, you want to be confident that it actually has played that role over time. That's what we have in mind when we plug funds into Morningstar categories. We assign funds to categories based on the past three years' worth of style boxes. (Fund firms are required to provide shareholders with a list of their funds' portfolio holdings every quarter, but some fund shops make their portfolios available even more frequently than that.) A single portfolio could reflect a temporary aberration—maybe the fund's holdings have been doing really well, so they have grown from small- to mid-cap as stock prices have gone up. But because a fund's category assignment is based on three years' worth of portfolios, it gives you a better handle on how the fund typically invests.

You'll see that our category system for U.S. and foreign-stock funds is closely related to our style box. On the U.S. stock side, we have categories corresponding with each of the nine squares of the style box, ranging from large value in the upper left corner to small growth in the lower right corner. Similarly, we have five style-based categories for diversified foreign-stock funds (i.e., those that don't focus on a single region), ranging from foreign large-value to foreign small/mid-growth. (Because there aren't quite as many foreign-stock funds in the U.S. as there are domestically focused funds, we don't have separate foreign-stock categories corresponding with all nine squares of the style box.) We also carve out some categories for specialized stock funds. To name a few, there are categories for health-care offerings, Japan funds, and energy funds. Morningstar slots funds into about 50 categories (see Figure 1.3).

Diversified Domestic Stock	Large Value	Mid-Cap Growth
	Large Blend	Small Value
	Large Growth	Small Blend
	Mid-Cap Value	Small Growth
	Mid-Cap Blend	
International Stock	Europe Stock	Foreign Large Blend
	Latin America Stock	Foreign Large Growth
	Diversified Emerging Markets	Foreign Large Value
	Diversified Pacific Stock	Foreign Small/Mid Growth
	Pacific Stock ex-Japan	Foreign Small/Mid Value
	Japan Stock	World Stock
Specialty Stock	Communications	Precious Metals
	Financial	Real Estate
	Health	Technology
	Natural Resources	Utilities
Hybrid	Conservative Allocation	Bear Market
	Moderate Allocation	Convertibles
Specialty Bond	High-Yield Bond	Emerging Markets Bond
	Multisector Bond	Bank Loan
	International Bond	
General Bond	Long-Term Bond	Short-Term Bond
	Intermediate-Term Bond	Ultrashort Bond
Government Bond	Long-Term Government	Short-Term Government
	Intermediate-Term Gov't.	
Municipal Bond	Muni National Long	Muni CA Intermediate/Short
	Muni National Intermediate	Muni NY Long
	Muni National Short	Muni NY Intermediate/Short
	Muni High-Yield	Muni Florida
	Muni Single-State Long	Muni Massachusetts
	Muni Single-State Intermediate	Muni Minnesota
		Muni New Jersey
	Muni Single-State Short	Muni Ohio
	Muni CA Long	Muni Pennsylvania

Figure 1.3   Morningstar's fund-category system.

On the bond side, our categories also relate back to the style-box system. For example, the high-yield bond category—home to so-called junk-bond funds—captures most of the funds that land in the low-credit-quality row of the style box. Meanwhile, our long-term government category includes all of the funds that buy U.S. Treasury and agency bonds with long durations.

As with the style box, Morningstar categories pick up where fund names and prospectus objectives leave off. They help you figure out how a fund actually invests, which in turn lets you know how to use it in your portfolio. If you're looking for a good core stock fund, you might begin your search within the large-blend category. Funds that land there usually invest in the biggest, best-established U.S. companies and buy stocks with a mix of growth and value characteristics. Thus, large-blend funds tend to be a decent bet in varied market and economic conditions. Although they may not lead the pack too often, neither are they apt to be left completely behind. (We discuss this subject in detail in Part Two.)

By targeting funds in different categories, you are much more likely to pull together a diversified portfolio than if you rely on funds' prospectus objectives to show you the way. An investor focusing exclusively on prospectus objectives might think he or she had a diversified mix in a portfolio that consisted of Dreyfus Premier Value (with a prospectus objective of growth), American Funds Investment Company of America (growth and income), and USAA Income Stock (equity-income). Diversified? Not so fast. According to their Morningstar categories, which take their underlying holdings into account, all three funds are actually large-cap value offerings.

As you might expect, different-style funds tend to behave differently in various market and economic environments, which is why the style-box and category system can be so handy. Knowing a fund's category can give you some indication of how it might perform in good markets and in bad. As a rule of thumb, the large-cap value group is considered the safest category because large-cap companies typically are more stable than small ones (the high-profile blowups of giants like Worldcom and Enron notwithstanding). And in down markets, when investors are concerned that stock prices could be too high across the board, large-value funds' budget-priced stocks don't have very far to fall.

Funds that land in the small-growth category, however, are usually the riskiest. The success of a single product or service can make or break a small company, and because small-growth stocks often trade at lofty prices, they can take a disastrous tumble if one of the company's products or services fails to take off as the market expects. These funds can deliver glittering riches in up markets, though: In 2004, the average small-growth fund returned 45%. (For more on the correlation between investment style and risk, see Chapter 3.)

Examining Sector Weightings

Checking a fund's style-box and category placement can go a long way toward helping you know what a fund is all about, but it may not tell the whole story. Not all funds that land in the same style box or even the same category will behave the same way. For example, both Marsico Growth and Fidelity OTC are popular funds that land in the large-cap growth category. Yet they have tended to own very different kinds of large-growth stocks. In the late 1990s, the Fidelity fund often dedicated more than half of its assets to technology-related stocks—as much as 75% at one point. Marsico Growth also staked a sizable amount in tech, but its position topped out at 40% of the portfolio.

What a difference those two approaches made! A heavy weighting in the tech sector was a boon in 1999, when investors adored technology stocks. Fidelity OTC soared an amazing 73% that year, whereas Marsico Growth gained 53%. A 53% gain is an impressive return in its own right, but if you had put $10,000 in each fund at the start of the year, your Fidelity OTC investment would have been worth $2,000 more than Marsico Growth at the end of 1999. But anything that produces such strong returns can also prove an Achilles' heel, and that's exactly what happened to Fidelity OTC. When tech collapsed in 2000, the Fidelity fund lost 26%, whereas Marsico Growth lost 16%. The moral of the story isn't that a technology-heavy fund like Fidelity OTC is automatically a bad idea, but that if your fund is inclined to make big bets on certain sectors, there's also a greater likelihood that your fund will suffer losses.

Morningstar calculates a fund's sector exposure based on the percentage of its portfolio that is committed to stocks in each of 12 industry groupings. We also cluster those 12 sectors into one of three supersectors: information, services, and manufacturing (see Figure 1.4). We developed the broader classification system because the sectors within our supersector groupings tend to behave in a similar way in various stock market environments. In the recent market downturn of 2000 through 2002, for example, every sector in our

☁ Information Economy	⊡ Service Economy	⊞ Manufacturing Economy
▚ Software	▨ Health Care	▬ Consumer Goods
▦ Hardware	▭ Consumer Services	✺ Industrial Materials
▤ Telecommunications	▤ Business Services	◔ Energy
◉ Media	$ Financial Services	♀ Utilities

Figure 1.4 Morningstar's sector breakdown. Twelve sectors are divided into three supersectors representing broader parts of the economy.

information supersector—hardware, software, telecommunications, and media —incurred terrible losses. If all the funds in your portfolio heavily concentrate their holdings in a certain supersector, it can be a strong indication that your portfolio needs exposure to other parts of the economy. Similarly, if you have a job in a technology-related field, you will want your portfolio to have plenty of exposure outside the information supersector because much of your economic well-being (through your job) is already tied to that area.

Examining Number of Holdings

To understand what a particular fund is up to, knowing the number of stocks it owns can be just as important as any of the other factors we have discussed. Whether your fund holds 20 stocks or hundreds of them will make a big difference in its behavior. (Because Securities and Exchange Commission regulations limit the percentage of its assets that a fund can commit to a single holding, fund portfolios rarely have fewer than 20 stocks.) For example, both Fidelity Contrafund and Janus Twenty land in our large-cap growth category. But the Janus fund, which typically holds fewer than 30 stocks, is likely to see a lot more gyrations in its performance—for better and for worse—than the Fidelity fund, which spreads its money across more than 500 stocks. If Janus Twenty's top holding, at 15% of assets, has a bad week or a bad year, the whole fund's performance is also apt to be poor. Meanwhile, trouble in Fidelity Contrafund's top stock, at 2.6% of assets, won't have as big an impact on the fund's total return.

The number of holdings in bond funds tends to have less of an impact on how they behave. All else being equal, however, a bond fund with more holdings is likely to be less volatile than one that is more concentrated in bonds from a smaller number of issuers. A bond fund is apt to be particularly risky if it both delves into lower-quality bonds and concentrates in a short list of holdings. That stands to reason, because the fund's fortunes are dependent on a small group of risky securities.

Checking Up on Trading Behavior

In addition to checking style boxes, categories, sectors, and number of holdings (phew!), a fund's turnover rate is another important factor when you're judging a fund's style. Turnover rates, which funds are required to include in their reports to shareholders, measure how much the portfolio has changed during the past year and shows approximately how long a manager typically holds a stock. For example, a fund with a turnover rate of 100% has a typical holding period of one year; a fund with 25% turnover holds a stock for four years on average.

Turnover is a pretty simple calculation: To figure it out, fund accountants just divide a fund's total investment sales or purchases (whichever is less) by its average monthly assets for the year.

A fund's turnover rate can give you important insights into a manager's style. It can tell you whether a manager tends to buy and hold, picking stocks and sticking with them for the long haul instead of frequently trading in and out of them. To give you a basis for comparison, stock funds on average have turnover rates of about 100%. We consider a fund's turnover rate to be notably modest when it's 25% or lower.

Eyeballing a fund's turnover can provide insights into a fund's risk level. Managers who keep turnover low often practice low-risk strategies, whereas high-turnover funds can be aggressive and much riskier. That gets back to investment style: As a rule of thumb, the more value-conscious your manager is, the more patient he or she will tend to be with the holdings in the portfolio. Meanwhile, growth-oriented fund managers often employ high-turnover strategies.

In addition to potentially jacking up a fund's risk level, high turnover can also spell tax consequences for investors. A manager who sells a stock at a profit incurs a taxable gain, and funds are required to distribute any capital gains to their shareholders (provided the manager can't offset that gain by realizing a loss from another holding in the portfolio). If you own the fund in a taxable account instead of a tax-sheltered vehicle like a 401(k) or Individual Retirement Account, you'll have to pay taxes on that capital-gain distribution. If the fund has a high turnover rate, the tax consequences could cut into returns you would otherwise pocket.

As if that weren't enough, high-turnover funds can incur higher trading costs than low-turnover offerings. When we say *trading costs* we're not just referring to the dollars that the fund pays its brokers to execute the trade (though those charges can cut into your returns, too). Rather, we're also referring to the fact that big funds can "move the market" when buying and selling their shares. Say a big fund like Fidelity Contrafund wants to get out of one of its largest positions in a hurry. Because Contrafund is flooding the market with shares, it may have to accept lower and lower prices for those shares as it unloads its position. The more the fund engages in such trading, the less attractive its average purchase and sale prices will be, and the less its shareholders will profit. (We probably shouldn't pick on Contrafund in particular—it has been a strong performer, despite its huge asset base and high-turnover approach. But in general, a fund that combines a high-turnover strategy with a big asset base is fighting an uphill battle.)

For all these reasons, we think you greatly improve your portfolio's odds of good long-term performance if you put the bulk of your assets in low-turnover funds. Figure 1.5 provides a list of some of our favorites. When shop-

Fund Name	Category	Turnover %
Selected American	Large Blend	3
Legg Mason Value	Large Blend	4
Tweedy, Browne Global Value	Foreign Small/Mid Value	8
Harbor International	Foreign Large Value	12
Oakmark Select	Large Blend	14
Clipper	Large Value	16
FPA Paramount	Small Value	16
Ariel Appreciation	Mid Blend	19
Fairholme	Mid Blend	23
American Funds EuroPacific Growth	Foreign Large Blend	25

Figure 1.5   Ten great low-turnover funds.

ping for stock funds, look for those funds whose turnover rates are lower than 50%, preferably much lower.

Generally speaking, turnover is a more significant factor for stock funds than it is for bond funds. In part that's because many bond funds employ short-term trading strategies that jack up their turnover rates but don't meaningfully affect their risk levels, tax efficiency, or trading costs.

Investor's Checklist: Know What Your Funds Own

▶ Use a fund's Morningstar style box as a visual guide to learn what the fund owns and how it's apt to behave in the future.

▶ When assembling a diversified portfolio, look for funds that land in a variety of Morningstar categories.

▶ Look in Morningstar's large-blend category for core funds that are unlikely to go too far out on a limb.

▶ Bond funds with limited interest-rate sensitivity and high credit quality are less risky than those that venture into longer-duration and/or lower-quality bonds.

▶ Check a fund's sector weightings relative to its category peers to see if the fund is betting heavily on a given area of the market.

▶ Funds that concentrate heavily in their top positions can generate big gains when their top picks pay off, but also stand to lose more if they don't.

▶ Put the bulk of your portfolio in low-turnover funds, which are generally less risky, more tax-efficient, and have lower trading costs.

2

Put Performance in Perspective

Now we can move on to the question most investors start with: How much money has the fund made? It's no wonder that this is the first thing people think about. People invest in hopes of making money, and returns tell you what the fund made in the past. Historical returns sell funds—that's why mutual fund ads in financial magazines or newspapers often feature big mountain charts showing the funds' returns.

Yet as hard as it might be to believe, a fund's past returns are not particularly predictive of its future returns. (The best predictor of good returns? Low costs. We talk more about the importance of low expenses in Chapter 5.) Nonetheless, a fund's past history can offer some clues about whether it's worth owning. In this chapter, we discuss where a fund's return numbers come from, and how to check whether a fund's return is satisfactory.

Understanding Total Return

To make sense of the return numbers in advertisements, fund-company literature, the newspaper, and on Morningstar.com, the first thing you should know is that these figures are based on a few notable conventions. For starters, the numbers are known as total returns because they reflect two things: market gains (or losses) in the stocks or bonds the fund owns—usually called the fund's capital return—and income received from those investments. Income comes from the dividends paid by stocks and the interest paid by bonds the fund owns. Together, those capital returns and income returns make up total returns. For example, Vanguard Wellington, a popular fund that splits its assets between stocks and bonds, earned an 11.17% total return in 2004. That was based on an 8.10% capital return (the amount the fund's stock and bond holdings gained in value during the year) plus a 3.07% income return (the total of the dividends the fund received from its stocks plus the coupon payments from its bonds for the year).

The total-return number is calculated on the assumption that shareholders reinvest any distributions that the fund makes. Mutual funds are required by law to distribute, or pay out, almost all income they receive (from dividend-paying stocks or interest-paying bonds) to their shareholders. They also must distribute any gains they realize by selling stocks or bonds at a profit. If you choose to reinvest those income and capital-gain distributions, and most investors do, you won't receive a check in the mail for those distributions but instead your money will go toward buying more fund shares. If you decide to take the money and run, your fund returns may be lower than those of someone who reinvested and got more shares.

Here's another important convention related to funds' total-return figures: Total-return numbers for periods longer than one year are typically represented as annualized, rather than cumulative, returns. (Morningstar shows investors each fund's annualized returns over the past 3, 5, and 10 years.) What's the difference? A fund's cumulative return is the total amount it has made—in percentage terms—over a given time frame. For example, if you put $10,000 into a fund that went on to return a cumulative 100% over the next three years, you'd have $20,000 at the end of that three-year period. An annualized return, meanwhile, is something like an average return over a given time period, except that it takes compounding into account. For example, an annualized return recognizes that if you made gains in the first year you owned a fund, you had more to invest at the beginning of the second year. In early 2005, Oakmark Select had a three-year annualized return of 8.19%. The fund never actually earned that exact amount in 2002, 2003, or 2004; instead, it lost 12.5% in 2002, gained 29% in 2003, and returned 9.7% in

2004. But if you had bought the fund in early 2002 and hung on for the next three years, your per-year earnings—otherwise known as your annualized return—would work out to be 8.19%.

Putting Returns in Perspective

The tricky thing about returns is that they're hard to evaluate in a vacuum. Here's an example: Say you own a fund that has gained an average of 10% per year for the past three years. You're feeling pretty good about your achievement—that is, until you chat with a coworker who claims to have a fund that has gained 13% per year.

Try not to be too hard on yourself, though. You may be much better at selecting funds than those numbers might suggest. Without context—unless you know what types of fund you and your coworker have—the numbers are meaningless. You may own a large-cap value fund that has been trouncing its peers. Meanwhile, your coworker owns a fund in the red-hot small-value category. His returns may look high, but his fund may actually be lagging far behind its small-value competitors.

To know how well a fund is doing, you need to make relevant comparisons. Use an appropriate yardstick such as a stock or bond index or a group of funds investing in the same kind of securities—the Morningstar categories that you read about in Chapter 1.

Using Indexes as Benchmarks

An index is the most common kind of yardstick—or benchmark—for judging fund performance. When you read a fund's shareholder report, you will always see the fund compared with an index, sometimes more than one. An index is simply a basket of securities, either stocks or bonds.

Ask someone to name a stock market index and odds are good that the answer will be the Dow Jones Industrial Average. You can't escape the Dow—it's the index that usually heads the stock report on the evening news. Although the Dow is familiar, it isn't a great performance benchmark for your mutual funds because it is extremely narrow; it includes just 30 large-company stocks. Most stock funds include many more holdings and do not focus solely on the market's largest companies.

Instead, the index you'll hear about most often in investing circles is the Standard & Poor's 500 index, which includes 500 major U.S. companies. Because Standard and Poor's chooses the stocks in the index to cover a range of industries, the S&P 500 has greater breadth than the Dow. Thus, it's a reasonable yardstick for many funds that focus on big, name-brand U.S. stocks.

Yet despite widespread use, the S&P 500 isn't a good benchmark for every U.S. stock fund. Although it encompasses 500 stocks, it's designed so that the companies with the biggest market capitalizations (the total value of their outstanding shares), such as Microsoft and General Electric, take up the greatest percentage of the index. As a result, such names tend to influence the index's performance. On days when these giants do well, so does the S&P 500.

That's why you wouldn't want to compare a fund that focuses mostly on small companies, such as Third Avenue Small-Cap Value, against the S&P 500 index alone. Small-company stocks make up a very small portion of the S&P 500, so it would be surprising if a small-cap fund performed much like the index at all. In 2004, Third Avenue Small-Cap Value gained 21%, while the S&P 500 gained just half that; in 1998 the fund actually lost money, while the index was up 29%. Those disparate returns reflect that small and large stocks often go their separate ways. In the late 1990s, large caps scored tremendous gains and small caps made relatively modest ones; then in the early 2000s, large caps ran into a brick wall and small caps came into their own.

Likewise, it makes little sense to compare a foreign-stock fund like Janus Overseas with the S&P 500. That fund owns only a smattering of U.S. stocks, focusing instead on foreign issues. And there's even less reason to judge a bond fund against the S&P 500, which includes only stocks.

So what indexes should you use to make appropriate comparisons? The S&P 500 may be the most widely used benchmark for large-cap stock funds, but the Russell 2000 Index, which is dedicated to small-capitalization stocks, is commonly used to evaluate small cap funds' performance. The Morgan Stanley Capital International Europe, Australasia, Far East Index (often called the MSCI EAFE), which follows international stocks, is the most common benchmark for judging foreign funds' performance. Taxable bond funds, meanwhile, typically gauge their performance alongside that of the Lehman Brothers Aggregate Bond Index. Dozens of other indexes segment the stock and bond markets even more. For example, they may focus on inexpensive large-company stocks or fast-moving small companies, regions of the world such as Europe or the Pacific Rim, or technology stocks. Figure 2.1 provides a summary of major indexes and what they track.

Morningstar also has its own line of indexes, which correspond with its U.S. stock style boxes. In addition to a broad market index, the Morningstar U.S. Market Index, we offer indexes for each of the nine squares of the style box (e.g., the Morningstar Mid-Cap Value Index), the three investment-style columns (e.g., the Morningstar U.S. Value Index), and the three capitalization rows (e.g., the Morningstar Large-Cap Index). You can see the performance of these indexes as well as their components by going to the home page on Morningstar.com.

Dow Jones Industrial Average	Computed by summing the prices of the stocks of 30 companies and then dividing that total by a value that has been adjusted over the years to account for the effects of stock splits on the prices of the 30 companies.
Standard & Poor's 500	A market capitalization–weighted index of 500 widely held stocks often used as a proxy for the stock market. Standard & Poor's chooses the member companies for the 500 based on market size, liquidity, and industry group representation.
Russell 2000	A commonly cited small-cap index that tracks the returns of the smallest 2,000 companies in the Russell 3000 Index.
Lehman Brothers Aggregate	A broad bond-market benchmark that includes government, corporate, mortgage-backed, and asset-backed securities.
Dow Jones Wilshire 5000	A market capitalization–weighted index of the most-active U.S. stocks. It measures the performance of the broad domestic market.
MSCI World	The Morgan Stanley Capital International World index measures the performance of stock markets in 23 nations: Australia, Austria, Belgium, Canada, Denmark, Finland, France, Germany, Hong Kong, Ireland, Italy, Japan, Malaysia, the Netherlands, New Zealand, Norway, Portugal, Singapore, Spain, Sweden, Switzerland, the United Kingdom, and the United States.
MSCI EAFE	The Morgan Stanley Capital International Europe, Australasia, and Far East index is widely accepted as a benchmark for international stock performance. It represents many of the world's major markets outside the United States and Canada.

Figure 2.1   Major indexes and what they track.

Using Peer Groups as Benchmarks

Indexes can be useful, but peer groups such as the Morningstar categories, which we discussed in Chapter 1, are an even better way to evaluate your fund's returns. That's because the categories allow you to compare your fund's performance with that of other funds that invest in the same way. An index may be a suitable benchmark because it tracks the same kinds of stocks that your fund invests in, but an index itself isn't an investment option. Your choice isn't between investing in a fund and an index but between a fund and a fund.

If you're trying to evaluate a fund that invests in large, cheaply priced companies, compare it with other large-value funds. Or compare those that buy only Latin America stocks with others that invest exclusively in Latin America. To find a fund's category, go to www.morningstar.com and type in the fund's name or ticker, or check its page in *Morningstar Mutual Funds*™ (found in most public libraries).

Armed with information about a fund's true peer group, or category, you're in a much better position to judge its performance. Say you owned T. Rowe Price Global Technology in 2004. At the end of that year, you might have been disappointed—your fund gained 10%, but lagged the S&P 500. Alongside that benchmark, your fund didn't fare particularly well. But the fund looked better versus its peers: T. Rowe Price Global Technology is a specialty-technology offering, and those funds on average only gained about 4% in 2004.

The fact that T. Rowe Price Global Technology lagged the S&P 500 in 2004 didn't so much reflect the fund's quality as it did the relatively weak performance of technology stocks that year. Like T. Rowe Price Global Technology, most technology sector funds focus exclusively on that sector; they don't have the latitude to load up on energy stocks or financials when they're hot. Thus, comparing such a fund to the index, which is broadly diversified across sectors, gave you no insight into how your fund really did. But comparing the fund with its category told you that it did just fine.

Understanding the Perils of Return Chasing

It can be frustrating when your fund is in the red or lagging other categories, even if it's doing well relative to its peer group. That frustration can lead to the most common and costly mistake investors make—chasing returns. They buy hot-performing funds in hot-performing categories, and after one fund or fund group turns cold, they sell it and jump into another hot fund or category. The catch is that by the time you've noticed the hot fund category and decided to make a switch, that category could be ready to cool off. Meanwhile, your once-lagging fund could be poised for an upturn. Simply put, there are never clear signals that it's time to buy one fund type or swap into another. Jumping around, therefore, often spells missed opportunities.

Morningstar's own studies support the notion of swimming against the tide rather than chasing hot returns. By tracking new money flowing into funds and fund sales, we have found that investors often buy or sell at just the wrong time. When everyone is buying a particular kind of fund, it's often a sign that the category is due for a fall. Meanwhile, those categories that investors are yanking their money from are often due for a rebound. Tech funds skyrocketed in 1999, and investors were tossing in new money hand over fist. The funds then crashed in 2000. Conversely, investors had little interest in small-cap value funds in 1999, but those funds came to the fore from 2000 through 2004.

Instead of switching among funds, we recommend building a portfolio of varied funds. That way, whatever the market is doing, at least some portion of your portfolio is likely to be doing well. It's not sexy, it's not a hot tip, but we know of no better way to improve your odds of being a successful long-term fund investor. (In Part Three, we explain how to build a portfolio that suits your goals and is also less likely to be tossed around by changes in the market.)

Focusing on Long-Term Returns

You can check a fund's returns relative to the average for its category in publications such as *Morningstar Fund Investor* or *Morningstar Mutual Funds* (many public libraries subscribe to these products) or on Morningstar.com. But which returns should you consider? How the fund did for the past 3 months, the past 10 years, or some period in between?

Because studies show that trading in and out of funds doesn't work, be a long-term investor and focus on a fund's returns over the past 5 and 10 years. Compare those returns with those of other funds in the category to get a clear view of performance. Although we wouldn't rule out a fund that was below par for one of those periods, there's little reason to buy a fund that's inferior for most periods.

Take a look at the fund's calendar-year returns versus its category, too. Don't get too hung up on uneven year-to-year returns relative to the peer group; after all, some of the best fund managers have performance that looks streaky when judged on a calendar-year basis. But eyeballing a fund's relative returns over a period of several calendar years can be a handy way to identify those offerings that may look good because of a couple of strong recent years but have little to recommend them overall. Many so-called bear funds (funds that short stocks) soared to the top of the charts during the decidedly bearish market of 2000 to 2002. A look at year-to-year calendar returns, however, reveals that prior to that winning streak, the funds had been a terrible place to invest.

Finally, ask how long the fund's current manager has been aboard the fund. Maybe the fund sports terrific long-term returns over every period, but the person who helped deliver those great returns has retired or moved on to another fund. In that case, the fund's long-term record may have little bearing on how it will perform in the future.

Checking Up on Aftertax Returns

Have you compared your fund to the appropriate peer group? Check. Verified that its returns stack up well relative to its peers over a variety of time periods? Check. But if you're planning to hold a fund in a taxable account, you still have a little bit of work to do when evaluating its past returns.

That's because the total-return figures you typically see don't include the bite taxes can take out of your return. When a fund distributes income or capital gains to shareholders, you, the shareholder, are required to pay taxes on those distributions (regardless of whether you were around to receive them or not!). And, of course, paying taxes cuts into your take-home return.

The difference can be significant. As of January 2005, Longleaf Partners had a 10-year annualized return of 14.60%—not too shabby. Van Kampen Comstock had an even better 10-year return of 14.90%. But if you take out taxes, the story is completely different. Longleaf Partners had a 12.54% return after taxes, whereas Van Kampen Comstock delivered a much smaller 10.50% aftertax return. If you were investing in a taxable account, the Longleaf fund would definitely be the better of the two.

The good news is that it's fairly easy to find out how well a fund has shielded investors from taxes. The Securities and Exchange Commission now requires funds to disclose what shareholders would have kept after they paid taxes. If you're buying a fund for a taxable account and not through a 401(k) plan or Individual Retirement Account, seek out the aftertax return numbers, because they'll matter most for you. You can find a fund's aftertax returns in the fund's shareholder report, and you can also see these numbers by going to www.morningstar.com and typing in the fund name or ticker. There you can get a fund's raw aftertax return and also see how that figure compares with the fund's Morningstar category peers. Many fund companies now report aftertax performance on their Web sites, too. (Aftertax returns assume the highest income tax rate. If you're in a lower tax bracket, the tax bite on distributions will be less, so your aftertax return will be higher than the reported figures.)

Investor's Checklist: Put Performance in Perspective

▶ See how a fund's return stacks up relative to an appropriate yardstick— either an index or a peer group of funds with a similar investment style —to determine whether its returns are good or bad.

▶ Employ a buy-and-hold strategy instead of chasing hot-performing funds.

▶ Check a fund's performance over several time periods—the longer the better.

▶ Eyeball a fund's year-to-year returns to see how consistent its performance has been.

▶ Make sure that the manager who built a fund's past return record is still on board before buying in.

▶ Pay attention to a fund's aftertax returns—available in its annual shareholder report—if you're buying a fund for a taxable account.

3

Understand the Risks

THERE'S AN OLD saying that investors are driven by two emotions: greed and fear. We covered greed in Chapter 2. Now it's time to explore the fear of losing money. Regrettably, most investors had to confront that fear head-on during the period from 2000 through 2002—the worst bear market since the Great Depression.

In the later years of the 1990s, when the stock market seemed unstoppable, it was difficult for investors to believe that there could be a downside. Many investors who knew that their investments might run into trouble figured that they could just grit their teeth through the rough patches. During the 1990s, after all, so-called market corrections typically only lasted a quarter or two, and then it was off to the races again.

Although many market watchers warned that certain sectors of the market—notably technology and telecommunications stocks—were ridiculously overpriced, few investors were prepared for the viciousness of the market downturn from 2000 through 2002. From its March 2000 peak through September 2002, the broad market was down 38.2%, and more daring fund categories suffered much worse losses. A $10,000 investment in the average large-cap growth fund in March 2000 would have shrunk to

$4,393, while the typical tech-fund investor saw a $10,000 investment shrivel to just $1,680. Ouch!

It's easy enough to say that those are just paper losses—you don't really lose the money until you sell. But such paper losses can keep investors up nights and often lead them to sell when their funds are losing money. They worry about how much worse things might get and whether they might lose everything. Investors know that in the past the markets have recovered, but it can be hard to keep that in mind in the thick of things. As a result, people often sell at the worst time, turning their paper losses into losses in fact.

To help you avoid those funds that are apt to keep you up at night, it helps to remember that funds that make big short-term gains also tend to incur big losses. You can't get big returns without taking on a lot of risk—witness the Internet-focused funds that flew high in the late 1990s and then came crashing down. Taking a close look at the fund's portfolio—using some of the tools we discussed in Chapter 1—can also help you know if a fund harbors risks that haven't yet been realized. Measures of a fund's past volatility—standard deviation, Morningstar Risk, and the Morningstar Rating™ (the star rating)—also can provide insight into how risky a fund is apt to become.

Evaluating Investment-Style Risk

In Chapter 1, we discussed the tools you can use to analyze a fund's investments: Morningstar style boxes and categories, sectors, concentration, and turnover. These are key factors to focus on when judging the kinds of risks a fund is taking on and whether it's right for you.

The Morningstar style box is a great way to find out how risky a fund is apt to be. Over the long term, large-value stock funds, which land in the upper left-hand corner of the Morningstar style box, tend to be the least volatile—they have fewer performance swings than other stock mutual funds. On the opposite end of the spectrum, funds that fall in the small-growth square are typically the most volatile group (see Figure 3.1).

A fund such as Van Wagoner Emerging Growth, which owns small, growth-leaning stocks, is likely to experience more dramatic ups and downs than one holding large, budget-priced stocks, like Vanguard Wellington. Van

Three-Year Standard Deviation
U.S. Stock Funds

Investment Style			
Value	Blend	Growth	
			Market Cap
15.30	14.76	16.02	Large
15.53	16.16	17.41	Mid
17.03	17.80	19.98	Small

Three-Year Standard Deviation
Taxable Bond Funds

Duration			
Short	Interm.	Long	
			Quality
3.07	5.28	6.73	High
3.93	5.55	6.37	Med
7.19	7.49	11.52	Low

Figure 3.1   Standard deviation, a measure of volatility, shows which investment styles have been the most (and least) risky over the past three years. The higher the number, the more volatile the funds in a given style box have been.

Wagoner Emerging Growth might deliver higher returns over the long haul, but its performance will tend to be much more erratic. Investors may have to go on a pretty wild ride to get those returns.

Similarly, our bond style box shows how risky your fixed-income fund is apt to be. Generally speaking, the safest square of the bond style box is the top-left square—home to funds with limited interest-rate sensitivity and high credit qualities. Such funds won't see their bonds drop in value too much if interest rates go up, and they focus on government and high-quality corporate bonds, meaning that there's little risk that the bonds' issuers will fail to keep up with their interest payments. Funds that fall into this square of the style box are often just a notch riskier than money-market funds. Meanwhile, the riskiest square is the lower right-hand corner of the box. Few funds occupy it, though—bond funds tend to take on credit or interest-rate risk, usually not both.

You can also use the style box to get a handle on whether a fund is likely to be more or less risky than its category peers. If you're looking at a technology fund that lands in the small-growth square of the style box, for example, you know it's likely to be more volatile than a fund that falls in the large-cap row. That's because, all else being equal, smaller-company stocks will tend to be more volatile than large-cap stocks.

Evaluating Sector Risk

In addition to considering a fund's investment style, it also helps to eyeball its sector positioning to gauge how vulnerable it is to a downturn in a certain part of the market. Investors who paid attention to sectors back in 1999 did themselves a huge favor. They could see that even though Fidelity OTC, a large-growth fund, had higher returns than Marsico Growth, another large-growth fund, it was also much more vulnerable to a downturn in just one stock sector.

As described in Chapter 1, Fidelity OTC's former manager made a big bet on technology stocks that was abundantly rewarded in 1999, then punished later on. The manager couldn't control how the market would feel about tech stocks, but he could decide how much sector-specific risk was acceptable for the fund. A fund that bets a lot on a single sector—particularly if it's a sector that houses a lot of high-priced stocks like technology—is likely to display dramatic ups and downs. As long as the manager's strategy doesn't change, that volatility will continue. Sometimes the fund will make money and sometimes it will be down, but its volatility will remain high, reminding investors that even though the fund may currently be making a lot of money, it also has the potential to fall dramatically.

Although there are no rules of thumb for how much is "too much" in a given sector, it's helpful to compare your fund's sector weightings with those of other funds that practice a similar style as well as with a broad-market index fund such as Vanguard 500 Index or Vanguard Total Stock Market Index. This is not to suggest that you should automatically avoid a fund with a big wager on an individual sector; in fact, some of the most successful investors are biased toward a market sector or two. (Exhibit A: Warren Buffett, whose Berkshire Hathaway is heavily skewed toward financials stocks, particularly insurers.) But you should be aware of a fund's sector biases so that you don't purchase another fund that also invests heavily in that same sector, thereby increasing your portfolio's risks even more.

Evaluating Individual-Company Risk

Just as a fund that clusters all its holdings in a sector or two is bound to be more risky than a broadly diversified portfolio, funds that hold relatively few securities tend to be more risky than those that commit a tiny percentage of assets to each stock. As mentioned, Janus Twenty has around 20 to 30 holdings, whereas Fidelity Contrafund had more than 500 stocks as of its last portfolio. If a few of Janus Twenty's holdings run into trouble, they can do a lot more damage to performance than a few of Contrafund's can. If Janus Twenty had its money spread equally among 20 stocks, each would count for 5% of the portfolio, but a single stock would account for just 0.20% of Contrafund's holdings. If one of Janus Twenty's picks were to go bankrupt, it would take a far bigger bite out of returns than if Contrafund got caught with the same bum stock. (For similar reasons, concentration should also be a consideration when evaluating corporate-bond funds, particularly those that focus on junk bonds.)

Because managers almost never spread the fund's money equally across every holding, along with checking a fund's total number of holdings, it's a good idea to check a fund's top 10 holdings to see what percentage of the assets are concentrated there. Even though a fund has 100 holdings, if the manager has committed half of the fund to the top 10, that fund could be a lot more volatile than one with the same number of holdings but less concentration at the top. Analytic Disciplined Equity and Franklin Blue Chip each own 75 stocks, but the Analytic fund has nearly 40% of its assets in its top 10 holdings, whereas the Franklin has just 23% parked at the top. Simply because its top holdings make up more of its portfolio, the Analytic fund is going to suffer more if its top holdings run into trouble than will the Franklin fund.

Assessing Past Volatility

Although conducting a fundamental analysis of a fund—checking its investment style and concentration in sectors and individual stocks—is one of the best ways to assess an offering's riskiness, past volatility is also a fairly accurate indicator of future risk. If a fund has seen lots of ups and downs in the past, it's apt to continue to have herky-jerky returns. Morningstar studies show that funds with high volatility in one time period usually exhibit similar volatility in subsequent time periods. Meanwhile, even-keeled funds continue to exhibit low volatility.

Doing the Gut Check

If you want to make sure that you're going to be comfortable with a fund you're considering, do a simple check to see whether you can tolerate those periods when the fund is in the red. Look at how much the fund has lost in the past and ask yourself if you could hold on during those periods. (You can find this information by typing in the ticker for a fund on Morningstar.com, or in the pages of *Morningstar Mutual Funds*, available in many public libraries.) Look at the years and quarters in which the fund has lost the most money. For example, if you had $10,000 in Janus Twenty at the beginning of 2000, your stake would've been down to $6,758 by year-end (the fund lost 32.42% for the year). The fund's worst quarter in recent years was a 24.6% loss in the first quarter of 2001. A $10,000 investment at the beginning of the quarter would have been worth $7,540 at the end. What would you have done if you didn't know when the fund would come back or whether it might go on to lose as much in the next quarter or year?

In principle, long-term investors can ignore such downturns. If you don't need the money for a decade or more, the downside should be less important. What matters is what you have at the end, not how you got there, right? Well, sort of. It's true that many rewarding funds have taken their shareholders on relatively wild rides. But by owning such a fund, you expose yourself to the risk that your fund could be at a low ebb when you need to start withdrawing your money to fund a particular goal, such as college or retirement. Moreover, owning an extremely volatile fund can spell unnecessary stress. Uncertainty is a problem for many investors. They would rather bail out than hang around to see what happens next. If, after looking at a fund's worst quarterly or annual losses, you know that such losses would cause you to sell the investment, it's probably not the fund for you. And even if you believe you could stick it out, would you suffer too much stress worrying about the fund? If so, don't buy it. Look for something steadier. Successful investing means not only making money but also being comfortable in the process.

Using Standard Deviation

But what if you want to quickly shop among a group of funds to figure out which is the least risky? Standard deviation is probably the most commonly used gauge of a fund's past volatility, and it enables quick comparisons among funds. Morningstar analysts like standard deviation because it tells investors just how much a fund's returns have fluctuated during a particular time period. Morningstar calculates standard deviations every month, based on a fund's monthly returns for the preceding 3-, 5-, and 10-year periods. Standard deviation represents the degree to which a fund's returns have varied from its 3-, 5-, or 10-year average annual return, known as the *mean*. By definition, a fund's returns have historically fallen within one standard deviation of its mean 68% of the time.

For example, as of early 2005, ICM Isabelle Small Cap Value had a mean of 9.90 and a standard deviation of 26.23 for the trailing three-year period. Those numbers tell you that about two-thirds (68%) of the time, the fund's annualized return was within 26.23 percentage points of 9.90%. That's a huge range of returns, from a 16.33% loss to a 36.13% gain. If you're a cautious investor, you would not get anywhere near that fund. You would be much happier with a fund that had a much lower standard deviation.

The catch is, standard deviation doesn't tell you much when you look at it in isolation. Knowing that a fund has a standard deviation of 25 for the past 3 years is meaningless until you start making comparisons. Just like returns, a fund's standard deviation requires context to be useful. If you're looking at a fund with a standard deviation of 15 for the same period, you know that the fund with the standard deviation of 25 is substantially more volatile.

An index can be a useful benchmark for a fund's volatility as well as for its returns. Say you're considering a fund that lands in Morningstar's large-cap blend category. The S&P 500 index is a good benchmark for that group because it emphasizes large companies with a variety of investment styles—growth, value, and everything in between. Through early 2005, the S&P 500 index's three-year standard deviation was 15.56. You can tell that the large-blend fund with a standard deviation of 25 has taken investors on a much wilder ride than the index. Unless it also has much higher returns to compensate for the stress of owning it, buying that fund would make little sense.

As with returns, you can also check a fund's volatility level by comparing its standard deviation with the average for its category. (You can find category-average statistics, including standard deviation, in *Morningstar Mutual Funds*.) In 1999, Janus Olympus had a three-year standard deviation of 31.91 while the typical large-growth fund had a standard deviation of 24.19. Janus Olympus also had much better returns than the average, but its high standard deviation indicated that it had been significantly more volatile than its typical competitor.

This was a warning sign that the fund could also lose a lot more than the average if things were to turn ugly. When large-growth funds fell an average of 14.6% in 2000, Janus Olympus dropped 21.6%. It dropped an additional 33% in 2001, versus a 23% loss for the typical large-growth fund, and shed another 24% in 2002.

Using Morningstar's Risk Rating

Standard deviation is useful because it tells you about the fund's past performance swings, and big swings usually beget more big swings. But standard deviation doesn't tell you whether the fund's swings were gains or losses, and that's an important distinction for most investors. Theoretically, a fund with extremely high returns year in and year out could have a standard deviation just as high as one that had posted fairly steep losses. Consider two small-cap funds: In early 2005, RS Emerging Growth had a standard deviation of 25.58, and Legg Mason Special's standard deviation was 25.43. Yet the Legg Mason fund's return for the past three years averaged 18% per year, whereas the RS fund's return averaged 4%. During that period, the Legg Mason fund's worst three-month loss was 15%. The RS fund lost as much as 23% in three months. The Legg Mason fund had, hands down, the better risk/reward profile, but standard deviation alone wouldn't have helped you choose it over the other fund.

That example illustrates why investors should look at the whole picture, not simply returns and standard deviation. Just as we want to know how successful a fund manager has been at making money for shareholders, we want to know how successful he or she has been at protecting them from losses. That's why Morningstar's risk rating not only looks at all variations in a fund's returns—just like standard deviation—but also emphasizes a fund's losses relative to its category peers. The formulas driving Morningstar's risk rating are complicated, but the underlying idea is straightforward: As investors, we don't like losing money! (You can find a fund's risk rating by going to Morningstar.com and typing in its name or its ticker.)

Morningstar's risk rating looks at funds' performance over a variety of time periods. We don't rate funds that are younger than 3 years old because shorter periods just don't give an adequate picture of a fund's performance. If a fund is 3 years old, its Morningstar risk rating will be based entirely on that

Age of Fund	Morningstar Rating Based on:
At least 3 years, but less than 5	100% 3-year rating
At least 5 years, but less than 10	60% 5-year rating 40% 3-year rating
At least 10 years	50% 10-year rating 30% 5-year rating 20% 3-year rating

Figure 3.2   How a fund's age factors into its Morningstar rating.

3-year period. For a 5-year-old fund, 60% of its risk rating is based on the past 5 years and 40% on the past 3 years. A 10-year-old fund's 10-year record will count for 50% of its risk rating, while the 5- and 3-year periods count for another 30% and 20%, respectively (see Figure 3.2). Morningstar looks at this combination of periods because we think long-term investing is important, but we also want to be sure that funds don't earn good ratings just on the strength of success years ago. We assign funds new risk scores every month.

Because we measure a fund's risk relative to other funds in its category, it's easy to compare funds that invest in the same way. The least risky 10% of funds in a category earn the Low risk designation, the next safest 22.5% are considered to have Below-Average risk, and the middle 35% are deemed to have Average risk. The next 22.5% are deemed to have Above-Average risk, while the final 10% are considered High risk. If you're contemplating a large-cap value fund with High Morningstar risk, you know that it has exhibited more volatility (including real losses) than 90% of large-value offerings.

Using the Morningstar Rating (The Star Rating)

Because investors are extremely concerned with losing money, a fund's risk rating counts for fully one-half of its overall Morningstar Rating (better known as the star rating). The other half of the Morningstar Rating looks at a fund's return relative to other funds in its category.

We calculate a fund's Morningstar return rating in much the same way as we do the risk rating. We use the same combination of time periods (3-, 5-, and 10-year returns go into the calculation). We also adjust a fund's returns for any sales charges to better reflect what real-life investors would have earned. And as with the risk rating, funds that rank in the top 10% of their categories on the return front earn a return rating of High; the next-best, 22.5% earn a return rating of Above Average, and so on. We repeat the process every month.

Once we have both a risk rating and a return rating for a fund, we put them together into an overall rating calculation. By combining Morningstar risk and return, we come up with a risk-adjusted return score for each fund in a category. We then rank the funds according to their scores. The highest-scoring 10% of funds within each category earn five stars, the next 22.5% get four stars, the middle 35% get three stars, the next 22.5% two stars, and the worst 10% receive a single star (see Figure 3.3).

The star rating allows you to skim over the huge number of available funds and narrow it down to a more manageable list of those that have done a good job of balancing risk and return. You can use the star rating to weed out funds that have been too risky for too little gain and focus your search on the better funds.

You can also use the star rating to monitor your holdings. You shouldn't automatically sell a fund if it drops a star. But if your fund's star rating drops below three, that's a good reason to dig in and find out what's going on with your holding. It may well be that your manager's style has simply been out of favor in the market and is due for an upswing, but it may also indicate a more fundamental problem.

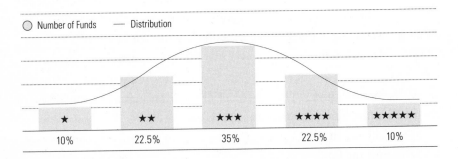

Figure 3.3   The distribution of star ratings within a category in the Morningstar rating system.

Before you start using the star rating there are a couple of important things to note about it. One is that it's purely quantitative. As much as we might enjoy the power to do so, Morningstar analysts don't award stars to funds they like or yank them off funds they dislike. (Fund managers sometimes ask our analysts what they can do to get more stars. We always tell them, make more money for your shareholders and give them a smoother ride.)

You should also know that if a management change occurs, the rating stays with the fund—it doesn't travel with the manager to a new fund. That means a fund's rating could be based mostly on the success of a manager who is no longer there. It's also worth noting that the star rating is based on how the fund did in the past. It won't predict short-term winners.

Finally, to use the star rating effectively, you first need to establish the kind of fund you want. The star rating will tell you whether one technology fund is better than another, but it won't tell you whether you should even be buying a technology fund or how much of your portfolio you should commit to it. (Parts Two and Three of this book are devoted to identifying the categories of funds you should invest in and building a portfolio.) Because we award five-star ratings in every category, funds that are inappropriate for most investors can earn the highest star ratings. Allianz RCM Global Technology garnered four stars as of early 2005—it notched spectacular returns during the late 1990s and also fared better than many rival technology funds during the sector's eventual collapse. Yet most investors simply don't need a fund that focuses specifically on the technology sector.

The star rating is a great first screen, but it's not the only piece of information you should consider when assessing a fund. Before buying a fund, instead of just asking, "Does it get five stars?" you should ask yourself the following five questions:

1. What does the fund own?
2. How has the fund performed?
3. How risky has the fund been?
4. Who runs the fund?
5. What does the fund cost?

We covered the first three in Chapters 1 through 3; the rest are covered in Chapters 4 and 5.

Investor's Checklist: Understand the Risks

▶ Use a fund's style-box placement as a rough gauge of its risk level. Large-value funds are typically the least risky U.S. stock funds, and small-growth funds are often the most risky. On the bond side, funds that focus on lower-quality longer-term bonds usually carry the most risk, while those that focus on high-quality short-term bonds are invariably the least risky.

▶ Some of the best managers concentrate heavily on a favorite sector or two, but be aware that big bets on individual sectors may also add to your fund's risk level.

▶ Scan a fund's number of holdings, as well as the percentage of assets it holds in its top 10 positions, to see how much company-specific risk it harbors. Also take company-specific risk into account when evaluating lower-quality bond funds.

▶ Get a handle on whether a fund is appropriate for you by checking its worst historical return period—either its worst quarterly or annual loss. If you would not be able to hang on through that type of loss, steer clear.

▶ Use backward-looking volatility measures, including standard deviation and the Morningstar risk rating, to help determine how volatile a fund has been relative to rival funds.

▶ Check the Morningstar rating (a.k.a. the star rating) to quickly size up a fund's historical risk/reward profile.

4

Get to Know Your
Fund Manager

LET'S SAY YOU followed the first three chapters of this book and have found a fund with a mix of good returns without too much risk. You also have a good understanding of the type of securities your manager is buying. But if the manager who earned that great record is gone, you could be in for an unpleasant surprise.

Because managers are vital to a fund's success or failure, Morningstar analysts spend a lot of time talking with them, either on the phone or in person. Every time we write a fund analysis, and sometimes in between analyses, we try to talk to the manager.

The manager can shed light on strong or poor performance and give us insight into why the fund's portfolio looks the way it does. Maybe the manager expects the economy to take a turn for the better and is emphasizing the sectors that will benefit most. That tells you that the fund could be poised for a strong run or could run into trouble if the economy slows.

By interviewing many managers with similar investment strategies, we can also ferret out the best investment arguments and build a level of confidence in a particular manager's investment rationale. If we hear five different managers all talking about the latest trendy stock—and it happens more often than you might think—we get skeptical about any claims they make about uncovering great companies others have overlooked. We're also wary of fund companies that always try to put a positive spin on performance or hype up their strategies to make them sound better than they are. Over the years, we have noticed that managers of better-performing funds are typically the most straightforward about what is and is not working in their portfolios.

In addition to taking stock of the manager's rationale for positioning the portfolio, our analysts also pay attention to the structure of the firm and the resources the manager can draw upon when picking securities. Is the manager backed by scores of analysts, as is the case at most Fidelity funds? Or is the fund largely a one-person show, heavily reliant on the talents of a single individual? Knowing the answers to these questions can help you know how worried you should be if a fund manager decides to leave the firm or retire, and that's why our analysts' research into a fund's management extends to the firm as a whole.

There's another reason that Morningstar analysts maintain regular contact with fund managers and conduct regular visits with fund-management companies. In addition to sizing up the manager's investment process and the depth of his or her research team, our analysts also spend time evaluating the shareholder friendliness of each fund shop. Has the firm focused on serving its shareholders well, or has it put its own interests before those of fundholders, rolling out trendy fund types and overcharging its investors, for example? Because we at Morningstar believe that the shareholder friendliness of an investment firm is of critical importance when making investment decisions, we've recently rolled out stewardship grades to help investors quickly size up the quality of the firm. These grades focus on what we consider to be the key determinants of a firm's shareholder friendliness: costs, board quality, management ownership and compensation structure, regulatory issues, and corporate culture.

Evaluating management—either of a company or a fund—is the point at which investing becomes more art than science. You won't find management skill neatly summed up in a data point; you must use your judgment. By looking at a few key criteria, you can improve your portfolio's performance, find managers who will stick around, invest with firms that are apt to put your interests on par with their own, and feel more comfortable about the funds in your portfolio.

Understanding Types of Fund Management

Before you can judge the quality of your manager, you need to know the two types of fund management (and one subtype; see Figure 4.1). The most straightforward fund-management structure is the single-manager approach. These are the managers who, like former Fidelity Magellan manager Peter Lynch, become the stars of the fund industry. A manager like Lynch or Bob Stansky, who holds Lynch's old post at Fidelity Magellan, is listed as the fund's sole manager. Of course, even a sole manager seldom works in total isolation. Stansky gets plenty of market research and stock ideas from Fidelity's stock analyst staff. But Stansky is the one who picks the stocks that go into Magellan's portfolio and who decides when to cut them loose. He's the key decision maker at the fund.

Then there's the management team, popularized by fund companies like American Century and Putnam. The team may consist of two or more

Solo Management	Describes a fund that is managed day-to-day by just one person. That person is responsible for all key decisions affecting the fund's assets.
Management Team	Describes a fund that is managed jointly by two or more persons. Also can be used to describe a fund that strongly promotes its team-managed aspect or team culture.
Multiple Managers	Describes a fund that is managed independently by two or more persons. Often, this term is used to describe funds that have divided net assets in set amounts among the individual managers. In most cases, multiple managers are employed at different subadvisors or investment firms.
Subadvisor	Describes cases in which the fund company employs another company, called the subadvisor, to handle the fund's day-to-day management. In these instances, the portfolio manager generally works for the fund's subadvisor and not the fund company.

Figure 4.1   The various management arrangements a fund can have.

comanagers who work together to select the fund's portfolio holdings. Sometimes one manager will make the final call on what to buy or sell, or each manager may have greater say about investments that land in his or her area of specialization. In other cases, the process is more democratic and each manager has equal say.

Finally, and much less common than the other two types of management structures, there is the multiple-manager system. In this system, a fund's assets are divided among a number of managers, each of whom works independently of one another. American Funds is the group best known for using this approach, though Fidelity has also recently taken this tack on a few of its funds. So-called all-star funds, such as those offered under the Managers and Masters' Select names, also use the multiple-manager system. These funds hire name-brand managers from different fund groups and portion out assets among them. These hired guns are known as subadvisors.

There are advantages and disadvantages associated with each of these management setups. For example, naming a single manager makes it clear who's ultimately accountable for managing shareholders' money. It's also easier for investors to get information about an individual than about a nameless, faceless committee. On the flip side, team-managed and multimanager funds are likely to have greater continuity, which can help smooth transitions if one manager leaves. Multimanager funds may also have the ability to handle more in assets than can funds run by a single manager or management team. If there are several managers employing different management styles, as is often the case with multimanager approaches, the managers can spread the incoming assets among different types of securities. That, in turn, means it's less likely the fund will affect the prices of its stocks and bonds when it's buying and selling. (We discuss asset growth in more detail in Chapter 15.)

Evaluating Quality and Quantity of Experience

There's no reason to settle for an inexperienced manager when there are hundreds of funds with skilled, seasoned management. In fact, most investors do have experienced managers working for them. In a past study, we looked at the 25 largest funds, which represent about one fourth of all mutual fund assets, and found that the typical big fund boasts a veteran team with more than eight years' tenure at the fund. That figure significantly understates management's experience, because it usually represents only the time a manager has spent at the fund, not the manager's total years in money management.

You can find a manager's tenure in a variety of places, including a fund company's Web site or on Morningstar.com. Our one-page fund reports, found in *Morningstar Mutual Funds*, also contain information on other funds the manager runs. Check to see when and where the manager's career in investing began and when he or she began managing money. A good rule of thumb is to search out managers who have logged at least 10 years as an analyst or manager; at a bare minimum, you want a manager who was on board during the bear market from 2000 through 2002 as well as the heady days of the late 1990s. That way you'll be able to see how he or she navigated those extreme environments. If the fund manager previously ran other funds, take a good look at the records of those funds to see how they fared against others in their peer group.

Experience is not the only thing that matters, though. Where a fund manager learned about investing is as important as total tenure. Look for managers who learned to invest from great managers, or who cut their teeth at firms with lots of great funds. The manager might have come up through the ranks at a giant, high-quality firm like Fidelity or American Funds or a high-quality boutique like Longleaf or Davis/Selected. If the manager learned his or her craft at a firm with lots of inferior funds, however, you have good reason to be skeptical about that manager's abilities.

Assessing the Firm's Resources

Managers are not lone wolves, and whether a fund succeeds or fails depends on the quality of its analysts and traders as well as its manager. Every sizable fund is the product of all three groups working together.

Fund giants like Fidelity employ hundreds of analysts and scores of portfolio managers. Other firms have very little analyst support and the managers rely heavily on research produced by big Wall Street brokerage firms. The problem with relying on Wall Street is that it's almost impossible to outsmart the market using widely available research reports. A few managers can do it, but that's not the norm.

It can be tricky to get a handle on the depth of a firm's research bench, but many fund companies will provide the number of analysts at the firm or even biographies of those analysts. Quantity isn't the same as quality, but it does at least let you know that there's a complete organization behind the manager.

The key way to get a handle on the quality of a manager's support team is to look at the records of funds from the same firm. If you're considering buying a growth fund, be sure to check out all the growth funds managed by a family to see if the firm excels at growth investing. You might find that the fund you're considering is a gem but it's surrounded by mediocrity. That's a sign that the fund is just getting by on the strength of a good manager (or luck) and will deteriorate if the manager leaves. The Legg Mason funds run by Bill Miller have always stood out above the rest of the firm's funds. This is not luck—it reflects that Miller is head and shoulders above his colleagues, and if he were to leave that would be a cause for concern. The best firms have great investors throughout the organization—whether they are analysts, managers, or chief investment officers.

Morningstar's analysts also like to size up a firm's trading abilities, particularly if the firm has big funds that may need to buy and sell huge blocks of shares at once. Firms that have sophisticated trading operations are able to execute their trades with the least possible impact on their stocks' share prices—they can unload a large number of shares without driving the stock's price way down, and they can buy without driving up the share price substantially. We also look favorably on those fund companies that try to keep their trading costs to a bare minimum. American Century, for example, pays less than one cent per share, on average, to execute its trades, while the industry average is five cents per share. (We discuss fund expenses—including trading costs—in Chapter 5.)

Assessing Shareholder Friendliness

Evaluating the investment abilities of a fund manager and the depth of the resources he or she draws on is, of course, a key way to find a winning mutual fund. But if you were paying attention to the fund scandal of 2003 and 2004, when many of the mutual fund industry's best-known firms were accused of ethical lapses and even illegal activity, you know that eyeballing a fund company's investment results doesn't tell you all you need to know about the quality of a fund firm. Because some fund shops have demonstrated a pattern of engaging in activity that runs counter to shareholders' interests, it's important to ask whether the organization, as Vanguard founder Jack Bogle has put it, values salesmanship over stewardship. Does the firm take its responsibility to fund shareholders seriously and actually put their interests first?

Answering those questions was the impetus for Morningstar's Stewardship Grades, which we rolled out in 2004. The grades are designed to make it easier for investors to compare the corporate-governance track records of funds they own or are considering buying. The letter grades consider the fund's performance in the following five key areas.

Regulatory Issues

For the regulatory component of the stewardship grade, we examine each firm's record to determine if it has run afoul of regulators. For example, was the firm one of the many that allowed large investors to engage in improper trading of fund shares at the expense of smaller investors? (Such improprieties were the focus of the fund scandal of 2003 and 2004.) Have regulators accused the firm of any other improprieties that had the potential to harm fund investors? We also look at the gravity of the allegations and the subsequent reforms that the firm has undertaken.

Board Quality

Quick, who owns Fidelity Magellan? We wouldn't blame you if you said "Fidelity," but that's not correct. Instead, fund shareholders own the fund, just like any other corporate shareholders, and rely on a fund board to represent their interests. The board, acting on behalf of shareholders, has hired Fidelity to run Magellan and has negotiated the fund's fees. Some boards take these responsibilities seriously, while others have chosen to look the other way as investment-management firms have launched lousy funds, hiked expenses, or left underperforming managers on the job. Because boards are in place to represent fund shareholders' interests, our stewardship grades evaluate directors' performance within that role. We also consider factors such as the number of funds that directors oversee, the relationships between directors and fund firms, and whether trustees are investing alongside fundholders. (For example, we like that all ICAP board members are paid in fund shares.)

Manager Incentives

In addition to considering a fund's regulatory history and the quality of its board, our stewardship grades also take manager incentives and ownership into account. That's because performance incentives can have a strong influence on whether a fund is a good fit for long-term investors. A fund manager who is paid to beat an aggressive benchmark over a one-year period, for example, might be inclined to take much bigger risks than he or she otherwise would. In a similar vein, the stewardship grades also consider whether a manager owns the fund (or owns others from within the family). Not only is management ownership an important reflection of whether that individual has conviction in his or her own process, but managers who invest alongside fund shareholders are also more likely to pay closer attention to issues like expenses and taxes than ones who do not. We don't believe it's a coincidence that firms like Longleaf Partners, which requires that all employees invest in Longleaf's funds, have shown themselves protective of fund shareholders' best interests. Figure 4.2 includes funds whose managers invest heavily in them.

Expenses

The amount that a management company charges fund shareholders often speaks volumes about the priority the firm accords the interests of fund shareholders versus those of company stakeholders. That's why our stewardship grade looks at each fund's expense level relative to its rivals, as well as trends in expenses, to gauge whether a firm is appropriately passing on economies of scale to a growing fund's shareholders. Importantly, the scoring for this factor is within category and within distribution channel because we want to compare apples to apples. For example, we compare the expenses of a no-load large-value fund with those of other no-load large-value offerings.

Longleaf Partners	Third Avenue Value
Muhlenkamp	Tweedy, Browne Global Value
Selected American/Davis New York Venture	

Figure 4.2   Funds whose managers heavily invest in their own funds.

Corporate Culture

No, we're not talking about dress codes or broadly assessing how a firm operates. Rather, we're focusing on how shareholder focused management is by looking for tangible evidence that a firm has a deep-rooted understanding of its role as a fiduciary. This is the most subjective component of the grade by virtue of the sheer number of factors that can influence the depth of a firm's commitment to its fundholders. Among other factors, our analysts assign the corporate culture component of the grade by evaluating criteria such as the quality of shareholder reports, a firm's willingness to close funds at appropriate asset levels, and the pattern of new fund launches. We examine how fund companies deal with these issues to gauge whether they have consistently placed the long-term interests of fund shareholders front and center—where they belong. We've also taken a close look at firms' usage of redemption fees and the ability to retain key personnel.

Finding the Right Fund Companies for You

Because knowing your fund family's capabilities is critical to picking strong-performing funds, here are thumbnail descriptions of some of the best-known fund companies (as well as a few boutiques), along with pros and cons of each.

AIM

Known best for its growth funds, AIM's growth lineup generally held up fairly well during the 2.5-year bear market that began in March 2000, though it suffered markedly at the onset. That behavior illustrates a characteristic of AIM's earnings growth focus, which feeds off trends. In other words, the funds don't do well at market inflection points. In fact, several of AIM's growth funds were left behind 2003's rally.

Given the funds' continued preference for premium-growth stocks and tolerance of high price multiples, we continue to expect streaky performance from AIM's growth funds. On AIM's value offerings—yes, AIM offers some value funds and has for years—we also expect streaky performance. That's because the patient value managers often buy controversial stocks that can take a couple of years to pan out. These funds also tend to be more concentrated than their growth counterparts.

AIM absorbed the Invesco lineup of funds after the latter firm's funds posted terrible bear-market performance and Invesco became enmeshed in the fund-trading scandal of 2003 and 2004. Most of the former Invesco funds subsequently merged into AIM offerings with similar strategies.

Overall, AIM is one of the more-adventurous shops around. Investors here should likely be willing and able to endure some swings in performance.

Strengths: AIM has a few standout funds whose managers look for growth but pay attention to their stocks' price tags. AIM Mid Cap Core Equity is one of our favorites within this group.

Weaknesses: Investors seeking small-value options won't find them here. And while expenses here are generally below average among funds sold through financial advisors, they could be lower given the firm's assets under management.

American Century

Although American Century is best known as a shop that uses computerized models to pick growth stocks, the firm has been placing greater emphasis on its analyst resources over the past several years, and it has successfully expanded its lineup to include some fine value, foreign, and bond funds.

On the growth-stock side, American Century practices a strategy known as momentum investing. The aim is to find companies with accelerating growth rates in the hope that the market doesn't fully appreciate the degree of positive change at the firm. Computers can screen for a host of momentum factors such as profit growth, earnings growth, and earnings that exceed expectations. The catch is that companies with accelerating profits tend to trade for high prices, and that makes them vulnerable to jarring price drops when their earnings fall short of expectations.

The firm is best known as a no-load fund family, though most of its funds also have share classes designed for those using financial advisors. American Century's expenses aren't the lowest around, but the firm has worked to keep its trading costs as low as they can be. American Century's executives have also been vocal opponents of so-called soft-dollar arrangements, whereby fund shops pay higher prices for their trade execution in exchange for stock research and other goodies.

Strengths: American Century is a classic B student. Although only a few of the firm's funds would make the top of our buy lists (its value-oriented funds, including American Century Value and Equity-Income, are standouts, and some of its bond funds are also topnotch), most of the firm's funds are respectable.

Weaknesses: The firm has improved fundamental research capabilities, but it still has a ways to go before it can stand with the best on that front. Moreover, while many American Century funds are sensibly managed, their costs are generally higher than offerings from rival no-load firms such as T. Rowe Price, Vanguard, and Fidelity. American Century Giftrust has been a notable laggard for several years.

American Funds

The watchword here is long-term. The privately held American Funds gets managers focused on the long haul and shelters them from any pressure to chase investment trends. As a result, the funds generally win out in the end even if they endure periods of looking extremely unfashionable. American does a great job of keeping managers and analysts at the firm for their entire careers. As a result, it boasts some of the longest-tenured managers in the industry. Adding to the firm's long-term success is the fact that fund expenses are the lowest of any advisor-sold firm. Also, the firm never chases a quick buck by launching trendy funds that bring in a ton of cash but may not be in shareholders' best interests. Remember how it seemed as if everyone had an Internet fund by early 2000? The American Funds group did not. And their funds largely avoided the overhyped stocks that later crashed to the earth when the bubble burst and accounting scandals scarred the market.

For every one of its 26 mutual funds, American divvies up assets among a handful of independently acting managers. At most firms, a team-managed approach means that a group of managers swap ideas and come to a consensus, but American cobbles together managers with different styles and lets them loose. That gives American funds diversification among both strategies and stocks. American has never closed a fund to new investors because the firm believes it can always carve out another chunk and turn it over to another manager. That said, the firm has seen a torrent of new assets come in the door over the past few years. American says that it has promoted some analysts to management posts and isn't struggling to invest the new assets, but it's clear that entrenched managers are running more than they ever have before. We'd like to see the firm articulate a closing policy for some of its largest funds, including Growth Fund of America.

Strengths: American's fundamental research skills are second to none, and it shows across the board in its funds. Fundamental Investors and EuroPacific Growth, to name just a few, have produced outstanding performance without undue volatility. We also like American Funds' innovative take on emerging markets, the New World fund, which combines developed and developing markets.

Weaknesses: The fund doesn't have much in the way of small-cap exposure: SmallCap World, its one small-cap option, is nothing to write home about. And if you're looking for a fairly aggressive fund, you'll have to look elsewhere because American doesn't go there. The shop also faced regulatory scrutiny in early 2005, with regulators alleging that the firm had improper arrangements with brokerage firms to sell its funds and that it failed to clearly disclose these arrangements to shareholders or directors. The company has contested the charges, however.

AXP

Long the fund-world's doormat, AXP, the fund management arm of American Express, is beginning to show signs of life. In 2002, the firm built an excellent new unit in Boston, hiring two ex-Fidelity managers. Those new managers have, in short order, built a large staff of individuals with some impressive resumes. The team in Boston runs AXP's domestic large-cap funds, and the firm has also picked some excellent subadvisors, including Davis (of Davis Selected Advisors), to take over some long-suffering funds. In addition, in 2003 the firm acquired highly regarded British asset manager Threadneedle to run its international offerings. The funds that are still at the firm's Minneapolis branch don't inspire confidence, though, as they're run by the same crew that turned in dismal performance in the past. The firm's funds are sold through AXP's extensive network of financial advisors.

Strengths: Large-cap funds such as AXP Growth, which is being steered by the new Boston-based team, are worth a look, as are some of the AXP Partners funds, which are managed by superb subadvisors.

Weaknesses: Skip AXP's bond funds. Although the firm's fixed-income operation has seen some notable strategic and managerial changes over the past few years, we're still a long way away from recommending the funds.

Columbia

Columbia's management team has worked hard to put the past behind it, and that's been necessary on several levels. First, the firm has been reeling from its involvement in the market-timing scandal. In February 2005, Bank of America, Columbia's parent, agreed to pay $675 million, including fee cuts of $160 million at the funds, to settle charges with the New York Attorney General and the SEC that the firm had market-timing and late-trading agreements. (These arrangements occurred separately at the Nations funds and at Columbia before the two merged in 2004.) That was the biggest fine in the scandal, which was fitting given that the abuses were among the broadest and worst committed anywhere. To its credit, the massive complex has not only paid up, but they've cleaned house, beefed up compliance, and vastly improved disclosure. Going forward the shop has another sizable challenge: consolidating the sprawling lineup of funds that results from serial mergers and putting firmly in place a coherent and unified investment process. The funds in the complex may now share the Columbia brand, but it's a conglomeration of previously independent shops, including Columbia, Liberty, Galaxy, Colonial, Stein Roe, and Pacific Horizon—plus boutiques Marsico and Wanger Asset Management. The shop has started to whittle down the number of funds from more than 120 to a target of about 75 in the next couple of years. They've also centralized the management and research staffs. Still, one has to consider the shop a work in progress, particularly given that a number of funds under the Columbia umbrella have been lackluster performers at best.

Strengths: With more than 100 funds, there are a number of solid offerings scattered about. The centers of gravity for investment prowess, though, are two largely autonomous boutiques: Marsico and Wanger Asset Management (home of the Acorn funds).

Weaknesses: While the shop's on the right track, stability is going to be an issue for some time. Which funds—and even which managers—will remain in place five years from now is a question no one can truly answer.

Davis/Selected

This family of funds—more of a boutique than a full-service fund shop—is built on a fundamentals-driven, buy-and-hold investing ethos. Although mainly associated with value investing and financials stocks in particular, the firm will invest in any sector. Management is loath to sell a stock and will allow appreciating stocks to move into the growth side of the style box without selling.

The firm is owned by the Davis family, which collectively has a king's ransom invested in the firm's funds. Given that, we think it's no coincidence that Davis/Selected is among the most shareholder-friendly shops around. The firm recently rolled out a new, low-cost share class for investors who buy directly through the firm rather than using a fund supermarket, and its funds have historically been extremely tax-efficient. The Davis funds are advisor sold, while funds carrying the Selected name are geared toward no-load investors.

Strengths: Our favorites in this lineup are the large-cap Selected American and Davis New York Venture. We're also fans of Selected Special, a go-anywhere fund that relies heavily on input from Davis/Selected's analyst team.

Weaknesses: Davis focuses on what it does well and leaves the rest to others. Thus, the firm has little in the way of bond or international offerings, and doesn't do aggressive growth at all. We would also avoid the expensive Davis Government Bond.

Dodge & Cox

Talk about utilitarian! This fine value-oriented shop has just four funds: Stock, Balanced, Income, and International, all of which are standouts in their respective categories. Dodge & Cox is the ultimate example of a firm that has let investment excellence—rather than marketing flash—attract investors. The firm, which has a huge institutional investment-management business, doesn't advertise at all. Its expenses are also extremely low.

Strengths: We'd heartily recommend any Dodge & Cox fund, though the firm's Stock and Balanced funds are currently closed to new investors.

Weaknesses: Although it would be tempting to leave Dodge & Cox in charge of one's entire portfolio, the firm doesn't offer a money market fund. And while Dodge & Cox has closed both its Balanced and Stock offerings, current investors in those funds continue to send in assets at a good clip. Thus, neither offering is particularly nimble.

Dreyfus

One of the most venerable names in the mutual fund industry, Dreyfus hasn't managed to maintain its elite reputation in recent years. It especially struggled when the market favored growth investing in the 1990s, but performance has been better lately. Some of its value-leaning choices have become industry standouts, especially Dreyfus Midcap Value. And its subadvisory relationship with Fayez Sarofim, a Texas-based investment firm esteemed for its buy-and-hold investment approach, means Dreyfus is able to offer its clients a handful of very good long-term core offerings. Overall, though, Dreyfus' lineup is a mixed bag and includes a number of undistinguished funds, particularly in the large-cap blend space. Nor does Dreyfus offer a comparative advantage in terms of its expenses, which are just average.

Strengths: Dreyfus Appreciation, whose subadvisor Fayez Sarofim employs a consistent focus on mega-cap steady-growth firms, is the Dreyfus lineup's jewel in the crown. Dreyfus Midcap Value, while volatile, is also a standout.

Weaknesses: Dreyfus has several lackluster large-cap funds whose results pale alongside inexpensive index offerings.

Fidelity

This privately held colossus offers the advantages and disadvantages that come with its girth. The positive aspect of its heft is that Fidelity has hundreds of very bright managers and analysts conducting excellent fundamental analysis.

In addition, Fidelity passes the economies of scale on to investors in the form of low expense ratios.

The downside is that managing hundreds of billions of dollars limits the flexibility of Fidelity's fund managers. Just as asset bloat can hinder an individual fund, it can hinder a fund family, too. The firm left open some of its biggest funds, including Magellan and Low-Priced Stock, longer than it should have, meaning that the managers are apt to have a tough time delivering standout performance going forward. The fund is tempting fate with the giant Contrafund; although Will Danoff continues to do a spectacular job, the fund's girth will present an increasing challenge for him.

The firm's huge number of portfolio managers also means that analysts spend a lot of time repeating themselves to all the managers interested in their stocks. (To make sure analysts' research has an impact, Fidelity compensates analysts based on how much their picks contribute to fund performance and how well analysts communicate with managers.) One other problem: Fidelity has to constantly fend off poachers trying to hire away its smart young analysts and managers. In 2002, AXP Funds pulled off a coup when it lured a few of Fidelity's rising stars and two analysts to head a new unit running large-cap AXP funds; Fidelity has also lost a number of top managers to hedge funds over the years.

Size has made Fidelity's funds more mild-mannered than in the past. You won't get any unpleasant surprises from Fidelity funds, but you're not likely to see many funds crush their indexes, either. Expect Fidelity funds to quietly outperform over the long haul.

Fidelity funds are primarily sold through no-load channels, but the firm also has an extensive lineup of offerings geared toward financial advisors.

Strengths: Fidelity's U.S. stock funds aren't exciting, but the group's large-cap funds are generally well-run, dependable vehicles. The firm has also had success with its smaller-cap offerings, particularly the giant Low-Priced Stock, but asset bloat is an ongoing worry and the firm's small-cap staff is quite lean given the funds' size. The firm's government and high-quality corporate bond funds are wonderfully conservative portfolios. The firm's fixed-income managers avoid making market bets and simply stick to researching companies and selecting bonds that appear undervalued. The firm's municipal-bond operation is also one of the fund world's best. In an effort to compete with indexing giant Vanguard, Fidelity reduced the expense ratios on a number of its index funds to 0.10% in 2004; Fidelity made those few cuts permanent in early 2005.

Weaknesses: Fidelity runs a host of narrowly focused select funds, many of which investors should avoid. Funds like Fidelity Select Air Transportation and Fidelity Select Defense & Aerospace are really only of use to speculators who want to make a bet on an industry. Unlike some firms' sector offerings, Fidelity's sector funds are not designed as places for managers to stay for the duration of their careers. Rather, a sector manager is supposed to learn about the sector and then move on after a year or two to learn about another sector or run a diversified fund. Moreover, while Fidelity has historically done a solid job of running small-cap money, the firm has a tendency to let its small-cap and mid-cap funds grow too large. For a truly nimble small-cap offering, we'd look elsewhere.

Franklin Templeton/Mutual Series

The Franklin Templeton umbrella covers five distinct groups under three names. Templeton is a value-oriented foreign-stock shop with a lineup of well-managed but often pricey funds. Under the Franklin name, you'll find some good municipal bond managers, a decent growth-stock group, and a separate small-value crew that runs Balance Sheet Investment and MicroCap Value.

Finally, the Mutual Series group runs outstanding low-risk deep-value funds out of New Jersey. The firm does rigorous balance-sheet analysis and seeks to buy stocks on the cheap. Over the years, the Mutual Series funds have produced excellent returns at very moderate risk levels. The big negative at these funds is that founder Michael Price left the firm after selling it to Franklin, and his successor, David Winters, departed in mid-2005.

Franklin's funds are sold primarily through financial advisors. The firm, which is publicly traded, ran into problems with securities regulators in 2004. In that year, state and federal regulators accused Franklin of allowing large clients to engage in improper trading of the firm's funds; Franklin has since settled the charges. The firm has also faced scrutiny for its so-called revenue-sharing practices, whereby a fund shop pays to be part of a brokerage firm's preferred-fund list.

Strengths: Thanks to combining the strengths of fund groups with different specialties, Franklin Templeton does a reasonable job of covering all the bases. Franklin runs some solid, income-oriented municipal-bond funds such as California Tax-Free Income and Federal Tax-Free Income. In addition, the huge Templeton Foreign, run by Jeff Everett, is a solid choice if you're in the market for a conservatively managed foreign value fund.

Weaknesses: Although we're big fans of the investment process at the firm's Mutual Series funds, we can't help but notice that the shop has seen a parade of manager defections over the past several years, and David Winters' recent departure is a huge blow. Meanwhile, the firm has let other funds, such as Franklin Small-Mid Growth, grow too large.

Harbor
Harbor, a division of Dutch asset manager Robeco, doesn't offer index funds, but it does offer moderate-cost actively managed funds run by outstanding subadvisors.

Strengths: Harbor Bond is run by fixed-income superstar Bill Gross, making it the cheapest way for no-load investors to gain access to the brain trust at PIMCO funds. Harbor International Growth is a topnotch growth-oriented foreign fund run by Jim Gendelman at Marsico, and Harbor Capital Appreciation is run by Sig Segalas' outstanding team at Jennison Associates.

Weaknesses: Although the institutional share classes of Harbor funds remain a great deal, expenses on the retail share classes of Harbor Capital Appreciation and International could be lower given their sizable asset bases.

Janus
The fund industry's golden child in the second half of the 1990s, Janus is still working to regain investors' trust following the one-two punch of terrible bear-market performance and the firm's entanglement in the fund scandal in 2003. In April 2004, Janus settled with industry regulators to resolve allegations that it had allowed several clients market-timing privileges in a number of its funds. The firm has since instituted some notable reforms, including a

new manager-compensation system that puts a greater emphasis on long-term performance. Janus has also made an effort to diversify its lineup somewhat. Although its funds had a near-exclusive focus on growth stocks in the second half of the 1990s, several of the inhouse Janus funds—including Janus World-wide, Core Equity, and Enterprise—are more valuation-conscious and diversified by sector than they once were. Janus also owns part of value specialist Perkins, Wolf, McDonnell, which runs Janus Small Cap Value and Janus Mid Cap Value.

Those strides have led to improved performance on several Janus funds. But while Janus has historically done a decent job of retaining key investment personnel, the firm has a new CEO and chief investment officer, and a few of its longest-tenured portfolio managers have left the firm in recent years. Janus got too big too fast and crashed in the 1990s, and it's still not clear the firm has adjusted to life as a large investment company.

Strengths: Despite its bear-market travails, Janus boasts a tightly knit group of managers and analysts and a research-driven culture. We're also impressed that none of the firm's many large-cap funds is inclined to hug the S&P 500. David Corkins, in charge of Janus Mercury since early 2003, has proved to be one of the firm's top managers, having steered Janus Growth & Income to marvelous gains before assuming his current post. Janus Twenty has also posted strong, although erratic, returns on manager Scott Schoelzel's watch.

Weaknesses: The firm's foreign funds are still works in progress.

Longleaf Partners

Founded by Mason Hawkins and Staley Cates, this Memphis firm is a stickler for value. A stock has to be trading at least 40% below management's estimate of intrinsic value before the firm will buy. If management does like a stock, it won't be shy about buying. Longleaf typically runs focused portfolios of just 20 or 30 names. This practice can make performance erratic, but over the long haul the firm has put up strong returns.

Strengths: Although all three Longleaf funds are closed to new investors, we'd gladly buy into any of them should they reopen. Longleaf is also an exceptionally shareholder-friendly firm. It has never launched a trendy fund to capitalize on market demand, and all of its employees must keep all of their equity investments in Longleaf Partners funds.

Weaknesses: Longleaf Partners International, while a superb performer within the foreign large-value category, has a steep expense ratio that dims its appeal.

Marsico

Founder Tom Marsico runs some of the better large-growth funds around. Marsico put up great returns at Janus before setting out on his own, and he has continued to produce strong relative performance since then. Marsico blends stock selection with top-down analysis (playing on macroeconomic trends) to make a pleasing mix. More recently, the firm has launched funds run by former Marsico analysts.

Strengths: Tom Marsico is the proven quantity here, so we favor his Marsico Focus and Marsico Growth funds. If you invest with a broker, you can find similar funds under the Nations Marsico label. Marsico International Opportunities is a fine growth-leaning foreign fund, but we'd like to see its expenses come down.

Weaknesses: Due to his superb long-term track record, Marsico's funds have attracted a huge amount of assets over the past several years. Although he focuses on highly liquid large caps, there's a risk that ongoing inflows will limit Marsico's ability to pack a lot of assets into his highest-conviction picks.

Merrill Lynch

Merrill Lynch's mutual fund operation has made some positive strides since Bob Doll took over as president and chief investment officer in 1999, but can't yet be counted among the mutual fund elite. Doll has helped modernize the firm's research, risk control and trading platforms, and has also improved the communication between managers and analysts. Another big improvement here is a compensation scheme that places greater emphasis on longer-term performance. Doll has made some key changes on the personnel front as well.

Still, Merrill's lineup is a work in progress. There are a number of funds with mediocre results, as well as some with narrow mandates that make them exceptionally volatile. Also, expenses are high on many of the firm's funds given their asset levels.

Strengths: Merrill Lynch Large Cap Core and Merrill Lynch Large Cap Value are particularly sound.

Weaknesses: The firm has a few holes in its domestic small- and mid-cap lineup. The international funds also need some work; Merrill Lynch Developing Capital Markets, an emerging-markets fund, is particularly weak.

MFS

MFS, which runs the industry's oldest mutual fund, has a full lineup of funds, but the shop is perhaps best-known for its large-growth offerings. As was the case at firms like Putnam and Janus, MFS' gutsier funds put up impressive returns in the late 1990s, but they crashed back to earth in 2000 with the onset of the bear market. Since then, MFS' growth-oriented managers are paying closer attention to valuation when selecting stocks for their portfolios. The firm also has beefed up its research effort by hiring some more-experienced analysts and firing some underperforming managers. Recent performance has been stronger, but it's too soon to say whether those results are sustainable.

MFS is also recovering from 2004's market-timing scandal, in which regulators found that the firm allowed fast-trading in some of its funds. (It's worth noting that MFS did not have any "sticky asset" deals, whereby large investors agree to invest certain sums in a fund company's offerings in exchange for the ability to quickly move in and out of its funds.) MFS has since brought in new senior management, strengthened the independence of its board of directors, and stopped using soft dollars to pay for third-party stock research.

Strengths: Although MFS is known for its growth investing, its value funds—specifically MFS Value and MFS Strategic Value—are among the firm's strongest offerings. It's worth noting, however, that two of the value team's longest-tenured members have retired in the past year.

Weaknesses: MFS is looking to some relatively inexperienced managers to turn around some funds with lackluster relative returns, including the flagship MFS Massachusetts Investors Trust and MFS New Discovery, a small-growth fund. We'd wait for these managers to prove their mettle before jumping in.

Oakmark

Oakmark uses a deep-value approach on all of its funds, seeking companies that are trading at big discounts to its managers' estimates of their intrinsic values. Oakmark is a highly research-intensive firm, and the managers know their companies inside and out. Generally speaking, this approach has produced strong long-term returns. However, the concentrated nature of the portfolios, combined with some managers' willingness to take on sector risk, has sometimes led to uneven performance.

Strengths: We're fans of Oakmark's domestic- and foreign-stock funds. The crown jewels here are Oakmark Fund and Oakmark Select, which are run by 2001 Morningstar Domestic Stock Manager of the Year Bill Nygren.

Weaknesses: We wouldn't recommend building a portfolio exclusively of Oakmark funds, because that would leave you without growth stocks or fixed income.

Oppenheimer

Oppenheimer isn't a bad choice for one-stop shopping. The firm, whose funds are sold through advisors, offers a diverse lineup covering various asset classes and investment styles. Managers and analysts work in teams based on their investment disciplines, such as growth, value, and global.

Oppenheimer's domestic-equity funds rarely shoot out the lights, but many of them offer a respectable risk/return profile. The fund's value lineup had been a weak area in the past, but the firm has taken steps to address the problem. It has brought in outside managers and analysts to build up the value team. The firm also brought in a new investment-grade bond team to take over a few middling fixed-income offerings. That team, which came from the former MAS division of Morgan Stanley, follows a disciplined process that places great emphasis on risk control. Finally, the firm's Rochester municipal-bond division has recently assumed responsibility for the firm's national and state tax-exempt funds.

Strengths: Under the guidance of Bill Wilby, Oppenheimer's global lineup is the firm's crown jewel. A unique theme-based approach to uncovering hidden gems across the globe has generally delivered superb results. Oppenheimer Capital Appreciation, a tame large-growth offering, is also worth a look.

Weaknesses: Many of the fund's municipal-bond funds have been lackluster performers, so we'd steer clear.

PIMCO

PIMCO's prowess in fixed-income management is second to none. PIMCO Total Return is by far the biggest bond fund around and it's also one of the best. PIMCO's size has enabled it to build a great staff of analysts, managers, and traders. In addition, its size has given its institutional share classes low expenses. We've twice named PIMCO's bond guru, Bill Gross, our Fixed Income Manager of the Year because of his uncanny ability to regularly turn in great results.

Strengths: If you invest through a 401(k) or a planner with a large practice, you might be able to buy into the low-cost institutional share class of PIMCO Total Return. If not, PIMCO subadvises Harbor Bond, a low-cost virtual clone of that offering. PIMCO also offers a suite of fine offerings designed to perform well in an inflationary environment, including PIMCO Real Return and PIMCO Commodity Real Return Strategy.

Weaknesses: PIMCO's shorter-term bond funds are fine if you can get into one of the institutional share classes, but the lettered share classes (A, B, C, and D shares) are too costly.

Putnam

Like Janus, Putnam has been struggling in recent years to recover from terrible bear-market losses at its growth funds as well as its involvement in the fund scandal. Regulators accused the firm of fraud in 2003, alleging that the fund company allowed some investors—including six of its own fund managers—to quickly trade in and out of its funds at the expense of long-term fundholders. When Putnam executives discovered the improper trading, they failed to properly discipline the employees. Putnam also failed to cut off market-timers in its 401(k) funds.

Putnam has taken considerable steps to put this episode behind it, including dismissing its former chief executive Larry Lasser. Ed Haldeman, the new CEO, engineered considerable improvement at Delaware Investments before joining Putnam about two years ago. Haldeman has improved compliance, cut fees, fired personnel involved in the unethical trading, and is working to improve performance at the firms' funds.

We're not giving Putnam a clean bill of health—it still has to prove that its lackluster growth offerings are on the mend—but the firm deserves credit for its efforts to reform its culture and deliver better results for investors.

Strengths: Putnam's value and blend funds are generally solid; New Value has been a particularly strong performer under manager Dave King's watch.

Weaknesses: Putnam appears to have its growth funds aimed in the right direction, but we wouldn't jump in just yet, particularly because the funds have seen significant management upheaval in recent years. The firm's international funds, once a real bright spot in its lineup, are no longer the strong options they once were, owing to a key manager's dismissal during the fund scandal.

Royce

Royce is one of the fund world's best small-cap shops. Traditionally the firm has had a value bias, but it now has plenty of blend funds and even a few growth offerings. Founder Chuck Royce and the firm's other managers and analysts are particularly skilled in this patch of the market. Legg Mason owns the firm, but hasn't shown an inclination to meddle in what Royce does well.

Strengths: Royce Premier, a small-blend fund, is a standout option. We'd also jump at the chance to buy the now-closed Royce Special Equity.

Weaknesses: The key concern regarding Royce is whether success will spoil the firm. Royce Total Return, for example, is a fine fund, but it's the largest actively managed small-cap offering still open to new investors. We'd like to see the firm take steps to close its funds proactively, before they become too large.

Scudder

This fund family has seen substantial turmoil over the past several years. In April 2002, Deutsche Asset Management acquired Zurich Scudder Investments (which had absorbed the Kemper Funds in 1997). That sparked the departure of several portfolio managers, and Deutsche's executive ranks endured substantial turnover as well.

Meanwhile, in January 2004, the firm revealed that it had previously allowed an investment advisory firm to market-time several of its foreign stock funds. While that arrangement was initiated under Deutsche's previous regime, it's not yet clear if the firm has rooted out all wrongdoers (the firm has not been charged by regulators).

Aside from the scandal, Scudder's current fund lineup—a sprawling one due to the various mergers—is a mixed bag. The firm has taken steps to eliminate redundant offerings and bring in new talent, but its best domestic-equity funds are subadvised by outside firms. Meanwhile, Scudder's fixed-income funds are generally solid, but the firm's international stock funds are only so-so.

Also, we're becoming concerned about the lack of stability here. Several executives have recently departed, and two new ones from parent company Deutsche Bank—which is likely unhappy with its investment at this point— were recently brought in. It's unknown what effect that might have on the funds, but it's difficult to get excited about them at this point.

Strengths: Scudder Dreman High Return Equity is a standout deep-value fund managed by one of the investing world's best-known contrarians, David Dreman. Scudder Flag Value Builder and Scudder Fixed Income are also terrific offerings.

Weaknesses: The lingering market-timing scandal and the continuing lack of stability—a result of the Deutsche/Scudder/Kemper mergers—provide plenty of reason to be wary.

TIAA-CREF

Known for managing teachers' pension funds, TIAA-CREF (Teachers Insurance and Annuity Association–College Retirement Equities Fund) has branched out into mutual funds. The funds are broadly diversified portfolios, some of which blend active with passive management. No niche products here.

Strengths: TIAA-CREF Equity Index is a solid total-stock-market fund with low costs; the firm's bond funds have also been superb.

Weaknesses: The actively managed portions of some TIAA-CREF funds have been mediocre. In addition, TIAA-CREF has recently moved to hike expenses in its actively-managed stock funds.

T. Rowe Price

T. Rowe Price offers mild-mannered style-specific funds. You'll find that T. Rowe Price's funds are among the more conservative options in just about any category because they all adhere to risk-reducing strategies. The funds avoid big stock or sector bets, and even T. Rowe Price's growth funds are wary about buying stocks with a lot of price risk. The firm has also done a great job of enticing managers to stick around.

Strengths: T. Rowe Price has fine offerings across the board. Its Equity Income fund, run by Brian Rogers for the past 20 years, is one of our favorite large-value offerings. We're also big fans of the firm's Growth Stock fund. T. Rowe Price Global Stock is also an offering to watch here, as manager Rob Gensler has amassed a tremendous record at the firm's telecom and media fund. If you want a specialized fund such as a regional or sector fund, an offering from T. Rowe makes a good choice because the firm tries to tone down the risk in volatile asset classes.

Weaknesses: T. Rowe's core bond offering, New Income, is an extremely competent fund, but it's not in the very top tier of intermediate-term bond offerings. T. Rowe Price International Stock has also failed to stand out. And while the firm is extremely shareholder friendly on the whole, it did launch a few technology sector funds just as tech stocks were peaking.

Tweedy, Browne

These value stalwarts are throwbacks to the Graham and Dodd investing style, in which Warren Buffett was also schooled. They look for cheap, well-run businesses. The biggest difference between Tweedy, Browne's funds and Longleaf's is that this team avoids big stock bets. Thus, you get a much smoother ride here. The firm's two funds—Global Value (a foreign-stock fund) and American Value, a mid-value offering—are both closed.

Strengths: For mild-mannered foreign-stock exposure, you can't go wrong with Tweedy, Browne Global Value. And while American Value has struggled over the past few years, we think its style could be due for a rebound. Both funds are closed, but well worth holding.

Weaknesses: Tweedy, Browne funds' fees are generally quite reasonable, but Global Value's expenses haven't come down even though its assets have risen dramatically.

Vanguard

This firm still bears the imprint of its founder, Jack Bogle, who was a zealot when it came to cutting costs and stumping for fund-shareholder rights. Notably, Vanguard's funds are invariably dirt-cheap, typically founded on prudent investment strategies, and run by a cast of experienced managers. The secret to the firm's enduring success in upholding this model has been its unique organizational structure: The various Vanguard funds own the advisor, The Vanguard Group, Inc., which provides its services at cost. Consequently, Vanguard has not wavered noticeably from its modus operandi of placing shareholder interests front and center, where they belong. In so doing, Vanguard has been able to support its current lineup—which is replete with strong performers—while introducing new funds in a judicious manner. The upshot for investors has been positive—Vanguard's stable is remarkable for its consistency across asset classes and investing styles. Simply put, there are few weak spots here.

Strengths: For index funds, bond funds, and tax-managed funds, Vanguard is tough to beat. The firm boasts some great actively managed funds, too, thanks to the firm's low costs and ability to choose solid managers. Among the actively managed Vanguard funds we like are Selected Value, International Growth, and the new Primecap Core.

Weaknesses: Aside from the solid Vanguard Explorer, a small-growth fund, Vanguard doesn't have a lot to offer in terms of actively managed small-cap funds.

Wasatch

These small-cap specialists are that rare boutique that can actually manage both growth and value funds well. Led by Sam Stewart, this closely held firm has produced outstanding results. We also like Wasatch's willingness to close funds while assets are still small. The downside to the firm's closing policy is that expenses are high on some of the firm's funds.

Strengths: Wasatch's U.S. small-cap funds are all closed, but we'd gladly buy any of them if they were to reopen. The firm's Heritage Growth fund, a mid- to large-cap growth offering, is a relatively new offering whose prospects are bright.

Weaknesses: The firm isn't trying to be all things to all people, so you'll have to look elsewhere for exposure to large caps or bonds.

Investor's Checklist: Get to Know Your Fund Manager

- ▶ Remember that evaluating fund managers can be as much art as science. You won't find quality of management summed up in a single data point.
- ▶ Look for a manager with experience. A rule of thumb is to stick with managers who have at least 10 years of experience. Also, favor managers who have learned from some of the best or cut their teeth at high-quality firms.
- ▶ Find out who is behind the manager. A fund manager needs a strong support staff for research and trading.

▶ Check out a wide range of funds at the firm to see if they are successful across the board. Be wary of fund companies that have only one star fund surrounded by mediocre offerings.

▶ Delve into whether the fund shop puts fund shareholders on an equal footing with company stakeholders. Investigate the quality and independence of its board, as well as the firm's record on matters such as fund costs and trendy fund launches.

5

Keep a Lid on Costs

ASK YOUR NEIGHBOR how much she pays for cable television service every month and she can probably tell you within a dollar. Ask her how much she pays for money management and she might not have any idea. Yet, she's probably paying five times more for money management than for cable. If you figure a 1% fee for a $150,000 portfolio, that's $1,500 a year. And if an advisor is managing her money, she might be paying another $3,000 to $5,000. After your home, your money-management fees may well rank among your top household expenses along with your car payments and food budget.

The tendency of investors to lose track of such a big figure is why money management is such a great business to be in. The fees are spread out over the year so that you hardly notice them, and you never receive a bill showing you exactly how much you owe. In any single year, your portfolio's appreciation or depreciation before costs is sure to be greater than the expense bill, so you're more likely to focus on your return than what you're paying in expenses. The catch is that those fees can add up to a small fortune from the time you buy your first fund to the time you make your last sale.

Funds are required to report their expense ratios on a regular basis to their shareholders. A fund's expense ratio shows you what percentage of a fund's assets are used to cover the costs of managing the fund, including management fees, administrative charges, and, where applicable, charges called 12b-1 fees, which were designed to cover a fund's marketing and distribution costs. A $50 million fund with a 1% expense ratio, for example, is charging all of its shareholders $500,000 per year to run their money, whereas a $50 million fund with a 1.5% expense ratio is charging all of its shareholders $750,000 to run the fund. Because expense ratios are calculated uniformly among funds, it's easy to look at two offerings and make apples to apples comparisons. And when you see total return figures reported for a mutual fund, you can rest assured that those returns factor in the fund's expense ratio.

Unfortunately, however, a fund isn't required to show you exactly what it will cost you to own it—in dollars and cents, based on the size of your own investment—in a given year. Nor do fund expense ratios reflect all of the other costs associated with owning that investment, including the fund's trading-related costs, any sales charges you might pay to buy and sell the fund, and any taxes you might have to pay because you own the fund. Even if an investor wanted to focus on costs, the complexity of fund expenses would make it difficult to get a sense of the actual dollars and cents you'd shell out if you owned a given fund.

Avoiding the Rearview Mirror Trap

Before we delve into the particulars of other fund-related expenses, let's first discuss why a fund's costs are so critical. If all funds cost the same or if paying more ensured better management, costs wouldn't matter. Fund expense ratios vary widely, however, and high-cost funds don't have better managers than low-cost funds. Investors too often ignore costs because they make the mistake of driving while looking through the rearview mirror. They look at a chart showing past fund performance and reason that if the fund at the top managed to overcome its expense ratio in the past, why shouldn't it be able to in the future? The problem is that for every high-risk, high-cost fund that hits it big, there are 10 more that fail. You seldom notice the losers because they generate little coverage in the same way that television news reports about lottery jackpot winners do not give equal time to the millions of people who failed to win any money. What's more, high-cost funds that made big, losing bets often are merged into funds with better records, so they won't even show up when you search for them today.

Looking through the windshield rather than the rearview mirror, you can see that expense ratios are the clearest thing ahead. You can't know which sectors will perform well or whether your fund manager will jump ship, but you have a very good idea what a fund's expense ratio will be in the future. In general, expense ratios show little change from year to year unless a fund's asset base changes dramatically or regulators force the fund shop to make fee cuts. (During the mutual fund scandal of 2003 and 2004, the New York Attorney General's office penalized several high-profile firms by forcing them to cut their funds' expenses.) For example, Janus Twenty lost 24% in 2002 and soared 25% the following year, but its expense ratio hardly changed. Expenses are the easiest part of fund returns to control.

It wouldn't merit much attention if the difference between a cheap and an expensive fund only added up to a few dollars after 20 years. However, the power of compounding interest makes small sums grow very large over time. Compare the results of the supercheap Vanguard 500 Index, which costs 0.18%, with the reasonably priced Fidelity Discovery at 0.84%, and the rather pricey Federated Kaufmann (A shares) at 1.95% (see Figure 5.1). If you were to invest $10,000 in each fund and each produced 10% annualized returns before taxes over the ensuing 20-year period, you would end up spending a little over $1,000 in fees for Vanguard 500, $4,500 for the Fidelity fund, and $9,100 for the Federated fund (assuming the funds' expense ratios stay where they are now). When you factor in the effects of compounding—which means that because you're giving up less of your initial investment to costs, money in the

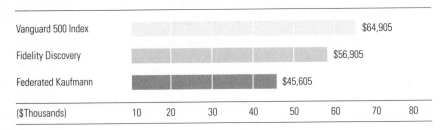

Vanguard 500 Index							$64,905	
Fidelity Discovery						$56,905		
Federated Kaufmann				$45,605				
($Thousands)	10	20	30	40	50	60	70	80

Figure 5.1 Hypothetical growth of a $10,000 investment after 20 years. This example assumes that each fund generated a 10% return before expenses.

cheapest fund has the potential to grow faster and larger than money in the more expensive fund—the gap in final dollar values would be even greater. Thus, a $10,000 investment in Vanguard 500 would have grown to $64,905 at the end of 20 years (assuming a 10% annualized return), while Federated Kaufmann would have grown that sum to just $45,605—a gap of $19,300! If you had invested $100,000, you could add a zero to that figure ($190,000) and if you had $1 million in the fund, you would be talking about a $1.9 million gap.

This hypothetical scenario works in practice, too: Funds with higher expense ratios tend to lag cheaper funds. In a 2002 study published in *Morningstar Mutual Funds*, our colleague Scott Cooley divided all of the funds in each Morningstar category into one of four groupings based on their expense ratios in 1996: the highest cost 25%, the next highest cost 25%, the second cheapest 25%, and finally, the cheapest 25%. He found that in all categories, low-cost funds outperformed high-cost funds over the subsequent five-year period. For small-company growth funds, for example, the cheapest 25% produced annualized five-year returns of 8.47% between 1996 and 2001, whereas the highest cost 25% produced returns of 6.97% over that five-year stretch. For large-blend funds, the advantage was a narrower but still significant— 1.2% a year.

But what about all of those funds that have managed to trump their peers even though they charge a lot? Doesn't that show that manager skill matters more than expenses? Not so fast. Because investors who choose high-cost funds often do so because these offerings have produced strong past performance, Scott took a closer look at this group of high-cost over-achievers in an effort to see whether their good fortunes would persist. He pored through Morningstar data to find those funds with high expenses but top 25% returns in the period from 1991 through 1996. He then compared that group's subsequent five-year performance with the subsequent five-year returns of low-cost funds that had landed in their categories' bottom 25% from 1991 through 1996. Over the ensuing five years, from 1997 through 2001, the cheap funds with lousy track records whipped the high-cost funds with strong past returns.

People often assume that paying more means you get higher quality. It's a pretty good bet that a car that costs $50,000 is a better vehicle than one that costs $15,000, after all, even though you may not think it's worth the additional cost. In the fund world, however, a cheap fund is just as likely to be run by an outstanding manager as is a pricey one. For example, American Funds Washington Mutual, which employs an outstanding crew of experienced managers, currently charges 0.64% a year. Vanguard Primecap, which is also run by a brilliant team, currently charges a mere 0.46%. Harbor Bond, run by Morningstar's two-time bond fund manager of the year Bill Gross, charges just 0.57%.

Comparing Expense Ratios

Now that we've established the importance of paying attention to expense ratios, let's talk about what you should be looking for. First, be aware that fund expense ratios often vary by fund type. In general, the lower returning the asset class, the less you should be prepared to pay in annual expenses. For example, money market funds and money market alternatives, such as ultrashort-term bond funds, often charge 0.50% or less in annual operating expenses—the cheapest of the cheap in the mutual fund world. In part that's because these funds don't cost a lot to run (after all, it doesn't take a lot of research to pick high-quality bonds with very short maturities) and it's also because fund companies know that there's not a lot of opportunity to dramatically beat one's rivals within these asset classes. If one fund shop's money market fund is charging 1% in expenses while most of its rivals charge 0.50%, there are very few ways the manager of the pricey fund can make up that expense disadvantage.

Beyond money market and ultrashort funds, conventional bond funds are the next cheapest fund type; you can find lots of terrific core fixed-income funds that charge less than 0.75% in annual expenses. More specialized bond-fund types, such as high-yield or emerging-markets bond funds, might charge slightly more, but in general you should try to keep your bond funds' expense ratios to 1% or lower. Think of it this way: If a bond fund is yielding 5% (and that's a pretty good yield these days), your fund's total return is apt to be somewhere in the 5% neighborhood, too. If you're paying more than 1% in expenses, you're surrendering a full 20% of your return!

Stock funds typically charge more than bond funds, with some offerings charging upwards of 2% in annual expenses. That's too much. If you're looking for a large-company stock fund to anchor your portfolio, you can find plenty of terrific offerings that charge less than 1% in annual expenses. You may have to pay slightly more for more specialized stock fund types—including international, small-company, or sector-specific funds—but you should think long and hard before paying 1.5% in annual expenses for any fund type.

Figure 5.2 provides a survey of the average expense ratios for each type of fund.

Understanding Sales Charges

Although we've just gone on and on about why you should take care to keep your costs low when investing in funds, we would disagree with those who say that all investors should only consider no-load funds. (No-load funds are those that you can buy and sell without paying a sales charge; load funds, conversely, carry sales charges and are typically available to those who invest with a broker or planner.) True, we'd concede that your overall investment costs will generally

Category	Average Expense Ratio %
Large Value	1.15
Large Growth	1.31
Large Blend	0.99
Mid-Cap Value	1.29
Mid-Cap Growth	1.39
Mid-Cap Blend	1.32
Small Value	1.31
Small Growth	1.44
Small Blend	1.33
Conservative Allocation, Moderate Allocation	1.21
Foreign, Europe, Japan, and World	1.71
Emerging Markets (incl. Latin America and Pacific/Asia)	2.08
All Sector Funds	1.81
Bond	1.12
High-Yield Bond	1.28
Emerging Markets, Multisector, and International Bond	1.34

Figure 5.2   Comparison of average expense ratios.

be lower if you go the no-load route, and we've known many investors who have crafted terrific portfolios of no-load funds. But if you're not comfortable putting together an asset allocation plan, selecting specific funds, and monitoring that portfolio, then paying an advisor or broker to do it for you can be money well spent, even if it means paying a sales charge to buy or sell.

That's not to say that you shouldn't carefully scrutinize any sales charges you pay, however—you should. These charges are taken out of your investment automatically; you will not be writing a check to cover them, so you might not even realize that you're paying them or know how large they are. But the type of sales charge you pay can have a big effect on your overall portfolio's return. And in recent years fund-industry regulators have turned up several instances in which investors were overcharged when buying and selling fund shares through brokers. For these reasons, it pays to know how the different sales charges work and to grill your broker about why you're paying the type of sales charge you're paying.

Although the alphabet soup can be inconsistent from family to family, fund companies often identify the different cost structures available as A, B, and C shares.

Funds that carry front-end loads are usually called A shares. The fund's sales charge is simply taken out of your initial investment up front. So if you put $10,000 into one of Putnam funds' A share classes, many of which carry a 5.25% load, you will pay $525 in commissions and invest $9,475 in the fund. Front loads typically range from 3% to 5.75%. If the fund's annual expenses are relatively low, A shares are often the best deal for long-term investors who are buying through a broker or advisor.

B shares usually carry deferred loads, meaning that you will not pay sales charges until you sell the fund. The charges also decline each year you hold the fund. Although B shares might sound like a good deal—and some unscrupulous brokers go so far as to tell investors they're not paying a load by opting for the B shares—B shares usually are not the best choice for most investors. In fact, a few fund shops—including Franklin Templeton—have stopped selling B shares altogether. B shares are often a bad deal for investors because they include stiff annual fees, called 12b-1 fees, which are part of your fund's expense ratio. (12b-1 refers to a fee that fund companies are allowed to charge to cover the costs of marketing and distributing their funds.) Brokers often like to sell B shares because they can receive that 12b-1 fee year in and year out, but those high ongoing costs can be a big drag on your bottom line. Thus, if your broker suggests that you consider the B share class of a given fund, be sure to ask your broker whether the A shares might not be a better choice for you. And if you do opt for B shares, at the very least you should look for back-load shares with conversion features. In this type of fund, the back-load shares effectively become front-load shares for investors who have owned the fund for a certain number of years, and front-load shares almost always have lower 12b-1 fees.

Funds with level loads are usually called C shares. They have no initial sales charge (or a relatively modest one of 1% or 2%). However, these funds further compensate the broker who sells you the fund by charging an annual fee (typically about 1%) each year you stay in the fund. That's good for the broker, but it means higher annual costs for shareholders.

For example, Scudder funds' C shares don't have an initial sales charge, but they carry heavier annual expenses than the firm's A and B shares. Level-load shares might make sense for an investor who intends to hold a given fund for a very short time period, but they're particularly bad choices for long-term investors. It's better to pay one lump sum up front than to have your return eaten away each year by higher expenses.

Unfortunately, the list goes beyond A, B, and C shares. You'll also see I shares at some firms; these are usually for institutional investors and have lower costs but require very high minimums, such as $1 million. And occasionally you'll spot R shares, S shares, or Z shares. These typically are the former no-load shares of a fund that has been taken over by a load fund shop; they're often closed to new investors. Finally, some no-load funds have specially designated share classes for large investors or retirement plans. (By the way, you should know that we recognize how confusing all of these different letters and arrangements must seem to ordinary investors. That's why we wrote a column several years back on Morningstar.com, pleading with fund companies to "Stop the Share-Class Madness." It didn't help.)

In addition to making sure that you opt for the right share class for you, be sure to ask your broker if you qualify for a reduced load based on the size of your investment. Most fund shops charge smaller loads if your investment hits a breakpoint, such as $75,000 or $50,000, and you may be able to count several accounts as one for that purpose. (Some brokerage firms got in trouble recently for failing to provide these discounts to investors who qualified for them, so your broker should be well aware of the issue and more than willing to tell you the breakpoints.)

There is absolutely no reason to pay a load if you're picking your own funds. For nearly any load fund out there, you can find a reasonable no-load alternative. And given the bite a sales charge takes out of your investment, you can often get better returns even if the no-load fund isn't quite as good as the load one.

Paying Attention to Hidden Costs

As important as it is to pay attention to a fund's expense ratio and sales charges, those two fees don't tell you all you need to know about what it will cost to own that fund. For example, other fund-related expenses come out of your return but aren't reflected in the fund's expense ratio.

Take brokerage commissions. Your manager has to pay these costs when he or she buys or sells stocks and bonds for the portfolio, but fund companies don't have to include these costs when calculating fund expense ratios. You'd expect funds' trading costs to be lower than what you or I would pay to execute a trade; after all, funds are typically trading large numbers of shares, so they should be able to negotiate volume discounts, right? Well, yes and no. Unfortunately for fund shareholders, some fund shops pay more than they need to for trades because they receive research and other goodies in exchange for paying higher commissions. And under a practice called *directed brokerage*, which regulators banned in 2004, some fund shops paid inflated trading commissions in exchange for having their funds placed on that brokerage firm's "preferred list."

Funds also face so-called market-impact costs. That means that if your manager is trying to buy or sell a big block of a given stock, there's a chance that the fund will have to accept a less advantageous price for that security than if he or she were buying or selling fewer shares. For example, say your manager is trying to buy 1 million shares of a certain small-company stock. If only 100,000 shares of that stock typically change hands each day, that means it will take your fund manager a minimum of 10 days to complete your fund's trade. In the meantime, the stock could get more and more expensive, reducing the amount of money that your manager can make in it.

So if these costs aren't included in a fund's expense ratio, how can you try to keep track of them and limit them? We have a couple of suggestions. To keep fund trading costs from dragging on your bottom line, we'd urge you to focus on those funds that simply don't trade much. Index mutual funds, especially those that focus on large-company stocks, generally limit their trading costs, because they simply mirror the holdings in a given market benchmark. You could also look for those actively managed funds with low turnover rates, an indication that their managers like to buy their holdings and hang on. A fund with a turnover rate of 25% or less, indicating that the manager completely makes over the portfolio every four years, will generally have lower trading costs than one with a turnover rate of 100%.

What about limiting market-impact costs—the risk that your manager will obtain a less than advantageous price for your fund's securities? A couple of different characteristics tend to put a fund at a greater risk for racking up these hidden costs. First, because high-turnover funds trade frequently, it only stands to reason that they run a greater risk of affecting securities' prices when they buy and sell. And funds that traffic in small-company stocks, which invariably have fewer outstanding shares than large-company stocks, could also see market-impact costs erode their returns. Finally, market-impact costs tend to be a bigger problem for funds with large asset bases than for tiny, nimble funds, simply because the manager of the big fund has to step up and buy or sell a greater number of the outstanding shares of a given security than does the manager of a tiny fund. We're not saying that you should automatically dismiss a fund simply because it has a large asset base, high turnover, or focuses on small-company stocks. But if you're considering a fund that has more than one of these risk factors, you would do well to consider whether market-impact costs could eventually drag on your own bottom line.

Minding Tax Efficiency

Tax costs can also take a bite out of your bottom line. In fact, despite the many advantages of the mutual fund format, the tax treatment of funds is one key drawback. Keep taxes in mind when managing your portfolio—for example, when deciding whether to hold a given fund in your taxable account or a tax-sheltered vehicle like a 401(k).

As a fund shareholder, taxes can hit you in several different ways. First, if you sell a fund from a taxable account after you've made a gain in it—for example, you invested $10,000 five years ago and you now have $20,000—you must pay taxes on that gain. By the same token, if you get an income distribution from a fund—say, your bond fund pays you income and you spend that check to cover living expenses or reinvest in the fund—you have to pay taxes on that payout. In these respects, a mutual fund is no different than owning stocks and bonds directly.

But you can also be on the hook for taxes if you haven't sold a single share of a given fund. That's because when funds themselves sell holdings and realize capital gains, they're required to pass on those capital-gains payouts to their shareholders, who in turn must pay taxes on those gains. That applies even if you don't actually take that money and spend it, and instead are reinvesting your fund's income and capital-gains payouts back into the fund.

So how can you limit the effect that taxes will have on your portfolio? Start by focusing on what you can control. Of course, you can do your part by limiting the amount of trading you do in your taxable account. Fund investors who use buy-and-hold strategies tend to be more successful than those who trade a lot. Employing a low-turnover strategy also has the salutary effect of limiting the amount of capital gains you have to pay taxes on, and in turn means that you'll have more money working for you in the market.

In addition to limiting your own trading in your taxable account, you can take care to ferret out those funds that have historically done a good job of keeping the tax collector at bay. So-called tax-managed funds are explicitly managed to limit the effects of taxes. Managers in charge of these vehicles often trade very little and actively work to offset capital gains by realizing losses from other holdings in the portfolio. Municipal bond funds, whose income payouts are exempt from federal (and in some cases, state) taxes can also be a good bet for taxable accounts. In addition, certain funds that use very low turnover strategies—say, those with turnover rates of 10% or less—make sense for taxable accounts. Because the manager isn't doing much buying or selling, the fund isn't likely to be realizing sizable capital gains.

Morningstar provides a few separate statistics to help you get your arms around a fund's tax-related costs and determine whether it's best suited for a tax-sheltered or taxable account. All of these statistics are available on the *Morningstar Mutual Funds* page (available in public libraries) or on the Tax Analysis page for each individual fund on Morningstar.com.

To help investors determine how tax-efficient a fund has been in the past, we provide a tax-adjusted return for each fund over the past 3-, 5-, and 10-year periods. Basically, the tax-adjusted return depicts an investor's gain (or loss) after accounting for all income payouts and short- and long-term capital-gains distributions. (For the purpose of this statistic, we assume investors are paying the maximum tax rates for each type of distribution.) For example, as of early 2005, Legg Mason Value's three-year tax-adjusted return was identical to its pretax return; because manager Bill Miller trades very little and works to limit the tax collector's cut, investors in taxable accounts have pocketed every bit as much as investors who own the fund in tax-sheltered accounts. N/I Numeric Investors Small Cap Value has also been a fabulous performer but it has surrendered a big share of its return to taxes. The fund's three-year pretax return, through January 2005, was 20.51%, whereas its tax-adjusted return was 15.11%—more than five percentage points less!

Along the same lines, we also provide what we call a tax–cost ratio for each fund. Basically, the tax–cost ratio expresses the percentage-point reduction in annual returns lost to taxes. (Again, for the purpose of this statistic we assume that an investor is in the highest tax bracket.) Thus, the bigger that number is, the less appealing the fund is for taxable accounts. In that respect, a fund's tax–cost ratio is similar to its expense ratio: Lower is better! (Unlike the expense ratio, however, the tax–cost ratio is not deducted from a fund's published returns.)

Finally, to help investors determine how tax-friendly a fund is apt to be in the future, we also provide a statistic called potential capital-gain exposure. Essentially, potential capital-gain exposure shows you what percentage of a fund's net assets would be subject to taxation if the fund were to liquidate today. (This number, like tax-adjusted returns and the tax–cost ratio, can be found in the Tax Analysis section for each fund on Morningstar.com or in *Morningstar Mutual Funds*.) A higher number indicates that the manager has been content to hang on to his or her winners, so the fund has a lot of unrealized gains on its books. While a high potential capital gain exposure figure needn't be perceived as an imminent threat, would-be investors should know that if a new manager came aboard the fund or if the manager were forced to sell shares to meet investor redemptions, shareholders could be on the hook for a tax bill. Where a negative number appears, the fund has unrealized losses that it can possibly use to offset future gains.

Investor's Checklist: Keep a Lid on Costs

▶ Be a cheapskate. When you look for funds, focus on low costs. Look for bond funds that charge less than 0.75% and stock funds that charge less than 1.00%. (You may have to pay more for more specialized stock and bond funds, but core funds should fall within these parameters.)

▶ Check out the expense ratios of the funds you already own. If some are more costly than is the norm for their categories, see if you can switch to lower cost options.

▶ If you're working with a broker, find out how much you're paying and make sure the advice you are getting is worth the price.

▶ If you plan to buy a load fund and hold on for the long haul, funds with front-end loads (often referred to as A shares) are generally the best deal.

▶ Be on the lookout for hidden costs. High-turnover funds generally have higher trading costs and could also be vulnerable to so-called market-impact costs. Small-company funds, particularly those with big asset bases, may also be vulnerable to market-impact costs.

▶ If you're holding a fund in a taxable account, look for one that's geared toward limiting the tax collector's cut. Tax-managed funds, municipal bond funds, and ultralow-turnover funds all fit the bill.

6

Find the Right Core Stock Funds for You

SAY YOU'VE IDENTIFIED a fund that stacks up well on all of the major counts—its returns have been solid, it's not too risky, it boasts an experienced manager, and its costs are reasonable. But there's still no guarantee that it's the right fund for you. To know that, you need a better understanding of how a fund is investing and whether its strategy is compatible with your goals.

Because a core stock fund or two should form the foundation of nearly every investor's portfolio, you should spend extra time understanding the nuances of your core funds' strategies. At Morningstar, we strongly believe that investors are more successful when they buy a fund with the intention of hanging on to it for many years. Thus, it's essential that you understand the strategy your core stock fund is employing and believe that it makes sense for you and your goals. If you understand and believe in your fund's approach—whether you own a fund run by a bargain-hunting manager or an ultracheap index fund that's content to shadow a given market benchmark— you're much more likely to use it wisely, hanging on when the fund hits a rough patch, for example.

Identifying Core Stock Funds

At the risk of stating the obvious, a fund that's an appropriate holding for an investor with a 45-year time horizon is probably going to be pretty different from one that's the right pick for a retiree. But at the heart of nearly every investor's portfolio, no matter what his or her time horizon is, should be at least one or two stock funds that can be considered core holdings. We discuss some specific strategies for allocating your assets among different fund types in Part Three of this book, but in general at least 75% of your equity holdings should be in so-called core stock funds.

When we talk about core funds, we're typically referring to those funds that are broadly diversified across sectors and individual stocks. Moreover, funds that we consider core don't typically put the bulk of their assets in racy small-company names, but rather focus on large-company stocks. Why the obsession with large caps? For starters, such issues typically display less volatility than smaller stocks (the strong recent performance of small-cap stocks notwithstanding). It's also because most investors don't want their core stock holdings to be dramatically out of step with the broad U.S. stock market. Because the U.S. market, as represented by the Dow Jones Wilshire 5000 index, currently has about 70% of its assets in large-cap stocks, it stands to reason that your anchor stock holding(s) should also put the lion's share of assets in large-company stocks. For most investors we'd recommend that the bulk of their equity assets be in funds that land in Morningstar's large-growth, large-blend, or large-value categories.

Foreign-stock funds that land in Morningstar's foreign large-blend, foreign large-value, and foreign large-growth categories also make good core-holding material. (We discuss foreign-stock fund investing in more detail in Chapter 7.) Alternatively, a no-nonsense way to obtain core equity exposure is to buy an all-in-one fund that combines stocks and bonds in a single package. (We discuss these funds and other strategies for simplifying your investment life in Chapter 12.)

Understanding Value Funds

One of the key choices to make when selecting a core stock fund is deciding between those that favor value stocks, growth stocks, or something in the middle. (For more details on how we define investment style and why we think it's important, see Chapter 1.)

To illustrate the difference between the growth and value styles of investing, it might help to think about the real estate market. One real estate buyer —think of him as the value investor—might prefer the cheaper house on the less desirable side of town. Sure, it needs some fixing up, and the neighborhood's not the best. But the house is close to downtown, which is beginning to enjoy a renaissance. At some point, he figures, the house's price will rise sharply, so he's willing to wait through some lean years. By contrast, a growth investor considers it ridiculous to languish in substandard housing waiting for a revival that might never come. She would prefer the house in the neighborhood that has long been considered your area's most desirable. Sure, prices are high there—they always have been. But that's because the neighborhood is centrally located, boasts the area's best schools, and features well-built homes with lots of amenities. The growth investor believes that a home in this area will always be desirable, so she's willing to pay a relatively high price for it today because she knows someone will pay her even more for it when she wants to sell.

Of course, not all value funds (or growth funds, for that matter) are identical. Different people have different definitions of what's a great value. Maybe you call your shoes a deal because you paid only $14.99 for them at a discount store. Your friend, meanwhile, says her designer shoes, at $125, are a value buy because she got them for less than full price. Fund managers who buy value stocks express similar differences of opinion. All value managers buy stocks that they believe are worth significantly more than the current price, but they'll argue about just what makes a good value. How a manager defines value will determine what the portfolio includes and how the fund performs.

For example, look at sibling funds Vanguard Windsor and Vanguard Windsor II. They are both large-cap value funds, but their performance in recent years has differed dramatically. In 2001's value rally, Windsor gained 5.7%, while Windsor II lost 3.4%. In 2002, however, Windsor dropped 22.3% while Windsor II lost nearly 7 percentage points less. Why? Because their managers use very different approaches. Specifically, Windsor's managers focus on beaten-down industries they believe are due for a rebound, and they buy stocks that are the cheapest of the cheap. What's more, lead manager David Fassnacht isn't afraid to add to stocks that other investors are fleeing or to build sizable positions in troubled companies. The Windsor team's interest in beaten-up names has really stung at times. The fund entered 2002 with a 3% stake in WorldCom and nearly a 2% stake in Adelphia Communications, and the team added to both names when they fell early in that year. Those stocks proved extremely painful in 2002 as both plunged further and further in response to concerns about off-balance-sheet debt and their eventual bankruptcies.

Windsor II, meanwhile, also emphasizes cheap stocks, but its managers pay more attention to the companies' profitability. The Windsor II managers also favor those companies that pay big dividends, because it considers those dividend payouts to be an indication of a company's financial stability. As a result, the fund holds fewer deeply out-of-favor investments than Windsor does. That strategy hurt Windsor II in 2001 but helped it in 2002. For a closer look at how two funds can implement value strategies in different ways, check out

Top 10 Holdings for Vanguard Windsor (Portfolio Date: 12-31-04)	% of Net Assets
Citigroup	5.06
Bank of America	3.65
Comcast	3.35
Tyco International	3.24
Fannie Mae	2.46
Wyeth	2.41
Applied Materials	2.32
Pfizer	2.19
Time Warner	2.16
TJX Companies	2.02

Top 10 Holdings for Vanguard Windsor II (Portfolio Date: 12-31-04)	% of Net Assets
Wells Fargo	2.99
Occidental Petroleum	2.70
Citigroup	2.63
ConocoPhillips	2.46
Bank of America	2.48
Altria Group	2.48
JP Morgan Chase	2.43
Cendant	2.42
ChevronTexaco	2.06
Imperial Tobacco Group	2.05

Figure 6.1   Different definitions of value have led these funds to different portfolios.

the top 10 portfolio holdings for the two funds in Figure 6.1. A few of the holdings are the same, but most are not.

Value strategies divide into the relative-value and absolute-value camps; some value managers also look for stocks with high dividend yields. There are variations within each camp; in fact, Vanguard Windsor and Vanguard Windsor II both practice relative-value strategies.

Understanding Relative-Value Funds

Fund managers practicing relative-value strategies favor stocks that look cheap relative to some benchmark. In other words, value is relative (much like your friend was able to rationalize that her $125 shoes were a good buy because they were marked down from $200!). These benchmarks can include one or more of the following measures:

▶ *The Stock's Historical Price.* Companies selling for lower prices than usual—as represented by a lower-than-normal price/earnings, price/cash flow, price/book, or price/sales ratio—can be attractive buys for value managers. Often, these companies' prices are lower due to some type of bad news, to which the market often overreacts. When drug stocks like Merck and Pfizer took a tumble in 2004 and early 2005 because of bad news regarding their arthritis drugs, for example, many bargain-hunting managers, including the skippers of Vanguard Windsor and Windsor II, saw the plunge as a buying opportunity. They noticed that the stocks' price ratios were lower than they had been in many years and had confidence the companies could overcome their current problems.

▶ *The Norms for the Company's Industry or Subsector.* A manager may believe that a company is undeservedly cheap compared with its competitors in that same line of business. For example, in early 2005, Legg Mason Value manager Bill Miller added to his fund's stake in health-care insurance provider Aetna, arguing that there was no reason for the firm to trade at a big discount to rival UnitedHealth, which Miller also owned. Occasionally this thinking can backfire; after all, it may turn out that the rival firm *is* overpriced.

▶ *The Market.* In this case, a solid company may be dragged down because its whole industry is out of favor. This scenario is common in so-called

American Funds Washington Mutual	Sound Shore
Dodge & Cox Stock	Vanguard Growth and Income
ICAP Select Equity	Vanguard Windsor
Janus Mid-Cap Value	Vanguard Windsor II

Figure 6.2   Funds that follow relative-value strategies.

cyclical sectors—those that do best when the economy is growing but founder when the economy cools off. Energy, basic materials, and manufacturing companies are often considered cyclical, as are many technology hardware names. For example, in mid-2004 Vanguard Windsor began buying the stocks of semiconductor-related companies, which had tumbled due to concerns that companies weren't spending on technology gear to the extent that some market watchers thought they would.

In general, relative-value funds have a decent shot of delivering strong performance in a variety of market conditions—not just when truly cheap stocks are in demand. For example, although technology stocks soared in the late 1990s, leaving many value funds on the sidelines, certain relative-value funds actually performed reasonably well during that stretch because they had delved into tech names they considered cheap within that sector, which was pricey overall. The key drawback to the relative-value approach is that these funds might also have more exposure to volatile sectors, with technology and telecommunications being the prime examples. (See Figure 6.2 for a selection of relative-value funds.)

Understanding Absolute-Value Funds

Managers such as FPA Capital's Bob Rodriguez, Third Avenue's Marty Whitman and Curtis Jensen, and the teams at Oakmark and Longleaf Partners follow absolute-value strategies, and are typically considered stricter value practitioners than the relative-value set. (Warren Buffett, while not a fund manager, is perhaps the best-known practitioner of an absolute-value strategy.) Absolute-value managers don't compare a stock's price ratios to that company's historic norms, those of other companies, or the market. Instead, they try to figure out what a company is truly worth and they want to pay substantially less than that figure for the stock. If it's not selling for substantially less, then they're simply not interested, even if the stock is selling at a lower price than all of its rivals or the average for the S&P 500.

Absolute-value managers determine a company's worth using several factors, often looking at the company's assets, balance sheet, and growth prospects. They also study what private buyers have paid for similar companies. Determining a company's private market value is a key tool for Bill Nygren, who's made Oakmark Select and the Oakmark Fund among the most compelling funds for value-oriented investors.

As a general rule of thumb, absolute-value managers often focus on companies in traditional value sectors, including financials firms, basic-material and manufacturing companies, and energy firms. But some of these funds will also venture into traditional growth sectors—including technology, health care, and retail—if they find a company they think is selling at a discount to what it's truly worth. For example, Third Avenue's Marty Whitman and Curtis Jensen have long made a habit of buying semiconductor makers when they're in the dumps. And in recent years—even into 2005—Oakmark's Bill Nygren increasingly ventured into onetime growth stocks like Time Warner, Gap, and Disney.

Absolute-value managers may be willing to make more dramatic sector bets than their relative-value counterparts. For example, while some relative-value managers strive to keep their portfolios' sector weightings roughly in line with those of the S&P 500 Index, it's rare to find an absolute-value manager who's at all concerned with such considerations. For example, most absolute-value funds avoided tech stocks during the late 1990s. That big antitechnology bet meant that these offerings missed out on that sector's huge runup, but it also left them better positioned than relative-value funds when the sector eventually tanked. Some absolute-value managers have also piled assets into cheap stocks that have stayed depressed. That problem—also known as the *value trap* in investment circles—illustrates one of the key dangers of investing in cheap stocks: You might be buying cheap stocks that just get cheaper.

If you own an absolute-value fund, be prepared to wait out some dry spells and don't expect your fund to move in line with a broad market index such as the S&P 500. Managers who follow strict value strategies tend to be a determined lot, and they're generally not swayed by market fads. It can take a while for an extremely undervalued stock to pay off, particularly if it's in a

Clipper	Mutual Qualified
FPA Capital	Oakmark
Harbor Value	Oakmark Select
Longleaf Partners	Scudder Dreman High Return Equity
Mutual Beacon	Third Avenue Value
Mutual Shares	

Figure 6.3   Funds that follow absolute-value strategies.

segment of the market that's badly out of favor. Over long time periods, however, absolute-value strategies have often helped funds deliver strong long-term returns. (For a selection of absolute-value funds, see Figure 6.3.)

Understanding Income-Oriented Value Funds

Another subset of value funds are those that focus on companies with high dividend yields. Such funds may also use absolute- or relative-value strategies in addition to seeking stocks with high income payouts. These funds' managers take that approach for a few reasons. First, as we noted in the case with Vanguard Windsor II, some fund managers may consider a company's ability to pay out part of its earnings in the form of a dividend to be an important sign of financial strength. Other income-oriented managers might consider a high dividend yield to be a good sign of a cheap stock. (A company's dividend yield is calculated by dividing its dividend by its stock price, so if a company's share price is declining, its dividend yield will invariably be on the rise.) Finally, some value managers focus on dividend-paying stocks because they're catering to investors who are looking to their mutual funds for a regular income stream. This last group is a declining subset of stock funds, however, largely because most common stocks deliver little in the way of income these days.

Knowing When Value Investing Works

Although value investing makes a lot of intuitive sense (after all, most sane people would agree that it's better to buy a cheap stock than a pricey one), it doesn't pay off all the time. Both value and growth stocks can be subject to major performance swings. Although value strategies fared well in the early to mid-1990s as companies climbed out of the recession, growth stocks dominated the market in the last few years of that decade. Value-oriented investors did so badly in 1998 and 1999 that some commentators proclaimed the death

American Funds Washington Mutual	This fund offers just about everything a conservative value fund should: a veteran management team plying a mild-mannered strategy, a low expense ratio, and decent tax efficiency.
Clipper	This fund's management team has built a superb record by assembling a concentrated portfolio of companies that are trading at substantial discounts to their estimates of intrinsic value. Its exacting discipline has held it in good stead over time.
ICAP Select Equity	Manager Rob Lyon loads up on just 20 companies with reasonable valuations and improving growth prospects. He trades rapidly, making this a more appropriate holding for a tax-advantaged account.
Oakmark	One of Morningstar's favorite stock pickers, manager Bill Nygren buys mid- and large-cap stocks that are trading at discounts to their estimated intrinsic values. Nygren's record on this fund has been superb.
Oakmark Select	Like manager Bill Nygren's other charge, Oakmark, this fund invests in undervalued stocks. It's much more concentrated than its sibling, however, typically holding 15 to 20 names at a time.
Sound Shore	Management here builds a portfolio of 40 or so mid- and large-cap companies trading at large discounts to their historic price multiples. Using this strategy, the veteran team has built a fabulous long-term record.
T. Rowe Price Equity-Income	Veteran manager Brian Rogers' conservative approach has kept the fund out of trouble in down markets. Like American Funds Washington Mutual, this is a risk-averse dividend-paying fund.
Vanguard U.S. Value	Grantham, Mayo, Van Otterloo, a topnotch institutional firm, runs this offering for Vanguard, using quantitative models to pick this fund's stocks. Low costs are a key attraction.

Figure 6.4   Our favorite large-cap value funds.

of value investing. While tech stocks went on a tear, cheaper industrial manufacturers and basic-material producers, tobacco stocks, and weaker financial
issues got left out in the cold. The result was a dramatic shakeup in the investment business. At the low point for value—spring 2000—famous hedge-
fund manager Julian Robertson folded up his shop, Oakmark Fund's value
stalwart, Robert Sanborn, was nudged aside, and Fidelity's dean of money
managers, George Vanderheiden, retired.

But just when it seemed as if things could not get much worse, value
managers got the last laugh. Value funds held up much better than growth
funds during the painful bear market from March 2000 to March 2003, and
they kept up pretty well in the ensuing rally, too. As a result, for the five-year
period ending in early 2005, the typical large-value fund had a roughly 7% annualized gain, whereas the typical large-value fund lost nearly 9%.

Although value funds generally show less volatility than growth funds,
that doesn't guarantee safety. In many previous market downturns, such as the
cyclicals and financials decline of 1990, the utilities debacle of 1994, and the
Asian crisis of summer 1998, value funds lost as much or more money than
growth funds. See Figure 6.4 and Figure 6.5 for our favorite large- and mid-
cap value funds.

Janus Mid Cap Value	Lead manager Tom Perkins is a discriminating bargain hunter. The fund is certainly capable of posting losses, but it has put up one of the best long-term records in the category.
Vanguard Selected Value	This fund features experienced management, a great record since the current lead manager took the helm in 1999, and low expenses. Its portfolio is a bit concentrated, however, so investors should be prepared to ride out some rough patches.
Weitz Value	Manager Wally Weitz has a true contrarian streak and will often hold cash if he can't find enough cash flow–generating companies trading cheaply. Investors here need patience, but Weitz has proved his mettle over time.

Figure 6.5   Our favorite mid-cap value funds.

Understanding Growth Funds

Value and growth are often considered opposites in investing, and for good reason. Most growth managers are more interested in a company's earnings or revenues and a stock's potential for price appreciation than they are in finding a bargain. In general, growth funds will have much higher price ratios than value funds. That's because growth managers believe that if a company has what it takes to create high-quality products and services, investors will be willing to pay a higher and higher price for it in the future.

That's the general philosophy behind growth investing. But it's worth noting that growth-fund managers, like their value-oriented counterparts, practice different styles. Those styles will affect how the fund performs—and how risky it is.

Understanding Earnings-Driven Funds

The majority of growth managers use earnings-driven strategies, which means they use a company's earnings growth as their yardstick for determining how quickly the company is growing. They want a company whose earnings are growing significantly faster than those of the average company in its sector or the market as a whole.

Within this group of growth managers, earnings-momentum managers are by far the most daring. You might say their mantra is "Buy high, sell higher." Momentum investors buy rapidly growing companies they believe are capable of delivering an earnings "surprise," such as higher-than-expected profits or other favorable news that will drive the stock's price higher. These managers will likely sell a stock when its earnings slow. That can be the harbinger of a later earnings disappointment—a negative earnings surprise—that will drive the stock's price down.

Earnings-momentum managers typically pay little heed to the price of a stock. Instead, they focus on trying to identify companies with accelerating earnings, as well as catching upswings in stocks that have already shown price gains. These funds, therefore, can feature a lot of expensive stocks as long as earnings continue to grow at a rapid rate. Funds that hold many expensive stocks are often said to carry a lot of *price risk* because if bad earnings news or some other event makes other stockholders jump ship, the prices of such stocks can plunge dramatically.

One of the best-known proponents of the earnings-momentum approach is the American Century group of funds. Founder Jim Stowers II began running the family's funds with an earnings-momentum style in 1971. Other prominent momentum players are Garrett Van Wagoner, manager of Van Wagoner Emerging Growth, as well as the fund companies AIM, Turner, and PBHG. These funds have delivered impressive returns in friendly markets: Van Wagoner Emerging Growth gained a stunning 291% in 1999. Since then, though, it has been bleeding red ink. The fund lost 20.9% in 2000, another 59.7% in 2001 and another 65% in 2002. After a revival in 2003, it sank 16% in 2004. Van Wagoner's fund is the most extreme example of the earnings-momentum style. Other earnings-momentum funds won't be quite as streaky, and in fact have the potential to be rewarding long-term investments.

However, the key problem with earnings-momentum funds, in Morningstar's experience, is that most investors have trouble sticking with them for the rough stretches. That's why earnings-momentum funds may not serve as worthy core holdings for most investors. Because of poorly timed purchases and sales, the typical dollar in PBHG Growth lost an average of 1.4% annually over the 10-year period through early 2005, compared with a gain of 3.9% per year for an investment made at the beginning of the period and held for the duration. When we studied other momentum funds, the pattern was the same. In 9 out of 10 major momentum funds, investors' actual returns were significantly lower than their reported performance figures would suggest. If you're going to buy a momentum fund, make sure you can stomach significant downturns. Following a disciplined dollar-cost averaging strategy—whereby you invest a set amount of money into a fund at regular intervals, say, every month—is one way to smooth out some of the bumps that come with the momentum territory and to avoid jumping in and bailing out at exactly the wrong times. For a selection of momentum funds, see Figure 6.6.

AIM Aggressive Growth	American Century Ultra
AIM Constellation	Brandywine
AIM Weingarten	PBHG Growth
American Century Giftrust	Turner Midcap Growth
American Century Heritage	Van Wagoner Emerging Growth
American Century Select	Vanguard Growth Equity

Figure 6.6   Funds that follow momentum strategies.

Understanding Revenue-Driven Funds

Not all growth stocks have earnings. In particular, stocks of younger companies—often those in the technology and biotechnology areas—may not produce earnings for years, because they're spending more than they're taking in. Some growth managers will buy such companies if they're generating strong revenues. (Revenues are simply a company's sales; earnings are profits after costs are covered.) Because there is no guarantee when firms without earnings will turn a profit or if they ever will (think of the many Internet companies that went under in 2000), this approach can be risky. Janus funds, for example, owned some stocks with no earnings in the late 1990s. They earned stunning returns when the market was still bullish, but they lost more than many competitors when the market turned ugly from 2000 through 2002. Many managers who focused on companies' revenue growth in the late 1990s have since abandoned their strategies because many of the stocks in their portfolios imploded in the dot-com bust. As with earnings-momentum funds, such offerings tend to be too volatile to serve as core holdings for most investors.

Understanding Blue-Chip Growth Funds

In general, blue-chip growth funds can serve as fine core holdings for investors' portfolios. Their managers look for companies growing in a slow but steady fashion. The slow-and-steady group has historically included such blue-chip stocks as Wal-Mart and Procter & Gamble. As long as these stocks continue to post decent earnings, the managers tend to hold on to them. Blue-chip growth funds often have more modest price ratios than other growth-oriented funds, and often fare relatively well in slow economic environments because they favor large companies that aren't dependent on economic growth for their success. But when reliable growers take the lead, as they did in 1998 and during the heyday of the Nifty Fifty in the late 1960s and early 1970s, these funds endure as much price risk as the more aggressive funds. Funds known for following this moderate earnings growth strategy include ABN AMRO/Montag & Caldwell Growth and Dreyfus Appreciation.

Another great example of the slow-and-steady style is Smith Barney Aggressive Growth. Manager Richie Freeman looks for companies with good product pipelines, company managers who own big slugs of their own stocks, and positions in dynamic industries. Once he finds these companies, he hangs on to them. The fund's average holding period is nearly 10 years, and some of the fund's biggest long-term winners have been in the portfolio for longer than that. Although Smith Barney Aggressive Growth has much longer holding periods than the average growth fund, many of the most successful growth managers let their winners ride. We often hear portfolio managers say that taking profits too early is one of the biggest mistakes growth investors can make.

Knowing When Growth Investing Works

Different growth strategies fare well in different market environments. Blue-chip growth strategies generally work best when investors are concerned about economic weakness. Manufacturing and basic-material stocks will suffer when economic growth slumps, but companies with steadier growth and products and services that are considered necessities generally hold up quite well.

Funds using more aggressive-growth strategies, such as earnings-momentum offerings, often need the backdrop of a more buoyant economic environment to thrive. That's because their stocks are often extremely expensive; to justify buying such pricey names, investors need to be confident about both the companies themselves as well as the broad economy. For example, aggressive-growth funds came on strong in the great bull market at the end of the 1990s, coinciding with a strong U.S. economy. Thanks largely to the implosion in tech stocks, however, such funds fell far behind their blue-chip growth counterparts as the economy weakened in 2000, 2001, and 2002. For a listing of our favorite large-cap growth funds, see Figure 6.7. Our favorite mid-cap growth funds are listed in Figure 6.8.

Understanding Blend Funds

Although some of the best-known mutual fund managers use either growth or value approaches, a giant group of fund managers splits the difference between these two investment strategies. We say such managers are using blend strategies, because their approaches combine aspects of both value and growth styles. Some of the fund world's biggest stock offerings are blend funds, including Fidelity Magellan, Vanguard 500, and Fidelity Growth & Income. The blend group is home to pure index funds and indexlike funds, but it's also home to bold stock-picker's funds such as Legg Mason Value, Vanguard Primecap, and Selected American/Davis New York Venture.

Fidelity Capital Appreciation	Fidelity veteran Harry Lange will sometimes range outside style and capitalization boundaries to find names that meet his growth criteria. Over time, Lange has delivered for his shareholders, and expenses here are pleasingly low.
Harbor Capital Appreciation	Manager Sig Segalas likes high top-line growth rates, but he won't go whole-hog into such names. The fund didn't perform as well as we would have liked during the bear market from 2000 through 2002, but its long-term record is stellar.
Marsico Focus	A series of smart calls has made this fund one of the best in any category. Manager Tom Marsico marries top-down calls with top-notch bottom-up stock picking.
T. Rowe Price New America Growth	Manager Joe Milano has demonstrated a willingness and ability to look outside traditional growth areas such as technology and biotech to unearth atypical picks. The result is a portfolio aggressive enough to hold its own in up markets, but one that retains some ability to play defense in tougher climates.
Vanguard Growth Equity	Manager Bob Turner looks for stocks with high growth rates, favorable momentum characteristics, and positive technical indicators. Although that strategy has led to a high level of volatility, we continue to recommend it for its discipline in sticking with a bold approach.
ABN AMRO/Montag & Caldwell Growth	Manager Ron Canakaris looks for mega-cap growth stocks that are selling below his estimates of fair value. Investors willing to sacrifice topflight gains in growth rallies for less painful losses in slumps will be happy here.

Figure 6.7   Our favorite large-growth funds.

Within the blend category, the most common management style is the so-called growth at a reasonable price approach (GARP). Managers who seek growth at a reasonable price try to strike a balance between strong earnings and good value. Although similar to the blue-chip growth style we discussed earlier, blend funds differ in subtle ways. Some managers in this group find moderately priced growth stocks by buying stocks momentum investors have

Brandywine	This fund remains a mix of contradictions. Its strategy involves momentum but also deep research. Its turnover is quite high, and yet it's one of the least volatile members of the mid-cap growth category. What's different here is that Brandywine's deep research team watches firms' business momentum, not stock price momentum. Its managers buy and sell quickly to stay ahead of rivals.
Turner Midcap Growth	Despite the fund's dramatic downside risks, we remain fans of its reasonable expenses and tight focus on mid-growth stocks.
Wasatch Heritage Growth	We made this fund a pick as soon as it launched in June 2004, even before we saw its portfolio. We did so largely because we trust Wasatch's somewhat contrarian yet moderate stock-picking approach. While the firm has never wandered outside of its small-cap hunting ground before, its plan to focus on larger firms previously owned in Wasatch's small-cap funds seems sensible.

Figure 6.8   Our favorite mid-cap growth funds.

rejected; often, these companies have reported disappointing earnings or other bad news and their stock prices may have dropped excessively as investors overreacted by dumping shares. GARP managers also look for companies that Wall Street analysts and other investors have ignored or overlooked and that are therefore still selling cheaply. As with value investors, GARP investors try to find companies that are only temporarily down-and-out and that have some sort of factor in the works (commonly called a catalyst) that seems likely to spark future growth. Prominent funds with GARP strategies include Fidelity Magellan and Fidelity Dividend Growth. Funds that follow the GARP strategy are listed in Figure 6.9.

For a look at our favorite large-blend and mid-cap blend funds, see Figures 6.10 and 6.11.

Fidelity Dividend Growth	Selected American
Fidelity Magellan	T. Rowe Price Blue Chip Growth
Gabelli Growth	T. Rowe Price Growth & Income

Figure 6.9   Funds that follow growth at reasonable price (GARP) strategies.

Fidelity Dividend Growth	Manager Charles Mangum's contrarian-growth approach puts the fund out of step with the market at times, but he's a topnotch stock picker with a fine long-term record here.
Oak Value	This fund's managers take a cue from Warren Buffett, favoring companies with understandable business models, solid managements, and strong free cash flows.
Selected American	Owing partly to its big financials stake, this fund has delivered uneven returns at times, but manager Chris Davis and Ken Feinberg have delivered fine results over the long haul.
Vanguard 500 Index	This offering is great core-holding material: Its portfolio is broadly diversified, tax efficiency is high, and costs are very low.
Fidelity Spartan 500 Index	At 0.10%, this fund's expense ratio is cheaper than the Vanguard fund's. However, the Fidelity offering requires a minimum initial investment of $10,000 and $1,000 for subsequent investments.
Vanguard Total Stock Market Index	Because it tracks the Dow Jones Wilshire 5000 Index (a broad market benchmark), this ultralow-cost offering owns stocks of every size, sector, and valuation range in one fell swoop.
Fidelity Spartan Total Market Index	At 0.10%, this Fidelity total-market fund is half as pricey as Vanguard's. But as with Fidelity's S&P 500 offering, this fund requires relatively high minimum and subsequent investments.
Vanguard PRIMECAP Core	The same talented management team runs the fund using a very similar—not to mention highly successful—strategy they've long employed at sibling Vanguard PRIMECAP.

Figure 6.10   Our favorite large-blend funds.

Knowing When Blend Investing Works

If you're not sure whether the value or growth style of investing appeals to you most, blend funds are a good way to hedge your bets. That's because, as we've already noted, value and growth investment styles tend to swing in and out of favor. If you own a blend fund, you improve your chances of having

Ariel Appreciation	Manager John Rogers has the heart of a contrarian, picking up stocks that are out of favor and giving his holdings time to regroup. Expect the fund to hold its picks for at least three years.
Fairholme Fund	Manager Bruce Berkowitz and team thrive on venturing into unloved areas when they can find good businesses and trustworthy company managers. It's a true stock picker's fund. Big industry and sector bets are common.
Selected Special	Chris Davis and Ken Feinberg took over this fund from Elizabeth Bramwell in May 2001, and they've allowed their talented analyst team to play a key role. The fund is now a wide-ranging mid- and large-cap offering that isn't afraid to walk on the wilder side of the category.
TCW Galileo Value Opportunities	This fund is probably the boldest of our mid-blend picks. Its veteran managers run a pretty focused portfolio and readily dive into unloved areas.
Vanguard Mid Capitalization Index	This fund recently changed its benchmark from the S&P MidCap 400 Index to the MSCI U.S. Mid Cap 450 Index, but it's not likely to lose its appeal. The change to the new index is bound to give it some overlap with the S&P 500, but the fund remains a great diversifier.

Figure 6.11   Our favorite mid-blend funds.

something in your portfolio that's working well no matter what. For example, many blend funds got a piece of the action in the late 1990s, when tech shares were going up and up and up; blend funds generally fared better than value offerings during that stretch. But blend didn't suffer as much as pure growth funds in the aftermath, when tech shares imploded. That all-weather appeal is partly what makes blend funds such popular choices for the core holdings in investors' portfolios.

Deciding between Style-Specific and Flexible Funds

Just as it's up to you to decide how to allocate the core of your portfolio among value, growth, and blend styles, you also must decide whether to build a portfolio that's composed of flexible funds or funds that focus exclusively on a specific type of stock.

Style-specific funds have certainly gotten a lot of attention in recent years. In fact, it's safe to say that if he were still running a fund today, legendary manager Peter Lynch might get pulled over by the style police. That's not a slight on Lynch's taste in clothing—it's a point about his investing style. The former head of Fidelity Magellan was an opportunist. Sometimes he liked growth stocks. Other times, value investments held more allure. Large companies struck his fancy, but occasionally so did smaller firms. Today, financial advisors, investors, and the media look down on such flexible managers. They would rather have managers who stick to one part of the Morningstar style box: They want style-specific managers.

At first glance, Morningstar may appear to be on the side of the style police. After all, we categorize funds by their investment styles, such as large growth or small value. But that doesn't mean we only like funds that tend to stay in the same part of the style box year in and year out. Style-specific funds have their charms, but flexible funds also have advantages. Neither one is inherently better than the other. There are great and terrible funds in both camps.

Lynch isn't the only fund-industry luminary who has insisted on having the freedom to pursue his best ideas, wherever they might lead him. Take celebrated First Eagle Global manager Jean Marie Eveillard, who retired at the end of 2004 following a fabulous career as an investment manager. Eveillard preferred smaller stocks, but enjoyed his greatest successes by delving into larger companies or bonds when they fell into deep disfavor. Recent examples include McDonald's, Tyco International, and Latin American bonds after a serious currency scare. And even with U.S. funds, some of the best managers, including another Fidelity star, Contrafund's Will Danoff, are drifters who refuse to tether themselves to any one section of the Morningstar style box. The positive aspect of this approach is that your fund has the potential to thrive in all sorts of market environments. But flexible funds have their downside: They can make building a portfolio tricky. After all, if a fund is a small-cap fund one year and has large-company tendencies the next, how can investors be sure that their portfolios are really diversified? No wonder advisors, investors, and the media are wary of flexible funds.

Style-specific funds, meanwhile, tend to cleave to one bin of our style box. They always invest in, say, small-value stocks, or mid-cap growth stocks. Index funds relentlessly stick to one part of the style box, and families like

Putnam and T. Rowe Price offer actively managed funds that tend to stay put. It is much easier to build and monitor a portfolio of style-pure funds. If you select four funds precisely because they invest in different ways, you want to be confident that they will continue to invest that way. Thus, you're always sure that you're diversified.

Rather than steering clear of flexible funds entirely, we'd argue that flexible and style-specific funds can peacefully coexist in a portfolio. For example, you might consider using style-specific funds at the core of your portfolio. If you treat them as building blocks to meet your asset-allocation goals but save a portion of assets for flexible funds, your overall asset allocation will not get too far out of line.

And if you do make room for more flexible funds, be sure to monitor them carefully. Keep an eye on where and why your flexible fund's manager is moving. And if you choose to devote significant assets to more than one flexible fund, keep track of how much you have in each investment style. If all your flexible-fund managers are favoring large-growth stocks, you may want to assume they know more than you do and let them ride. But perhaps you should temper that bet somewhat by cutting back there and adding to other parts of your portfolio.

Deciding between Active and Passively Managed Funds

It's the $64,000 question of mutual-fund investing: Are actively managed funds better or worse investments than index funds? In a nutshell, actively managed funds employ portfolio managers who try to outsmart the market by over- and underweighting certain stocks or sectors. Index funds, however, are content to hold exactly the same stocks—in exactly the same proportion—as a given market benchmark. For example, Vanguard 500 Index tracks the S&P 500 Index, and if the S&P allots 3.41% to General Electric, so will Vanguard 500.

The pro-indexing argument usually comes down to this: Most actively managed funds don't beat their inexpensive index-fund competitors, so your odds of investing in a superior fund are much better if you just buy an index offering, which may also offer the advantage of ultra-low costs. The argument for active management is that some funds do beat the index options: Why not go for the best returns you can get?

We'd say both arguments are correct. We aren't being wishy-washy—it's a matter of where index investing and active management are most effective.

Morningstar's managing director Don Phillips often advises investors to think of the mutual fund universe as a horseshoe. Because both index funds and active managers have their merits, consider buying the former to give your portfolio low-cost exposure to the large stocks that dominate the market and where active managers have had the most trouble beating the benchmark. Then use excellent actively managed funds for the parts of the market your index funds don't cover. Even if you go with one or the other, you can build great portfolios by sticking to the ends of the horseshoe and buying the best of either group.

Morningstar studies show that indexing tends to be more effective in some investment styles than in others (see Figure 6.12). Funds that focus on large-cap U.S. stocks invest in the most closely watched stocks in the world. It's close to impossible for these managers to know anything about Microsoft or General Electric that hordes of Wall Street analysts and other fund managers don't also know. That's why index funds are so hard to beat in that area—they go along for the ride, while many active managers can end up outsmarting themselves. Low costs are also a huge help. Index funds don't have to hire a bunch of analysts to dig through financial statements or visit factories. Vanguard 500 Index, for example, charges shareholders just 0.18% per year (that's 18 cents for every 100 dollars you have in the fund), and Fidelity's S&P fund charges only 0.10% per year. The typical large-blend fund, meanwhile, costs 1.22% per year. That means every year Vanguard 500 Index and Fidelity Spartan 500 Index have a

Fund Category vs. Index	Fund Category Return +/− Index			
	1-Year	3-Year	5-Year	10-Year
Large Growth vs. Russell 1000 Growth	1.53	2.03	3.35	-0.18
Large Blend vs. S&P 500	0.55	2.40	2.47	-2.40
Large Value vs. Russell 1000 Value	-2.30	-0.76	-1.23	-2.88
Mid Growth vs. Russell Midcap Growth	-3.56	-0.92	4.43	-0.89
Mid Blend vs. Russell Midcap Index	-2.25	-0.87	1.36	-1.29
Mid Value vs. Russell Midcap Value	-6.82	-0.63	-0.05	-2.06
Small Growth vs. Russell 2000 Growth	0.95	0.10	2.23	3.10
Small Blend vs. Russell 2000	3.24	0.92	3.86	0.87
Small Value vs. Russell 2000 Value	1.46	0.31	-1.47	-0.18

Figure 6.12   How fund categories have performed versus corresponding indexes. Data as of March 31, 2005.

roughly one-percentage-point edge on most of their rivals. Those two funds can make a bit less than the average large-blend fund before expenses and still come out ahead after subtracting costs.

Funds that venture outside the large-cap arena have many more stocks to choose from—there are more than seven hundred U.S. mid-cap stocks and more than four thousand small caps to sort through. And more important, those stocks receive far less attention from the financial community. So it's more likely that a manager could ferret out an underappreciated gem in the mid- or small-cap area than he or she could in the large-cap realm.

Likewise, foreign-fund managers have thousands of foreign stocks to choose among. They can even decide to avoid investing in some countries entirely. But if the index includes a struggling market, the index fund has to invest there. For example, the Japanese market struggled through much of the 1990s. If you were a foreign-fund manager, an easy way to stay ahead of the major foreign indexes and index funds was to hold fewer Japanese stocks than the index. That said, the long-term data on foreign indexing is scant. With foreign markets arguably becoming more efficient, meaning that there's more readily available data on a bigger percentage of stocks, we'd expect active managers of large-cap foreign-stock funds to begin having a tougher time beating foreign-stock benchmarks such as the MSCI EAFE Index. It's worth noting that most broad index funds (with the prominent exception of Vanguard Total International Stock Market Index) track the EAFE index, which has no exposure whatsoever to Korea, Taiwan, Brazil, India, or other markets MSCI classifies as emerging. That makes them dramatically different than nearly all other international funds, most of which devote at least a small percentage of assets to global leaders like Samsung (Korea), successful generic-drug makers in India and Israel, and tech giants in Taiwan.

Although a lot of us at Morningstar tend to invest at least part of our portfolios in actively managed funds, an all-index-fund portfolio is a reasonable strategy for people who don't want to make a full-time job out of analyzing funds. You could certainly do much worse. By opting for an index fund, especially one with very low costs, you are generally assured that the fund will be competitive over the long haul, even if it doesn't dominate its category. You also don't have to worry much about your fund manager leaving. After all, he or she isn't picking the fund's holdings. And if you're paying close attention to your portfolio's asset mix, you can be confident that your fund won't suddenly change its style when you look away. (We discuss more tips for simplifying your investment life in Part Three of this book.)

If you want to invest in actively managed funds, focus your search efforts on fund categories where active managers have a better chance of beating their relevant benchmarks. But whatever portfolio slot you're trying to fill, always compare your actively managed options with index funds that track the same stock arena. If the active funds aren't doing better, there's no reason to choose them over an index option.

Choosing an index fund isn't necessarily a snap, though. More than 200 index funds ply their trade in 24 different investment categories. (See Figure 6.13 for a list of common indexes and the funds that track them.) To complicate matters, the index funds in some investment categories (such as large blend) track different benchmarks. The following suggestions will help you choose an index fund that meets your needs.

Know What Index Your Fund Follows

Vanguard 500 Index, Fidelity Spartan Total Market Index, TIAA-CREF Equity Index, Domini Social Equity, and Schwab 1000 all land in the large-cap

Index	What It Tracks	Index Funds
S&P 500	500 of the largest U.S. stocks	Vanguard 500 Index Fidelity Spartan 500 Index Schwab S&P 500 Select T. Rowe Price Equity Index 500
S&P MidCap 400	400 mid-cap stocks that are too small to make the S&P 500	Dreyfus MidCap Index Federated Mid-Cap Index
Russell 2000	2,000 small-cap stocks that are too small to make the Russell 1000	Merrill Lynch Small Cap Index
Lehman Brothers Aggregate Index	Broad bond market index that includes government bonds, corporate bonds, mortgage-backed securities, and asset-backed securities	Vanguard Total Bond Market Index Merrill Lynch Aggregate Bond Index

Figure 6.13   Major indexes and the index funds that track them.

blend category. But they each track different indexes: the S&P 500, the Wilshire 5000, the Russell 3000, the Domini Social Equity Index, and the Schwab 1000 Index, respectively.

The differences can be significant. Domini Social Equity tracks a custom-made benchmark. It focuses only on those 400 companies that pass its social screens. (It doesn't own firms that manufacture alcohol, tobacco, or firearms, for example.) Knowing what index a fund tracks gives you a handle on the risks and returns you can expect and how they differ from those of other index funds. Don't buy Domini's fund if you dislike Microsoft: It constituted more than 5% of assets and was the fund's largest holding in early 2005. Meanwhile, Microsoft was a relatively measly 2.6% of Vanguard 500 Index and was the third-largest position after General Electric and ExxonMobil. Thanks to big positions in growth sectors such as technology, services, and retail, Domini Social Equity outpaced Vanguard 500 Index and other large-blend index options during the bull market of the late 1990s. But it has been more volatile, too, and lost a lot more than the S&P 500 from 2000 through 2002.

Thanks to the variety of index funds, you have much more flexibility than a decade ago, when tracking the S&P 500 was about your only option. Today, you can build a well-balanced portfolio made up entirely of index funds.

Know the Tax Effects

One of the most common myths about indexing is that all index funds are tax efficient. Funds that buy the biggest stocks, such as Vanguard 500, do boast terrific tax efficiency; as of July 2002, Vanguard 500 Index's shareholders kept about 94% of their pretax earnings over the 10-year period ending in early 2005.

Vanguard 500 Index tends to be tax efficient because it only has to sell stocks when they drop out of the index. Stocks that leave the index usually are small players (most companies drop out of the index precisely because they have become too small)—no stock after number 231 accounts for more than 0.10% of the S&P 500 index. When S&P 500 index funds sell these smaller positions, they don't reap sizable taxable gains. Also, the taxable income distributed by the fund tends to be modest—in early 2005, Vanguard 500 Index's latest income distribution figure (known as its yield) for the past 12 months was just 1.75%.

Don't expect tax efficiency from funds tracking other indexes, though. For example, shareholders of Vanguard Extended Market Index, which tracks the

Wilshire 4500 Index of small- and mid-cap stocks, kept an average of 84% of their pretax returns over the trailing 10-year period ending in early 2005. The challenge for this and other small- and mid-cap index funds is that stocks grow too large and are removed from the index. The index fund has to sell that stock. That spells a taxable gain: For the stock to have grown too big for the index, it has to have gone up in price—the fund will be selling the stock for more than it paid. The fund is required to distribute that profit to shareholders, who then have to pay taxes on it.

Know the Costs

Another common assumption about indexing is that all index funds are cheap. Because they don't demand the resources of active management, they certainly ought to be. But some index funds charge surprisingly high annual expenses. Consider this: Morgan Stanley charges 1.46% for the B shares of its S&P 500 Index fund. That's a huge amount when you consider that, as noted previously, the comparable offerings from Vanguard and Fidelity both cost less than 0.20% per year.

Using Exchange-Traded Funds as an Index Fund Alternative

Another passively managed investment option began to create a buzz a few years back: exchange-traded funds, or ETFs. Giant asset managers such as Barclays Global Investors rolled out scores of new offerings in 2000, and Vanguard launched its own version (called VIPERs). State Street is another player in the ETF world, with its streetTracks brand of ETFs. So-called Spiders, which track the S&P 500, have more than $50 billion in assets, while Nasdaq 100 Trust Shares have more than $20 billion in assets. One of the most successful new fund launches of 2004 was streetTracks Gold, which raised more than $2 billion in assets within months of its launch.

Like index mutual funds, ETFs are baskets of securities that are designed to give you diversification in a single shot; they track sector-specific, country-specific, or broad-market indexes. But like stocks, ETFs trade on an exchange. That means that investors can trade ETFs throughout the trading day, unlike mutual funds, which investors can only buy or sell at the price at the close of the day. Investors can also sell ETFs short and buy them on margin. Anything you might do with a stock, you can do with an ETF.

You might consider an exchange-traded fund if you like to trade a lot, if you're particularly concerned with limiting taxes, if you are inclined to make one big lump-sum investment and let it ride, or if you're looking for a cost-effective way to gain exposure to a single market niche not served by a conventional mutual fund. Otherwise, you're apt to find that an index mutual fund will serve your needs just as well. You'll definitely want to stick with a plain-vanilla mutual fund if your investing strategy involves making lots of small purchases—which, by the way, is a great way to invest! That's because you'll have to pay a brokerage commission each time you buy or sell an ETF, and all of those commissions, no matter how little you're paying, will quickly cut into your fund's return.

Here are the pluses and minuses of ETFs for determining if these options are right for you:

Advantages

▶ *Greater Flexibility.* These funds trade throughout the day, so you can buy and sell them when you want and can easily switch from one to another. When you buy a mutual fund, however, you're buying at the end-of-day net asset value (NAV) (or share price), no matter what time of day you place your order.

▶ *Potential for Lower Expenses.* The iShares S&P 500 Index, for example, has an expense ratio of just 0.09%. On a $10,000 investment, you would save $9 a year by choosing iShares S&P 500 Index (an ETF) over Vanguard 500 Index. The latter charges 0.18% per year for its services and Vanguard also levies an annual fee of $10 for smaller account holders, which increases the iShares' edge.

▶ *Tax-Friendly Structure.* With a regular mutual fund, investor selling can force managers to sell stocks to meet redemptions, which can result in taxable capital-gains distributions being paid to shareholders who stay on board. But when you buy or sell an ETF, you're often buying or selling existing shares in an exchange with another investor. That shields the fund from the need to sell stocks to meet redemptions. This should make ETFs more tax-efficient than most mutual funds, and they may therefore hold a special attraction for investors in taxable accounts. Keep in mind, however, that ETFs can and do make capital-gains distributions, because they must still buy and sell stocks to adjust for changes to their underlying indexes.

Disadvantages

▶ *Potential for Price Discrepancies.* Because ETFs trade like stocks, there can sometimes be a brief discrepancy between the share price of an ETF and the value of its holdings. Due to ETFs' unusual structure, large investors can—and usually do—keep ETFs' prices in line with their NAVs using a technique known as arbitrage. Heavily traded issues such as SPDRs (which track the S&P 500) and Qubes (which track the Nasdaq 100 index) typically trade right around the value of their underlying securities.

▶ *Trading Costs.* The expense advantage of ETFs may also prove to be more mirage than fact for many investors. Because ETFs trade like stocks, you have to pay a broker's commission whenever you buy or sell an ETF, just as with a stock. If you plan on making a single, lump-sum investment that you hold for years, then it may pay to choose an ETF. However, even assuming a low commission of $8 per trade, a single lump-sum investment of $10,000 in the iShares S&P 500 Index would need to be held for nearly two years to beat Vanguard 500 Index's total costs over the same period.

The companies offering ETFs tout low expenses as one of their key benefits. But if, like many investors, you invest small sums of money at regular intervals, brokerage costs mean you could actually end up paying far more for investing in an ETF than in a comparable mutual fund. Also, investors who want to trade frequently would save money with a regular mutual fund versus an ETF. (We still don't think frequent trading makes any sense, however.)

Top 10 ETFs by Asset Size	Index Tracked
SPDR Trust Series 1	S&P 500
Nasdaq 100 Trust	Nasdaq 100
iShares MSCI EAFE	MSCI EAFE
iShares S&P 500	S&P 500
MidCap SPDR Trust	S&P MidCap 400
iShares MSCI Japan Index	MSCI Japan
DIAMONDS Trust	Dow Jones Industrial Average
iShares Dow Jones Sel Dividend	Dow Jones Select Dividend Index
iShares Russell 2000 Index	Russell 2000
iShares Russell 1000 Value	Russell 1000 Value

Figure 6.14   The 10 largest ETFs and the indexes they track.

The bottom line: ETFs' cost advantages aren't always as large as they might seem, and trading costs can quickly add up. If you are in the market for a fund that tracks a broad index such as the S&P 500, or want to invest regular sums of money, it's tough to make a case for choosing an ETF over one of the existing low-cost mutual-fund options.

Figure 6.14 shows the most popular ETFs, in terms of assets.

Investor's Checklist: Find the Right Core Stock Funds for You

▶ All value managers buy stocks that they think are inexpensive, but they often take different routes toward that goal. When you buy a value fund, make sure you understand where it lands on the value spectrum and how it fits in with the rest of your portfolio.

▶ Not all growth funds are created equal. Some fund managers focus on companies with improving earnings growth, while others specialize in momentum or revenue growth. Still others focus on companies with a track record of growing their earnings on a consistent basis.

▶ Blend funds split the difference between the growth and value investment styles. Therefore, they can make a lot of sense as core stock funds for your portfolio.

▶ Don't rule out using flexible funds that roam into different areas of the style box. Although they can be tricky to slot neatly into a portfolio, flexibility can be an advantage for a talented manager.

▶ Remember that the choice between indexing and active management doesn't have to be either/or. You can create a successful portfolio using either strategy, or by combining the best of both worlds.

▶ If you have a lot of money to work with and plan to invest a lump sum, ETFs can be cheaper and more tax-efficient than index mutual funds. But because you have to pay a commission to trade them, they're not the best choice if you like to invest smaller sums at regular intervals.

7

Move Beyond the Core: Using Specialized Stock Funds

THE KEY TO a successful fund-investing plan is to make sure that you've selected appropriate, high-quality stock and bond funds to serve as the foundation of your portfolio. But what if you want to add some oomph once you've assembled your core positions? Real-estate and foreign-stock funds can reduce your portfolio's overall volatility level. Others, such as small-cap and sector funds, add some spice, potentially boosting your returns.

Using Foreign Funds in a Portfolio

French champagne and Italian shoes aren't the only imports dear to Americans. By early 2005, U.S. investors had poured nearly $900 billion into international funds that primarily buy stocks of foreign companies. What's the attraction? For starters, foreign-stock funds' returns can be alluring. In 2004, the typical foreign-stock fund gained more than 19%, while the S&P 500 index rose only about half as much. Then, there's the diversification that foreign investing may offer. Foreign markets are often influenced by different factors than the U.S. market, so adding foreign funds to your investment mix gives you a better chance of always owning something that's performing well.

The addition of foreign stocks can actually reduce your portfolio's overall volatility level. Moreover, while some investment pundits consider foreign stocks to be riskier than U.S., we'd disagree with that assertion. There's absolutely no reason that a blue-chip foreign company such as Nestlé or Toyota should be any more volatile than its U.S.-based competitor. For all of these reasons, we'd argue that the typical U.S. investors' foreign-stock weighting is lower than it should be.

Good news: The process of picking a foreign fund is much like choosing a fund that invests in the United States. As with U.S. stock funds, you should size up how a foreign-stock fund invests before looking at returns or Morningstar ratings. You can then set reasonable expectations for the investment, uncover its hidden risks, and avoid surprises. Foreign funds plug into the same style box and sector framework that we use to analyze domestic-stock funds. That means you can use what you have learned about U.S. funds in scrutinizing foreign options. Just as in the domestic-fund realm, foreign funds that invest in large-cap stocks make solid core holdings, whereas funds that focus on small- and mid-cap issues usually work best in a supporting position within your portfolio. Figures 7.1 through 7.4 show our favorite foreign-stock and world-stock funds.

To help identify the best foreign-stock fund for you, start by asking the following questions. You can find most of the answers to these questions on a report on Morningstar.com, in *Morningstar Mutual Funds* (available in many public libraries), on the fund family's Web site, or in the fund's shareholder report.

What Is Its Style?

Not so long ago, investors delving into international stocks didn't pay too much attention to what investment style a foreign fund used. That's because most foreign-stock funds bought reasonably priced stocks of the world's largest companies, taking what was essentially a growth-at-reasonable-price approach. International-investing pioneers such as the managers at EuroPacific Growth, the world's largest foreign-stock fund, had profited for years and even decades by using such strategies. In the 1990s, though, Janus and American Century met with great success when they began applying the same aggressive-growth-focused strategies they used at home to investing abroad. Their styles were still novel among foreign-stock

American Funds EuroPacific Growth	This giant fund's many managers put together a broad, diversified portfolio. Not only do its long-term returns easily beat the category average, but its volatility has been milder than the norm. Relatively low expenses are another attraction.
Fidelity Spartan International Index	There's no telling if indexing will beat the better active managers over time, but in a large-blend category, an index fund is typically a quite formidable competitor. Low costs add to this fund's appeal.
Vanguard Total International Stock Market Index	Unlike other index funds, this fund invests in other index funds: Vanguard European Stock Index, Vanguard Pacific Stock Index, and Vanguard Emerging Markets Stock Index. The fund's exposure to emerging markets sets it apart from most other foreign-stock index trackers.

Figure 7.1   Our favorite foreign large-blend funds.

investors. Meanwhile, Templeton and First Eagle were using value strategies abroad.

To help address the diversity of foreign-stock fund styles, Morningstar plots each fund's portfolio holdings on its investment-style box grid, just as we do for U.S. stock funds. (For an overview of our style-box methodology, refer to Chapter 1.) And as with U.S. stock funds, we look at foreign stock offerings' style-box placement over the past three years to help determine their category placement. We break diversified foreign-stock funds into one of five groups: foreign large blend, foreign large growth, foreign large value, foreign small/mid-value, and foreign small/mid-growth. (The reason we have fewer than nine foreign-stock boxes is because there still aren't that many small- and mid-cap international funds.)

The investment style you choose should depend on how much risk you can handle and the other funds in your portfolio. If your U.S. stock funds lean toward growth stocks, consider a foreign fund that's more inclined toward value. If you think you might sell if a fund endures a substantial drop, steer clear of foreign funds that emphasize small companies; they tend to be more volatile than funds that focus on large firms. Bear in mind, however, that small-cap stocks are generally better diversifiers than foreign large-cap stocks, because foreign blue chips tend to be big multinationals and often perform much like U.S.-based multinationals.

Does the Fund Own Emerging-Markets Stocks?

In 2003, some international funds posted eye-popping returns of 50% or more. Their secret? Stocks of companies that operate in less developed markets such as Brazil. Owning emerging-markets stocks has its benefits. In addition to generating occasionally topnotch returns, emerging-markets securities can add more diversification to a U.S. portfolio than stocks from developed international markets such as Germany and the United Kingdom.

There's a price for the exhilarating highs and the diversification that emerging-markets stocks can add: the threat of steep losses. Concerns about political and economic stability, which are usually less pronounced in developed markets than in developing ones, can cause investors to flee, driving down stock prices. In 2000, for example, the MSCI Emerging Markets index was in a freefall: It shed more than 30% for the year. That wasn't the first time emerging markets had tanked, either: The emerging-markets benchmark dropped 13% in 1997 and another 28% in 1998. As with small-cap choices, if you don't think you'll handle such events well, avoid funds that focus solely on emerging-markets stocks.

Dodge & Cox International Stock	This fund only opened for business in March 2001, but members of the seasoned management team have had much success at Dodge & Cox Stock. A buy-and-hold orientation should help keep a lid on turnover, and through December 2004, the fund's expense ratio was a pleasingly low 0.82%.
Harbor International	Following a strict value discipline even when venturing outside traditional value sectors, longtime manager Hakan Castegren has racked up stellar returns over the course of his 16-year tenure. In 2002, Harbor rolled out an Investor share class of this offering. That fund's minimum initial purchase amount is just $2,500, and its expense ratio remains reasonable.

Figure 7.2   Our favorite foreign large-value funds.

But if you really want to avoid emerging-markets stocks entirely, you'll need to do more than just shun funds dedicated to emerging markets. You should also check the country exposure of mainstream diversified international funds you might be considering, because many of these offerings also buy emerging-markets stocks. In 2004, the average foreign-stock fund held more than 8% of its assets in emerging-markets names. Many excellent foreign funds do invest in emerging markets, so some exposure isn't generally cause for concern; in fact, it can be a good thing. But if you're a cautious investor and you see that 15% or 20% or more of the fund is in developing markets in Asia, Eastern Europe, or the Pacific Rim, it may be a good idea to look for another fund.

Does It Concentrate in a Specific Region?

While you are examining a fund's country exposure, get a feel for whether the fund prefers a few markets or a particular region (a handful of funds are dedicated to certain geographic regions or even single countries) or whether it casts a wider net. Morningstar places international funds that focus on a single region in one of these regional categories: Europe stock, Latin America stock, Japan stock, Pacific/Asia stock, and Pacific/Asia ex-Japan stock (such funds focus on all Asia and Pacific Rim markets excluding Japan).

Even mainstream international funds are often heavily skewed toward a particular region. For example, as of late 2004 Janus Overseas had a third of its

Artisan International	There's no doubt that the fund, which has roughly $10 billion in assets between its retail and institutional share classes, is not as agile as it once was. But we think manager Mark Yockey's go-anywhere style—which applies to sector, geography, and market cap—provides room for him to maneuver.
Harbor International Growth	Although this fund struggled under a prior manager, Jim Gendelman of Marsico Capital Management has given it a new lease on life. Harnessing Marsico's research, Gendelman builds a bold portfolio and doesn't hesitate to diverge from the MSCI EAFE Index.

Figure 7.3   Our favorite foreign large-growth funds.

assets in Asia (excluding Japan) and another 12% in Latin America. Concentrating in a single region or country can increase your fund's volatility level. It's comparable to a fund that focuses heavily on a single sector. If you're a conservative investor, find funds that own stocks from a wide variety of markets.

Does It Buy U.S. Stocks?

For some funds, the world is their oyster. The managers of these offerings, called world-stock funds, have free rein to unearth good stock picks wherever they find them—in the United States as well as overseas. In theory, world-stock funds have the potential to be the ultimate core funds. After all, if you have a great stock-picker at a fund's helm, why artificially limit him or her to buying only U.S. or foreign stocks? The American Funds Group has long taken a global approach to managing many of its funds, and shops like First Eagle, Oppenheimer, Vanguard, and Oakmark also run topnotch world-stock funds.

Unfortunately, for every great world-stock fund out there, there are two or three others that are thoroughly mediocre. Many of the best international

American Funds New Perspective	This fund provides exposure to global market leaders. It invests primarily in growth-leaning companies, but management's attention to price multiples, a broadly diversified portfolio, and a comparatively high cash stake have kept volatility in check.
Oakmark Global	This fund is an aggressive value choice. Its managers prefer highly out-of-favor companies whose stocks are trading at steep discounts to their estimates of intrinsic value. The fund's portfolio has a go-anywhere quality, so its geographic allocations aren't fixed, and it also invests across the market-cap spectrum. The fund's portfolio separates it from the pack, as do its results.
Oppenheimer Global	Theme-based, growth-oriented stock picking has been the key to this fund's success. However, the fund's longtime manager was recently promoted and will cede direct responsibility for this fund in the near future. While we think the new manager is capable, we'll be watching carefully, as he has big shoes to fill.

Figure 7.4   Our favorite world-stock funds.

managers don't run a world-stock fund, so if you limited your international search to that category you'd be eliminating a strong bunch. And in many cases, fund shops have rolled out world-stock funds by simply blending together the portfolios of their firms' already-existing—and not particularly distinguished—foreign and U.S. stock funds. The result? A not particularly distinguished world-stock fund.

If you're considering a world-stock offering, make sure that its manager has demonstrated the ability to get the most out of its flexible format. You'll also want to assess how that world-stock fund fits with other U.S. and foreign-stock funds you happen to own; you may find that the world-stock fund doesn't offer anything you don't have already. In many cases, it's also more cost-effective (in terms of the expense ratio of your overall portfolio) to buy separate foreign- and U.S. stock funds instead of a world-stock offering.

What Is Its Currency-Hedging Policy?

When fund managers buy foreign stocks, they're also effectively investing in the foreign currency in which the stock is denominated. Even if a British stock goes nowhere, a fund can still make a gain for its U.S. shareholders if the pound strengthens relative to the dollar. So a foreign stock's return is really a combination of two factors: the performance of the stock itself and the performance of the country's currency versus the U.S. dollar.

Suppose you buy a Japanese stock, Sony. The stock itself rises 10%. But the yen (Japan's currency) falls 15% against the U.S. dollar. As a U.S. investor, you have lost money on that investment. Why? Because even though the stock price has risen, the currency's value has fallen. What if the yen rises 10% instead? Then you get the 10% rise in the stock's price and the 10% rise in the currency.

The effects of currency swings have been on full display over the past decade. During the second half of the 1990s, the U.S. dollar was nearly unstoppable. Because foreign stocks are denominated in foreign currencies, most foreign-stock managers had a hard time beating their U.S.-focused counterparts once you factored in the effects of declining foreign currencies versus the buck. But that trend has reversed itself over the past few years. As the dollar has slid precipitously in value versus most foreign currencies, foreign-fund managers have looked invincible. In 2003 and 2004, foreign funds pocketed not only the gains from the stocks they held, but also gains that foreign currencies have scored versus the dollar.

However, some managers take the currency component out of the equation altogether by hedging their foreign currencies. That is, they effectively trade their exposure to foreign currencies for U.S. dollars. In our preceding example, suppose you buy Sony, but hedge your currency exposure by buying a contract (known as a *future* because it's a commitment to conduct the transaction at some future time) to sell Japanese yen and buy U.S. dollars. Sony's stock rises 10% and the yen falls 10% against the dollar. What's your return? Because you hedged your currency exposure, it is 10%—the change in the yen doesn't affect your return.

Several academic studies have indicated that currency hedging has only a minimal effect on returns over very long time periods. But over shorter spans, hedging can make quite a difference in a fund's performance. Janus Worldwide, for example, was nearly unstoppable in the second half of the 1990s, in no small part because then-manager Helen Young Hayes consistently hedged the fund's foreign-currency exposure, helping the fund benefit from the strong U.S. dollar.

Because we think it's important to invest for the long term, we don't believe it matters much whether a fund hedges its currency exposure or not. We focus instead on how consistent a fund is in its policy. To avoid the unexpected losses that can accompany badly timed currency plays, stick with funds that have consistent hedging policies—those that almost never hedge or those that almost always do. Unfortunately, foreign funds aren't currently required to disclose many details about their currency-hedging policies. Morningstar analysts usually discuss a fund's currency strategy in their writeups of funds in *Morningstar Mutual Funds*, and you can also call the fund company's customer service number to ask about the fund's policy. Tweedy, Browne Global Value is a fund that consistently hedges its foreign-currency exposure, while funds from American Funds and Fidelity do not.

Does It Use Fair-Value Pricing?

Foreign funds can be particularly vulnerable to short-term traders, whose activity can cut into the gains of longer-term investors. That's where fair-value pricing and redemption fees come in.

To help understand what fair-value pricing is and why some foreign funds use it, it helps to first consider why someone would specifically target foreign funds for rapid-fire trading. Mutual funds, unlike stocks, bonds, and ETFs, are priced just once a day. Thus, when foreign markets close for the day, a fund company is able to tote up the value of its international funds' holdings and arrive at the funds' net asset values. Due to time-zone differences, a foreign fund's price might be set for that day well before the U.S. market has ceased trading. For an Asian fund, that can happen well before noon U.S. Eastern time. That gives short-term traders—often called *market-timers*—a window of opportunity to react to late-breaking news in the United States that could affect foreign markets on the following day.

For example, say it's a sleepy day in foreign markets, and most foreign funds end the day with their values pretty much unchanged. Toward the end of trading in the United States on that same day, however, Intel issues a very optimistic report about its earnings, sending U.S. tech shares soaring. The market-timer knows Asian tech shares are a slam-dunk to rise the following morning (because foreign markets often respond the next day to news in the United States), so before the end of the U.S. trading day, he phones in an order to buy a foreign fund that's heavy on Asian tech names. Because that foreign fund's price was set earlier in the day, before U.S. stocks went up, the market-timer is essentially obtaining a "stale price" for the fund's holdings. When the foreign fund rises the next day, he can sell it and pocket a quick—and nearly risk-free—profit. In so doing, he's cutting into the profits of longer-term shareholders. To be prepared for withdrawals from these rapid-fire traders, the fund's manager may carry a large cash stake, thus diluting gains for loyal long-term shareholders.

That's why some fund shops use a mechanism called *fair-value pricing*, which is designed to ensure that their funds' holdings reflect their current value, even if the securities aren't currently trading. (Nonforeign funds might also use fair-value pricing to help determine a value for holdings that don't trade a lot, so that their net asset values are as accurate as possible.) In the foregoing example, a fund that used fair-value pricing would update the prices of its foreign-stock holdings after foreign markets had already closed, to reflect how the stocks and bonds in that portfolio would've responded to developments in the U.S. market had foreign markets still been open. (In essence, the fund shop has to make its best guess to determine the securities' value, because the stocks' and bonds' home markets are closed.) That, in turn, reduces the market-timer's incentive to benefit from time-zone discrepancies between foreign and U.S. markets. He won't pocket a gain by selling the next day, because the fund has essentially already priced in the next day's gain.

Some fund shops—including Fidelity and T. Rowe Price—have been using fair-value pricing for years. And many others adopted fair-value pricing in the wake of the fund scandal that erupted in 2003, as regulators sought to crack down on short-term trading that was hurting longer-term investors. Unfortunately for investors, fund companies aren't required to disclose whether they're using fair-value pricing. Some fund companies include their fair-value pricing policies on their Web sites, though, and Morningstar analysts often mention a firm's fair-value pricing policy in their individual fund reports on Morningstar.com and in *Morningstar Mutual Funds*, found in many public libraries. In general, though the process isn't always precise, we like to see a foreign fund use fair-value pricing at least some of the time.

Does It Charge a Redemption Fee?

Essentially, redemption fees are tolls you must pay if you sell the fund within a certain period of time after you purchased it. They are another tool that international funds often use to keep short-term traders out.

Although we're no fans of costs on our mutual funds, buying an international fund with a redemption fee is a great idea if you're a long-term investor. Because these fees are typically only imposed on investors who buy and sell a fund over a relatively short period of time—typically within two or three months, but sometimes longer—there's a good chance that you'll never have to pay one if you're a buy-and-hold investor. And because redemption fees are penalties for early withdrawal that are paid back into the fund—instead of to the fund company—the fees actually benefit long-term investors.

Like fair-value pricing, redemption fees are designed to deter rapid-fire traders by washing out any gains they might earn by buying and selling over short time frames. Redemption fees have been around a long time, but many fund shops that didn't have them began to impose them after the fund scandal, which centered around rapid-fire buying and selling of fund shares, came to light back in late 2003. And those shops that were found to be waiving their redemption fees for favored large investors are being much more careful now.

Redemption-fee information appears in the Fees and Expenses section of Morningstar.com's Reports as well as in a fund's prospectus.

Using Small-Cap Funds in a Portfolio

In recent years, small has been beautiful. As of early 2005, the best three-year returns among diversified U.S. stock fund categories belonged to the small-value and small-blend groups, which had gained an average of 15% and 12% per year, respectively. Small-cap stocks also trounced large during the bear market from 2000 through 2002. As large-cap stocks incurred horrifying losses during that period, many small-company funds actually posted tidy gains. It was as if no one told these guys that there was a bear market going on!

The fact that small-cap stocks have beaten their large-company rivals in recent years illustrates the benefits of diversification. Nonetheless, it's also important to note that small-cap stocks' success in the bear market turned the normal pattern on its head. In previous bear markets, big-cap stocks tended to fare better than small ones. If they don't abandon stocks altogether, nervous investors tended to flee to the safe haven of familiar blue-chip names. The late 1990s ruled out that option, though. Big names led the market on the way up, and because their price multiples were sky-high, they were among the first to drop as investors turned cautious. For investors who still wanted stock exposure, smaller issues appeared to be a good deal.

Although taking that approach would've beaten the bear, going whole-hog into small-cap funds wouldn't have been a prudent response, any more than staking everything in large-growth funds was the smartest way to run with the bulls. Investors who do either inevitably run into trouble when the bears stop prowling or the bulls stop running.

It makes sense to be especially circumspect with small stocks, because they can be a lot more volatile than large caps with the same investment style. Small-value funds tend to have more dramatic ups and downs than their large-cap counterparts, small blend is more volatile than large blend, and so on. In the late 1990s, small caps looked pretty sorry compared with their larger counterparts. In fact, the typical small-company fund lost money in 1998, even as the S&P 500 posted a 29% gain. Your best bet is to own a mix of large and small stocks. You will benefit when the market favors one type of stock without missing out completely when investors turn to the other. For

FPA Paramount	This fund has improved markedly since its current comanagers, Eric Ende and Steven Geist, took over in mid-2000. The previous manager's snafus here make for a large tax-loss carryforward that can be used to balance future gains, so the fund is a great choice for taxable accounts.
Third Avenue Small-Cap Value	This fund is run by Curtis Jensen rather than company founder Marty Whitman, but it's a chip off the old block. Jensen is a picky investor who will hold cash if he can't find enough stocks to satisfy his criteria, and he's not shy about wandering off the beaten value-investing path.

Figure 7.5   Our favorite small-blend funds.

most investors, smaller stocks should represent between 10% and 20% of the stock portion of their portfolios.

Figures 7.5 and 7.6 list our favorite funds in two of the three small-cap stock fund categories. (Because most of the best small-value funds were closed in the first half of 2005, Morningstar doesn't currently have any top picks within this group.)

When you're looking for the right small-cap fund for your portfolio, ask the same five questions we discussed in the first five chapters of this book. Here are two more questions to consider.

Masters' Select Smaller Companies	Litman/Gregory Advisors divvies up assets equally among five topflight managers with experience running concentrated small-cap portfolios. Each picks 8 to 15 stocks according to his own investing style. That all-star lineup and Litman/Gregory's history of acting in the interests of shareholders make up for the fund's brief track record.
Vanguard Explorer	This offering's lineup of five managers has produced a diversified portfolio that has performed well in varied market climates. Though the fund doesn't shoot the lights out in growth-driven years such as 2003, it holds up better than rival funds in tough markets.

Figure 7.6   Our favorite small-growth funds.

How Big Is the Fund?

More so than with other mutual funds, asset size—the amount of money the manager has to invest—matters with small-cap funds. Bigger funds are harder for managers to run and they're not likely to enjoy the same level of performance as smaller, more nimble funds because a small-cap manager needs to buy small companies. A manager with a lot of money to invest either has to find more good ideas (and idea 150 may not be as good as idea 35) or has to invest more money in the same stocks. The problem with the latter approach is that many small-cap stocks don't have a lot of shares floating around to buy or sell, and there are practical and legal limits to how much of a company a fund can own. All told, it could be hard for the manager to find a home for all that money he or she wants to put to work. When a fund has too much in assets, the number of holdings will increase significantly or the manager will be forced to put the money to work in larger-cap stocks. Or both. The result could be a fund that's very different from the one that generated strong returns in its early years. Fidelity Low-Priced Stock provides an extreme example of how asset bloat can change a fund. Manager Joel Tillinghast has always run a portfolio that's well diversified across individual stocks. But by early 2005, the $36 billion fund had more than one thousand individual stocks, each accounting for no more than 2% of assets. And whereas the fund once focused largely on small-cap stocks, mid caps and even large caps increasingly pepper the fund's top holdings.

In general, small-cap funds whose asset bases start to float above $1 billion can become unwieldy. For funds that focus on micro-cap stocks (the very smallest companies in the market), that threshold may be more like $500 million. Be on high alert for asset bloat if your small-cap manager likes to concentrate a big percentage of assets in individual stocks or if he or she uses a high-turnover style. (For a discussion of how these factors can affect a fund's so-called market-impact costs, see Chapter 5.)

Funds that grow too large aren't often disasters—after all, they wouldn't have gotten large in the first place if they didn't have talented managers—but their returns may drift toward the category's middle if they've become bloated. You might also find that their styles have mutated and they no longer fill the role in your portfolio that you bought them to fulfill.

What Is Its Closing Policy?

If you find an appropriate small-cap fund, the next logical question is: Will the fund company be willing to close it if it gets too big for the manager to run efficiently? Most fund companies haven't been very good about doing this. After all, it isn't easy to turn away money on which the fund company earns fees (through the expense ratio investors pay). That said, there have been encouraging signs: As small-cap funds suddenly became popular from 2000 through 2004, fund companies such as Wasatch did close small-cap stock funds to prevent excessive cash from undermining their strategies.

When searching for a small-cap fund, check the prospectus for information on whether and when the fund might close. You can also call the fund's customer-service line and ask about plans to close it. We prefer those companies, such as Wasatch and Turner, that tend to close their funds before trouble arises. Such shops determine how much in assets they can successfully run and decide at the start that they'll close when they hit that level.

Using Sector Funds Wisely (Or Not at All)

Do You Need a Sector Fund? This is an easy question to answer: No one needs a fund focused on a single industry sector. The main reason sector funds can be pointless investments is that a portfolio of diversified funds should give you exposure to most major market sectors, and there's no need to double up.

Our examination of sector funds also suggests that they can be more trouble than they're worth. One giveaway that sector funds are often more profitable for fund companies than for investors is that these funds tend to launch when a sector is red-hot. That's when a fund shop can pull in the most money by encouraging investors to jump on a trend. It's also usually the worst time to buy a fund. Nearly two dozen technology funds debuted in 1999. Investors who bought in made some gains right off the bat, but they suffered huge losses in 2000 and after. Many ended up selling during the bear market, missing tech stocks' rebound in 2003.

That pattern of buying too late is a common one with sector-fund investors, and it relates directly to these funds' extreme performance swings. At the end of February 2005, six of the 10 funds with the best five-year returns were sector funds of various stripes (notably, real estate and natural resources). That's a common pattern—for most periods, sector-focused funds tend to have the highest returns. The sectors will change but the leaders will usually have relied on just one or two industries to help them build their impressive return records.

The downside of that great return potential is—you guessed it—the potential for far higher risk. The standard deviation (the variation of a fund's monthly returns for the preceding 36 months around its average monthly return for the period) of the typical technology fund is double that of the S&P 500. That volatility is apparent if you compare the list of leading funds over various time periods. At the end of 1999, 9 of the 10 funds with the best 10-year returns were technology funds, but by early 2005, no tech fund cracked that list.

As if overlap with other fund holdings and extreme performance gyrations weren't enough, sector funds also tend to be expensive relative to diversified funds. Because they usually don't have much in the way of assets, they don't benefit from the economies of scale that can enable funds to keep annual expense ratios down. Further, fund companies seem to think they can justify higher expense ratios because these funds require more specialized research. We don't really buy that, because most fund families also use the research they put into their sector offerings when running their diversified funds. Sector-fund investors are often effectively subsidizing a fund company's research efforts.

If you can't resist the temptation to bet on a sector via a sector fund, be smart about it. One smart strategy is to dollar-cost average into your sector fund. The discipline of dollar-cost averaging—essentially, making small purchases at regular intervals rather than plunking down a lump sum all at once—means you can lower the average cost of your shares, resulting in higher total returns. The strategy is even more effective with highly volatile investments such as sector funds.

When you have identified a sector in which you want to invest, use the criteria you learned in Chapters 1 through 5 to pick a solid fund. In addition to the questions you would ask about performance, risk, portfolio holdings, management, and costs before buying any fund, ask three more questions that apply specifically to sector funds.

Is the Sector Out of Favor?

If you're determined to invest in a sector fund, it pays to take a contrarian tack rather than chasing trends. Precisely because investors typically *don't* have such good timing, you can often outperform by buying what most investors are selling. The biggest sales likely will be in the sector categories that have posted the worst returns during the past 12 months.

Morningstar's annual Unloved Funds study is founded on that very principle. In conducting the study over the past decade, we've found that more than 75% of the time, the three stock-fund categories with the biggest asset outflows in a given calendar year tend to outperform the S&P 500 over the ensuing three-year period. And the unpopular categories, as a group, beat the popular categories—those that have been seeing lots of new cash come in the door—more than 90% of the time. That doesn't mean you should automatically rush into whatever group is most out of favor, though. Do some research, including reading Morningstar's analyses of the funds, to make sure you understand why the group is unloved and to confirm that it has good potential.

How Diversified Is It?

Some sector funds focus on a single industry within their sector. For example, Fidelity Select Electronics lands in Morningstar's specialty-technology group, but it's quite focused on a single key industry within the tech sector, semiconductors. If you're considering buying a sector fund, read its prospectus to see if it is dedicated to just one industry within a broader sector; you can also examine a fund's portfolio holdings and shareholder report. Also be aware that even if a fund doesn't claim to be a subsector fund, it might still be heavily focused on one industry. Amerindo Technology, for example, has tended to heavily emphasize Internet stocks and have little or nothing in computers and other technology hardware. And even if the fund doesn't focus on one subsector, check to see if it owns just a small number of stocks, which can also spell a high degree of volatility. Only a few holdings need to run into trouble to trash a fund's return.

Does It Charge a Redemption Fee?

As is the case with international funds, sector funds frequently charge redemption fees designed to keep short-term traders out. If you're a long-term investor (and if you've gotten this far in the book, you're already aware that we think that's the way to go), it's worthwhile to actively seek out a sector fund with a redemption fee. (For more details on redemption fees and why we think they're a good idea, check out the section on international funds earlier in this chapter.) If you do insist on trading frequently, use an ETF and hope your profits more than cover the commissions to buy and sell.

Figure 7.7 lists our favorite sector funds.

Davis Financial	This fund owns about 30 names and makes big bets on stocks and industries it likes best. Its style can lead to disappointing short-term results, but its managers have put up solid long-term numbers.
T. Rowe Price Financial Services	Over the long haul, this fund has benefited from both savvy stock selection and a well below average expense ratio. Manager Michael Holton is off to a good start.
T. Rowe Price Health Sciences	This offering shows T. Rowe's adventurous side. Although manager Kris Jenner invests in large-cap names, he favors smaller-cap drug and biotech stocks.
PIMCO Commodity Real Return	This fund provides investors direct exposure to commodities. Though this fund will likely be extremely volatile, commodities exposure can actually improve a portfolio's risk/reward profile.
American Century Global Gold	This fund boasts a seasoned management team and reasonable expenses.
Vanguard Precious Metals & Mining	We like this fund for its experienced management, ultralow costs, and relatively broad diversification.
Fidelity Select Technology	This fund boasts low expenses relative to its peers and offers investors reasonably broad exposure to the technology sector.
Allianz RCM Global Technology	Managers Walter Price and Huachen Chen have run money in this style together for going on 20 years, and they've been very successful here since this fund's launch in late 1995.
Eaton Vance Utilities	This fund is a good choice for investors seeking exposure to large-cap utilities and telecom fare with a sprinkling of energy and foreign holdings for diversification.

Figure 7.7   Our favorite sector funds.

Using Real-Estate Funds in a Portfolio

Although we stand by our claim that no one really needs a sector fund, some funds are so useful that they merit further consideration. Real-estate funds can add a lot of variety to a portfolio. They're technically sector funds, but they play such a distinct role in a portfolio that they deserve to be treated separately.

The average real-estate fund has a strikingly low correlation with the S&P 500 index. That means that when the S&P 500 goes up or down, real-estate funds probably won't move in sync with the index. That makes real-estate funds appealing when large-cap stocks are down. The real-estate group is even less attuned to the bond market, with a negative correlation versus the Lehman Brothers Aggregate Bond index. (That means that the index and the real-estate category are likely to move in opposite directions.)

In other words, real-estate funds do not behave much like large-cap U.S. stocks, which is what most long-term investors have (or at least, ought to have) as the core of their portfolios. Nor do the funds behave much like bonds, which are the common choice to stabilize a stock portfolio. Adding a real-estate fund to a portfolio of stock and bond funds could add greater variety, resulting in steadier performance. A glance at the real estate group's performance from 2000 through 2002 highlights this benefit: Most U.S. stock funds were underwater, but the typical real-estate fund gained nearly 25% over that stretch. Most bond funds posted gains over that period, but they were modest compared with real estate's success.

The real-estate category's solid showing is partly attributable to the high dividend yields of many real-estate securities. Most funds in the category invest predominantly in real estate investment trusts (REITs), which pool together investors' money and invest in income-producing property or mortgage loans. REITs bring in a lot of income, but they're required by law to pay out most of that income as dividends to shareholders. That consistent yield can bolster returns during rallies and offset losses in down years. Moreover, unlike other diversification mainstays such as gold and foreign funds, the yields of real-estate funds prevent them from being exceptionally volatile. Real-estate funds are also more tax-efficient than other income offerings such as bond funds because, for accounting reasons, part of their dividend is con-

Morgan Stanley Institutional U.S. Real Estate	Management has often found undervalued assets in many parts of the real estate market, leading the fund to amass one of the most consistent records in the category. Notably, the fund is the only real estate option in Morningstar's 401(k) plan.
Security Capital U.S. Real Estate	Even though its concentrated portfolio means mistakes are costly, we're confident that the fund's experienced management team and deep research resources will win out. If real-estate stocks take a breather, we think this fund is well-equipped to ferret out what value remains.

Figure 7.8   Our favorite real-estate funds.

sidered a return of capital. That means not all of the yield paid by a real-estate fund will be treated as income and taxed at that higher rate, whereas all of the yield from a bond fund is likely to be taxed as income.

That doesn't mean that you should use real-estate funds in place of any bond holdings, however. Although they're not as wild as gold funds, they're too volatile to provide the kind of sanctuary a bond fund would offer. When the economy buckles, the funds can suffer severely, as their average 14% loss in 1990 proved. Nevertheless, if you want to diversify a long-term portfolio that is currently tilted heavily toward large-cap stocks, you'd be well-served by putting a small stake of your overall portfolio into a real-estate fund.

Figure 7.8 shows our favorite real-estate funds.

Using Commodity Funds in a Portfolio

A real-estate fund would be our top choice for investors seeking to diversify their portfolios with a sector fund, but one other category of funds has caught our attention over the past few years: commodity funds. These funds don't generally buy commodities directly, but rather buy derivatives that give their portfolios exposure to fluctuations in the price of commodities such as oil, wheat, metals, and hogs.

Commodities-focused funds aren't widely available—only a handful of fund shops offered them as of March 2005. But like real-estate funds, they exhibit a very low correlation with the U.S. stock market.

As stand-alone investments, commodities funds are ridiculously volatile. But when used as a very small piece of a broader portfolio, these funds' limited correlation with the stock market means they can actually reduce that portfolio's overall volatility level and potentially improve its return potential. Commodities funds also have the potential to help stave off the ravaging effects that inflation can have on your stock and bond holdings. In an inflationary environment, any income from your stock and bond holdings is worth less tomorrow than it was today. That's not the case with commodities, which invariably gain in value when inflation is on the rise.

Be careful, though: Many commodity prices have climbed sharply in the past couple of years, so as with anything else, don't expect that trend to keep up indefinitely.

Investor's Checklist: Move Beyond the Core: Using Specialized Stock Funds

▶ To help find a foreign fund that complements your other holdings, you'll need to delve into its investment style. We plot foreign funds' portfolios on the same nine-box grid we use to classify U.S. stock funds.

▶ For straightforward foreign-stock exposure, pick a fund that focuses on big companies in developed markets and doesn't make big bets on emerging markets or single countries.

▶ Opt for funds that consistently hedge or don't hedge their foreign currency exposure.

▶ Favor those foreign-stock funds that are doing their part to keep short-term traders out. Ask whether a fund employs fair-value pricing and whether it imposes a redemption fee.

▶ Small-cap funds add diversification and may boost returns. Watch out for the added risk, though.

▶ Beware of asset growth in small-cap funds. Some funds aren't hampered much by lots of money, but for many funds, assets greater than $1 billion can spell trouble.

▶ No one needs a sector fund: They're costly, risky, and often redundant with other funds you already own.

▶ If you are determined to buy a sector fund, plan to use a dollar-cost averaging strategy. Also, focus your attention on those sector groups that have been out of favor, not those that have been hot.

▶ Real-estate and commodity funds can be great portfolio diversifiers because they don't behave like ordinary stock or bond funds.

8

Find the Right Core Bond Fund for You

SAY YOU'RE AT a dinner party and someone starts bragging about his car. It's a safe bet that he's talking about a sports coupe or maybe an SUV. Could it be a minivan? Not likely. ("I swear, you can fit a couple dozen bags of groceries and still have room for a month's worth of dry cleaning! And there have to be at least half a dozen cup holders, not to mention. . . .")

Bond funds are the minivans of the investing world. People talk about stock funds because those funds are often exciting. Bond funds mostly aren't exciting. Our bond analysts would heartily disagree with that assessment—they find bond funds utterly compelling. We concede that the ins and outs of how the funds invest can be interesting, but when it comes to dramatic performance, in gains or losses, bond funds don't begin to compare with stock funds. In fact, that unstimulating performance is a big part of what makes bond funds such useful investments.

To learn how to choose a bond fund, you first need to understand how bonds work. The essential difference between a bond and a stock is that when you buy a stock, you become part owner of the company. Buy a share of Ford and you own a fraction of Ford. It's a small fraction—there are about 1.8

billion shares of Ford floating around out there—but you do own a piece of the company. When you buy a bond, you are loaning money to the company (or, in the case of Treasury bonds, you're loaning money to the government). Your loan lasts a certain period of time—until the date when the bond reaches maturity—and you get a certain dividend payment on a regular basis (commonly known as a coupon) as interest on the loan. Thus, the essential issues to consider when investing in bonds are how much interest or yield the bond pays, how long until the bond matures (that translates into interest-rate risk), and how confident you are that the business or government can repay the loan (known as credit quality).

Understanding Interest-Rate Risk

As we noted in Chapter 1, two key forces govern the performance of bonds and bond funds: interest-rate sensitivity (or duration) and credit quality. (The two factors are the key determinants of a fund's placement within Morningstar's style box for bond funds, which we also described in Chapter 1.) Duration is a key consideration for bond-fund investors because bond prices move in the opposite direction of interest rates. When rates fall, bond prices rise. Why does that happen? When rates drop, older bonds carrying higher yields (because they were issued when prevailing interest rates were higher) become more valuable to investors than newly issued bonds with lower yields. The opposite happens when interest rates rise: The prices of existing bonds, issued when rates were lower, get depressed because investors would rather buy the new bonds with higher yields. To determine how dramatic a fund's rises and falls might be, check out its duration. The longer the duration, the greater a fund's sensitivity to interest-rate changes.

Duration boils down the three risk factors of bonds: maturity, the cash flows from coupons and principal, and current interest rates. To help illustrate how these three factors come into play, it might help to think of a bond as a pro-basketball player's contract. In negotiating his first contract, a top draft pick wants a salary that will stay competitive with what's offered across the NBA. Looking at different contract proposals, he'll consider the length of a contract (its maturity), the salary (the yield, or coupon), and wages across the league (current interest rates). He will also take into account any clause that would permit his contract to be terminated early. In the bond world, those are terms that allow the bond issuer to "call" the bond, paying off bondholders before it matures. An issuer might call a high-interest bond, for example, because it can issue new bonds with a lower interest rate, thereby saving itself a lot of money.

Suppose the player is offered a five-year contract at $1 million a year. He likes the coupon, but he's nervous about the long-term commitment. If he signs the contract and the average NBA salary spikes up, his salary will be less attractive than it was and may even be below average for the league. Duration factors in these kinds of trade-offs and produces a risk measure that investors can use for comparisons. Of two bonds, the one with the longer duration will be more vulnerable to a change in interest rates.

One of the less-than-intuitive aspects of duration is that it's expressed in years, just like maturity. The trouble is, duration isn't nearly as concrete a concept as maturity. Take a bond with a maturity of 11 years and a duration of 8.5 years. At the end of 11 years, we know that something happens: The issuer pays off the bond. The issuer isn't on the hook for any more coupon payouts, and bondholders get back their principal (the amount they loaned, otherwise known as the bond's *face value*). But what happens after 8.5 years, the length of that same bond's duration? Nothing, really. Instead, duration is a useful abstraction: The longer a bond's duration, the more it responds to changes in interest rates. As a general rule of thumb, every one-percentage-point change in prevailing interest rates will cause a fund's price to change by the amount of its duration. For example, if prevailing interest rates went from 3% to 4%, a fund with a duration of 8 years would be expected to lose 8% of its value. And by extension, a bond fund with a duration of four years should be half as sensitive to a change in interest rates as a bond fund with a duration of eight years.

Understanding Credit-Quality Risk

In addition to interest-rate risk, bond funds also face credit risk, which is the risk that the issuers of the funds' bonds may not be able to repay their debts. Think of it this way. If your no-good brother-in-law who hasn't held a job in six years wanted to borrow $50 from you, you would probably wonder if you would ever see that $50 again. You would be far more comfortable loaning money to your super-responsible kid sister. The same dynamic occurs between companies and investors. Investors eagerly loan money to the government or to well-established companies that seem likely to repay their debts, but they think twice about loaning to firms without solid track records or that have fallen on hard times. Because people have greater doubts about the ability of those businesses to repay their debts, the borrowers will have to promise higher interest rates to obtain money.

Judgments about a firm's ability to pay its debts are captured in its credit rating. Credit-rating firms, such as Moody's and Standard & Poor's, closely examine a firm's financial statements to get an idea of whether a company is closest to being a no-goodnik or a debt-paying good citizen. They then assign a letter grade to the company's debt. In Standard & Poor's system, AAA indicates the highest credit quality and D indicates the lowest. So if you hold a bond rated AAA, odds are excellent that you'll collect all your coupons, and then you'll receive your principal when the bond reaches maturity. Bonds rated AAA, AA, A, and BBB are considered investment-grade, meaning that it's very likely the company that issued the bonds will repay its debts. Bonds rated BB, B, CCC, CC, and C are noninvestment-grade, or high-yield (also known as junk), bonds. That means there is serious concern that the bond issuer will not uphold its obligations to pay interest to its bondholders. The lowest credit-quality rating, D, is reserved for bonds that are already in default.

If you're going to buy a bond with a low credit-quality rating (one that might not pay its promised coupons and return all your principal), you'll want an incentive. To encourage you, the bond will offer the higher yield mentioned earlier. All other things being equal, the lower a bond's credit quality, the higher its yield. That is why you can find high-yield bond funds with yields of 8% or more, while you're lucky to earn 5% on most investment-grade bond funds. Because investment-grade issuers are more likely to meet their obligations, investors give up higher income for that greater certainty that the issuer will make good on its obligations.

Credit quality also affects a bond's performance. Lower-rated bonds tend to underperform—or drop in price—when the economy is in recession or when investors think the economy is likely to fall into a recession. Recessions usually mean lower corporate profits and thus less money to pay bondholders. If an issuer's ability to repay its debt looks a little shaky in a healthy economy, it will be even more suspect in a recession. That's why high-yield bond funds usually take a hit when investors are worried about the economy. Because most high-yield bonds are issued by businesses and are affected by the economy, a high-yield bond fund offers less diversification for a stock-fund portfolio than do other bond funds.

Buying Core Bond Funds

For the core bond-fund holdings in most investors' portfolios, bond funds with short- and intermediate-term durations—ranging up to about six years—are the way to go. They're less volatile than longer-duration funds and offer nearly as much return.

And just as we think most investors would do well to select bond funds with low to moderate interest-rate sensitivity for their core fixed-income holdings, we'd urge you to take a similarly moderate tack when it comes to credit quality. You needn't stick with Treasury-bond funds for the whole of your fixed-income portfolio (the U.S. government is the most creditworthy issuer around, but Treasury yields also tend to be lower than any other bond type), but we would suggest putting the bulk of your bond portfolio—say, 75% or more—into funds with investment-grade ratings or better.

Morningstar's intermediate-term bond category—which tends to encompass broadly diversified bond funds that don't take on extreme credit-quality or interest-rate risk—is an ideal place to start for most investors looking for a core fixed-income fund. Most of the top-tier bond shops, including PIMCO, Vanguard, Fidelity, Metropolitan West, and Western Asset, have sturdy intermediate-term bond funds as their family flagships. For investors who are saving for a goal that's close at hand, Morningstar's short-term bond category is a good place to look for core bond exposure. Vanguard and Fidelity all manage topnotch short-term funds that could serve as worthy core holdings for investors seeking a bond fund with limited interest-rate-related volatility. (See Figures 8.1 through 8.3 for our favorites.) We'd also recommend that investors—and not just those in the very highest tax brackets—investigate whether municipal-bond funds make sense for their portfolios. (The next section provides some guidance on how to know if a municipal bond fund makes sense for you and how to select one.)

When you're looking for a bond fund, follow the standard guidelines for picking a fund from the beginning of this book. Pay special attention to these three points, as well.

Look for Low Costs

A penny-pinching mentality is a must when evaluating bond funds. Because bonds typically return less than stocks over the long haul, their costs become a heavier burden. As if high expenses cutting into your returns weren't bad enough, high-cost bond funds are often riskier than low-cost bond funds. Expenses get deducted from the yield the fund pays to its shareholders, so managers of high-cost funds often do hazardous things to keep their yields competitive with cheaper funds, such as buying longer duration or lower quality bonds, taking on leverage, or betting on derivatives. In doing so, they increase the fund's risk. Managers with low expense hurdles, in contrast, can offer the same yields and returns without taking on extra risk. Plenty of terrific bond funds carry expense ratios of 0.75% or less.

Focus on Total Return, Not Yield

Many bond fund investors are in the habit of focusing on yield. If you're looking for income in retirement, it's natural to focus on yield—it tells you some-

Fidelity Short-Term Bond	Most investors want their short-term bond fund to be a conservative investment that won't lose much money, and this fund matches that description exactly. Like Fidelity's other bond funds, this one simply focuses on adding incremental gains through issue selection. We also like its modest expense ratio, which is a must with yields as low as they are today.
Vanguard Short-Term Bond Index	This fund is designed to track the Lehman Brothers 1–5 Year Government/Corporate Index and thus sticks to a mix of government bonds and investment-grade corporate issues. It doesn't carry much credit risk and boasts a solid long-term record. Ultralow expenses make it difficult to beat.

Figure 8.1   Our favorite short-term bond funds.

Metropolitan West Total Return Bond	The investment-grade corporate-bond market's 2002 travails took much air out of this fund's sails, but we remain fans of the fund and its management. The team sports some of the best brains in the industry, as well as a solid, deep bench of sector specialists.
Dodge & Cox Income	This fund has booked several great years, including 2002, when its management team was named as Morningstar's Fixed-Income Manager of the Year. The fund gets a lift from low expenses, proving that you don't have to pay big bucks for good active management.
Vanguard Total Bond Market Index	This fund is not flashy, but it doesn't need to be. Its superlow expenses make it tough to beat over any extended period of time. Designed to track the Lehman Brothers Aggregate Bond Index, this fund actually beats its benchmark by a small margin during most trailing periods.
FPA New Income	This fund's management team, led by Bob Rodriguez, is one of the best in the business. It takes a contrarian tack and is more than willing to pile into unloved sectors of the bond market, often with impressive results.
PIMCO Total Return	Bill Gross, named Fixed-Income Manager of the Year in 1998 and 2000, has made this fund a star. Although Gross shies away from most risky bets and sticks primarily to high-quality bonds, this fund has one of the best records in the intermediate-term bond category.
Western Asset Core	While Southern California neighbor PIMCO grabs more of the bond world's attention, Western Asset Management deserves much recognition for the record it has assembled with its funds, including this offering. Low expenses and a deep and experienced research effort lend it considerable appeal.

Figure 8.2   Our favorite intermediate-term bond funds.

Vanguard Long-Term Investment-Grade Bond	You can trace a lot of this fund's success back to its tiny expense ratio. That gives it a head start over just about everyone else. It also allows the fund to compete with its rivals while maintaining a relatively high-quality profile. The fund is subadvised by the renowned Wellington Management Co. and skipper Earl McEvoy. The fund's high rate sensitivity is a critical component here and could weigh on returns if inflation concerns push long-term interest rates higher.

Figure 8.3   Our favorite long-term bond fund.

thing about the size of the checks you'll get when the fund makes its regular income distributions. But chasing yield can have its penalties. Some funds use accounting tricks to prop up their yields while at the same time your principal value, or NAV, may be declining. For example, managers may pay more than face value for high-yielding bonds and distribute that entire yield as the bonds depreciate to face value, or they actually dip into your principal in order to pay out a high yield. (In that case, part of what appears to be higher income is effectively the fund paying you back your own money! You're robbing Peter—you—to pay Paul—also you.) That payout will be reflected in a NAV, or share price, that shrinks over the years.

Instead of judging a bond fund by its yield alone, evaluate its total return: its yield plus any capital appreciation (capital appreciation comes from bonds increasing in value if interest rates change) plus compounding of those gains over time. Yield will be the lion's share of a bond fund's return; you just want to be sure that the fund isn't cutting into NAV to produce that yield. Funds with superior long-term returns relative to other funds in their peer group are your best bet.

Seek Some Variety

You wouldn't choose a fund that buys only health-care stocks as your first equity fund, so why should your first (and perhaps only) bond fund be a narrowly focused Ginnie Mae fund? (Ginnie Mae funds focus on bonds backed by mortgages that the Government National Mortgage Association has guaranteed.) Yet many investors own bond funds that buy only government bonds, or Treasuries, or mortgages. For your core bond exposure, consider intermediate-term, broad-based, high-quality bond funds that hold both government and corporate bonds. You can get higher total returns plus the stability that diversification affords.

Determining if Municipal Bond Funds Are Right for You

If you're in one of the higher tax brackets, you might consider municipal-bond funds for the core of your bond portfolio. States, cities, and local governments issue municipal bonds, or muni bonds, to raise money. They use the proceeds to improve roads, refurbish schools, or even build sports complexes. The bonds are usually rated by a major rating agency, such as Standard & Poor's or Moody's, based on the quality of the issuer. Unlike income from bonds issued by corporations or the federal government, income from municipal bonds is exempt from federal income taxes; the income may also be exempt from state income taxes if you happen to live in the same state as the state issuing the bond. So when examining a municipal bond's yield, it's important to take the implicit tax advantage into account. Muni bonds usually pay lower rates specifically because of their tax benefits. (Their yields are even higher once you factor in the tax savings.)

You don't need to be in a tax bracket that would allow you to drive a Jaguar or to shop routinely at Neiman Marcus for the tax-protected income from a muni fund to be a good deal for you. That's because income from taxable bonds, unlike dividends or capital gains that you might earn from your stocks or stock funds, is taxable at your ordinary income-tax rate. So if you can save on your bond funds' tax bill by buying munis, your take-home return will be that much higher. Say, for example, you're an investor in the 28% tax bracket. You want to know which investment offers you a better yield: a corporate-bond fund yielding 7% or a muni-bond fund yielding 6%. After taxes, the muni fund is the higher-yielding investment: Take 28% in taxes off the corporate-bond fund's 7% yield, and you're left with an aftertax yield of a bit more than 5%.

Consider the following points when searching for a suitable muni fund. You can find this information in a fund's report on Morningstar.com, in its shareholder report or prospectus, in *Morningstar Mutual Funds* (available in public libraries) or on the fund family's Web site.

Look for Intermediate-Term Durations

Just as with taxable bond funds, if you're looking for an all-purpose muni fund to anchor your portfolio, you probably will want an intermediate-term option. Like most bond funds, a municipal bond fund's value rises and falls depending on changes in interest rates. To determine a fund's interest-rate risk, check its duration. (A fund with a long duration will land in the right-hand column of Morningstar's bond style box.) A long duration usually means more potential for short-term gains and losses. Vanguard Long-Term Tax Exempt's duration has been roughly twice that of Thornburg Limited-Term Municipal National over the past several years. No wonder the Vanguard fund lost nearly twice as much as the Thornburg fund (2.5% vs. 1.39%) when interest rates rose in the second quarter of 2004. But given that rates have generally been on a downward trend since 2000, the Vanguard fund's longer-duration portfolio helped its annualized return outpace the Thornburg fund's over the past five years, gaining an annualized 7.24% versus a 4.69% return for the Thornburg fund. Our suggestion: Choose the happy medium and opt for a fund with an intermediate duration. For investors with shorter-term horizons, we'd suggest they look to a short-term municipal bond fund; T. Rowe Price, Vanguard, USAA, and Fidelity all field excellent short-term muni offerings.

Look for Solid Credit Quality

Just like funds that hold bonds issued by businesses, some municipal-bond funds are vulnerable to credit problems and bond defaults (i.e., the issuers of the bonds they own could fail to pay up on their obligations). Some aren't, though. Vanguard Insured Long-Term Tax Exempt, for example, only buys bonds that are insured against credit problems. Insured bonds earn AAA ratings (the highest) and are highly sensitive to interest-rate movements, but they generally yield less than lower-quality bonds. At the other end of the credit spectrum lies Franklin High Yield Tax-Free Income, which invests heavily in low-rated or nonrated, high-yielding municipal bonds.

For most of the 1990s, the strong economy masked the risks of high-yield municipal bonds. With the economy strong, such funds had the wind at their backs, and Morningstar's analysts got into plenty of arguments with the fund companies' managers, who couldn't understand why we were warning investors about the funds' risks when they were scoring great returns. The average high-yield muni fund returned about 3% more per year than the average high-quality offering during the decade ending December 31, 1999. After the economy slowed and slipped into recession, though, more municipalities threatened to default on their debts, which hurt the performance of high-yield muni funds.

When it comes to deciding how much credit-quality risk you're willing to put up with, we recommend a middle-of-the-road approach. If you're buying a municipal-bond fund for the core of your portfolio, favor those offerings with average credit qualities of AA. They have enough high-quality bonds to skirt most credit scares but are still flexible enough to snap up higher-yielding, lower-rated issues. If you're inclined to be more cautious, a fund dedicated to AAA rated or insured bonds is best.

Know Your State's Tax Rate

Some municipal bond funds can offer you shelter from both state and federal taxes. That's because while some municipal-bond funds invest all over the country, others focus on a single state. National muni funds offer geographic diversification and can seize opportunities from New York to New Mexico. Single-state funds, on the other hand, can provide residents of those states with income that's exempt from both federal and state taxes. (National muni funds only give you the federal tax break.) A Californian doesn't pay state income tax on the income from a California muni fund. Choose a single-state fund if you live in a high-tax state. Otherwise, go national for the diversification benefits.

Seek Low Costs

Costs are important for all bond funds, but especially for municipal-bond funds. In any given year, the difference between the highest- and lowest-returning muni funds can be minuscule. A small cost advantage, therefore, goes a long way. Invest in a muni fund with an expense ratio of less than 0.75%.

Avoid AMT, If Need Be

You can still owe taxes on the income of municipal-bond funds if you're exposed to the Alternative Minimum Tax (AMT) and the fund you own holds bonds subject to this tax. The AMT is designed to ensure that wealthy individuals pay at least some tax, but you could be subject to AMT even if you aren't in one of the higher tax brackets. For example, if you cash in a lot of employee stock options, you may be subject to AMT. Check out Tax Topic 556 ["Alternative Minimum Tax"] on the Internal Revenue Service's Web site, refer to IRS Form 6251 "Alternative Minimum Tax—Individuals," or ask an accountant to determine if the AMT could be a problem for you.

Fund managers buy municipal bonds subject to the AMT because those securities tend to yield more than non-AMT bonds. If you're concerned about the AMT, choose a muni fund that specifically avoids bonds subject to the tax, such as T. Rowe Price Tax-Free Income. The prospectus will indicate if the fund has a mandate to avoid such bonds. Funds with "Tax-Free" or "Tax-Exempt" in their names must keep 80% or more of their assets in bonds not subject to the AMT or any other federal tax.

Fidelity Spartan Short-Intermediate Municipal	This fund has been a strong performer in the muni-national short category for a number of years. Fidelity's municipal-bond research capabilities, the fund's reasonable price tag, and Mark Sommer's steady approach all argue in this fund's favor.
T. Rowe Price Tax-Free Short-Intermediate	This fund is a solid all-around offering and has delivered steady results over the long term. The fund's restrained approach, combined with its below-average expense ratio, makes it a solid pick for conservative muni investors.
USAA Tax-Exempt Short-Term	Manager Cliff Gladson's picks have hit their mark more often than not. And with the fund's expense ratio below average, we're quite comfortable recommending it.
Vanguard Limited-Term Tax-Exempt	Ultralow expenses are the key here. And because of that expense advantage, the fund doesn't need to take on lots of extra credit risk to keep up with the group's more aggressive members.
Vanguard Short-Term Tax-Exempt	This fund is the more conservative of our two Vanguard muni short picks. It is just a small step up from a money market fund and boasts very low volatility. Its net asset value can and does fluctuate, though, and short-term losses are a possibility.

Figure 8.4   Our favorite national municipal short-term funds.

Fidelity Spartan Intermediate Municipal Income	Fidelity's muni shop has just gotten better and better, and this portfolio is a poster child for its progress. Its strategy may be a tad conventional, but Fidelity knows how to do it right. That includes pairing the fund with a nice, low expense ratio.
USAA Tax-Exempt Intermediate-Term	Despite assuming greater than average credit risk—it holds many more mid-grade issues than its average rival—this fund has consistently been able to keep volatility in check.
Vanguard Intermediate-Term Tax-Exempt	Are you tired of this story yet? Vanguard equals supercheap bond funds, and you really don't need much more than that. The portfolio has a huge head start on just about everyone else, so even a mistake here is almost never enough to derail it.

Figure 8.5   Our favorite national municipal intermediate-term funds.

Fidelity Spartan Municipal Income	Manager Christine Thompson was our choice for 2003 Fixed-Income Fund Manager of the Year. With a modest price tag and analytics that match up against any other firm's, this fund is a terrific choice.
Franklin Federal Tax-Free Income	This is the largest muni-national long-term fund for good reason. As has been the case with many of its siblings, this fund has earned an enviable record of solid returns and moderate volatility.
Vanguard High-Yield Tax-Exempt	In some ways, this fund has its cake and eats it too. Although it doesn't carry enough low-quality paper to be considered a high-yield muni fund by Morningstar, this fund's low costs allow it to offer a yield that is competitive with that of many members of the high-yield municipal category without taking on as much credit risk.
Vanguard Long-Term Tax-Exempt	This fund represents Vanguard's incredible cost advantage married to the muni world, where costs matter more than just about anywhere else. The fund makes occasional credit and interest-rate shifts, but they don't seem to affect the portfolio's long-term record—which is stellar—as much as its cheap profile.

Figure 8.6   Our favorite national municipal long-term funds.

In Figures 8.4 through 8.6, we provide a sampling of our favorite national municipal bond funds.

Investor's Checklist: Find the Right Core Bond Fund for You

▶ Bonds with longer durations are more sensitive to changes in interest rates. Funds that own such bonds can rise significantly in value when rates drop or lose value when rates rise.

▶ Bonds with lower credit qualities pay higher yields to compensate investors for the risk of default on their obligations. Funds that own these bonds are particularly vulnerable to a weakening economy.

▶ For the core portion of your bond portfolio, focus on intermediate-term funds that own both government and corporate bonds. If you're saving for a goal that's close at hand, you'll want to select your core bond fund from one of Morningstar's short-term bond categories.

▶ Costs take a big bite out of bond fund returns. Look for low-expense funds.

▶ Focus on a fund's total return, which reflects income return plus capital return. Income can be appealing, but not if it comes at the expense of your principal.

▶ If you need tax protection, buy a municipal bond fund that doesn't make big interest-rate or credit-quality bets. One dedicated to your state can shelter you from state and federal taxes.

9

Move Beyond the Core: Using Specialized Bond Funds

THE KEY TO bond-fund investing is understanding what your funds can and can't do. A basic high-quality bond fund can act as a good balance to a stock portfolio, but it shouldn't be expected to outperform a stock fund over a long period of time. (Because high-quality bonds promise much more certain returns than stocks, they do not have to offer such high returns to attract investors.) And because interest rates almost never stand still, a bond fund should not be expected to turn in positive returns every single year, either. That's where bond funds with different focuses, such as international or emerging-markets bond offerings, or those with some credit sensitivity, such as junk bond funds, can be a welcome elixir. These specialized funds may be riskier than the core fund types we discussed in the previous chapter, but they also have the potential to amplify your portfolio's returns.

Using High-Yield Bond Funds

If you are expanding your bond-fund horizons, high yield is one of the first areas to consider. High-yield bonds are often called lower-quality bonds, or junk bonds. No matter what the name, these bonds offer much more income than Treasuries or other high-quality corporate bonds. That's because they have more risk that their issuers may not be able to make the interest payments or pony up the principal they originally promised to return. (Hence the term *junk bond*.) If the economy slows down or if the companies fall into trouble, they may not be able to keep their end of the bargain.

Given that credit risk, not interest-rate risk, is their Achilles' heel, a junk-bond fund could be a good complement to a high-quality bond fund, which is generally more sensitive to interest-rate changes. Funds favoring high-grade bonds with far-off maturities can be volatile when interest rates change. But because junk bonds offer so much more income and often have shorter maturities, they typically aren't as sensitive to interest-rate shifts as higher-quality, longer-duration bonds are. When interest rates shot up in 1999, the average long-term government bond fund lost more than 7%. The average junk bond fund, which is far less vulnerable to interest-rate movements, actually gained 4.2%. High-yield bond funds can therefore be a good supplement to a core intermediate-term fund that owns Treasury bonds, high-quality corporate bonds, and mortgages, all of which offer high credit quality. Junk-bond funds will behave more like stock funds, though, so keep them to no more than 15% of your bond exposure.

When shopping for a junk-bond fund, examine a fund's credit quality. (This information is available from the fund company and from the Morningstar.com Reports for individual funds.) Is the fund investing in the upper tiers of junk (say, bonds with credit qualities of BB and B), or is it dipping lower for added yield? Check, too, to see if the fund owns any convertible bonds (bonds that convert to stocks), or bonds from emerging markets. Some high-yield funds may even include stocks in their portfolios. These elements are likely to make the fund more volatile. Finally, examine how the fund performed during tough markets for junk-bond funds. That will give you a sense of how risky the fund could be in the future. Junk-bond investors experienced trying periods in 1990 and, more recently, in the third quarter of 1998, as well as in 2000 and 2002. In the 1990s and again in 2003 and 2004, junk bonds performed quite well in the strong economy. But an economic slowdown can spell underperformance for these funds. Whereas all other categories of bond funds made money as the economy began faltering in 2000, the average high-yield bond fund actually lost 7.6%.

Figure 9.1 shows our favorite high-yield bond funds.

Eaton Vance Income Fund of Boston	This fund has turned in solid results in recent years. Good issue selection and sector allocation kept it from crashing when the high-yield market slumped in mid-2002, while its stash of lower-quality bonds helped it participate during the market's two-year rally.
Northeast Investors	This fund's performance will sometimes look out of step with the high-yield group, but its managers are among the longest tenured around. A low expense ratio adds appeal. High-yield purists beware, though: The fund also owns some stocks and emerging-markets debt.
PIMCO High Yield	More conservative than most high-yield bond funds, this offering can lag when the junk market gets hot. Still, it has a big, big following and billions in assets. It generally buys no bonds rated below B.
Vanguard High Yield Corporate	This fund stays in the shallow end of the high-yield bond pool. It doesn't take on as much credit risk as its typical peer, so volatility is relatively mild. Low costs have given it that luxury.

Figure 9.1   Our favorite high-yield bond funds.

Using Ultrashort Bond Funds

Ultrashort funds land at the opposite end of the risk spectrum from junk-bond funds—they're about as safe as a bond fund can get. These funds can serve an equally worthwhile role in your portfolio, however, typically delivering higher yields than you'd earn on a money market fund without taking on substantially more risk.

Unlike a money market fund, in which your NAV will stay fixed at $1, ultrashort funds' NAVs can and do fluctuate based on the value of their holdings. That means you can lose money in an ultrashort fund. Any such losses are apt to be quite minor, however; in fact, the biggest monthly loss incurred by the average ultrashort fund was just 2.4%, back in 1987.

In general, we're fans of this asset class, particularly given that money market yields have been particularly puny over the past several years. The key thing to remember when venturing into the ultrashort group is the impor-

Fidelity Ultra-Short Bond	This fund is relatively new, but we think it makes a strong case for itself. It is managed by Andrew Dudley, who has had much success at Fidelity Short-Term Bond; boasts a reasonable expense ratio, which should provide a sustainable advantage for the fund; and sticks with high-quality bonds, which limits its overall credit risk.
Payden Limited Maturity	This fund's very modest price tag, broadly diversified portfolio, and overall cautious profile make it a very good choice for investors in search of more yield than a money market fund can offer. The fund carries more risk than money market funds do, but for those comfortable with a little principal volatility, we think it's a solid pick.
SSgA Yield Plus	This fund is one of the category's least rate-sensitive funds, so we expect it to hold up better than most during rising-rate environments. Overall, we think this fund's low volatility makes it a good money-market alternative for those who don't mind small fluctuations in principal.

Figure 9.2 Our favorite ultrashort bond funds.

tance of pinching pennies. Remember, a fund's expense ratio is deducted directly from its yield, so the less you pay in expenses, the more you get to pocket. And in this group, fractions of a percentage point separate the winners from the also-rans, so it's usually a good idea to opt for the cheapest fund you can find. (If you're planning to hold the fund for awhile, you'll also want to make sure the fund isn't just temporarily waiving expenses.) Fidelity, Schwab, and Payden all offer topnotch ultrashort funds.

Our favorite ultrashort bond funds are shown in Figure 9.2.

Using Inflation-Indexed Bond Funds

Inflation-indexed bonds are the holy grail of income investing, as they offer a guarantee that your returns won't be ravaged by high inflation. The principal value of an inflation-indexed bond rises with inflation, something that's almost as certain as death and taxes. Conversely, an inflation-indexed bond's value can fall in a deflationary climate, but not below the bond's face, or par, value. Inflation-indexed bonds won't perform very well when inflation looks tame and conventional bonds are zooming up in price, and they're not immune to interest-rate-related volatility. But we still think they're an important addition to the bond investor's toolkit.

Most funds focusing on inflation-indexed bonds stick with the highest quality bonds—those issued by the U.S. Treasury (Treasury Inflation-Protected Securities, commonly referred to as TIPS). A small number of other bonds issued by government agencies and corporations also try to keep pace with inflation. As of early 2005, the top inflation-indexed bond funds included Vanguard Inflation-Protected Securities, Fidelity Inflation-Protected Bond, and PIMCO Real Return.

Such funds can be a great idea for your bond portfolio because they address a key problem of all bond funds: Inflation cuts into any returns you make. Bonds do not deliver big gains, so the impact of inflation is more noticeable than it is for stock funds. Even a low inflation rate will gradually erode your bond fund's returns, an important consideration if you are relying on your bond fund for income.

Using Bank-Loan Funds

There's almost no better place to pick up a lot of income with low day-to-day volatility than with a bank-loan fund (also called *prime-rate funds* or *floating-rate funds*). Prime-rate funds invest in leveraged bank loans. Banks typically make these loans to companies (most of which have poor credit profiles) and then sell the loans to institutional investors and mutual funds. The yields on the loans rise and fall along with short-term interest rates, so their prices tend to remain relatively stable. That's how bank-loan funds keep their NAV volatility at the low end of the risk spectrum

Sound too good to be true? In some ways, it is. Bank-loan funds come with plenty of caveats. For starters, most charge relatively high fees when compared with the average bond fund. Further, some use investment leverage, which boosts both gains and losses. Leverage is essentially borrowing to invest. That way a fund can get 25% more bond exposure, for example, than it would without borrowing. That can increase the fund's gains by 25%, but it also increases the losses by that much.

Another drawback to bank-loan funds is that most of them have restrictive redemption policies. In late 2002, Fidelity launched the first bank-loan fund that allows daily redemptions, but most other bank-loan funds will only let you redeem your shares every quarter or so. And if too many people want to cash out when you do, you may not be able to sell as many shares as you would like. (You can buy at any time, though.) Bank-loan funds may also charge redemption fees because the market for corporate loans is still relatively illiquid, making it tough for these funds to sell these loans to meet shareholder redemptions.

Finally, although bank-loan funds display little sensitivity to interest-rate shifts, that doesn't mean they'll never lose money. Most bank-loan funds were hurt by slight principal losses in 2000, 2001, and 2002, as a number of borrowers defaulted on their obligations. Thus, while we'd concede that bank-loan funds' promise of relatively high income payouts and limited interest-rate sensitivity is appealing, we'd take care to limit a bank-loan fund to a small slice of your portfolio. Also, be careful about owning a high-yield and a bank-loan fund together, as both types of offerings can be vulnerable to losses during economic downturns.

For our favorite bank-loan funds, see Figure 9.3.

Eaton Vance Floating Rate	This fund is relatively new, but Eaton Vance has a long history managing bank-loan funds. Overall, the fund is a bit more defensive than its average bank-loan peer.
Fidelity Floating-Rate High Income	This fund is a relative newcomer to the bank-loan category, but we like it for its low expense ratio and its research capabilities. The fund is also the only no-load option for bank-loan investors. We expect more competitors to enter this space given this fund's growing asset base, but Fidelity's growing experience will be a valuable asset here.

Figure 9.3 Our favorite bank-loan funds.

Using World Bond Funds

Although the United States is one of the major issuers of bonds, it makes up less than half of the global debt market. So should investors be looking abroad for bond investments? Not necessarily. That's because many domestically focused bond funds also delve into international bonds; PIMCO Total Return's Bill Gross, for example, boosted that fund's returns in 2004 by delving into European bonds.

If you are determined to venture into a world-bond fund, however, bear in mind that these funds come in a lot of different variations. Some invest only in foreign bonds, while others take a more global approach and include U.S. securities in their portfolios. Some stick to developed markets; others are more bold and dabble in emerging-markets debt. Some funds stick to government-issued securities—sovereign debt—while others invest in corporate bonds. And most important, some funds hedge all or part of their foreign-currency exposure back into the dollar, limiting or eliminating the impact of currency fluctuations on their returns, while others don't hedge.

Whether to buy a hedged or unhedged offering is the biggest decision facing investors looking to delve into international-bond funds. As the dollar has weakened versus most major foreign currencies in recent years, many investors have ventured into foreign bonds as a way to take advantage of a weaker greenback. When a foreign currency gains against the dollar, interest and principal payments made in that foreign currency can buy more U.S. dollars, boosting returns substantially. For example, T. Rowe Price International Bond, which sticks to high-quality securities and doesn't hedge its currency exposure, gained a whopping 22% in 2002 as the dollar dropped. That can cut both ways, though. When a foreign currency drops in value versus the dollar, those interest and principal payments are worth less when translated back into dollars. That same T. Rowe Price fund lost 3% in 2000 while the average intermediate-term bond fund posted a gain of 10%. Over the long term, unhedged and hedged funds have delivered similar returns, but investors in unhedged funds have had to put up with close to three times as much volatility over that time period than those who stuck with hedged offerings.

While world-bond funds aren't required to disclose whether they hedge, most discuss their currency policy in their prospectuses or shareholder reports. And Morningstar analysts are also likely to discuss funds' hedging policies in their Analyst Reports.

Using Emerging-Markets Bond Funds

Emerging-markets bond funds are the high-yield funds of international debt. Whereas world-bond funds largely focus on debt from well-established markets such as Europe and Japan, emerging-markets bond funds buy debt from Latin America, Asia's developing economies, and Eastern Europe. True, many such countries have instituted important economic and political reforms over the past several years, resulting in credit-quality upgrades for some of their debt. But investors still need to be aware that these markets are fraught with potential pitfalls. Argentina defaulted on its bonds as recently as 2001, for instance. While that extra risk means that these bonds typically yield more than those from more developed markets, they also come with a lot more volatility. The average emerging-market bond fund gained an eye-catching 30% in 2003, but lost a jarring 21% in 1998 when Russia defaulted on its debt.

In short, emerging-markets bond funds aren't for the faint of heart, and most investors probably don't need one at all. Like world-bond funds, they can potentially add some diversification to U.S.-focused portfolios, and their yields may also look tantalizing relative to other fixed-income offerings. But be aware that many U.S.-focused bond funds might also dabble in emerging markets, so if you have a wide-ranging U.S. bond fund, world-bond offering, or a multisector-bond fund, you could be duplicating exposure to some of these risky countries by adding a dedicated emerging-markets bond fund.

And if you're looking for exposure to foreign currencies, you usually won't find it here; most emerging-markets debt is denominated in dollars. While emerging-markets debt denominated in local currencies has been increasingly available, the currency risk adds volatility to an already-volatile asset class. In addition, emerging-markets funds can be costly, so if you're determined to buy an offering from this group, be sure to find one with reasonable costs. Finally, watch out for funds that layer on extra risks by concentrating heavily in a single region or venture into the lowest-rated credits to add yield.

See Figure 9.4 for our favorite world and emerging-markets bond funds.

PIMCO Foreign Bond (Hedged)	This fund offers high-credit-quality international exposure, with most of its currency exposure hedged back into the dollar. Though the fund doesn't offer the same amount of diversification as an unhedged fund, it usually provides a much calmer ride for those who want to add international flavor to their domestic fixed-income portfolios.
T. Rowe Price International Bond	This fund sticks to high-quality foreign bonds and keeps its currency exposure unhedged. That means it will lag when the dollar is strong and rally when the dollar is weak. In addition, it tends to be less correlated with U.S. fixed-income markets than the average world-bond fund.
Fidelity New Markets Income	This fund's moderate approach has served it well. Manager John Carlson doesn't typically make big country or sector bets, he avoids local-currency debt, and he runs a more diversified portfolio than many of his peers.
PIMCO Emerging Markets Bond	As it has in other areas of fixed income, PIMCO has demonstrated that it's a formidable competitor in the emerging-markets bond arena. Manager Mohamed El-Erian is a seasoned veteran, and the fund is also supported by five comanagers and PIMCO's extensive research staff.

Figure 9.4   Our favorite world-bond and emerging-markets bond funds.

Using Multisector-Bond Funds

Multisector-bond funds try to harness some of the specialized bond types we've just discussed into a single, well-diversified package. Most split their assets among a high-quality U.S. sleeve, a junk-bond component, and international bonds. Because these three asset classes have historically had limited correlation with one another, the idea is to deliver a higher payout than you'd get with a plain-vanilla bond fund without taking on substantially higher risk.

A handful of multisector funds have delivered on that promise. T. Rowe Price Spectrum Income, for example, is an ideal choice for an investor in search of a well-diversified bond portfolio in a single shot, and Loomis Sayles

Bond's Dan Fuss has also made great use of the flexibility that the multisector format affords.

In general, however, we're not big fans of the multisector-bond group, because many multisector managers chase the highest-yielding securities, giving their funds a fairly high level of volatility. In addition, multisector funds also tend to be quite costly relative to conventional bond funds. Well-diversified intermediate-term bond offerings such as PIMCO Total Return or Metropolitan West Total Return Bond have the latitude to delve into the sectors that multisector funds target, but they charge far less for their services and don't chase bonds simply because their yields are attractive.

Investor's Checklist: Move Beyond the Core: Using Specialized Bond Funds

▶ If you've already built a solid foundation for your bond portfolio, you might consider adding a junk-bond fund. Steer clear of those high-yield funds that focus on the junkiest bonds, though.

▶ Ultrashort-term bond funds can be a useful parking place for your short-term money. These funds' yields are typically higher than money market fund yields, while their volatility isn't substantially higher. Low expenses are a key consideration for ultrashort funds.

▶ Inflation-indexed bond funds can be a useful addition to your portfolio, because they help protect it from one of bonds' natural enemies: inflation, which erodes the purchasing power of conventional bonds' income payouts.

▶ Bank-loan funds offer the promise of tantalizing yields and limited interest-rate sensitivity. These funds tend to behave poorly in weak economic environments, however, and may carry restrictions that could make them unattractive to some investors.

▶ World-bond and emerging-markets bond funds can be used to diversify a U.S.-focused bond portfolio, and their yields may also be higher than U.S.-focused funds. Be sure to keep them to a small slice of your portfolio, however, because these funds can also be quite volatile.

▶ Multisector-bond funds typically combine high-quality U.S. bonds, foreign bonds, and junk bonds in a single portfolio. However, beware of multisector funds that are chasing risky securities in an effort to pump out an attractive yield.

10

Match Your Portfolio to Your Goals

SELECTING WORTHWHILE FUNDS without taking a step back and thinking about what you're trying to achieve and how you're going to achieve it is a little like trying to build a house without a blueprint. You're apt to end up with a hodge-podge of different-style funds that, while reasonable investments on their own, don't add up to a pleasing whole.

The investing equivalent of a blueprint is an asset-allocation plan—your own target mix of stocks and bonds, as well as cash holdings, that you can rely on to help you achieve your goals. If you're tempted to make emotional, maybe even irrational, moves in response to the market's short-term movements, an asset-allocation framework can help keep you steady.

Start by thinking about how various asset classes are apt to behave. Stocks offer the prospect of greater returns over the long haul than bonds and cash, but they also carry a lot more risk. If you have a long time horizon, say more than 10 years, you will probably want to dedicate the majority of your portfolio to stocks. If you're saving to purchase a house within a few years, you'll want to tilt your portfolio more toward bonds, which can provide income while keeping your principal relatively safe.

Also, consider what stage of the investing life cycle you're in. A person in his or her 20s who is putting money away in a 401(k) plan is in the accumulating stage, and will probably want to stash at least 80% of assets in stocks. Middle-aged investors should take a more conservative stance if saving for retirement. A mix of 60% stocks to 40% bonds would be a reasonable choice for a 50-year-old with a fair amount of risk tolerance. Finally, retirees should focus on keeping the wealth they have built and will want to limit their stock exposure to about 20% to 40% of assets.

These are just general guidelines, though. To help arrive at an asset-allocation plan that's specifically geared toward you and your goals, you'll need to examine a number of variables, including how long you have until you'll need to start paying for that goal, your current savings rate, and estimated returns for each asset class, among other factors.

Taking Stock of Your Goals and Time Horizon

Maybe you're investing for retirement, for your child's education, or for a vacation home. Whatever your goals, articulating them should be the first step in creating your own financial plan.

If you're like most people, you're juggling a few financial goals at once, some close at hand and some further in the future. For portfolio construction and monitoring purposes, it usually makes sense to construct separate portfolios, with distinct mixes of stocks, bonds, and cash, geared toward each goal and time horizon. Or if you have goals with similar time frames—for example, you hope to buy a second home around the time you retire—you could build a portfolio that's geared toward that particular time horizon and would address both goals at once.

Your goals, in turn, determine how long you'll be investing (also called your *time horizon*) and how much of your investment you can put at risk. The closer your goal, the less you can afford to lose and the more you should focus on preserving what you have made instead of on generating additional gains. For example, if you and your spouse are in the market for your first house, you'll want to make sure to park your investments in a safe place, such as a money market fund. After all, you can't afford to have your down payment fund shrink by 20% over the space of a couple months, because you could need to tap into it at any time. But if you hope to retire in 25 years, you can afford to put most of your savings in higher-risk investments that also have the potential to deliver higher returns.

You'll also want to figure out how much money your goal requires. Some goals are easier to quantify than others—for example, it's easier to ballpark how much a new house will cost next week than it is to determine how much you'll spend during retirement in the year 2030. Because most of us have no idea what our goals will cost, we tend to squirrel away money without knowing whether we're saving enough to meet a specific need. For example, some financial-planning experts say we need 80% of our preretirement income to live comfortably once we stop working. In reality, many thrifty retirees make do on less. Others, meanwhile, spend their retirements traveling or taking up expensive hobbies. (Golf, anyone?) They spend more in retirement than they did while working.

You'll also want to bear inflation in mind when calculating how much you'll need to reach your goals. Based on historical inflation rates, you'll actually need $161,270 in 10 years to have the same buying power that you get with $120,000 today. When it comes to retirement planning, many advisors use a 2%, 3%, or 4% inflation rate. College costs, however, have been growing well ahead of inflation. Some advisors assume that college costs will continue to rise by about 10% per year.

Projecting Rates of Return

Another set of variables to consider when determining your target asset allocation is how much help you can expect from the stock and bond markets. True, it's impossible to forecast future market returns with a high degree of accuracy. But you do need some sort of estimate to do any reasonable sort of planning. Looking at historical stock- and bond-market returns can help you make that estimate, which will aid you in figuring out how much you need to devote to each asset class.

During the 1990s, as the S&P 500 was routinely posting double-digit gains, it was easy to be optimistic about future stock-market returns. With stocks going up and up and up, many investors assumed that there was little merit in putting any money into bond funds or conservative stock offerings—stocks, and tech stocks in particular, seemed like the way to go. (In fact, Morningstar analysts were routinely criticized for questioning the merits of ultraaggressive funds or recommending conservative offerings.)

But given that historical stock-market returns are in the neighborhood of 10%, it was easy to see that the 1990s' bull market was unsustainable, and that it was a good strategy to devote at least some of your portfolio to bonds. As stocks cratered from 2000 through 2002, investors who had staked too much of their assets in equities suffered horrific losses, while those who had made room for bonds saw their plans remain on track.

When projecting returns for stock and bonds, be conservative. Lately some market prognosticators have been arguing that 8% might be a more reasonable projection for stock returns over the next decade, given currently high prices in the market. Meanwhile, prevailing bond-market yields tend to be a decent predictor of future bond-fund returns. In March 2005, the 10-year Treasury note was yielding 4.5%, so bond-market returns in the 4% neighborhood over the next 10 years would be realistic.

You'll also want to take inflation rates into account when projecting returns. Although inflation is currently mild, it's not unreasonable to assume that inflation could claim 3% or 4% of your portfolio's return.

Assessing Your Savings Rate

Thinking about the markets' future rate of return might leave you feeling a little bit helpless—after all, you can't possibly control stocks' and bonds' ups and downs. There is, however, a variable that's entirely within your control: how much you invest. Putting even a little bit more money aside each month can have a powerful effect on your long-term wealth. For example, say you had planned to invest $500 a month in a fund that earned 6% annually for the next 20 years. In 2025, at the end of that time period, you'd have more than $231,000—not too shabby. But say you cut out Starbucks, brought your lunch each day, and managed to set aside an additional $100 a month for investing. At the end of that 20-year period, your nest egg would be nearly $50,000 larger—$277,224.

Your savings rate has a direct impact on how you'll allocate your assets. If you're willing to set aside more money to invest, you won't have to put as much of your portfolio in risky stock funds and can enjoy a smoother ride from your portfolio.

Crunching the Numbers

So you've taken stock of all of the key variables—your savings goals, time horizon, the markets' historical returns, and your own rate of savings. Now what? It's time to use these variables to help arrive at an appropriate asset allocation for each goal and time horizon.

If you're comfortable using a financial calculator, you can plug in some of the variables we've just discussed to help arrive at an appropriate asset allocation. Say, for example, you've determined that you'll need $2 million to retire in 20 years, and you can save approximately $50,000 a year. (Lucky you!) By entering those variables into a financial calculator, you'll find that you'll need to earn 6.77% on your money in order to hit your goal. Given projected equity returns of 8% to 10% and projected bond returns of 4%, that scenario would argue for a balanced portfolio that's tilted toward equities. If you're hoping to make a $25,000 down payment on a house in five years and have already set aside $20,000, you'll need a more modest rate of return to hit your goal—just 4.56% even if you don't save any more money. In turn, you could comfortably keep most of your portfolio in bonds.

For a more precise read on an appropriate asset allocation for you, avail yourself of one of the many asset-allocation tools available online. Morningstar's version of this planning software is called Asset Allocator, available to premium users of Morningstar.com. Using historical returns for various asset classes, it helps you figure out how likely you are to meet your goal given the amount of money you have to invest, your time horizon, and the asset mix of your choice. For example, if you want to save $35,000 to put down on a house purchase within the next five years and you intend to keep most of your assets in bonds, the program will tell you how likely you are to reach that goal if you save $200, $300, or $400 per month. You can adjust each of those variables to suit your needs.

Making Up for Shortfalls

Okay, what if you've plugged the numbers into a financial calculator or turned to an asset-allocation tool on the Web and found out that your chances of meeting your goal are slim. Don't give up. You can do four things to improve your chances:

1. *Invest more now.* In general, the more you invest up front, the more you can make over the long haul. The bigger your initial investment, the faster you will reach your target.
2. *Increase your monthly contributions.* As we noted earlier, investing a small amount more each month will move you more quickly to your goal.
3. *Extend the number of years to your goal.* If you can't put in more money, maybe you can wait a few more years before drawing on your portfolio. A longer time horizon creates the opportunity for additional compounding of your returns.
4. *Become more aggressive.* If you can't invest more money or time, try changing your portfolio mix by making it lighter in cash and bonds and heavier in stocks. Do so with care, however. In recent years, many soon-to-be retirees have paid a steep price for having too much in stocks.

Avoiding the Market-Timing Trap

Of course, you could forget the complexities of asset allocation by simply owning only those securities that are doing the best at any particular time. You could hold nothing but large caps when they are strong, switch to small caps when they have their day in the sun, and rotate into bonds when stocks are hopeless. Unfortunately, such a strategy is all but impossible to pull off. Studies by Morningstar and academic researchers have shown over and over again that so-called market timing is not effective.

An article in the February 2001 issue of *Financial Analysts' Journal* made this point effectively. The authors studied the difference between buy-and-hold and market-timing strategies from 1926 through 1999, mapping all the possible market-timing variations between 1926 and 1999, with different switching frequencies. They assumed that for any given month, an investor could either be in T-bills or in stocks, and then calculated the returns that would have resulted from all the possible combinations of those switches. Then they compared the results of a buy-and-hold strategy with all the possible market-timing strategies to see what percentage of the timing combinations produced a return greater than simply buying and holding.

Only about a third of the possible monthly market-timing combinations beat the buy-and-hold strategy. When the authors looked at quarterly switching over five-year periods, the results got even worse for the timers: Only one-fourth of the timing strategies beat buy-and-hold strategies. Annual results were even more grim: One-fifth of annual timing strategies beat buy-and-hold strategies.

If you try to time the market, the odds are stacked against you, especially when you consider the effect of trading costs. What's more, the bulk of the returns (positive and negative) from any given year come from relatively few days in that year. This means the risk of not being in the market is also high for anyone looking to build wealth over a long period of time.

Instead of getting caught up in market timing, it's better to hold an assortment of asset classes tailored to meet your needs. By diversifying among investments with different behaviors, you can get the returns you need to meet your goals and keep volatility in check. No matter what the market conditions, odds will be good that at least some part of your portfolio is doing relatively well and may even be prospering. Figure 10.1 provides a visual depiction of different categories' returns at various periods in time, while Figure 10.2 shows you how closely correlated various fund categories are.

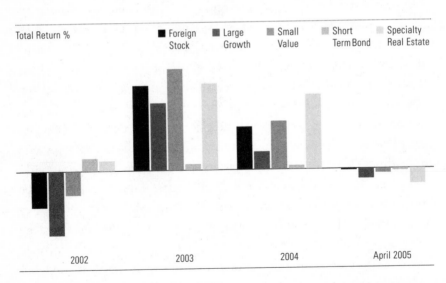

Figure 10.1 By diversifying among a variety of funds, you can prosper in good markets and gain some protection in bad ones.

↓ Category Correlation →	①	②	③	④	⑤	⑥	⑦	⑧	⑨
① Large Blend	1.00								
② Large Growth	0.96	1.00							
③ Large Value	0.98	0.88	1.00						
④ Mid-Cap Blend	0.90	0.88	0.90	1.00					
⑤ Mid-Cap Growth	0.86	0.92	0.81	0.96	1.00				
⑥ Mid-Cap Value	0.90	0.85	0.94	0.98	0.88	1.00			
⑦ Small-Cap Blend	0.76	0.74	0.77	0.94	0.90	0.92	1.00		
⑧ Small-Cap Growth	0.77	0.83	0.74	0.94	0.96	0.86	0.96	1.00	
⑨ Small-Cap Value	0.72	0.69	0.76	0.90	0.83	0.92	0.98	0.90	1.00

Figure 10.2 Morningstar category correlations based on three-year R-squareds as of March 31, 2005. The higher the number, the stronger the correlation.

That's why we think that finding the best asset mix is crucial if you want to meet your goals. In fact, it can be just about as important as choosing great funds.

Investor's Checklist: Match Your Portfolio to Your Goals

▶ Every investor should have an asset-allocation plan—a target stock/bond/cash mix based on his or her goals, time horizon, savings rate, and historical market returns.

▶ To help arrive at a customized asset-allocation mix that takes into account all of the key variables, use one of the many great asset-allocation tools available on the Web.

▶ If you've crunched the numbers and it looks like you'll fall short of your savings goal, don't despair. You can always invest more now, increase your monthly investment contributions, extend the number of years to your goal, or tip more of your portfolio into stocks. (Be careful about the last route, though.)

▶ Don't get caught up in the loser's game of trying to time the market. Instead, pick the right mix of assets to meet your needs and stick with a disciplined investment plan.

II

Put Your Portfolio Plan into Action

Now it's time to turn your blueprint into reality. When building a broad portfolio, start with core funds, which we discussed in Chapters 6 and 8. They can serve as a foundation, giving you a lot of diversification in a single package, and they tend to be reliable year in and year out. Core funds won't usually deliver eye-popping gains over short periods, but they aren't likely to be terrible, either. That makes them easier to stick with during rough times, and they'll help shore up your portfolio when your other funds are struggling. In short, they will provide your portfolio with a solid foundation.

Choosing the right type of core fund (or funds) for you gets back to your ideal asset allocation. All portfolios should have exposure to both core-stock and -bond funds, but your asset-allocation framework tells you what percentage you should have in each.

For core stock-fund exposure, we generally recommend large-cap U.S. stock funds, because those stocks represent the heart of the domestic economy. Large-cap stocks make up about 70% of the dollar value of all U.S. stocks.

Large-cap blend funds, which own big companies that tend to show both growth and value traits, are core stalwarts. Many broad market index funds would fit the bill here. Large-value and more conservative large-growth funds (such as the blue-chip growth funds we discussed in Chapter 6) can also make serviceable core holdings.

Don't rule out foreign- or world-stock funds when building the foundation of your portfolio; that way you won't be staking everything on the U.S. market. (By Morningstar's definition, foreign-stock funds invest outside the U.S., whereas world-stock funds graze across foreign and U.S. markets.) The fund should focus on the world's developed markets and invest in larger-cap companies, just as your core U.S. funds do. (Before investing in a foreign fund, be sure to check out Chapter 7, which includes a section on international investing.)

For core-bond-fund exposure, we recommend that most investors stick with those funds that invest in high-quality bonds with intermediate-term maturities. Many such funds land in Morningstar's intermediate-term bond-fund category. Like large-blend stock funds, intermediate-term bond funds are usually well-diversified and versatile.

If you're in search of a core bond holding and have only a short period of time before you'll need to begin tapping your assets (say, five or fewer years), you may want to choose a fund from one of Morningstar's short-term bond categories. Funds that focus on short-term bonds may not return as much as those that focus on intermediate- or long-term bonds, but they will do a better job of holding your principal value steady.

If you're in a higher tax bracket, opt for a municipal-bond fund for your core bond holding—the income you get can be exempt from both federal and state income taxes. Focus on those muni funds that favor high-quality intermediate-term bonds; as with taxable bond funds, there is no need to take on extra interest-rate or credit-quality risk for a shot at a modestly higher return. Here, too, focus on low-cost, intermediate-term choices. Chapter 8 provides more information on selecting a solid core bond fund.

Making Room for Noncore Holdings

There's no hard-and-fast rule governing how large the core of your portfolio ought to be. But you'll want to put at least 70% to 80% of your portfolio in core holdings. After all, these are the solid, long-term investments you're relying on to help you reach your goals.

So where do the rest of your assets go? Into noncore investments. Noncore funds aren't trying to be all things to all people; they're not as diversified or versatile as core funds. Instead, they focus on a specific part of the market. These funds aren't absolutely essential, but they can add variety to your overall portfolio, enhancing its returns and helping to temper its overall volatility. Small- and mid-cap funds, specialized foreign funds, junk-bond funds, and sector funds are all noncore funds. (For a discussion of these and other noncore fund types, see Chapters 7 and 9.)

Although you shouldn't put a significant portion of your portfolio in any one of these investments, they allow for the possibility of extraordinary returns. Of course, they also generally carry a higher level of risk. But

Core Role	Supporting Role	Specialty Role
Conservative Allocation	Convertibles	Pacific/Asia ex-Japan Stock
Moderate Allocation	Bank Loan	Diversified Pacific Asia
International Hybrid	High-Yield Bond	Europe Stock
Short-Term Bond	Long Government	Japan Stock
Short Government	Long-Term Bond	Emerging Markets Bond
Muni National Short	Ultrashort Bond	World Bond
Muni National Intermediate	Multisector Bond	High-Yield Muni
Intermediate-Term Bond	Small Value	Specialty-Communications
Intermediate Government	Small Blend	Specialty-Financial
Large Value	Small Growth	Specialty-Health
Mid Value	Diversified Emerging Mkts	Specialty-Natural Res
Large Blend	Foreign Small/Mid Value	Specialty-Precious Metals
Mid Blend	Foreign Small/Mid Growth	Specialty-Technology
Large Growth		Specialty-Utilities
Mid Growth		
Foreign Large Value		
Foreign Large Blend		
Foreign Large Growth		
World Stock		

Figure 11.1   The role of different fund categories in your portfolio.

as long as you limit the size of the riskier portion of your portfolio, you aren't likely to threaten the bulk of your nest egg. Just be sure to put together a reliable core first. Figure 11.1 provides a list of fund roles within a portfolio.

Building Portfolios for Short-Term Goals

Believe it or not, saving for short-term goals can be one of the trickiest parts of investing. Some short-term investors are inclined to stash too much in stocks, thereby risking a precipitous drop in their principal values right before they'll need to tap their money. Others play it too safe, sticking with ultrasafe CDs and money market funds that offer limited upside potential.

If you'll need to begin tapping your assets within five years, the key is to strike a happy medium. You want to see your money grow, at least modestly, but preserving it should be job one. Thus, your portfolio should focus largely on bond and money market funds. Any stock funds in your portfolio should be quite conservative, if you have them at all.

For the core of your short-term portfolio, focus on finding a high-quality intermediate-term bond fund that's well diversified across bond-market sectors. Several fine actively managed funds fit the bill, including PIMCO Total Return and Dodge & Cox Income. For low-cost total bond-market exposure, you might also consider a bond-market index fund such as Vanguard Total Bond Market Index.

In addition, make room for a shorter-term bond fund that you can begin tapping as your goal draws near. Ultrashort-bond funds invest mainly in short-term Treasury, mortgage-backed, and corporate bonds, and tend not to feel much pain when interest rates rise.

If you're willing to take on a little more risk than an ultrashort fund, you might also consider steering at least part of your short-term portfolio toward a short-term bond fund. Just be aware that you could lose money if interest rates rise: In 1999, the average short-term bond fund lost 0.70%. Steer clear of short-term bond funds that take on excessive credit risk. Many short-term bond funds rely on mid-quality corporates (rated A or BBB) to boost their distributed yields. But that can hurt their returns when investors become wary of companies with shaky finances, as they did in 2002.

Once you've anchored your portfolio with appropriate core bond holdings, you can consider spicing it up a bit. To help reduce the corrosive effect that inflation can have on bond-fund returns (those bond interest payments don't buy what they used to!), you could consider a fund that buys inflation-protected bonds.

Fund Name	Category	% of Assets
Dodge & Cox Income	Intermediate-Term Bond	25.00
Vanguard Total Bond Market Index	Intermediate-Term Bond	15.00
T. Rowe Price Equity-Income	Large Value	15.00
ABN AMRO/Montag & Caldwell Growth	Large Growth	15.00
Vanguard Inflation-Protected Securities	Intermediate Government	5.00
Fidelity Short-Term Bond	Short-Term Bond	10.00
Northeast Investors	High-Yield Bond	5.00
Dodge & Cox International	Foreign Large Value	5.00
Selected Special	Mid Blend	5.00
Portfolio Total	—	100.00

Portfolio Analysis

Asset Allocation (%)

● Cash	10.80
● US Stock	31.01
● Non-US Stock	6.64
● Bonds	50.98
● Other	0.58

Equity Style (%)

Value	Blnd	Grwth	
20	35	26	Large
9	6	3	Med
0	0	0	Small

Fixed-Income Style (%)

Short	Intrm	Long	
54	29	10	High
0	0	0	Med
8	0	0	Low

Sector Weightings (%)

Information	15.88	Service	41.18	Manufacturing	42.94
Software	1.89	Health Care	14.04	Consumer Goods	15.90
Hardware	5.87	Consumer Services	8.45	Industrial Materials	14.63
Media	5.09	Business Services	5.00	Energy	9.96
Telecomm	3.03	Financial Services	13.69	Utilities	2.46

Figure 11.2 A sample short-term portfolio (geared toward investors with time horizons of roughly five years).

If you own any stock funds in your short-term portfolio, keep the total position size relatively small, and favor those offerings whose managers employ conservative strategies. Focus on funds that are well diversified and have managers who are price conscious (i.e., they don't want to overpay for stocks). Large-cap value or large-cap blend funds would be ideal stock holdings for a shorter-term portfolio.

For a look at a model short-term portfolio composed of some of Morningstar's favorite funds, see Figure 11.2.

Building Portfolios for Intermediate-Term Goals

Perhaps your daughter will leave for college in six years and you're only beginning to invest for the big event now. Here's how to invest for a goal that's 5 to 10 years away.

Because intermediate-term investors want to see their money grow but don't want to have to deal with extreme volatility, they should put 25% of the money in a safety net of a bond fund or cash and the remaining 75% in stock funds. Those worried about risk might want to place 35% of their portfolios in bonds or cash.

Large-cap blend funds make the most sense for the core-stock portion of an intermediate-term investor's portfolio. Intermediate-term investors might also consider tipping part of their portfolios into a small-company or foreign fund for an extra measure of diversification. For a core fixed-income holding, look for a versatile intermediate-term bond fund.

When you're within a few years of your goal, you'll want to shift to the short-term strategy discussed earlier because at that point the risk required for bigger gains is too great. You need to preserve what you have made rather than run the risk of having to draw on your portfolio when it's down.

For a look at a model intermediate-term portfolio composed of some of Morningstar's favorite funds, see Figure 11.3.

Building Portfolios for Long-Term Goals

If you have a time horizon of 10 years or more, you can afford to take a few more risks with your portfolio. Because your main objective is to make sure that your nest egg grows, keep 75% or more of your assets in stock funds,

Fund Name	Category	% of Assets
Vanguard 500 Index	Large Blend	25.00
Vanguard Total Bond Market Index	Intermediate-Term Bond	25.00
Oakmark Fund	Large Blend	15.00
Dodge & Cox International	Foreign Large Value	10.00
Metropolitan West Total Return Bond	Intermediate-Term Bond	10.00
Fidelity Capital Appreciation	Large Growth	10.00
Weitz Hickory	Small Blend	5.00
Portfolio Total	—	*100.00*

Portfolio Analysis

Asset Allocation (%)

- Cash — 4.80
- US Stock — 51.10
- Non-US Stock — 10.58
- Bonds — 33.28
- Other — 0.24

Equity Style (%)

	Value	Blnd	Grwth	
	24	31	25	Large
	6	6	6	Med
	1	0	0	Small

Fixed-Income Style (%)

	Short	Intrm	Long	
	0	100	0	High
	0	0	0	Med
	0	0	0	Low

Sector Weightings (%)

Information Economy	23.70	Service Economy	44.78	Manufacturing Economy	31.52
Software	2.80	Health Care	10.69	Consumer Goods	11.51
Hardware	9.09	Consumer Services	11.17	Industrial Materials	12.00
Media	8.87	Business Services	4.61	Energy	6.49
Telecommunications	2.95	Financial Services	18.31	Utilities	1.52

Figure 11.3 A sample intermediate-term portfolio (geared toward investors with time horizons of 10 years or fewer).

which, over longer time frames, offer better appreciation potential than do bond funds.

And because risk control is much less of a consideration with a long-term portfolio than it is with a short- or intermediate-term portfolio, you can also afford to dedicate a bigger share of your stock portfolio to funds that employ risky, but potentially higher returning, strategies. (This advice only applies if you're confident that you can ride out the bumps and not sell when your funds hit a rough patch.) For example, you might consider a fund whose manager maintains a portfolio that's highly concentrated in its top holdings; Marsico Focus, ICAP Select Equity, and Oakmark Select are all terrific concentrated stock-picker's funds. Noncore fund types, including smaller-cap offerings, may also play a bigger role in your long-term portfolio.

Fund Name	Category	% of Assets
Harbor Capital Appreciation	Large Growth	20.00
Artisan International	Foreign Large Growth	15.00
Western Asset Core Bond	Intermediate-Term Bond	15.00
ICAP Select Equity	Large Value	10.00
Selected American	Large Blend	10.00
Oakmark Fund	Large Blend	10.00
Turner Midcap Growth	Mid Growth	10.00
Third Avenue Small-Cap Value	Small Blend	5.00
Masters' Select Smaller Companies	Small Growth	5.00
Portfolio Total	—	*100.00*

Portfolio Analysis

Asset Allocation (%)

● Cash	10.03
● US Stock	60.22
● Non-US Stock	20.60
● Bonds	8.58
● Other	0.58

Equity Style (%)

Value	Blnd	Grwth	
18	26	29	Large
3	7	11	Med
2	2	2	Small

Fixed-Income Style (%)

Short	Intrm	Long	
	100		High
			Med
			Low

Sector Weightings (%)

Information Economy	24.41	Service Economy	50.34	Manufacturing Economy	25.24
Software	5.06	Health Care	9.59	Consumer Goods	8.82
Hardware	9.51	Consumer Services	12.49	Industrial Materials	8.26
Media	7.10	Business Services	6.61	Energy	7.64
Telecommunications	2.68	Financial Services	21.64	Utilities	0.52

Figure 11.4 A sample long-term portfolio (geared toward investors with time horizons of 10 years or more).

For the core-bond component of a long-term portfolio, a sturdy intermediate-term bond fund fits the bill, providing broad bond-market exposure in a single package. Alternatively, an investor saving for a long-term goal might consider a broad income-oriented fund for his or her core bond exposure; T. Rowe Price Spectrum Income and Fidelity Strategic Income are two we particularly like.

For a look at a model long-term portfolio composed of some of Morningstar's favorite funds, see Figure 11.4.

Knowing How Many Funds Are Enough

Most of us collect something. For some, it's wine. For others, it's baseball cards. Still others collect clothes. Some people collect investments. Over the years, we've talked to many investment enthusiasts who have amassed portfolios with 50 or even 75 individual mutual funds.

Although diversification is generally desirable in investing, it's possible to overdo it. For one thing, you can easily lose sight of the financial forest for the trees. You wind up owning funds because they looked appealing when you bought them, but you may not be clear on how they're contributing to your goals. An investor with 50 mutual funds would face a monumental task just remembering all those names, never mind figuring out why he owns them and how they all work together.

Perhaps an even bigger negative associated with owning too many funds is that you could end up with a portfolio that looks and acts a lot like a broad market index such as the S&P 500, but costs a lot more—in terms of annual expenses—than an index mutual fund.

So how many funds do you need to achieve adequate diversification? Morningstar studied just this topic. We constructed hypothetical portfolios ranging from 1 to 30 funds, using every possible type of fund. For example, the 30-fund portfolios consisted of every 30-fund combination we could come up with. We then calculated five-year standard deviations for each of those portfolios. (As you learned in Chapter 3, a high standard deviation means there's the potential for big gains or losses, whereas a lower number indicates a less volatile portfolio.)

As you'd expect, single-fund portfolios had the highest standard deviation, delivering either the biggest gains or the heaviest losses. So owning

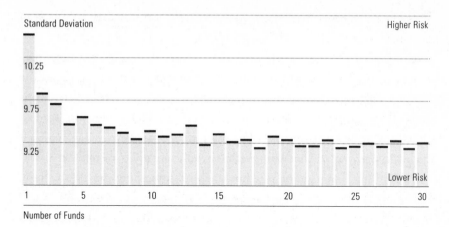

Figure 11.5   How the number of funds in a portfolio affects standard deviation.

just one fund can be a risky bet. Add another fund and the standard deviation drops significantly. Returns may be lower, but the downside is less severe, too.

As Figure 11.5 shows, after 4 funds, the effect of adding another fund diminishes. Adding a fourth fund helps reduce the overall portfolio's volatility, but not dramatically so. After 7 funds, things have mostly leveled out and after 10 funds, a portfolio's standard deviation stays nearly the same regardless of how many funds you add. Thus, once you own between 7 and 10 funds, there may be no need for more. In fact, the more funds you own, the more likely you are to own at least a couple that do practically the same thing.

Avoiding Overlap

Say it's late 1999 and you own a dozen funds, including Janus Twenty, Janus Fund, Janus Overseas, Janus Mercury, Janus Olympus, and American Century Ultra. You might be feeling pretty smug; those funds returned an average of 73% that year.

Yet the reason for these funds' good fortunes was also about to become their undoing—namely, they all had feasted on a similar group of pricey large-cap growth stocks, which fell precipitously in the ensuing bear market. Those funds lost an average of 21.7% in 2000 and went on to fall even further in 2001 and 2002.

Unfortunately, such stories were all too common during the bear market—investors had loaded up on a lot of like-minded funds and paid the price later on. The lesson? You don't want to find out too late that your funds all own the same type of stocks or bonds. That's why you need to know how your funds invest. Morningstar.com's Instant X-Ray tool is a quick and easy way to check for overlap in your portfolio, or to see if a fund you're thinking about adding is redundant with something you already have. You simply enter all your stock and fund holdings and then click on "Show Instant X-Ray." You'll see how your portfolio is distributed across each square of the Morningstar style box, across sectors, and among cash, bonds, and U.S. and foreign stocks.

In addition to checking up on investment-style and sector overlap, pay attention to whether your funds are all loading up on the same stocks. Imagine if, in early 2002, you owned two or three funds that each held a significant percentage of their money in Enron. Without realizing it, you might have had significant exposure to one of the biggest corporate bankruptcies in history. It's entirely possible that more than one of your funds will own the same stock, of course—and that wouldn't be necessarily problematic. What you don't want is a large chunk of the same stock showing up in multiple funds. Consider this: At the end of 2004, the top 15 holdings of Fidelity Magellan and Fidelity Growth & Income—two widely held large-blend funds—had 10 stocks in common (see Figure 11.6). If something goes wrong in one of those stocks, more than just one of your funds would be affected. Likewise, if you own individual stocks, be aware that your funds may also own those same stocks—it could spell additional risk.

If you're worried about duplication of investment styles, sectors, or individual stocks, pay scrupulous attention to what funds own before you add them to your portfolio, and check up on them frequently to stave off overlap. In addition, remember the following tips.

▶ *Don't buy multiple funds run by the same manager.* Zebras don't change their stripes, and managers rarely change their strategies. Fund managers

Top 15 Holdings for Fidelity Magellan (% Net Assets as of 12-31-04)		Top 15 Holdings for Fidelity Growth & Income (% Net Assets as of 12-31-04)	
❶ General Electric	3.91	❶ General Electric	4.03
❷ American Intl Group	3.25	SLM	4.03
❸ Microsoft	3.09	❺ ExxonMobil	3.66
❹ Citigroup	2.96	❸ Microsoft	3.16
❺ ExxonMobil	2.48	Verizon Communications	2.57
Viacom	2.38	UnitedHealth Group	2.40
❻ Home Depot	2.30	SBC Communications	2.34
❼ Bank of America	2.13	❽ Pfizer	2.21
❽ Pfizer	2.11	❾ Wal-Mart Stores	2.12
Tyco International	1.91	❷ American Intl Group	2.04
Johnson & Johnson	1.79	Altria Group	2.02
❾ Wal-Mart Stores	1.67	❹ Citigroup	1.94
❿ Wells Fargo	1.64	❼ Bank of America	1.78
Intel	1.55	❿ Wells Fargo	1.55
Lowe's Companies	1.51	❻ Home Depot	1.50

Figure 11.6   Ten of the top 15 holdings are the same in these two prominent funds.

have ingrained investment habits that they apply to every pool of money they run—you won't find a manager buying growth stocks for one fund he runs and value stocks for another. So if you buy two funds by Famous Manager A, chances are you'll own two of the same thing.

▶ *Don't overload on one boutique's funds.* Some fund families, such as Fidelity, T. Rowe Price, and Vanguard, offer lineups of funds that span several investment styles. Other shops, often called *boutiques*, prefer to specialize in a particular style. Oakmark means value; Wasatch usually operates in small-cap territory. Boutique families are often excellent at what they do, but it's doubtful whether owning three funds from the same boutique will give you anything more than you would get with one of them.

▶ *Watch for overlap in your large-cap holdings.* Large-cap stocks and funds make great core holdings, but they're perhaps the greatest source of overlap in many portfolios. Why? The pool of large companies is relatively shallow. Only about 250 of all U.S. stocks can be classified as large cap.

The remaining thousands of stocks qualify as mid- or small-cap issues. So if you own multiple large-company funds, there's a high possibility of overlap. That's also true if you hold both individual large-cap stocks and large-cap funds. It's hard to think of any justification for owning more than one large-blend fund. Once you have picked up a large-value and a large-growth fund—or a single large-blend fund—start looking at options in other parts of the style box.

▶ *Take the four corners approach.* The Morningstar style box can be a diversifier's best friend. Not only will the style box tell you whether your manager focuses on large-value stocks or small-cap growth issues, you can also use it to identify funds that bear little resemblance to one another. Owning funds in each corner of the box (large value, large growth, small value, and small growth) can be a straightforward way to ensure that you've built a diversified portfolio. Morningstar studies show that these fund categories have low correlations with each other: The four corners can all behave differently over the same time period. When the broad market tumbled in 2000 and 2001, large-growth funds suffered most, losing a cumulative 35% for the two years. Small growth dropped 12%, while large value eked out a 2% gain and small value zoomed 39%. Each group has led or faltered during other periods. If you own a large-value fund from your favorite fund company, choose its large-growth, small-value, or small-growth offerings to add something new.

Investor's Checklist: Put Your Portfolio Plan into Action

▶ Build a solid foundation for your portfolio by investing in reliable core funds.

▶ If you're saving for a goal that's five or fewer years away, stake the bulk of your portfolio in bond funds. If you make room for stock funds in your short-term portfolio, make sure that they're fairly cautious types.

▶ If you're building an intermediate-term portfolio (i.e., you intend to begin tapping your assets in five or 10 years), you can afford to strike a balance between stocks and bonds.

► If you're saving for a goal that's 10 or more years in the future, the bulk of your assets should be in stocks. Your long-term portfolio might also include exposure to funds with riskier strategies, such as those that concentrate heavily in their top holdings or that buy small-cap stocks.

► Don't obsess about the number of funds you own. But if you own a lot of funds, make sure they don't overlap too much.

12

Simplify Your Investment Life

BILL MILLER, WHO in 2004 led Legg Mason Value Trust to its 14th straight year of surpassing the S&P 500 Index, is widely regarded as one of the brightest minds on Wall Street. A true contrarian, Miller often makes bold moves, buying stocks that everyone else is seemingly fleeing in droves.

So what on earth do smaller investors like us have to learn from a power broker like Miller? Quite a lot, as it turns out.

No, we're not suggesting you sink a big portion of your portfolio into a single holding or buy stocks when they're in serious trouble—that kind of stuff *is* usually best left to the pros. Instead, you should emulate Miller on a more basic level. Like most of the best money managers, including Warren Buffett, Miller is heavily invested in a rather short list of holdings—just 34 securities at last count. And because he has researched his companies thoroughly and focused on well-managed firms that have what it takes to grow and grow, he holds many of his picks for years.

Most of us would do well to adopt a similarly streamlined approach to running our own portfolios. After all, wouldn't you prefer to have a portfolio devoted to a short list of those investments in which you have the highest degree of confidence, one that you can hold through thick and thin, no matter what the market serves up?

True enough, building such a portfolio is easier said than done. Life is messy, and as our financial lives get more complicated, most of us end up managing multiple accounts—our own 401(k) plans and those of our spouses, IRAs, 529s, and various taxable accounts, for example. But by following a few guidelines, you can set up a minimalist portfolio that you can really count on.

Sticking with the Basics

Bill Miller and most other top portfolio managers will tell you that there's a lot of day-to-day "noise" in the market, most of which has little to no bearing on the actual value of their holdings. Individual investors would do well to adopt a similar mind-set when building their own portfolios.

True, it's hard to open the business section without seeing an article about the falling dollar, spiking oil prices, or China's growth. But should you run out and buy an investment that's specifically designed to focus on one of those trends, such as a sector or regional fund? Probably not. Any such offerings tend to be expensive and exceptionally volatile, and individual investors have a record of buying them high and selling them low.

A better strategy, particularly if you're aiming to build a high-quality, low-maintenance portfolio, is to avoid these niche offerings altogether and instead focus on finding great core mutual funds—broadly diversified offerings with reasonable costs, seasoned management teams, and solid long-term risk/reward profiles. If you've done that, you can pretty much tune out the day-to-day noise and let your manager decide whether the next big thing is worth investing in. Check out Chapters 6 and 8 for some of our favorite core-stock and -bond funds.

Investigating One-Stop Funds

Of course, finding solid core funds is only part of the battle. Establishing and maintaining an asset mix suited to your particular investment objectives is another big task. That's why one-stop funds, particularly target-maturity funds, which "mature," or grow more conservative, as your goal draws near, make sense for so many investors. Because these are funds of funds that provide exposure to stock offerings (both foreign and U.S.), bond funds, and cash in a single package, they're ideally suited to investors looking to build streamlined portfolios.

And for busy people who don't have a lot of time to babysit their investments, target-maturity funds are ideal. Not only do they arrive at a stock/
bond/cash mix that's appropriate for your time horizon, but they also gradually make that asset allocation more conservative as the target date draws near.
You simply buy a fund that matches your target date—say, your child's anticipated college enrollment date or your planned retirement date—and tune out.

In Figures 12.1 and 12.2, you'll see our favorite funds in the conservative-
and moderate-allocation categories, which is where Morningstar places most
one-stop funds.

T. Rowe Price Personal Strategy Income	The fund is designed to provide one-stop exposure to most asset classes. Each stock or bond component mirrors one of T. Rowe Price's offerings. An added plus: T. Rowe Price doesn't charge any additional expenses on top of the underlying funds' costs.
Vanguard Tax-Managed Balanced	This sturdy fund could easily serve as an investor's sole taxable holding. It invests half of its assets in stocks se- lected to match the key characteristics of the Russell 1000 Index, emphasizing those issues with low dividend yields. The bond portion consists of intermediate-term, high-quality municipal issues. The fund uses trading techniques, such as selling losers to offset gains, to mini- mize capital gains.
Vanguard Wellesley Income	Comanager Jack Ryan, who runs the equity portion of the fund, is a yield-oriented contrarian. The fund typically has little exposure to growth-oriented sectors such as technology. The fund's bond stake (about 60% of assets) used to have a very long duration (a measure of interest- rate sensitivity), but Earl McEvoy, who runs the bond portion of the portfolio, now manages against a bench- mark with a shorter duration.

Figure 12.1   Our favorite conservative-allocation funds.

American Funds Income Fund of America	There's a reason this income-focused fund is the largest balanced fund around. A seasoned team of portfolio counselors divides assets between dividend-paying energy, utility, and financial-services stocks and high-quality debt, with a small sleeve of high-yield bonds for added spice. Over the long term, that stance has resulted in strong total relative returns, a generous yield, and below-average volatility. Expenses are a bargain at 57 basis points, too.
Fidelity Asset Manager	Tamer than many of its peers, this fund keeps a relatively light 50% of assets in stocks and typically maintains a modest cash stake. From there, lead manager Dick Habermann makes minor tactical adjustments to the fund's asset mix to take advantage of market currents. Although it's posted two subpar returns in 2003 and 2004, we still have plenty of confidence in management. Charles Mangum, who runs the stock portfolio, has built a stellar long-term record using the same strategy at Fidelity Dividend Growth.
Pax World Balanced	This fund would be one of our favorites even without its socially conscious investment guidelines. Manager Chris Brown builds the equity portfolio with a growth tilt and runs a relatively high-quality bond portfolio. The fund has delivered admirable long-term gains with below-average volatility.
Vanguard Target Retirement 2025	This fund is designed for investors who don't want to be bothered with modifying their asset allocation as they near retirement. Thus, its stock/bond mix—which is currently about 60/40—slowly becomes more bond-heavy over time.
Vanguard Wellington	This fund plies a value-oriented, dividend-focused approach, typically holding large stakes in utility and energy names boasting plump yields. Although that tack can leave the fund behind bolder, growth-minded peers in rallying markets, deft stock selection has generally steadied performance.

Figure 12.2   Our favorite moderate-allocation funds.

Indexing

If you'd like to simplify your investment life but aren't ready to cede as much control as you're required to with a target-maturity fund, index funds could be your answer. With an indexing approach, you accept the market's return (or rather, the market's return less any fund expenses) rather than trying to beat it.

With index funds, you don't have to worry about manager changes. Or strategy changes. You always know how the fund is investing, no matter who is in charge. Many investors find indexing boring, especially the mutual-fund hobbyists out there. But even fund junkies admit that index funds are the lowest-maintenance investments around. The real work with indexing comes at the start, when you're choosing the funds that make up your portfolio. Before doing so, check out Chapter 6, which includes a section on index funds.

Taking the Best and Leaving the Rest

Simplifying your investment life isn't terribly complicated if you're managing a single retirement portfolio for yourself. But life is messy, with most investors juggling multiple portfolios and multiple goals at once. In addition to your own 401(k) plan, for example, you might also be overseeing an IRA for yourself and your spouse, a child's college-savings plan, and your household's taxable assets.

If you're like many investors, you're running each of these various accounts as well-diversified portfolios unto themselves. That's not unreasonable. But to help counteract portfolio sprawl, consider managing all of your accounts that share the same time horizon as a single portfolio, a unified whole. In so doing, you'll be able cut down on the number of holdings you have to monitor, and you'll also be able to ensure that each of your picks is truly best of breed.

For example, say your spouse's retirement plan lacks worthwhile bond holdings but has a few terrific core equity-fund choices; yours has several solid bond picks. If that's the case, you may want to stash all of your spouse's assets in the stock funds while allocating a large percentage of your own 401(k) plan to bond funds.

The key to making this strategy work is to use tools such as Morningstar.com's Portfolio Manager and Instant X-Ray, which let you look at all of your accounts together, as a single portfolio. That way, you can see if your overall portfolio's asset allocation is in line with your target, and you can also determine whether you're adequately diversified across investment styles and sectors.

Jotting Down Why You Own Each Investment

Simplification gurus preach that writing down our goals helps us organize our lives to meet those goals. The same can be said for investing: By writing down why you made an investment in the first place, you're more likely to make sure that the investment meets its original goal. If it isn't doing what you expected by sticking with a specific investment style and producing competitive long-term returns, you'll be ready to cut it loose. Noting why you bought the fund—to get large-cap growth exposure and consistently above-average returns from a manager who has been in charge for several years, and so on—will help to instill discipline and eliminate some of the emotion that so often gets in the way of smart investing.

Say you bought Fidelity Contrafund to cover the costs of your daughter's education in 15 years. You chose the fund because it earned a Morningstar Rating of 5, reflecting a good combination of returns and risk; its expenses were lower than the category average; and the fund didn't risk a lot on the technology stocks that so many other growth funds were feasting on. Those are all good reasons. So you shouldn't even consider selling the fund unless it falls short on these points.

To take the opposite case, maybe you bought Scudder International Equity because you wanted some international exposure and you were attracted by its long-tenured management and consistent performance. But since 1999, the fund's performance has been a lot less impressive and it has also undergone a few management changes. The fund lagged the foreign-stock group in four of the five calendar years since 2000. Since the fund is no longer meeting your main reasons for buying it, selling would be a reasonable choice. Other legitimate reasons to sell would be that a fund has hiked its expense ratio, or assets have gotten so bloated that performance starts to suffer. (For a thorough review of the factors that might prompt you to sell a fund, see Chapter 15.)

Consolidating Your Investments with a Single Firm or Supermarket

By investing with only one fund supermarket or fund family, you eliminate excess complexity, cutting back on paperwork and filing. And the consolidated statements you'll receive can make tax time much easier, too. Instead of pulling together taxable distributions and gains from different statements, you'll have them all in one place.

If you want to stick with just one fund family, consider one of the big ones, such as Fidelity, Vanguard, or T. Rowe Price. These no-load families are all relatively low cost, with Vanguard being the cheapskate champion, and each offers a diverse lineup of mutual funds. If you would rather pick and choose among fund families, then a mutual fund supermarket might be your best option. Fund supermarkets bring together funds from a variety of fund groups. (For more on fund supermarkets, see Question 13 in the Frequently Asked Questions at the back of this book.)

Putting Your Investments on Autopilot

You may pay your electric and water bills automatically—why not invest the same way? You won't have to send a check out every month, every quarter, or every year. There's an added benefit to investing relatively small amounts on a regular basis (also called dollar-cost averaging): You may actually invest more than you would if you plunked down a lump sum, and at more opportune times. When you're dollar-cost averaging, you're putting dollars to work no matter what's going on in the market. You have effectively put on blinders against short-term market swings: Whether the market is going up or going down, $100 (or whatever amount you choose to invest) is going into your fund every month no matter what. That's discipline. Would you be able to write a check for $100 if your fund had lost 15% the previous month? Maybe not. But that would mean $100 less working for you when your investments rebounded.

Figure 12.3 shows how automatic investing can enable you to buy cheaper shares on average, which will spell stronger returns. An investor who put in $600 up front in January would have gotten 60 shares at $10

Month	Investment ($)	NAV ($)	Shares Purchased
January	100	10	10
February	100	9	11.1
March	100	11	9.1
April	100	8	12.5
May	100	9	11.1
June	100	12	8.3
Total Result of Investment	600 →	12 ×	62.1 = $745.20

Figure 12.3   How dollar-cost averaging works.

per share. Those shares were worth $12 in June, so her investment was worth $720. If she had dollar-cost averaged her investment, putting in $100 per month, she would have purchased some of her shares on the cheap and wound up with 62.1 shares in June. At $12 per share, she would have had $745.20, $25 more than if she had invested a lump sum at the beginning.

Be careful about using a dollar-cost averaging program if you use a broker or advisor to buy and sell shares, however. If you're paying a front-end load, you'll pay that amount on each and every investment. Perhaps more important, by making smaller purchases you might not be eligible for sales-charge discounts that are frequently available to those who are investing larger sums.

Investor's Checklist: Simplify Your Investment Life

► Avoid faddish funds designed to capitalize on short-term market trends. Instead, stick with core stock and bond funds that you don't need to babysit.

► Consider all-in-one funds, particularly target-maturity funds, which grow more conservative as you get close to your goal.

► Index funds make great choices for investors who don't want to spend a lot of time managing their portfolios.

► If you have several portfolios geared toward the same time horizon, manage them as a unified whole, emphasizing the best options available to you in each account.

▶ Whenever you make an investment, write down why you bought it. If it no longer fits your reasons for buying, it's probably a good candidate for selling.

▶ Consolidate your investments with a single fund family or fund supermarket.

▶ Simplify your life by setting up an automatic investment plan. Dollar-cost averaging takes the emotion out of investing and should produce better returns over time than buying and selling erratically.

13

Be Savvy When Seeking Advice

MAYBE YOU NEED help solving a particularly knotty financial problem, such as exercising your company stock options without getting murdered on taxes. Or perhaps your portfolio's bear market performance was so poor—and its rebound so lackluster—that you've realized you need guidance to get it back on track. Or maybe, to paraphrase the title of a recent bestseller, you're just not that into it. Whatever the reason, you've decided to seek the help of a financial planner. That can be a sensible move, especially if you have no time, interest, or aptitude for financial matters (and many very smart people fit one of those descriptions).

Unfortunately, your work isn't over once you've decided to ask for outside help. Certain Web sites, including www.fpanet.org and www.napfa.org, can help you find a financial planner in your geographic area, and you might also consider asking friends and relatives if they've found a planner they trust. But even if a financial professional comes highly recommended, you owe it to yourself to conduct your own due diligence to ensure that the person is a good fit for you and your goals.

Here are some key steps to take to evaluate whether a certain planner is right for you.

Establish Your Goals

Before you set out to find a planner, an essential first step is determining your goals. Are you looking for assistance with every stage of your financial life, from selecting insurance to investment planning to managing your taxes? Or are you seeking help with a specific problem, such as a one-time portfolio overhaul? Knowing how much—or how little—assistance you need will go a long way toward finding the right person to help you reach that goal.

Understand the Different Types of Advice

Wealth manager. Financial consultant. Financial planner. Welcome to the Wild West of financial advice. Because there are currently very few regulations surrounding the credentials one needs to proffer financial advice, don't let a fancy title lull you into a false sense of security. Certain individuals calling themselves financial planners are primarily in the business of selling securities and may have little substantive educational background in providing financial advice. Additionally, they are not necessarily bound by a fiduciary duty to put you in the best investments for your needs.

Similarly, don't be unduly impressed if there's an alphabet soup of designations following a certain individual's name. Some financial-planning-related designations require an extremely rigorous course of study and ongoing education, while others do not.

Finding an individual with the right background and educational experience gets back to what you're trying to accomplish. If you're seeking broad financial-planning assistance, your best bet is to seek out a Certified Financial Planner (CFP), a Chartered Financial Consultant (ChFC), or a Certified Public Accountant-Personal Financial Specialist (CPA-PFS). Individuals who have earned the right to use one of those designations have passed a series of courses and/or exams relating to a broad range of financial-planning topics, including taxes, investments, and insurance.

If your planning needs are more focused, you might seek out individuals whose designations relate specifically to that area. For example, if you need tax-planning help, look for a Certified Public Accountant (CPA) or enrolled agent. If you're looking for someone with specific expertise in analyzing individual securities, you'll probably want to look for someone who has earned the right to use the Chartered Financial Analyst (CFA) designation. Many financial professionals have earned more than one of these designations, and many large financial-planning firms employ individuals with a broad range of specialties and designations.

Check Up on Regulatory and Disciplinary History

In addition to checking credentials, take the time to make sure that any planner you're considering has never faced disciplinary action for unlawful or unethical behavior in his or her profession. Unfortunately, this can be tricky work, as not all planners and advisors are regulated by the same entities. Registered investment advisors must file what's called a form ADV with either the state or the SEC. In it, you can see details about the advisor's practice as well as any past regulatory transgressions. The National Association of Securities Dealers' (NASD) Web site also has a handy tool called NASD BrokerCheck that lets you view a given broker's employment history and find out if he or she has ever run afoul of NASD regulations.

Assess Experience Level

In addition to making sure that an individual has completed a rigorous course of study in financial planning and hasn't run afoul of regulators, you'll also want to interview prospective planners to ensure that they've had hands-on experience with your specific problem or issue. How long has the individual been in practice? Does the profile of his or her typical client match yours? Ask the planner to provide you with references. Call those references. True, few planners will give you the names of any dissatisfied clients. But by asking clients what type of advice the planner provided and whether they were satisfied with it, you'll have a better sense of whether that planner is a good fit for you and your needs.

Understand the Costs

Figuring out how much good financial advice will cost you is almost as confusing as discerning what the various designations mean. In general, planners and advisors get paid in one of three ways. First, they can charge you a percentage of your assets on an ongoing basis (say, 2% a year, not including brokerage costs or any expenses associated with mutual funds). Other planners charge a dollar rate on a per-job or hourly basis. Finally, others earn commissions on any products they sell you. Some planners may use a combination of these fee structures—for example, a planner might charge you an hourly rate to set up your plan and also put you in funds on which he or she earns a commission.

Knowing which fee structure makes the most sense for you relates directly to your needs and what you're trying to accomplish. If you're seeking soup-to-nuts asset management on an ongoing basis, it may be more cost-effective to pay your advisor an annual percentage of your assets rather than paying for advice a la carte. If, however, you need help with a focused goal—say, a one-time portfolio overhaul—you may want to seek out a planner who charges a flat fee. If you're not investing a huge sum of money, it may be more cost-effective for you to pay for financial-planning advice via commissions.

When interviewing prospective planners, don't be shy about asking for details about how they're compensated. You should also feel comfortable asking for an estimate of the costs of any work to be performed. Insist that the estimate be inclusive of any commissions the planner will earn when buying and selling the specific securities he or she is recommending.

Inquire about Investment Approach

If you're seeking help with your investments, ask the planner some questions about his or her investment philosophy. What criteria does he or she use to pick individual securities? It can be a red flag if the planner is focusing strictly on past performance and not considering more fundamental factors, such as the quality of the fund family or manager. What role do expenses play in the advisor's fund selection? (If the answer is "none," that's another red flag.) What would prompt the planner to sell a given fund? Does he or she employ a buy-and-hold philosophy or trade frequently? (Remember: Very few investors are able to outdo the market's return by trading frequently or chasing performance, so be skeptical of any advisor who claims to be able to do so.)

Weigh the Intangibles

Last but not least, ask yourself how well you and this person click on a personal level. No, your planner needn't be someone you'd want to hang out with in your free time. But you should feel that you can trust this person. If you don't, move on to someone you can.

Investor's Checklist: Be Savvy When Seeking Advice

▶ Many individuals can call themselves financial planners, but they might have very different credentials. For most general financial-planning needs, seek out a Certified Financial Planner (CFP), a Chartered Financial Consultant (ChFC), or a Certified Public Accountant-Personal Financial Specialist (CPA-PFS).

▶ Conduct a background check to make sure that any financial professional you're considering hiring has never faced disciplinary action for unlawful or unethical behavior within his or her profession.

▶ Inquire about experience. Has the planner assisted someone in your specific situation before? Ask for references and call them.

▶ Ask to see an estimate of how much the planner will charge you.

▶ Inquire about the planner's investment style. Does he or she employ a buy-and-hold philosophy or trade frequently? If the latter, look elsewhere.

Schedule Regular Checkups

As WE NOTED in Chapter 12, investors would do well to tune out the "noise" in the market, because day-to-day market action invariably has very little bearing on whether your portfolio will get you to your goals. If you've taken care to assemble a portfolio that suits your goals and time horizon, there's very little reason to spend time trading in and out of funds. Over the years we've seen investors inflict far greater damage on their portfolios by trading too frequently than by not trading enough.

Still, savvy investors should set aside time for regular portfolio checkups throughout the year to ensure that their portfolios are on the right track. Even if nothing has changed about your investments, it's still important to make sure that your portfolio's asset allocation is where you need it to be. For most investors, we recommend a brief quarterly review, accompanied by a more thorough examination once a year. If in your annual review you determine that your portfolio's allocations are out of whack with your targets, you'll want to consider making some changes (a process often called *rebalancing*).

Conducting a Quarterly Portfolio Review
Every quarter, conduct a minireview to look for major portfolio developments. Not only will this make your annual review less time-consuming, but

it will also tip you off to any burgeoning trouble spots that might require action during your annual portfolio checkup.

The goal of the quarterly minireview is to check for major changes or trends within your holdings and portfolio overall. It's not meant to be a substitute for the more thorough annual review; nor is it meant to trigger major buy or sell decisions. To keep your quarterly review short and to the point, you'll need to review only a few items within three key areas of your portfolio:

1. Performance-Related Data
- ▶ Overall portfolio return for past three months and for the year to date.
- ▶ Biggest gainer and loser for past three months and for the year to date.
- ▶ Best and worst performers relative to an appropriate benchmark, such as the appropriate mutual fund category.

The first question you'll probably want answered when you conduct your quarterly review is: "How much money did I make?" (Or, possibly, "How much money did I lose?") The key here is not to put too much emphasis on the gains or losses of a single quarter. More important than knowing your overall return in a short, three-month time period is determining which holdings contributed the most, and the least, to that return. These are the holdings that you may need to adjust (either buying more or selling) during your year-end checkup.

Also, keep in mind that it's not just absolute returns that matter. Your worst-performing holding, in absolute terms, may actually be doing better than any of its peers. If that holding is playing an important diversification role in your portfolio, you may end up keeping it even though its style is out of sync with the broad market. That's why it's important to note each holding's performance ranking relative to the appropriate category or index.

2. Portfolio Allocations
- ▶ Asset allocation.
- ▶ Investment style allocation.
- ▶ Stock sector percentage.

In each quarterly review, you'll want to check on your asset allocation to see if, and how, the big picture of your portfolio has changed. You'll also want to check to see whether your portfolio's breakdown among the various squares of the Morningstar style box has changed and investigate your overall portfolio's sector weightings. Striking alterations over a three-month time span don't indicate that it's time to buy more of a given holding and sell another. But by keeping tabs on major portfolio-related changes as they develop, you'll make your year-end review easier and will be tipped off to trends before your overall portfolio changes too dramatically.

3. Fundamental Changes and News
▶ Manager or strategy changes.
▶ Expense-ratio changes.
▶ Fund company news (mergers or acquisitions).

This part of the quarterly review is probably the most important, and could require you to do a little additional digging if it turns out something has changed about one of your funds. If, for example, you find that your mutual fund has undergone a manager change, you'll want to learn about the new manager's background and what changes, if any, he or she intends to make to the portfolio. A management change in and of itself isn't a "sell" signal, but it does entail further investigation. (For more details on how to interpret such fundamental changes, see Chapter 15.)

Conducting an Annual Portfolio Review
Although you can conduct your quarterly checkup fairly quickly, be sure to set aside a decent chunk of time for your annual review, because you'll need to determine whether you need to make any changes. A Web-based portfolio tool, such as Morningstar.com's Instant X-Ray, can help you quickly size up where your portfolio is right now.

As you conduct your annual portfolio review, you should check the percentage of your portfolio that is devoted to the following areas:

▶ Cash, stocks, and bonds.
▶ Various investment styles, such as "large value" or "small growth."
▶ Key sectors.
▶ Specific individual securities.
▶ Foreign exposure.

Asset mix. Even if you take a hands-off approach to your portfolio, you'll find that your mixture of cash, stocks, and bonds shifts over time. Stocks typically post better returns than bonds or cash, and therefore may continue to grow in importance in your portfolio if left untouched. When the market is in the doldrums, the opposite may be the problem: Your stock portfolio loses money, leaving your equity allocation smaller than you'd like. And no matter what happens in the market, you'll probably want to shift your portfolio into more conservative investments as your draw closer to your goals. Thus, it's important to pay close attention to the balance of stocks, bonds, and cash to make sure it's in sync with your targets.

Keeping tabs on your stock and bond mix and making adjustments if you need to is hands-down the most important thing you can do to keep your portfolio's volatility in check and to protect the gains you have made. Excessive stock exposure will make your portfolio much more vulnerable to stock market slumps. At the other extreme, parking too much in bonds could hinder you from getting the long-term returns you need to meet your goals.

Investment style. Just as your stock/bond mix can change over time, your portfolio's investment-style mix can also shift. In a given year, different kinds of stock funds can perform very differently from each other—that's the reason you want to hold a variety of stock funds in your portfolio. In the late 1990s, large-growth funds posted the best returns of any style category. As a result, such funds grew to be considerably larger portions of investors' portfolios than was ideal. Investors who weren't paying attention to their portfolios' investment-style mixes suffered tremendously in 2000 and 2001, when large growth turned into the worst-performing style category.

Your portfolio mix can shift for other reasons, too. For example, in 2004 and 2005, many value managers began to emphasize stocks that had typically been considered growth names, arguing that that part of the market was too compelling to overlook. Thus, it's possible that your value manager is currently holding some of the same names that your growth fund owns, and your overall portfolio is skewed toward growth stocks.

To help assess your portfolio's investment-style mix, compare its style-box breakdown to that of a broad stock-market index fund such as Vanguard Total Stock Market Index. You needn't build a stock-fund portfolio that's a mirror image of the index (if you wanted to do that, you might as well buy an inexpensive index fund). But you do want to be aware of any sizable, unintended investment-style bets in your portfolio, and consider making adjustments if need be.

Sector exposure. As part of your annual portfolio review, conduct a regular checkup of your sector exposure. If you find your portfolio skewing heavily toward one industry or another, consider scaling back on the fund (or funds) responsible for the overweight. (Alternatively, if a value-oriented fund is responsible for your portfolio's overweighting in a given market sector, you could wait for the manager to trim the position.) Focusing on one or two areas of the market might pump up your returns temporarily, but it will also leave you dangerously exposed to downturns in those areas.

Concentration in individual securities. While Microsoft, General Electric, or (for many investors) your employer's stock may play an important role in your portfolio, you'll want to know exactly how much you're devoting to such holdings. Checking on *stock overlap* will help to ensure that you don't inadvertently go into one year with 15% or more of your assets dedicated to the best-performing stock of the previous year, which could be ready for a downturn.

To accurately assess the largest stock positions in your portfolio, you'll need to add together any individual stocks you own and any exposure from the top holdings of your mutual funds. It's not unusual to discover that many of the most popular mutual funds are investing in the same securities. Use the Stock Intersection tool in Morningstar.com's Portfolio Manager to see the largest stock positions in your portfolio based on your individual stock holdings and the top holdings of your funds. If you have more than 5% of your portfolio in a single security, consider scaling back on the fund that's heavy on that holding, or trimming your position in the stock if you own it directly.

Foreign exposure. Finally, in your annual portfolio review look at the percentage of your portfolio devoted to specific countries or regions of the world. Your foreign-stock funds may change weightings frequently, and you will want to keep tabs on how each fund's weighting works with other holdings that you own. Even some domestic-equity funds are allowed to invest outside the United States, so don't rely solely on the word "foreign" or "global" to spot a fund's international ambitions. In early 2005, domestic-stock fund managers were routinely telling Morningstar analysts that they were finding stock valuations more attractive overseas than in the United States.

In addition to assessing your portfolio's allocation to foreign stocks, also examine single country or emerging-markets exposure. Check your exposure to the often-erratic Japanese market as well as to developing regions such as Latin America, the Pacific Rim, and Eastern Europe.

Rebalancing

So you've conducted your annual review and determined you need to make some adjustments to get your portfolio's weightings back in line with your targets. That process is called *rebalancing*.

On the surface, rebalancing seems counterintuitive. If some of your holdings have been thriving and are taking up a greater share of your portfolio, why not just let them run? The short answer is risk.

Imagine that in early 1995 your ideal portfolio was a 50/50 mix of stocks and bonds. To simplify things, you put $10,000 in Vanguard Total Stock Market Index and $10,000 in Vanguard Total Bond Market Index. If you then let them ride for five years, you would have had 69% in stocks and 31% in bonds.

You would have made a lot of money, because stocks were thriving during that period, but an additional 19% of your portfolio would have been vulnerable to a downturn in stocks. Your portfolio would have lost a cumulative 10.5% as the stock market dropped in 2000 and through 2001. If you went into the market downturn with your portfolio split equally between the stock and bond funds, you would have lost just 2.7% for the period.

The asset mix you came up with originally was the best one for meeting your goals. If that gets out of whack, then you don't have the right portfolio for you anymore, and it makes sense to restore the mix. Not only should you rebalance when your asset allocation gets out of line with your targets, which is often a function of time, but you should also consider doing so if your portfolio's investment style, sector positioning, or individual-stock weightings become too extreme.

Still, rebalancing can be challenging psychologically. It requires you to take money from your best-performing funds and divert it to the ones that are lagging and may even be losing money. Remember, though: When you rebalance, you're not selling off everything—you're merely lightening up on the funds that have done well. In effect, you're protecting the gains that you made by taking some money off the table. And by shifting money into the funds that haven't done as well, you're potentially getting more shares on the cheap, which can enhance your returns.

The common rule is to rebalance your portfolio once a year. Just choose a date such as January 1 (or maybe a different date, depending on how you like to usher in the new year) and review and rebalance your portfolio then. You could rebalance your portfolio more often, but our research indicates that more frequent rebalancing, such as every three or six months, doesn't do much to limit volatility.

Alternatively, you could rebalance when your portfolio's asset allocation veers from your targets by a certain percentage, say, 5% or more.

When rebalancing, it's essential to pay attention to the tax ramifications. After all, you'll be selling your winners, so you're apt to be on the hook for capital-gains taxes. One tax-efficient way to rebalance is not to cut back on your winners at all, but rather to send new cash to your losers. You can also limit the tax collector's cut if you concentrate your rebalancing efforts in your tax-sheltered accounts, such as your IRA or 401(k).

If you do rebalance a taxable portfolio, pay attention to when your funds make their annual capital-gains distributions. Most funds make them sometime between October and December. (You can contact your fund company in the fall to find out the scheduled distribution date.) If you sell after a distribution, you'll be paying taxes on shares that you later got rid of. Better to sell beforehand. When you're buying shares, do so after distributions have been made. Otherwise you could wind up getting a taxable distribution on shares that you have owned for just a matter of days.

Investor's Checklist: Schedule Regular Checkups

▶ Conduct a quick portfolio review each quarter to help anticipate any changes you'll need to make at year-end.

▶ Conduct a more thorough portfolio review once a year, analyzing your asset allocation, investment-style mix, sector weightings, and positions in individual stocks.

▶ Rebalance by first reviewing your portfolio's mix of cash, bonds, and stocks; its mix of investment styles and sectors and country exposure; and its concentration in individual stocks.

▶ Pay attention to the tax ramifications of rebalancing. Rebalance by putting new money to work (rather than selling) and concentrate your rebalancing efforts in your tax-sheltered accounts. If you rebalance a taxable account, pay attention to your funds' capital-gain distribution dates.

15

Know When to Sell

SMART INVESTORS ALWAYS take a fresh look at their holdings. They do not fall in love with their funds or get angry at them—they simply reassess their investments' potential. Mutual funds change and you have to be ready to sell when those changes indicate a problem.

Or maybe your fund didn't change—you did. Perhaps you've decided that a fund is simply too risky for you. Or possibly—on a happier note—a fund helped you reach your goal, and now you need to shift that money into a more conservative investment as you begin tapping your assets.

As we noted in Chapter 14, it's important to check up on your funds periodically to make sure the status quo hasn't changed. Is the manager still in place? Could an influx of new assets cramp his or her style? Is anything notable going on with the fund family? And perhaps most important of all, does the fund still fit with your asset-allocation plan?

If you do spot a red—or even a yellow—flag, investigate further before selling. Also, be sure to take tax and transaction consequences into account before cutting a fund loose. If you have owned your fund for a long time, you may have built up significant gains, resulting in a tax hit when you sell. Or if you use the services of a broker or investment advisor, you may have to pay a sales charge to sell a fund and buy another one. If you sell your struggling fund and swap into a new one, you'll be in the hole from the start. (Morningstar.com has a tool called Trade Analyzer to help you figure out the tax aspects of a swap.)

Evaluating Performance Weakness

Although one year of underperformance may be nothing to worry about, it can get frustrating to watch your fund fall behind the competition for two or three years or more. Before cutting a fund loose, be sure that you're comparing your underperformer to an appropriate benchmark, such as its Morningstar category or a suitable index. Check to see whether the performance shortfall is a recent development or part of a sustained pattern of performance weakness. For example, a below-average three-year ranking might actually result from just one off-year combined with two decent ones. It's a mistake to pull the plug on a fund based on short-term performance.

In addition, you should conduct a thorough investigation of why the fund is lagging. Spend some time digging into whether the fund is merely undergoing a rough patch for its style or whether there's a more serious problem going on. All too often, investors bail out of struggling funds only to see performance rebound shortly thereafter. So check to see if the fund's manager is still in place, and that he or she is still employing the same strategy that brought your fund success in the past. Is there upheaval at the fund-company level—for example, is your fund company merging with another firm? Or have investors flooded your once-nimble fund with assets?

Believe it or not, strong outperformance may be an even bigger reason to consider selling than dramatic underperformance. That's because outsized gains can often indicate that a fund is taking big risks. If your intermediate-term bond fund is returning more than 10% per year, for example, it's probably taking on more risk to achieve that return than you would expect to come from the "boring" part of your portfolio. See where those outsized returns are coming from and determine if that could spell trouble.

Knowing What to Make of Manager Changes

As we discussed in Chapter 4, actively managed mutual funds are only as good as the fund managers and analysts behind them. Because the fund manager is the person who is most responsible for a fund's performance, many investors wonder if they should sell a fund when their manager leaves. The short answer is, it depends.

A fund company will often claim that a manager change is just incidental and that everything is business as usual. That may be the case, but it pays to be skeptical. To help evaluate the potential impact of a management change, look at factors such as whether the departing manager was the only person at the helm or worked as part of a team. Also consider what kind of analyst support the incoming manager can draw on. Is he or she relying on the research of scores of analysts or is the manager flying the fund solo?

Also, take a hard look at the incoming manager's experience, including his or her record running other mutual funds. If the replacement already has a long-term record at a similar fund, then it should be easy to figure out if he or she is a worthy successor. If it's a manager from the same firm who doesn't have much of a record, take a look at the record of other funds in the same asset class. Some families have deep benches and can replace departing managers fairly effectively. In other cases you'll find that the firms do a lousy job at most of their funds in an asset class and you were holding the only good one. If that's the case, it may be time to bail out.

Bear in mind that some types of funds will be less affected by manager changes than others. For example, managers of index funds are not actively choosing stocks; they're simply mimicking a benchmark. Thus, even though there's some talent involved in tracking an index as closely as possible, manager changes at index funds are less important than manager changes at actively managed funds.

Finally, investigate whether the incoming manager plans to usher in a new strategy. Even if he or she has a proven record of success with that approach, the strategy shift could mean the fund is no longer a good fit for you—maybe the manager intends to buy smaller-company stocks and you bought the fund for large-cap exposure, for example.

Remember: Funds aren't stocks. A manager change won't affect the value of your fund overnight. You can and should take your time to investigate whether to make a change.

Assessing Strategy Changes

In general, a strategy change can be an even bigger cause for concern than a manager switch. It can be an indication that a once-successful portfolio manager has lost confidence in his or her style. And in the worst-case scenario, frequent strategy shifts can indicate that a fund lacks a well-defined style and the manager is simply trying to adjust to what's working in the markets at that time. The problem is that managers who chase trends will invariably be a day late and a dollar short. To beat the market, you need a fund that can stand by its strategy even when that leaves it temporarily out of fashion.

Fund managers don't always change strategies because they want to. Dramatic asset growth, which we discuss in depth later in this chapter, can force the manager of a smaller-cap fund to buy larger-cap stocks than he or she once did, to buy a larger number of stocks, or both.

No matter what the cause, strategy changes can leave you with a fund that no longer suits your needs. Presumably, you buy a small-value fund because you want exposure to small-value stocks. If the manager starts buying large-value stocks, you now have multiple large-value funds in your portfolio and no small-value fund. You may need to sell one of your large-value funds and pick another small-value one to restore your original balance of styles.

Be careful how you define a change in style, though. Sometimes a manager's stocks will change, but his or her strategy won't. Baron Asset is a case in point. The fund didn't migrate from the small-growth to the mid-cap growth category because manager Ron Baron began buying larger stocks. He still buys small-cap issues; he just holds on to them as they move into mid-cap or large-cap range. Similarly, Oakmark Fund manager Bill Nygren—a value maven—has been buying traditional growth stocks over the past few years, arguing that they represent a better value than conventional value issues. Neither fund's strategy has changed, even though their portfolios might now occupy a different square of the style box than they once did.

Monitoring Fund-Family Growth, Mergers, or Acquisitions

Maybe the family behind your fund is adding some new funds to its lineup. Or perhaps a bigger company is going to buy it. Why should you care? After all, won't your manager be there calling the shots? Such changes can matter a surprising amount, though, because they can distract managers from doing their job—running investors' funds.

Changes in fund-company ownership also can lead to a slowdown in performance. For example, we've seen plenty of instances where the acquiring fund company, eager to earn a return on its investment in a short time frame, hikes expenses or lets funds grow too large. It's also not uncommon for fund-company mergers to result in dramatic personnel shifts, with top skippers checking out shortly after a firm is sold to another company. In other words, your trusted manager may not still be running your fund—and sometimes he takes a few analysts with him to the new job, as well.

How can you find out if your fund companies are on the verge of change? For starters, regularly visit their Web sites for news of growth plans and new fund launches. You can also gain access to information on funds in the pipeline at the Securities and Exchange Commission's (SEC) Web site (www.sec.gov); before launching new offerings, fund families must register them with the SEC. And scan whatever fund company marketing materials jam your mailbox. Pay attention to what independent sources have to say about your funds and your fund families.

Evaluating Regulatory Problems

Although the fund industry had long been considered a squeaky-clean pocket of the financial-services industry, developments over the past few years prove that the admonishment "caveat emptor"—let the buyer beware—also applies to mutual fund investors.

The New York Attorney General's Office set into motion what is now called "the fund scandal" in late 2003, when it accused several mutual fund firms of allowing large clients to engage in improper trading of mutual funds to the detriment of rank-and-file investors. The scandal over improper trading quickly spread, and in a handful of cases, fund managers and fund-company executives were accused of making improper trades in their firms' own funds. Throughout late 2003 and 2004, state and federal regulators filed numerous charges against many of the industry's biggest firms, resulting in stiff fines, reforms (both forced and voluntary), and, in many cases, the ouster of top management.

More recently, regulators have been investigating sales practices in the fund industry, alleging that some fund shops made improper payments or directed trades to brokerage firms in exchange for having their funds appear on the broker's preferred list. In the years ahead, there are bound to be other instances of fund shops running afoul of regulators.

So what should you do if one of your fund firms is accused of a regulatory transgression? First, try to gather as much information about the matter as you can. If the SEC has filed an official complaint against the firm or if the firm has already settled with the SEC, you'll be able to find more information on the SEC's Web site (www.sec.gov). If a state regulatory body has brought enforcement action against a fund firm, you'll probably be able to find information about it on the Web site of that state's Attorney General's office. Morningstar.com is also a good source of information about this sort of news.

In addition, you'll want to evaluate what steps, if any, the firm has taken to address the situation. Has it imposed reforms designed to prevent a similar lapse from occurring again? Has it dismissed all of the individuals who were engaging in improper activities?

Most important, think about the firm's overall record of shareholder friendliness. Does the regulatory problem appear to be an isolated incident, or is it part of a broader pattern of the fund company putting its own interests ahead of fund shareholders'? If your fund shop also has a record of running costly funds, allowing funds to become bloated, and rolling out trendy new offerings with little investment merit, those are signs of a firm that may have higher priorities than the well-being of you, the fund shareholder. It could be time to take your hard-earned money to a different firm. We now include discussions of all of these issues—including each fund shop's corporate culture—in a feature we call Stewardship Grades. Morningstar's Stewardship Grades, which are available to Premium users of Morningstar.com, help get your arms around a lot of these issues at once. (We discuss the Stewardship Grade in Chapter 4.)

Monitoring Rising Expense Ratios

Morningstar has found that low expenses are one of the best predictors of fund outperformance, so when a fund jacks up its costs, that can be a very big red flag indeed. You can find plenty of great-quality core-stock funds that cost less than 1.00% per year in annual expenses, and many topnotch bond funds charge less than 0.75%. Thus, if you see that any of your funds' expenses have risen meaningfully beyond those levels, it's a reason to investigate further. You may want to give small-company and international-stock funds a little more leeway, but in any case, expenses of more than 1.5% should be cause for concern.

If you notice that your fund's expense ratio has risen, examine the fund's asset base. Has it fallen recently? Many funds employ so-called breakpoints, whereby expenses rise or fall when assets hit a certain level. Thus, if your fund has recently seen a lot of asset outflows, that might explain why expenses have gone up. You still may choose not to stick around in the fund, but at least you can point to a legitimate explanation for why expenses have risen.

Other funds—notably some from the Fidelity, Vanguard, and AXP fund families—employ so-called performance-based fees when calculating expense ratios. That means that the management fee—the amount the fund company earns for managing your assets—rises if the fund beats a given benchmark over a certain time frame and falls when it does not. Because performance fees help align fund-company interests with those of shareholders (the fund company gets a bigger paycheck if it performs well and a smaller one when it doesn't), you shouldn't necessarily be nervous about a larger expense ratio if it's triggered by such a fee.

If neither a performance fee nor asset outflows explains the hike in your fund's expense ratio, that's cause for concern—even more so if the increase pushes your fund's costs above those of offerings in the same category. It can indicate that the fund's board has failed to look out for shareholders' interests when negotiating with the management company. That can be a very good reason to shop around for another fund.

Keeping an Eye on Asset Growth

As funds attract new investors and grow larger, their returns often become sluggish, weighed down by too many assets. They lose their potency, and their returns revert to the average for their group. That phenomenon—often called *asset bloat*—occurs because the manager of a growing fund has to invest in more stocks, bigger companies, or both. If buying smaller-cap stocks or concentrating heavily in top holdings was key to the fund's success in the past, the fund could see performance become middling when the manager is forced to run the fund more like rival offerings.

A fund with a burgeoning asset base may also trade less frequently because its activities can affect a stock's price. Because the manager has a lot of money to throw at a single stock, that buying can drive up the stock price by upsetting the balance between supply and demand—more money will be chasing shares of that stock. It may be virtually impossible for a manager to buy all the shares he or she wants at one time, so the last share purchased could cost significantly more than the first. Because of this effect, a growing fund can create its own headwind, hurting performance by trading too frequently. Morningstar studies have also shown that funds may take on more risk as assets grow (see Figure 15.1).

To help stave off the effects of asset bloat, some funds stop accepting money from new investors when their assets grow too large. For example, an enormous number of small-company funds closed from 2002 through 2005. (In fact, Morningstar had no small-cap value analyst picks for much of that

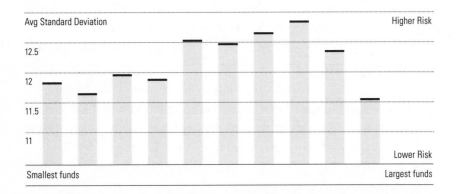

Figure 15.1   Asset size related to risk. As assets increase, many funds tend to take on more risk.

period because all of the best funds were already closed.) Ideally, a fund will close well before it is bloated, but many don't, because closing limits the amount of fees the fund company can bring in.

Morningstar has studied where asset growth can be the biggest problem, and the answer is funds that focus on smaller-cap or growth-oriented stocks. Funds that land in the small-growth category are the most vulnerable to asset bloat. Booming assets can also burden other small-cap or growth funds, but the negative effects may not be as great. Funds that built successful records using high-turnover strategies or concentrated approaches are also vulnerable to asset bloat.

Even if your fund's performance hasn't begun to slow down, it pays to stay attuned to how asset growth can affect your fund's strategy and how that offering fits within your portfolio. Calamos Growth is a recent example of a fund that has changed its tack to cope with ballooning assets. The fund has put up terrific returns for much of its life by focusing on mid-cap stocks and combining macroeconomic sector calls with bottom-up stock selection. As investors have flocked to the fund, however, its managers have put more money into larger-cap stocks. They've also doubled the number of holdings in the portfolio, thereby diluting the impact of their top positions. Even though the fund's performance hasn't slipped, investors who buy it today are getting a dramatically different offering than those who bought in five years ago.

Shrinking assets can be a different kind of warning sign. If a firm loses a lot of assets, it might have to cut back on staff. It's worth checking to see if the fund has the same amount of support that it had in years past. And as we noted earlier, fund expenses often go up when assets drop, which can be a big red flag in and of itself.

Evaluating Your Own Needs

As your objectives change, your investments should change as well. Suppose you start investing in a balanced fund (one that splits its assets between stocks and bonds) with the goal of buying a house within the next five years. If you get married and your spouse already owns a house, you may decide to use that money for retirement instead. In that case, you might sell the balanced fund and buy a portfolio of stock funds. Your goal and the time until you draw on your investment have changed. The investment should, too. For the same reason, bonds should become increasingly prominent in your portfolio as you near your goal.

You may also decide that a fund was simply not a good fit for you from the start. During the bear market, Morningstar analysts talked to scores of investors who were clinging to risky, technology-heavy funds. They were praying that their investments would claw their way back to break-even, and losing sleep in the process. Our usual advice? If you determine that a fund is simply too volatile for you to handle, cut your losses and move on, or at the very least sell the next time your fund rallies. Vow that in the future, you'll know your funds, know yourself, and never make the same mistake twice.

Evaluating Your Tax Situation

It's critical that you take taxes into account when deciding whether to sell. If you've held a fund for a long time and have earned strong returns in it, you could be on the hook for a big capital-gains bill that could offset any gains you might earn by switching into a more promising fund. If you think you can do better than your current fund but want to avoid the taxes, you might consider putting new money to work in a new fund. (Yes, we're suggesting you break the rule against fund overlap, but there's no sense in shifting everything to the superior fund when you will face a hefty tax bill as a result.)

However, if your fund is down enough, you can give yourself a tax break by selling. It could be a win-win deal. The IRS allows you to use $3,000 of capital losses in a particular year to offset ordinary income—which is taxed at much higher rates than capital gains—and capital losses that exceed the $3,000 threshold may be carried forward indefinitely. (Be sure to take into account any deferred loads or redemption fees when determining whether to recognize a tax loss. And keep in mind that if you work with a broker, you will also be paying a commission to invest the money.) Selling sooner instead of later is a particularly good idea if the fund looks poor for any of the reasons we've already discussed. You can even sell a good fund if you really need the tax break; just keep in mind that you can't buy it back for at least 30 days or the IRS won't let you take the tax writeoff. (You can, however, buy another fund that invests in a style similar to the fund you're selling.)

Investor's Checklist: Know When to Sell

▶ Watch out for excessive asset growth. Funds that focus on smaller companies or growth stocks and trade frequently are especially vulnerable to problems from asset bloat.

▶ If there's a manager change, answer these four questions:
  1. Is the manager solo or part of a team?
  2. What past experience does the new manager have?
  3. How successful has the fund company been at handling past changes?
  4. Does the fund company have a strong roster of managers and analysts?

▶ Big changes at the fund family may be a red flag. Watch out for the family launching lots of new funds or merging with or acquiring other fund companies.

▶ In deciding whether you should sell a fund, review the six good reasons for selling:
  1. You need to do basic portfolio rebalancing.
  2. Fundamentals such as the fund's investment style have changed.
  3. You misunderstood the fundamentals.
  4. Your investment goals have changed.
  5. You can use a tax writeoff.
  6. A fund has been too volatile for your taste.

16

Keep a Cool Head
in Turbulent Markets

SUPPOSE THAT YOU'RE planning on buying a car. You want to see great financing deals and sales, right? Automakers would prefer otherwise, but if you're buying, the cheaper the better.

Yet most people don't see things that way when stocks are down. If you're going to be buying stocks and holding them for at least five years, a bear market should see you cheerfully pursuing bargains or contributing more to your mutual funds so the managers can pick up deals on your behalf. Instead, investors tend to retreat, taking their money out of stock funds. When the market starts going up, then they buy. It's like waiting until prices and loan rates start going up to buy a car.

That example is courtesy of the great Warren Buffett. His point is that how you think about a bear market depends on whether you're a buyer or a seller. If you're building up your nest egg, think of yourself as a buyer: Low stock prices are good. For retirees and others making withdrawals from their funds, declining stock prices are bad news.

In fact, one key to investing success is understanding—and always remembering—how volatile stocks can be. Many investors simply don't appreciate how variable the stock market's returns have been. Take the oft-quoted statistic that over the long haul, stocks have delivered gains of roughly 10%. But in any given year, their returns frequently deviate from the norm.

In fact, although market commentators often refer to a 10% gain as a "normal" return, stocks hardly ever deliver that sort of increase in a single year. Between 1975 and 2005, there have been only two calendar years—1993 and 2004—in which the S&P 500 index achieved a return that was between 8% and 12%. During that time, the index's yearly returns ranged from a high of 37.5% (1995) to a loss of 22% (2002). And over the past three decades, the S&P 500 has posted an annual loss about one-fourth of the time.

That statistic highlights the importance of having an investment plan that works in both rising and falling equity markets. By keeping a cool head and sticking to sensible investing principles, investors can limit the bear-market damage to their portfolios and be positioned to benefit when stocks rebound.

Investing in Bear Markets

First off, it's important to know what *not* to do when stocks start falling: Don't try to time the market. Although plenty of so-called market strategists claim to be able to foresee the market's near-term direction, few, if any, manage to do so on a consistent basis. The events that move the market in the short term—currency crises, a terrorist attack, a series of surprisingly good (or bad) economic reports—are difficult to anticipate.

Elaine Garzarelli, the onetime star fund manager who correctly advised clients to sell stocks before the October 1987 equity-market crash, understandably reaped a whirlwind of favorable publicity after that call, but her subsequent money-management efforts were less successful. Her record during the 1990s was spotty at best, and she ultimately stopped trying to incorporate market timing into her fund-management strategy.

Garzarelli isn't alone. In fact, we don't know of any fund manager who has consistently added value by calling the near-term direction of the market. Given that fund managers have more resources at their disposal than the typical investor would have, their inability to execute market-timing strategies profitably should give average investors pause.

A mountain of evidence also suggests that in the aggregate, mutual-fund investors are lousy market timers. Time and again, they have pulled money out of equity funds after the market has already fallen and therefore haven't fully participated in the subsequent rebound. For example, equity funds suffered their greatest outflows ever, as a percentage of assets, in October 1987. Spooked by the dramatic 25% one-day drop in the market, investors sold in droves. Those fund investors therefore missed the S&P 500's 17.4% gain between December 1987 and February 1988.

Dollar-Cost Averaging

Because it's impossible to foretell the near-term direction of the market, the disciplined approach afforded by dollar-cost averaging is often the best course for investors trying to build wealth for their long-term goals. If you're putting money into the market at regular intervals, you're buying shares even when the market is down—usually a very profitable approach. By continuing to invest regularly (i.e., in your retirement plan) you can turn even difficult markets to your advantage.

Making Room for Bonds

In addition to maintaining a disciplined contribution schedule, it is also critical to properly diversify your portfolio both by asset classes and by investment styles. This is especially true for retirees and others who are taking distributions from their accounts and who need to avoid precipitous losses.

No matter what your time horizon, remember that bonds are a necessary part of any well-diversified portfolio. That was easy to forget between 1995 and 1999, when the S&P 500 delivered gains exceeding 20% in each year and bonds put up comparatively paltry return numbers. But in addition to providing the income needed by retirees and others, bonds can help stabilize a portfolio, as high-quality debt tends not to move in sync with equities. During times of stock-market turmoil, bonds often rally, as investors seek refuge from riskier assets. From May through July 2002, the S&P 500 suffered a punishing loss of more than 20%. But because interest rates fell, pushing up bond prices, most long-term government offerings gained at least a few percentage points (some gained several percent) for that three-month period. Of course, three months is a brief period, but it's not too brief for investors with all-stock portfolios to panic and sell at precisely the wrong time. Having some bonds to cushion the blow might just allow you to remain calm enough to weather the storm.

A comparison of Vanguard Total Stock Market Index and Vanguard Balanced Index vividly illustrates bonds' steady-Eddie natures. The former fund tracks the Wilshire 5000 Index of all regularly traded U.S. companies. The latter tracks that same index within the 60% of its assets, but it also stashes 40% of its assets in bonds that track the Lehman Brothers Aggregate Index of investment-grade debt issues. The pure-stock fund, Total Stock Market Index, delivered a 32% loss between April 1, 2000, and June 30, 2002. In contrast, the Balanced Index held up much better, losing just 13.5% during that period, thanks to its bond allocation.

Adding Foreign Stocks

Foreign equities and foreign bonds provide another source of diversification. Although the markets of the United States and other developed nations sometimes move in lockstep, that's not always the case, and international investing can add variety to a portfolio that may help in a bear market.

We don't expect the U.S. economy or its currency to crumble, but investing a portion of one's assets overseas buys insurance against just that. Could such an economic calamity afflict a major industrial country? Just ask Japanese investors. During the 1980s, the Japanese equity market posted gains that handily exceeded those in the United States. Articles about the superiority of the Japanese economic system, as well as its progressive labor/management relationships, filled the popular press in the United States. Japanese companies were thought to be more farsighted, and there was a consensus (not to mention a slew of best-selling how-to books) suggesting that the United States businesses would do well to emulate Japan.

Pity the poor Japanese investor who thought there was no need to invest overseas. From its peak in 1989 to June 30, 2002, the Nikkei index of Japan's major companies shed nearly three-fourths of its value, and in April 2005, it is still far below its peak. Income-hungry Japanese bond investors haven't done much better. With persistent deflation racking the Japanese economy, the nation's bond issuers haven't had to offer much in the way of a payout. Indeed, the yields of many high-quality Japanese issues have been near zero for years. Ask those long-suffering Japanese investors whether it makes sense to diversify and invest a portion of their assets overseas. We are willing to wager that most of them will say "Yes!"

During the 1970s, U.S. investors also benefited greatly from investing overseas. The Watergate political scandal, the bursting of the Nifty Fifty bubble in 1973 and 1974, and economic woes—including rising inflation and interest rates, as well as a weakening dollar—gave U.S. investors several body blows throughout the decade. The main index of foreign shares, MSCI EAFE, handily outpaced the S&P 500 during the period. Compared with those who invested exclusively in the United States, investors who diversified by purchasing foreign stocks and bonds achieved much better returns during that turbulent decade.

The recent bear market also reminded U.S. investors of the importance of diversifying their investments across borders. In 2002, the typical foreign-stock fund was down 1.2%, less than one tenth the loss experienced by the S&P 500 index. And foreign funds were down an annualized 3.8% for the trailing three years. The index's loss for the period was roughly two and a half times as much.

Diversifiying Across Investment Styles

Similarly, you can blunt your portfolio's losses during bear markets if you take care to diversify across funds that use different investment styles. Although many investors had their portfolios heavily concentrated in the large-growth funds that suffered especially steep losses when the bear bit between 2000 and 2002, there were plenty of places to hide. Small-value funds, which tend to own a lot of banks and industrials, rose 39% between April 2000 and June 2002. Funds that invest in real estate investment trusts (REITs) also prospered, in relative terms.

Does that mean small-value stocks and REITs will perform well in every market meltdown? No. It is difficult to predict, in advance, which segments of the equity market will hold up well during downturns. But we know that certain asset classes, ranging from REITs to small-value and natural-resources stocks, often perform differently from large-cap U.S. stocks. By spreading money across several of these largely uncorrelated segments of the market, investors can avoid suffering disproportionate losses in bear markets.

Planning for Taxes

Although we normally encourage investors to hold tight and continue contributing during market downturns, sometimes you can do yourself a favor by selling. We covered some reasons to sell a fund in the preceding chapter, but a big market downturn presents some selling opportunities that investors should not miss.

For one thing, if you're sitting on sizable unrealized losses in taxable accounts, you may wish to recognize some of those losses and give yourself a tax break. To be sure, selling a fund at a loss is no fun, but it is often sensible. What are the advantages of booking these losses? You may use capital losses on your fund or stock sales to offset up to $3,000 in ordinary income, and you can also use losses to offset gains elsewhere in your portfolio.

Selling funds at a loss may make sense even if you are comfortable with your current holdings. By recognizing losses now and gaining the tax benefit, you will have more dollars to invest at the depressed prices available in a bear market. You may be able to take the proceeds of the sale and direct them to better, lower-cost funds.

From a tax perspective, a bear market can also be a great time for investors to rebalance their portfolios. Maybe you realized that your portfolio tilted far too much toward growth funds, and now you want to spread this money across all types of equity offerings, including value funds. Because you may have a loss in your growth funds during a bear market, you can earn a tax benefit by selling them and shifting assets into value funds. In this situation, you're getting paid to rebalance.

Rebalancing

It's always important to rebalance, as we've noted in various spots throughout this book. But it can be particularly critical during times of great market turmoil, when various asset classes and investment styles may deliver markedly different returns.

An investor who had a well-diversified portfolio split 50/50 between stocks and bonds in March 2000 would have had a very different allocation by the end of 2002. Because bonds outperformed equities so handily during that period, that portfolio would probably be closer to 64% bonds and 36% stocks. When stocks rebounded in 2003, the bond-heavy portfolio performed worse than it would have if the investor had restored the 50/50 split. Furthermore, stocks have tended to deliver higher returns than bonds over long periods of time. A portfolio that has such a hefty bond weighting might be too conservative to deliver the long-term gains the investor needs.

Investing in Bull Markets

Okay, that's enough of the depressing stuff. Most of us invest because we want to make money, not because we want to win relative victories in bear markets. So what is the smart way to make money when the stock market is on the rise? As it turns out, a lot of the precepts that lead to successful investing in bear markets are also important when the bulls are charging.

Diversifying

At the risk of sounding like a broken record, diversification is no less important in a bull market than in a bear one. Ignore the market commentators and self-styled prognosticators who say they have identified the slice of the market that has outperformed and will continue to beat the market in the future. What they are really advocating is a strategy of buying when prices are already high, which is never a smart investment approach.

Rebalancing

Although a rebalancing plan makes sense for most investors regardless of the market environment, there is often a cost to rebalancing in a bull market. If one asset class or investment style handily tops another, you may have to sell some appreciated holdings to rebalance, thereby incurring some taxable capital gains.

The good news is that there are some tax-friendly ways to rebalance during a bull market. One is to use new contributions to rebalance your portfolio, as we discussed in Chapter 14. In this scenario, an investor who needed to increase an allocation to value funds in the late 1990s could have done so, at least in part, by directing new contributions to those offerings, instead of selling growth-fund shares at a gain.

You can also use taxable and tax-sheltered accounts in tandem to minimize the tax impact of rebalancing. An investor with a too-heavy stock allocation in the late 1990s might have sold off some equity funds in an IRA or

401(k) and redeployed that money into bonds. During a bull market, it makes sense to use a tax-protected account for rebalancing.

If rebalancing forces you to sell shares out of a taxable account, you may be able to use a technique called *specific-share identification* to cut your tax bill. That term refers to some fund companies' policies of allowing investors to select specific shares of a fund to sell. For example, if your fund currently has an NAV (net asset value, or price per share) of $20 and you own shares that you bought at $12.50 and $17 per share, sell the $17 shares. Your gain will be less and so will your tax bill.

Aside from taxes, another cost that deserves attention in bull markets is a fund's expense ratio. Investors tend to pay more attention to fund costs when returns are modest and expenses would eat up a higher percentage of their returns. But in actual dollars, a higher expense ratio costs more in vigorous bull markets than in times of more moderate returns because of the effects of compounding.

Investing During Inflationary Periods

The past 10 years have given investors a bird's-eye view of both a raging bull market and a brutal downturn. Not since the 1970s, though, have investors confronted an inflationary environment, in which the price of everything from food to gas to housing shoots up. Within such a climate, any gains you earn from your stock and bond funds buy less than they once did.

Although there are conflicting data about how big a threat inflation is right now, commodity prices have zoomed over the past few years amid a global economic recovery and torrid demand from rapidly growing economies such as China and India. The fact that the U.S. dollar has generally fallen over the past several years also portends inflation, as it now takes more dollars to buy imported goods than it did a few years ago.

We've already said that we think it's dangerous to completely rejigger your holdings to respond to the current market environment, but it would also be a mistake to ignore the potentially corrosive effects of inflation when putting together your portfolio. In Chapter 9 we discussed how funds that own inflation-protected bonds (TIPs) can make sense as part of a well-diversified portfolio, because the principal values of TIPs adjust upward along with inflation. Inflation-averse investors might also carve out a small portion of their portfolios for a commodity fund, which will benefit from the rising prices of everything from oil to metals to grains. Remember, though, that such funds can be exceedingly volatile, so you should limit your position to less than 5% of your overall portfolio. Also bear in mind that commodity funds tend to throw off a lot of income, so if possible, put it in a tax-sheltered account such as an IRA.

Keeping It Simple

As we've noted, certain investment precepts are sensible in both bull and bear markets. Keep a strong focus on the things you as an investor can control. Buy low-cost funds. Stick to an investment plan and continue to buy shares, even in a big market downturn. Maintain a well-diversified portfolio to lower risk and potentially enhance returns as well. Finally, remember that you have a tremendous amount of control over one of the most important factors that determine long-term investment success: how much you invest. By raising that amount even a bit, you can affect the consequences of a long-term stock-market trend that's not as strong as you had hoped. Moreover, you can avoid the poor investment decisions that often result when investors feel as if they haven't saved enough and therefore need to take extra-large chances to acquire an adequate nest egg. By following these guidelines, sticking to your plan, and just a little good fortune from all those outside forces you can't control, you'll be able to enjoy the benefits of meeting your long-term goals.

Investor's Checklist: Keep a Cool Head in Turbulent Markets

▶ Market timing doesn't work. Whether you are in a bear or bull market, stick to your long-term plan and rebalance accordingly.

▶ Dollar-cost averaging can be a particularly powerful way to invest in a down market because you are automatically buying as prices decline.

▶ Be sure to maintain a properly diversified portfolio, whatever the market. For most investors that means investing in a variety of stock types—large and small, growth and value, U.S. and foreign—and owning bonds for stability.

▶ Consider selling your losers during a bear market to give yourself a tax break.

▶ To limit taxes in a bull market, rebalance by investing new money and making the biggest shifts in tax-protected accounts.

▶ You can also limit bull-market taxes by selling higher-cost shares first to minimize the size of your taxable gain.

▶ Don't neglect expenses—they cost you whether the market is up or down.

▶ Consider the long-term effects of inflation on your portfolio. Think about devoting a slice of your portfolio to a TIPs fund and an even smaller piece to a commodity-linked fund.

PART TWO

Stocks

17

Making Room for Stocks

THE FIRST PART of this book addressed Morningstar's approach to selecting funds, and the second part focuses on Morningstar's stock-investing philosophy. But what about a more practical question: How do you determine whether to invest in stocks or funds? This is not an either/or question—most investors own a mix of funds and stocks. We'd advocate thinking about three questions when you're deciding how much of your portfolio to allocate to each:

1. How much time are you willing to invest in building and monitoring your portfolio?
2. How comfortable are you with volatility in the value of your portfolio?
3. What holes are you looking to fill in your portfolio?

Is Investing a Hobby or a Necessity?

Some folks invest in the stock market because they need to—it just makes more financial sense to put long-term savings into assets likely to produce a higher long-run return than a savings account at a bank—and some folks invest because they enjoy it. If you're in the former camp, and you either don't enjoy investing or you simply don't have much time to spend on your investments, stick with mutual funds. Successfully researching and buying individual stocks is simply more time-consuming than investing solely in funds, and it's not a guaranteed road to riches. In fact, if you invest in individual stocks without committing to thorough research and monitoring, you're likely to get burned. Funds are the perfect vehicle for someone with the need to invest—but neither the time nor interest.

How Strong Is Your Stomach?

Do you get anxious when your investments drop in value over a short time? Do you find yourself selling investments "at the bottom"—when the news is bad, the market is down, and your gut gets tied into a knot when you open your brokerage statement? If you do, think carefully before buying a bunch of stocks. Although a well-diversified portfolio of stocks will likely be no more volatile than a similar portfolio of funds, the individual stocks are almost certain to be much more volatile than the funds. Make sure you're comfortable with the additional short-term swings in value that stocks can have before you take the plunge.

What Are You Trying to Accomplish?

Assuming you've got the time and the interest, and assuming you're comfortable with stocks' greater volatility, try to be systematic about plugging individual stocks into your portfolio. One way to do this is to pick stocks in those areas of the market where you're knowledgeable and let funds do the heavy lifting in other areas. For example, if you work in a bank and you have a pretty good handle on what separates good banks from poor ones, you might try your hand at picking individual stocks in the financial-services sector, while using funds for the rest of your portfolio. Or, if you find yourself gravitating personally to a particular "style" of investing—value or growth—when picking stocks, complement those picks with funds in a different style.

Another factor to consider is that funds can do a better job than individual securities in some specialized areas of your portfolio. If you want some tax-free income, for example, it makes much more sense to buy a municipal bond fund than to try and assemble a portfolio of individual muni bonds. Or, if you want to increase your weighting in foreign stocks, you might be better off with a high-quality foreign fund than trying to pick foreign companies yourself—information you can trust on foreign companies is often harder to come by, and the accounting standards can be different.

The Morningstar Approach to Stock Selection

If you do intend to invest in individual stocks, you should be prepared to roll up your sleeves and do your homework because successful stock investing is not easy. One of the big myths of the bull market of the 1990s was that the stock market was essentially a savings account that returned 15% per year. You picked up a copy of *Fortune,* you watched a little CNBC, you opened an online account, and you were on the road to riches. Unfortunately, as many investors discovered when the bubble burst, things that look too good to be true usually are.

Picking individual stocks requires hard work, discipline, and an investment of time (as well as money). Expecting to make a lot of money with a little effort is like expecting to shoot a great round of golf the first time you pick up a set of clubs. There's no magic formula, and there's no guarantee of success.

That's the bad news. The good news is that the basic principles of successful stock-picking aren't difficult to understand, and the tools for finding great stocks are available to everyone at a very low cost—you don't need expensive software or high-priced advice to do well in the stock market. All you need are patience, an understanding of accounting and competitive strategy, and a healthy dose of skepticism. None of these is out of the average person's grasp.

Believe it or not, the basic investment process for stocks is quite simple: Analyze the company, and value the stock. If you avoid the mistake of confusing a great company with a great investment—and the two can be *very* different—you'll already be ahead of many of your investing peers. (Think of Cisco at 100 times earnings in 2000. It was a great company, but it was a terrible stock.)

Remember that buying a stock means becoming part owner in a business. By treating your stocks as businesses, you'll find yourself focusing more on the things that matter—like free cash flow—and less on the things that don't—like whether the stock went up or down on a given day.

Your goal as an investor should be to find wonderful businesses, and then to purchase them at reasonable prices. Great companies create wealth, and as the value of the business grows, so should the stock price in time. In the short term, the market can be a capricious thing—wonderful businesses can sell at fire-sale prices, while money-losing ventures can be valued as if they had the rosiest of futures—but over the long haul, stock prices tend to track the value of the business.

It's the Business That Matters

In the chapters that follow, we want to show you how to focus on a company's fundamental financial performance. Things like analyst upgrades and chart patterns may be fine tools for traders who treat Wall Street like a casino, but they're of little use to investors who truly want to build wealth by owning individual stocks. You have to get your hands dirty and understand the businesses of the stocks you own if you hope to be a successful long-term investor in individual stock.

When firms do well, so do their shares, and when business suffers, their stocks suffer as well. Wal-Mart, for example, hit a speed bump in the mid-1990s when its growth rate slowed down a bit—and its share price was essentially flat during the same period. However, Colgate-Palmolive became much more profitable during the late 1990s—thanks in part to the launch of a blockbuster new toothpaste—and its stock saw some dramatic gains at the same time. The message is clear: Company fundamentals have a direct effect on share prices.

Of course, this only applies over a long time period—in the short term, stock prices can (and do) move around for a whole host of reasons that have nothing whatsoever to do with the underlying value of the company. This is why we so firmly advocate focusing on the long-term performance of businesses, because the short-term price movement of a stock is completely unpredictable.

Think back to the Internet mania of the late 1990s. Wonderful (but boring) businesses like insurance companies, banks, and real estate stocks traded at incredibly low valuations, even though the intrinsic worth of these businesses hadn't really changed. At the same time, companies that had not a prayer of turning a profit were being accorded billion-dollar valuations.

The Long-Term Approach

Given the proclivity of Mr. Market to plead temporary insanity at the drop of a hat, we strongly believe that it's not worth devoting any time to predicting his actions. We're not alone in this. After talking to literally thousands of money managers over the past 15 years or so, we've discovered that none of the truly exceptional managers spend any time at all thinking about what the market will do in the short term. Instead, they all focus on finding undervalued stocks that can be held for an extended time.

There are good reasons for this. Betting on short-term price movements means doing a lot of trading, which drives up taxes and transaction costs. The tax on short-term capital gains can be almost double the rate of long-term capital gains, and constant trading means paying commissions more frequently. As we'll discuss in the next chapter, costs like these can be a huge drag on your portfolio, and minimizing them is one of the most important things you can do to enhance your long-term investment returns.

We've seen this borne out when we've done long-term studies of mutual fund returns: Funds with higher turnover—ones that trade more—generally post lower results than their more deliberate peers, to the tune of about 1.5% per year over 10 years. This may not sound like much, but the difference between a 10% return and an 11.5% return on a $10,000 investment is almost $3,800 after 10 years. That's the price of impatience.

Having the Courage of Your Convictions

Finally, picking individual stocks successfully means having the courage to take a stance that's different from the crowd. There will always be conflicting opinions about the merits of any company, and it's often the companies with the most conflict surrounding them that make the best investments. So as an investor, you have to be able to develop your own opinion about the value of a stock, and you should change that value only if the facts warrant doing so—not because you read a negative news article or because some pundit mouths off on TV. Investment success depends on personal discipline, not on whether the crowd agrees or disagrees with you.

Let's Get Started

When you do choose to buy individual stocks, we want to show you how to think for yourself, ignore the day-to-day noise, and make profitable long-term investment stock picks. Here's our road map.

First, we need to develop an investment philosophy, which is what we'll do in Chapter 18. We think that successful stock investing is built on five core principles: Doing your homework, finding companies with strong competitive advantages (or economic moats), having a margin of safety, holding for the long term, and knowing when to sell. We think that building a solid stock portfolio should be centered on these five ideas; once you know them, you'll be ready to start learning how to look at companies.

Second, we'll take a step back and review what *not* to do—because avoiding mistakes is the most profitable strategy of all. In Chapter 19, we'll go over the most common mistakes that investors make. If you steer clear of these, you'll start out ahead of the pack.

In Chapter 20, we'll show you how to separate great companies from mediocre ones by analyzing competitive advantages, which we call "economic moats." We'll explain how economic moats are what help great companies keep their top-tier status, and why they're a big part of what separates long-run winners from flashes in the pan. Understanding the sources of a firm's economic moat is critical to thoroughly analyzing a company.

Chapters 21 through 24 will show you how to analyze companies by reading their financial statements. First, we'll learn how financial statements work—what all those strange-sounding line items mean, and how the different statements fit together. Once we know how to read balance sheets and income statements, you'll learn a five-step process for putting all the numbers in context and finding out just how a solid a company really is. We'll also show you how to evaluate management.

In Chapter 25, we'll look at how you can detect aggressive accounting. You'll learn what red flags to watch out for, so you can minimize the odds of a big blowup in your portfolio.

In Chapters 26 and 27, we'll show you how to value stocks. You'll learn the underlying theory of investment value, when ratios like price-to-earnings are (and aren't) useful, and how to figure out whether a stock is trading for more or less than its intrinsic value. The cheapest stock isn't always the best investment, and what looks expensive may actually be quite cheap when viewed from another angle.

Chapter 28 presents two case studies. We'll apply the tools we've learned in the previous chapters to real-world companies, so you can see for yourself how the process of fundamental analysis works in practice.

In Chapter 29, you'll learn about the "10-Minute Test," a quick-and-dirty checklist that can help you separate firms that are unlikely to be worth your time from the ones that deserve a thorough, in-depth examination.

The structure of these chapters is the same as the basic investment process that we advocate: Develop a set of investing principles, understand the company's competitive environment, analyze the company, and value the stock. If you can follow this process while avoiding most big mistakes, you'll do just fine as an investor.

18

The Five Rules for Successful Stock Investing

It always amazes me how few investors—and sometimes, fund managers—can articulate their investment philosophy. Without an investing framework, a way of thinking about the world, you're going to have a very tough time doing well in the market.

I realized this some years ago while attending the annual meeting of Berkshire Hathaway, the firm run by billionaire superinvestor Warren Buffett. I overheard another attendee complain that he wouldn't be attending another Berkshire meeting because "Buffett says the same thing every year." To me, that's the whole point of having an investment philosophy and sticking to it. If you do your homework, stay patient, and insulate yourself from popular opinion, you're likely to do well. It's when you get frustrated, move outside your circle of competence, and start deviating from your personal investment philosophy that you're likely to get into trouble.

Here are the five rules that we recommend:

1. Do your homework.
2. Find economic moats.
3. Have a margin of safety.
4. Hold for the long haul.
5. Know when to sell.

Do Your Homework

This sounds obvious, but perhaps the most common mistake that investors make is failing to thoroughly investigate the stocks they purchase. Unless you know the business inside and out, you shouldn't buy the stock.

This means that you need to develop an understanding of accounting so that you can decide for yourself what kind of financial shape a company is in. For one thing, you're putting your own money at risk, so you should know what you're buying. More important, investing has many gray areas, so you can't just take someone else's word that a company is an attractive investment. You have to be able to decide for yourself because one person's hot growth stock is another's disaster waiting to happen. In Chapters 4 through 7, I'll show you what you need to know about accounting and how to boil the analysis process down to a manageable level.

Once you have the tools, you need to take time to put them to use. That means sitting down and reading the annual report cover to cover, checking out industry competitors, and going through past financial statements. This can be tough to do, especially if you're pressed for time, but taking the time to thoroughly investigate a company will help you avoid many poor investments.

Think of the time you spend on research as a cooling-off period. It's always tempting when you hear about a great investment idea to think you have to act now, before the stock starts moving—but discretion is almost always the better part of valor. After all, your research process might very well uncover facts that make the investment seem less attractive. But if it is a winner and if you're truly a long-term investor, missing out on the first couple of points of upside won't make a big difference in the overall performance of your portfolio, especially since the cooling-off period will probably lead you to avoid some investments that would have turned out poorly.

Find Economic Moats

What separates a bad company from a good one? Or a good company from a great one?

In large part, it's the size of the economic moat a company builds around itself. The term *economic moat* is used to describe a firm's competitive advantage—in the same way that a moat kept invaders of medieval castles at bay, an economic moat keeps competitors from attacking a firm's profits.

In any competitive economy, capital invariably seeks the areas of highest expected return. As a result, the most profitable firms find themselves beset by competitors, which is why profits for most companies have a strong tendency over time to *regress to the mean*. This means that most highly profitable companies tend to become less profitable as other firms compete with them.

Economic moats allow a relatively small number of companies to retain above-average levels of profitability for many years, and these companies are often the most superior long-term investments. Longer periods of excess profitability lead, on average, to better long-term stock performance.

Identifying economic moats is such a critical part of the investing process that we'll devote an entire chapter—Chapter 20—to learning how to analyze them. Here's a quick preview. The key to identifying wide economic moats can be found in the answer to a deceptively simple question: How does a company manage to keep competitors at bay and earn consistently fat profits? If you can answer this, you've found the source of the firm's economic moat.

Have a Margin of Safety

Finding great companies is only half of the investment process—the other half is assessing what the company is worth. You can't just go out and pay whatever the market is asking for the stock because the market might be demanding too high a price. And if the price you pay is too high, your investment returns will likely be disappointing.

The goal of any investor should be to buy stocks for less than they're really worth. Unfortunately, it's easy for estimates of a stock's value to be too optimistic—the future has a nasty way of turning out worse than expected. We can compensate for this all-too-human tendency by buying stocks only when they're trading for substantially less than our estimate of what they're worth. This difference between the market's price and our estimate of value is the margin of safety.

Take Coke, for example. There's no question that Coke had a solid competitive position in the late 1990s, and you can make a strong argument that it still does. But folks who paid 50 times earnings for Coke's shares have had a tough time seeing a decent return on their investment because they ignored a critical part of the stock-picking process: having a margin of safety. Not only was Coke's stock expensive, but even if you thought Coke was worth 50 times earnings, it didn't make sense to pay full price—after all, the assumptions that led you to think Coke was worth such a high price might have been too optimistic. Better to have incorporated a margin of safety by paying, for example, only 40 times earnings in case things went awry.

Always include a margin of safety into the price you're willing to pay for a stock. If you later realize you overestimated the company's prospects, you'll have a built-in cushion that will mitigate your investment losses. The size of your margin of safety should be larger for shakier firms with uncertain futures and smaller for solid firms with reasonably predictable earnings. For example, a 20% margin of safety would be appropriate for a stable firm such as Wal-Mart, but you'd want a substantially larger one for a firm such as Abercrombie & Fitch, which is driven by the whims of teen fashion.

Sticking to a valuation discipline is tough for many people because they're worried that if they don't buy today, they might miss the boat forever on the stock. That's certainly a possibility—but it's also a possibility that the company will hit a financial speed bump and send the shares tumbling. The future is an uncertain place, after all, and if you wait long enough, most stocks will sell at a decent discount to their fair value at one time or another. As for the few that just keep going straight up year after year—well, let's just say that *not making* money is a lot less painful than *losing* money you already have. For every Wal-Mart, there's a Woolworth's.

One simple way to get a feel for a stock's valuation is to look at its historical price/earnings ratio—a measure of how much you're paying for every dollar of the firm's earnings—over the past 10 years or more. (We have 10 years' worth of valuation data available free on Morningstar.com, and other research services have this information as well.) If a stock is currently selling at a price/earnings ratio of 30 and its range over the past 10 years has been between 15 and 33, you're obviously buying in at the high end of historical norms.

To justify paying today's price, you have to be plenty confident that the company's outlook is better today than it was over the past 10 years. Occasionally, this is the case, but most of the time when a company's valuation is significantly higher now than in the past, watch out. The market is probably overestimating growth prospects, and you'll likely be left with a stock that underperforms the market over the coming years.

We'll talk more about valuation in Chapters 9 and 10, so don't worry if you're still wondering how to value a stock. The key thing to remember for now is simply that if you don't use discipline and conservatism in figuring out the prices you're willing to pay for stocks, you'll regret it eventually. Valuation is a crucial part of the investment process.

Hold for the Long Haul

Never forget that buying a stock is a major purchase and should be treated like one. You wouldn't buy and sell your car, your refrigerator, or your DVD player 50 times a year. Investing should be a long-term commitment because short-term trading means that you're playing a loser's game. The costs really begin to add up—both the taxes and the brokerage costs—and create an almost insurmountable hurdle to good performance.

If you trade frequently, you'll rack up commissions and other expenses that, over time, could have compounded. Every $1 you spend on commissions today could have been turned into $5.60 if you had invested that dollar at 9% for 20 years. Spend $500 today and you could be giving up more than $2,800 20 years hence.

But that's just the beginning of the story because frequent trading also dramatically increases the taxes you pay. And whatever amount you pay in taxes each year is money that can't compound for you next year.

Let's look at two hypothetical investors to see what commissions, trading, and taxes can do to a portfolio. Long-Term Lucy is one of those old-fashioned fuddy-duddies who like to buy just a few stocks and hang on to them for a long time, and Trader Tim is a gunslinger who likes to get out of stocks as soon as he's made a few bucks (see Figure 18.1).

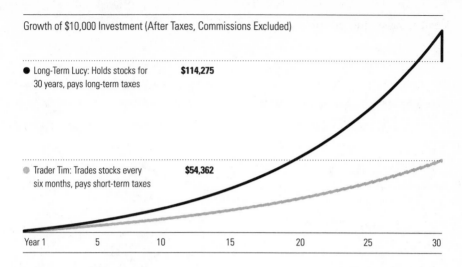

Growth of $10,000 Investment (After Taxes, Commissions Excluded)

● Long-Term Lucy: Holds stocks for   **$114,275**
   30 years, pays long-term taxes

● Trader Tim: Trades stocks every   **$54,362**
   six months, pays short-term taxes

Year 1   5   10   15   20   25   30

Figure 18.1   Tim turns over his portfolio every six months, incurring a 35% short-term capital gains tax. Lucy's gains are taxed at only 15% thanks to her buy-and-hold strategy, and more of her money compounds over a longer time. *Source:* Morningstar, Inc.

Lucy invests $10,000 in five stocks for 30 years at a 9% rate of return and then sells the investment and pays long-term capital gains of 15%. Tim, meanwhile, invests the same amount of money at the same rate of return but trades the entire portfolio twice per year, paying 35% short-term capital gains taxes on his profits and reinvesting what's left. We'll give them both a break and not charge them any commissions for now.

After 30 years, Lucy has about $114,000, while Tim has less than half that amount—only about $54,000. As you can see, letting your money compound without paying Uncle Sam every year makes a huge difference, even ignoring brokerage fees.

And since holding a single stock for 30 years may not be realistic, let's consider what happens if Lucy sells her entire portfolio every five years, reinvesting the proceeds each time. In this case, she winds up with about $96,000—which is not much less than $114,000 and is still much more than Tim's $54,000 (see Figure 18.2).

These examples look at just the tax impact of frequent trading—things look even worse for the traders once we factor in commissions. If we assume that Tim and Lucy pay $15 per trade, Tim nets only about $31,000 after 30

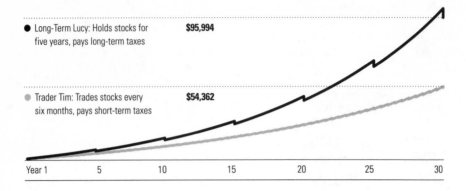

Growth of $10,000 Investment (After Taxes, Commissions Excluded)

- Long-Term Lucy: Holds stocks for five years, pays long-term taxes   **$95,994**

- Trader Tim: Trades stocks every six months, pays short-term taxes   **$54,362**

Year 1   5   10   15   20   25   30

Figure 18.2   Lucy decreases her holding period to 5 years from 30 years, but the benefit of lower taxes and a longer compounding period still nets her significantly more than Tim. *Source:* Morningstar, Inc.

years and Lucy nets $93,000, again assuming she holds her stocks for five years (see Figure 18.3).

The real-world costs of taxes and commissions can take a big bite out of your portfolio. Extending your average holding period from six months to five years yields about $62,000 in extra investment returns. Lucy gets a lavish reward for her patience, don't you think?

One final thought: To match Lucy's $93,000 portfolio value, Tim would need to generate returns of around 14% each year instead of 9%. That's the true cost of frequent trading in this example—about five percentage points per year. So, if you really think that churning your portfolio will get you five extra percentage points of performance each year, then trade away. If, like the rest of us, you were taught some humility by the bear market, be patient—it'll pay off.

Know When to Sell

Ideally, we'd all hold our investments forever, but the reality is that few companies are worth holding for decades at a stretch—and few investors are savvy enough to buy only those companies. Knowing when it's appropriate to bail

Growth of $10,000 Investment (After Taxes, Commissions Included)

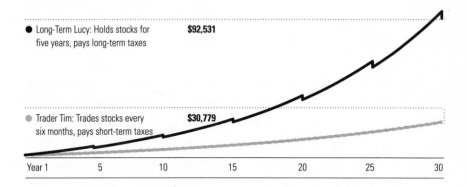

● Long-Term Lucy: Holds stocks for   **$92,531**
   five years, pays long-term taxes

● Trader Tim: Trades stocks every   **$30,779**
   six months, pays short-term taxes

| Year 1 | 5 | 10 | 15 | 20 | 25 | 30 |

Figure 18.3   When commissions are taken into account, Tim's returns suffer far more than Lucy's.
Source: Morningstar, Inc.

out of a stock is at least as important as knowing when to buy one, yet we often sell our winners too early and hang on to our losers for too long.

The key is to constantly monitor the *companies* you own, rather than the *stocks* you own. It's far better to spend some time keeping up on the news surrounding your companies and the industries in which they function than it is to look at the stock price 20 times a day.

Before I discuss when you *should* sell a stock, I ought to point out when you *shouldn't* sell.

The Stock Has Dropped

By themselves, share-price movements convey no useful information, especially because prices can move in all sorts of directions in the short term for completely unfathomable reasons. The long-run performance of stocks is largely based on the expected future cash flows of the companies attached to them—it has very little to do with what the stock did over the past week or month.

Always keep in mind that it doesn't matter what a stock has done since you bought it. There's nothing you can do to change the past, and the market cares not one whit whether you've made or lost money on the stock. Other market participants—the folks setting the price of the stock—are looking to the future, and that's exactly what you should do when you're deciding whether to sell a stock.

The Stock Has Skyrocketed

Again, it matters little how those stocks have done in the past—what's important is how you expect the company to do in the future. There's not *a priori* reason for stocks that are up substantially to drop, just as there's no reason for stocks that have tanked to "have to come back eventually." Most of us would be better investors if we could just block out all those graphs of past stock performance because they convey no useful information about the future.

So when should you sell? Run through these five questions whenever you think about selling a stock, and you'll be in good shape.

Did You Make a Mistake?

Did you miss something when you first evaluated the company? Perhaps you thought management would be able to pull off a turnaround, but the task turned out to be bigger than you (and they) thought. Or maybe you underestimated the strength of a company's competition or overestimated its ability to find new growth opportunities. No matter what the flub, it's rarely worth holding on to a stock that you bought for a reason that's no longer valid. If your initial analysis was wrong, cut your losses, take the tax break, and move on.

Have the Fundamentals Deteriorated?

After several years of success, that raging growth company you bought has started to slow down. Cash is piling up as the company has a tougher time finding profitable, new investment opportunities, and competition is eating away at the company's margins. Sounds like it's time to reassess the company's future prospects. If they're substantially worse than they used to be, it's time to sell.

Has the Stock Risen Too Far above Its Intrinsic Value?

Let's face it: The market sometimes wakes up in an awfully good mood and offers to pay you a price far in excess of what your investment is really worth.

There's no reason not to take advantage of other investors' good nature. Ask yourself how much more the market is willing to pay you than your estimate of the value of the stock and how likely it is that your estimate of its value could go up over time. You don't want to sell wonderful companies just because they get a little pricey—you'd incur capital gains and wouldn't be taking advantage of compounding. But even the greatest companies should be sold when their shares sell at egregious values.

Is There Something Better You Can Do with the Money?

As an investor, you should always be seeking to allocate your money to the assets that are likely to generate the highest return relative to their risk. There's no shame in selling a somewhat undervalued investment—even one on which you've lost money—to free up funds to buy a stock with better prospects.

I did this myself in early 2003 when I noticed that Home Depot was looking awfully cheap. The stock had been sliding for almost three years, and I thought it was worth about 50% more than the market price at the time. I didn't have much cash in my account, so I had to sell something if I wanted to buy Home Depot. After reviewing the stocks I owned, I sold some shares of Citigroup, even though they were trading for about 15% less than what I paid for them. Why? Because my initial assessment of Citigroup's value had been too optimistic, and I didn't think the shares were much of a bargain any more. So, I sold a fairly valued stock to purchase one that I thought was very undervalued.

What about my small loss on the Citi stock? That was water under the bridge and couldn't be changed. What mattered was that I had the opportunity to move funds from an investment with a very modest expected return to one with a fairly high expected return—and that was a solid reason to sell.

Do You Have Too Much Money in One Stock?

This is the best reason of all to sell because it means you did something right and picked a winner. The key is to not let greed get in the way of smart portfolio management. If an investment is more than 10% to 15% of your portfolio, it's time to think long and hard about trimming it down no matter how solid the company's prospects may be. (These percentages are a rough guide—you might be comfortable with more money in a single stock, or you might want to be more diversified.) It simply doesn't make sense to have too many of your eggs in one basket.

Investor's Checklist: The Five Rules for Successful Stock Investing

▶ Successful investing depends on personal discipline, not on whether the crowd agrees or disagrees with you. That's why it's crucial to have a solid, well-grounded investment philosophy.

▶ Don't buy a stock unless you understand the business inside and out. Taking the time to investigate a company before you buy the shares will help you avoid the biggest mistakes.

▶ Focus on companies with wide economic moats that can help them fend off competitors. If you can identify why a company keeps competitors at bay and consistently generates above-average profits, you've identified the source of its economic moat.

▶ Don't buy a stock without a margin of safety. Sticking to a strict valuation discipline will help you avoid blowups and improve your investment performance.

▶ The costs of frequent trading can be a huge drag on performance over time. Treat your stock buys like major purchases, and hold on to them for the long term.

▶ Know when to sell. Don't sell just because the price has gone up or down, but give it some serious thought if one of the following things has happened: You made a mistake buying it in the first place, the fundamentals have deteriorated, the stock has risen well above its intrinsic value, you can find better opportunities, or it takes up too much space in your portfolio.

19

Seven Mistakes to Avoid

In a lot of ways investing is like tennis. In tennis, having a killer serve and a great backhand will win you a lot of points, but any advantage that these skills confer can be quickly wiped out with a string of double faults or unforced errors. At the end of a five-set match, it's often the player with the least mistakes who wins. Just being able to consistently get the ball back over the net—no matter what your opponent throws at you—counts for a great deal.

Investing is pretty similar. Unless you know how to avoid the most common mistakes of investing, your portfolio's returns won't be anything to get excited about. You'll find that it takes many great stock picks to make up for just a few big errors.

So, before we dive into the company analysis process, I want to introduce you to seven easily avoidable mistakes that many investors frequently make. Resisting these temptations is the first step to reaching your financial goals:

1. Swinging for the fences.
2. Believing that it's different this time.
3. Falling in love with products.
4. Panicking when the market is down.

5. Trying to time the market.
6. Ignoring valuation.
7. Relying on earnings for the whole story.

Swinging for the Fences

This ties back to the importance of buying great companies with strong economic moats. Loading up your portfolio with risky, all-or-nothing stocks—in other words, swinging for the fences on every pitch—is a sure route to investment disaster. For one thing, the insidious math of investing means that making up large losses is a very difficult proposition—a stock that drops 50% needs to double just to break even.

For another, finding the next Microsoft when it's still a tiny start-up is really, really difficult. You're much more likely to wind up with a company that fizzles than a truly world-changing company, because it's extremely difficult to discern which is which when the firm is just starting out.

In fact, small growth stocks are the worst-returning equity category over the long haul. Why? First, the numbers: According to Professor Kenneth French at Dartmouth,[1] small growth stocks have posted an average annual return of 9.3% since 1927, which is a good deal lower than the 10.7% return of the S&P 500 over the same time period. Lest you sneeze at that 1.4% difference between the two returns, let me point out that it has an absolutely enormous effect on long-run asset returns—over 30 years, a 9.3% return on $1,000 would yield about $14,000, but a 10.7% return would yield more than $21,000.

Moreover, many smaller firms never do anything but muddle along as small firms—assuming they don't go belly up, which many do. For example, between 1997 and 2002, 8% of the firms on the Nasdaq were delisted each year. That's about 2,200 firms whose shareholders likely suffered huge losses before the stocks were kicked off the Nasdaq.

Believing that It's Different This Time

The four most expensive words on Wall Street are "It's different this time." History does repeat itself, bubbles do burst, and not knowing market history is a major handicap.

---

[1] Kenneth French, http://mba.tuck.dartmouth.edu/pages/faculty/ken.french/data_library.html.

In the spring of 2000, for example, the financial press started writing that semiconductor stocks were no longer cyclical. That turned out to be pretty close to the top in chip shares. A year later, energy stocks were all the rage, and many analysts were projecting their earnings to grow at 20% for the next several years. Then, the economy slowed, hurting the demand for power, and new plants came online, driving up the supply. As a result, energy stocks such as Mirant and Calpine tanked 50% to 60% even before the Enron debacle sealed their fate.

The point here is very simple: You have to be a student of the market's history to understand its future. Any time you hear someone say, "It really is different this time," turn off the TV and go for a walk.

Falling in Love with Products

This is one of the easiest investment traps to fall into. Who wouldn't have thought that Palm was a great investment after buying a Palm Pilot when they were first introduced a few years ago? It seems entirely logical, but the reality is that great products do not necessarily translate into great profits. For example, Palm was the first company to invent a handheld organizer that was relatively easy to use and affordable, but consumer electronics is simply not an attractive business. Margins are thin, competition is intense, and it's very tough to make a consistent profit.

Although great products and innovative technologies do matter when you're assessing companies, neither matters nearly as much as economics. Sure, Palm made a great device that millions of people purchased, and the firm even acquired one of its chief competitors, but the industry's dismal economics still caught up with the firm in the end—Palm lost hundreds of millions of dollars in 2001 and 2002, and as of mid-2003, the firm's shares had plunged more than 98% since they started trading in early 2000.

When you look at a stock, ask yourself, "Is this an attractive business? Would I buy the whole company if I could?" If the answer is no, give the stock a pass—no matter how much you might like the firm's products.

Panicking When the Market Is Down

Stocks are generally more attractive when no one else wants to buy them, not when barbers are giving stock tips. It's very tempting to look for *validation*— or other people doing the same thing—when you're investing, but history has shown repeatedly that assets are cheap when everyone else is avoiding them. (In the words of Sir John Templeton, one of the first investors to systematically scour foreign markets for bargains, "The time of maximum pessimism is the best time to buy.")

The most famous example of this is a *BusinessWeek* cover story from the 1979 that asked the question, "The Death of Equities?" not long before the start of an 18-year bull market in stocks.[2] More recently, *Barron's* featured Warren Buffett on its cover in late 1999, asking, "What's Wrong, Warren?" and bemoaning Buffett's aversion to technology stocks.[3] Over the next three years, the Nasdaq tanked more than 60%, and Berkshire Hathaway shares appreciated 40%.

We also see empirical—rather than anecdotal—evidence of this in a study that Morningstar has conducted every year for the past several years, in which we look at the performance of unpopular funds. After looking at which fund categories attracted the most money and which categories experienced the strongest outflows, we found something very interesting. The asset classes that everyone hated outperformed the ones that everyone loved in all but one rolling three-year period over the past dozen years.

The difference can be striking. For example, investors who went where others feared to tread and bought the three least-popular fund categories at the beginning of 2000 would have had roughly flat investment returns over the subsequent three years. That was much better than the market's average annual loss of about 15% over the same time period and miles ahead of the performance of the popular fund categories, which declined an average of 26% per year during the three-year period.

Going against the grain takes courage, but that courage pays off. You'll do better as an investor if you think for yourself and seek out bargains in parts of the market that everyone else has forsaken, rather than buying the flavor of the month in the financial press.

---

[2] "For better or for worse, then, the U.S. economy probably has to regard the death of equities as near-permanent condition—reversible some day, but not soon" from "The Death of Equities," *BusinessWeek*, p. 54 (August 13, 1979).

[3] Andrew Bary, "What's Wrong, Warren? Berkshire's Down for the Year, but Don't Count It Out," *Barron's*, p. 16 (December 27, 1999).

Trying to Time the Market

Market timing is one of the all-time great myths of investing. There is no strategy that consistently tells you when to be in the market and when to be out of it, and anyone who says otherwise usually has a market-timing service to sell you.

Consider an interesting study in the February 2001 issue of *Financial Analysts Journal,* which looked at the difference between buy-and-hold and market-timing strategies from 1926 through 1999 using a very elegant method. The authors essentially mapped all of the possible market-timing variations between 1926 and 1999 with different switching frequencies.[4]

They assumed that for any given month, an investor could be either in T-bills or in stocks and then calculated the returns that would have resulted from all of the possible combinations of those switches. (For the curious, there are 2^{12}—or 4,096—possible combinations between two assets over 12 months.) Then they compared the results of a buy-and-hold strategy with all of the possible market-timing strategies to see what percentage of the timing combinations produced a return greater than simply buying and holding.

The answer? About one-third of the possible monthly market-timing combinations beat the buy-and-hold strategy. You may be thinking, "I have a 33% chance of beating the market if I try to time it. I'll take those odds!" But before you run out and subscribe to some timing service, consider three issues:

1. The results in the paper cited previously *overstate* the benefits of timing because they looked at each year as a discrete period—which means they ignore the benefits of compounding (as long as you assume that the market will generally rise over long periods of time, that is).
2. Stock market returns are highly skewed—that is, the bulk of the returns (positive and negative) from any given year comes from relatively few days in that year. This means that the risk of *not* being in the market is high for anyone looking to build wealth over a long period of time.

---

[4] Richard J. Bauer Jr. and Julie R. Dahlquist, "Market Timing and Roulette Wheels," *Financial Analysts Journal,* 57(1), pp. 28–40.

3. Not a single one of the thousands of funds Morningstar has tracked over the past two decades has been able to consistently time the market. Sure, some funds have made the occasional great call, but none have posted any kind of superior track record by jumping frequently in and out of the market based on the signals generated by a quantitative model.

That's pretty powerful evidence that market timing is not a viable strategy because running a mutual fund is a very profitable business—if someone had figured out a way to reliably time the market, you can bet your life they'd have started a fund to do so.

Ignoring Valuation

This one came back to haunt many people over the past few years. Although it's certainly possible that another investor will pay you 50 times earnings down the road for the company you just bought for 30 times earnings, that's a very risky bet to make. Sure, you could have made a ton of money in CMGI or Yahoo! during the Internet bubble, but only if you had gotten out in time. Can you honestly say to yourself that you would have?

The only reason you should *ever* buy a stock is that you think the business is worth more than it's selling for—not because you think a greater fool will pay more for the shares a few months down the road.

We'll talk a lot more about the concept of intrinsic value and valuation more in Chapters 9 and 10. For now, just remember that the best way to mitigate your investing risk is to pay careful attention to valuation. If the market's expectations are low, there's a much greater chance that the company you purchase will exceed them. Buying a stock on the expectation of *positive news flow* or *strong relative strength* is asking for trouble.

Relying on Earnings for the Whole Story

At the end of the day, cash flow is what matters, not earnings. For a host of reasons, accounting-based earnings per share can be made to say just about whatever a company's management wants them to, but cash flow is much harder to fiddle with. The statement of cash flows can yield a ton of insight into the true health of a business, and you can spot a lot of blowups before they happen by simply watching the trend of operating cash flow relative to earnings. One hint: If operating cash flows stagnate or shrink even as earnings grow, it's likely that something is rotten.

We'll talk more about the importance of analyzing cash flow in Chapters 22 and 23 and I'll show you how to use it to detect potential accounting problems in Chapter 25.

If you can avoid these common mistakes, you'll be miles ahead of the average investor. Now, let's move from what you shouldn't do to what you should do. In the next chapter, I'll show you how to separate great companies from average ones by analyzing economic moats.

Investor's Checklist: Seven Mistakes to Avoid

▶ Don't try to shoot for big gains by finding the next Microsoft. Instead, focus on finding solid companies with shares selling at low valuations.

▶ Understanding the market's history can help you avoid repeated pitfalls. If people try to convince you that "it really is different this time," ignore them.

▶ Don't fall into the all-too-frequent trap of assuming that a great product translates into a high-quality company. Before you get swept away by exciting new technology or a nifty product, make sure you've checked out the company's business model.

▶ Don't be afraid to use fear to your advantage. The best time to buy is when everyone else is running away from a given asset class.

▶ Attempting to time the market is a fool's game. There's ample evidence that the market can't be timed.

▶ The best way to reduce your investment risk is to pay careful attention to valuation. Don't make the mistake of hoping that other investors will keep paying higher prices, even if you're buying shares in a great company.

▶ Cash flow is the true measure of a company's financial performance, not reported earnings per share.

20

Economic Moats

INVESTORS OFTEN JUDGE companies by looking at which ones have increased profits the most and assuming the trend will persist in the future. But more often than not, the firms that look great in the rearview mirror wind up performing poorly in the future, simply because success attracts competition as surely as night follows day. And the bigger the profits, the stronger the competition. That's the basic nature of any (reasonably) free market—capital always seeks the areas of highest expected return. Therefore, most highly profitable firms tend to become less profitable over time as competitors chip away at their franchises.

You can see this every day in the headlines. Why do generic drug firms employ armies of lawyers to look for patent loopholes? Because large pharmaceutical firms such as Pfizer and Merck are immensely profitable, and even one successful patent challenge will pay off in spades. Why were venture capitalists throwing money at every start-up firm in the networking industry during the late 1990s? Because Cisco was growing at 40% per year with operating margins of 25%. If a firm is generating big profits, it will surely attract competition.

The concept of economic moats is crucial to the way Morningstar analyzes stocks because a moat is the characteristic that helps great-performing companies to stay that way.

We've learned much about the subject by studying investment great Warren Buffett and Harvard professor Michael Porter, who first set down many of the main principles for analyzing competitive strategy and economic moats.

To analyze a company's economic moat, follow these four steps:

1. Evaluate the firm's historical profitability. Has the firm been able to generate a solid return on its assets and on shareholders' equity? This is the true litmus test of whether a firm has built an economic moat around itself.
2. If the firm has solid returns on capital and consistent profitability, assess the sources of the firm's profits. Why is the company able to keep competitors at bay? What keeps competitors from stealing its profits?
3. Estimate how long a firm will be able to hold off competitors, which is the company's *competitive advantage period*. Some firms can fend off competitors for just a few years, and some firms may be able to do it for decades.
4. Analyze the industry's competitive structure. How do firms in this industry compete with one another? Is it an attractive industry with many profitable firms or a hypercompetitive one in which participants struggle just to stay afloat?

Analyzing economic moats is complicated because there are a nearly infinite number of solutions to the problem of consistently making a buck when your competition wants to take it away, but the process is interesting for precisely the same reason.

Evaluating Profitability

The first thing we need to do is look for hard evidence that a firm has an economic moat by examining its financial results. (Figuring out whether a company might have a moat in the *future* is much tougher, but we'll give it a shot at the end of this chapter.)

What we're looking for are firms that can earn profits in excess of their cost of capital—companies that can generate substantial cash relative to the amount of investments they make. One easy way to do this is by using the metrics in the following questions. Although none of these measures are perfect by themselves—they're really a series of shortcuts—they generally do a good job of identifying which firms have economic moats and which ones don't when they're used together. If you're confused by the financial measures in this section, don't worry: I'll discuss them in detail in the next few chapters.

Does the Firm Generate Free Cash Flow? If So, How Much?

First, look at free cash flow—which is simply cash flow from operations minus capital expenditures. (We'll go over free cash flow more in Chapter 5. For now, just go to a firm's statement of cash flows, which you can find in its quarterly and annual financial filings, look for the line item labeled "cash flow from operations," and subtract the line labeled "capital expenditures.") Firms that generate free cash flow essentially have money left over after reinvesting whatever they need to keep their businesses humming along. In a sense, free cash flow is money that could be extracted from the firm every year without damaging the core business.

Next, divide free cash flow by sales (or revenues), which tells you what proportion of each dollar in revenue the firm is able to convert into excess profits. If a firm's free cash flow as a percentage of sales is around 5% or better, you've found a cash machine—as of mid-2003, only one-half of the S&P 500 pass this test. Strong free cash flow is an excellent sign that a firm has an economic moat.

What Are the Firm's Net Margins?

Just as free cash flow measures excess profitability from one perspective, net margins look at profitability from another angle. Net margin is simply net income as a percentage of sales, and it tells you how much profit the firm generates per dollar of sales. (You can find sales and net income on a firm's income statement, which should also be in each of its regular financial filings.) In general, firms that can post net margins above 15% are doing something right.

What Are Returns on Equity?

Return on equity (ROE) is net income as a percentage of shareholders' equity, and it measures profits per dollar of the capital shareholders have invested in a company. Although ROE does have some flaws—which we discuss in Chapter 23—it still works well as one tool for assessing overall profitability. As a rule of thumb, firms that are able to consistently post ROEs above 15% are generating solid returns on shareholders' money, which means they're likely to have economic moats. We'll go over ROE in more detail in Chapter 23.

What Are Returns on Assets?

Return on assets (ROA) is net income as a percentage of a firm's assets, and it measures how efficient a firm is at translating its assets into profits. Use 6% to 7% as a rough benchmark—if a firm is able to consistently post ROAs above these rates, it may have some competitive advantage over its peers.

When you're looking at all four of these metrics, look at more than just one year. A firm that has consistently cranked out solid ROEs, good free cash flow, and decent margins over a number of years is much more likely to truly have an economic moat than a firm with more erratic results. Consistency is important when evaluating companies, because it's the ability to keep competitors at bay for an extended period of time—not just for a year or two—that really makes a firm valuable. Five years is the absolute minimum time period for evaluation, and I'd strongly encourage you to go back 10 years if you can.

In addition, these benchmarks are rules of thumb, not hard-and-fast cutoffs. Comparing firms with industry averages is always a good idea, as is examining the trend in profitability metrics—are they getting higher or lower?

There's also a more sophisticated way of measuring a firm's profitability that involves calculating return on invested capital (ROIC), estimating a weighted average cost of capital (WACC), and then looking at the difference between the two. We'll talk more in Chapter 6, but don't worry if it seems too complicated for you. Using a combination of free cash flow, ROE, ROA, and net margins will steer you in the right direction.

Building an Economic Moat

Next, we need to determine why a firm has done such a great job of holding on to its profits and keeping the competition at arm's length. Although being in an attractive industry can certainly help, the strategy pursued at the company level is even more important. The mere fact that there are excellent companies in fundamentally unattractive industries (e.g., Southwest Airlines) tells us intuitively that this must be the case. Academic research suggests that a firm's strategy is roughly twice as important as a firm's industry when it's trying to build an economic moat.[1]

When you're examining the sources of a firm's economic moat, the key thing is to never stop asking, "Why?" Why aren't competitors stealing the firm's customers? Why can't a competitor charge a lower price for a similar product or service? Why do customers accept annual price increases?

When possible, look at the situation from the customer's perspective. What value does the product or service bring to the customer? How does it help them run their own business better? Why do they use one firm's product or service instead of a competitor's? If you can answer these questions, odds are good that you'll have found the source of the company's economic moat.

In general, there are five ways that an individual firm can build sustainable competitive advantage:

1. Creating *real product differentiation* through superior technology or features
2. Creating *perceived product differentiation* through a trusted brand or reputation
3. *Driving costs down* and offering a similar product or service at a lower price
4. *Locking in customers* by creating high switching costs
5. *Locking out competitors* by creating high barriers to entry or high barriers to success

Real Product Differentiation
This is certainly the most obvious type of economic moat—after all, wouldn't customers always pay more for a better product or service? Unfortunately, simply having better technology or more features is usually not a sustainable

---

[1] Anita McGahan and Michael E. Porter, "How Much Does Industry Matter, Really?" *Strategic Management Journal, 18,* p. 15 (1997).

strategy because there are always competitors hoping to build a better mousetrap. And because having the best product or service usually means charging a premium price, firms pursuing this strategy often limit the size of their potential market. Many customers will be satisfied with a slightly inferior product at a significantly lower price.

More important, it's just plain difficult to constantly stay one step ahead of competitors by adding features or improving a product, which is why few firms are able to use this strategy to create long-term excess profits. This is especially the case in many parts of the technology sector and in the consumer electronics industry—today's vendor of the latest and greatest server, storage system, or DVD player is likely not going to be tomorrow's leading player. Finally, constant innovation generally sucks up a large amount of capital in the form of research and development expenses, which can make a product-differentiation strategy very expensive.

Data-storage manufacturer EMC is a good example. In the mid-1990s, the firm had leapfrogged IBM in this fast-growing area of the technology sector and was winning new customers because its products had features that IBM's lacked. For several years, EMC raked in enormous profits by charging customers substantially higher prices than the competition for its technologically superior products. (In fact, EMC's prices were so high that customers nicknamed the firm "excess margin corporation.")

However, IBM and other competitors didn't give up. Eventually, IBM rolled out products that came pretty close to matching EMC's, and IBM priced them much lower in an effort to win customers back. As a result, IBM began regaining market share, and EMC's business suffered.

The lesson here is that although firms can occasionally generate enormous excess profits—and enormous stock returns—by staying one step ahead of the technological curve, these profits are usually short-lived. Unless you are familiar enough with the inner workings of an industry to know when a firm's products are being supplanted by better ones, be wary of firms that rely solely on innovation to sustain their competitive advantage.

Perceived Product Differentiation

Very often, however, a firm with consistently better products or services creates a brand for itself, and a strong brand can constitute a very wide economic moat. The wonderful thing about a brand is that as long as customers *perceive* your product or service as better than everyone else's, it makes relatively little difference whether it actually is different.

Tiffany is a fabulous example of the power of a brand to create excess economic returns. The simple fact that a piece of jewelry is packaged inside the famous little blue box allows Tiffany to charge a significant premium for its products. This example is fascinating because jewelry has so many objective standards—karats of gold, clarity of diamonds—that measure the quality of an individual piece. The fact that consumers will pay more for a virtually identical diamond ring from Tiffany than from a local jeweler is what defines a truly valuable brand: It increases a consumer's willingness to pay.

Thinking about brands and reputations in this way—whether consumers of a product or service are truly willing to pay more to buy the good from one firm instead of another—helps separate more valuable brands from less valuable ones. What matters is not the existence of the brand, but rather how the brand is used to create excess profits. In fact, brands aren't useful at all in some industries.

Think about companies such as Sony or Ford, both of which have well-known brands. But both firms have struggled to generate solid returns on capital over the past few years because they sell goods that are simply not very amenable to brand-driven price differentiation. Consumers are unlikely to pay much more for a Sony stereo relative to a product from Panasonic with similar features, and they're also unlikely to pay more for a Ford truck just because it has the Ford nameplate.

On the flip side, Abercrombie & Fitch has managed to convince legions of teenagers to pay $25 for a T-shirt just because it has "Abercrombie" on the front. How long this brand will remain strong is tough to predict, but there's no question that it's enabled Abercrombie to charge more for its products over the past several years. In fact, the durability of a brand is a critical component of any brand-based economic moat. Some brands—for example, Coke or Disney—last for generations, but some are much more fleeting.

When you're evaluating whether a strong brand really does create an economic moat, it's not enough to look at whether consumers trust the product or have an emotional connection to the brand. The brand has to justify the cost of creating it by actually making money for the firm, and sustaining a powerful brand usually requires a lot of expensive advertising. Therefore, unless the brand actually increases consumers' willingness to pay and those looser wallets translate into consistently positive returns on capital, the brand may not be worth as much as you'd thought.

Driving Costs Down

Offering a similar product or service at a lower cost can be an extremely powerful source of competitive advantage. It costs Southwest 25% less to fly one passenger one mile than the leanest of the major airlines, and it's that advantage that propelled the firm from a Texas upstart to a big-league player in 25 years. Low costs have fattened Dell's profit margins to such an extent that the firm has been able to expand its share of the PC market from around 6% in 1997 to more than 15% by year-end 2002—a big move in just six years.

Airlines and PCs are known as *commodity* industries, in which products are tough to differentiate. Low-cost strategies work especially well in these types of markets. Even in noncommodity markets, lower costs can bring large advantages as long as the cost advantage is sustainable and not temporary. However, it's not enough to just look at a firm's profit margins and say that such-and-such firm has lower costs than its competitors—you need to identify the sources of those cost savings, which can come in a variety of flavors.

In general, firms can create cost advantages by either inventing a better process or achieving a larger scale. Dell is the classic example of a firm with a process-based advantage. Building PCs only after they're ordered allows the firm to take advantage of the swift price erosion of PC components—parts don't sit in inventory losing value while the firm waits for orders to come in. Over time, Dell has continued to squeeze costs from its supply chain to the point where you could argue that Dell is no longer a technology firm, but rather a manufacturing one.

Process advantages can also be subtler. In the asset-management industry, you might think that Vanguard's size is what allows it to underprice its services—but there are other firms of comparable size with much higher fees. The key is that Vanguard is structured as a mutual organization that's collectively owned by fundholders, rather than a profit-maximizing corporation owned by shareholders. Because of this structure, Vanguard can plow back excess profits into cost-reducing activities, whereas traditionally structured asset management firms will either distribute excess profits to their managers in the form of fat bonuses or allow the cash to pile up on the balance sheet. In Vanguard's case, higher profits allow the firm to push costs down, which attracts more assets, which generates more profits, and so forth. This relatively unique structure means that it will likely be very difficult for any non-mutual asset-management firm to ever match Vanguard's low costs.

Scale advantages are often very difficult for competitors to match because they tend to build on themselves: The largest firms continue to drive down costs and prices, and smaller ones have an increasingly difficult time catching up. The most basic form of a scale advantage comes from simply leveraging fixed costs—in other words, spreading the cost of an asset such as a factory across an ever-larger sales base. Intel, for example, produces far more microprocessors in any given year than archrival AMD, which means its per-chip production cost is a great deal lower than AMD's.

Fixed costs don't have to be factories. For example, the trucks that make up the distribution network of package-delivery service UPS represent an enormous fixed cost that allows the firm to deliver to more locations at a lower cost than almost any other competitor. Although replicating a delivery network that serves only large metropolitan centers might not be too daunting a task for a potential competitor, replicating a network that can deliver to virtually any address in the United States would be another thing altogether. Because it costs UPS very little extra money to put an additional couple of packages on a truck that's already serving a particular delivery route, its profit on those extra couple of packages is high.

Locking In Customers

Customer lock-in, or creating high customer switching costs, is possibly the subtlest type of competitive advantage. Uncovering it requires a deep understanding of a firm's operations. Cost advantages, brands, and better products are all relatively easy to spot from the outside, but knowing exactly what makes it tough for a customer to switch from one firm to another can be difficult to find out. However, it can also be very powerful, which is why firms with high customer switching costs often have wide economic moats.

If you can make it difficult—in terms of either money or time—for a customer to switch to a competing product, you can charge your customers more and make more money—simple in theory, but difficult in practice.

Remember, a switching cost does not have to be monetary—in fact, it rarely is. Much more frequently, what deters customers from dropping a product or service in favor of a competing product or service is time. Often, learning how to use a product or service can require a significant investment of time, which means the benefits of a competing product have to be very large to induce a switch. A consumer might switch brands of tomato sauce because one tastes just a little better than the other, but a word-processing program would have to carry huge advantages over an incumbent program to induce a consumer to throw away the accumulated knowledge and spend time learning the new program.

Medical device firms such as Stryker and Zimmer are perfect examples of how firms can create high switching costs that help ensure customer retention. Both of these firms manufacture artificial joints such as hips and knees, and surgeons have to be trained on how to implant their products—a Stryker hip is different enough from a Zimmer hip that a surgeon can't just choose one or the other based on which is on sale that week. This training process is time-consuming for surgeons, which means surgeons tend to develop preferences for a particular company's products and stick with them. Therefore, Stryker, Zimmer, and their competitors tend to have relatively stable shares of the joint-replacement market—a firm would have to introduce a measurably better product to induce surgeons to incur the retraining costs needed to use the new product.

When you're looking for evidence of high customer switching costs, these questions should help:

▶ Does the firm's product require a significant amount of client training? If so, customers will be reluctant to switch and incur lost productivity during the training period.
▶ Is the firm's product or service tightly integrated into customers' businesses? Firms don't change vendors of mission-critical products often because the costs of a botched switch may far outweigh the benefits of using the new product or service.

- ▶ Is the firm's product or service an industry standard? Customers may feel pressure from their own clients—or their peers—to continue using a well-known and well-respected product or service.
- ▶ Is the benefit to be gained from switching small relative to the cost of switching? Bank customers, for example, often endure slightly higher fees because the lower fees they might get from moving to a competing bank are of less value than the potential hassle of moving their account.
- ▶ Does the firm tend to sign long-term contracts with clients? This is often a sign that the client does not want to frequently switch vendors.

Locking Out Competitors

Locking out competitors is the fifth strategy that firms can use to generate lasting competitive advantages. If done well, this can result in years of strong profits. If done *too* well, it can invite the scrutiny of the federal government on antitrust grounds—as Microsoft (and other firms) have discovered.

The most obvious way to lock out competitors is to acquire some kind of regulatory exclusivity, as many casinos do from state governments. Licenses and such are powerful deterrents to competitors—but because governments make the rules, they can also change them without warning. U.S. state governments have been known to raise the tax rates on the casinos they license after the casino facilities are in place and generating profits. Although the casinos were still protected from competitors, state governments were able to tax away a larger portion of their excess profits than the casinos initially expected.

Patents fall into the regulatory category as well because a patent holder is legally protected from direct competition for a set period of time. And as large pharmaceutical companies have demonstrated, patents can lead to years of extremely high profit margins. But although patents may deter competition, they tend to attract litigation, which can severely hamper the patent-holder's ability to earn excess returns.

A great example is Pfizer, which holds patents on some of the top-selling drugs in the world. These patents allow the company to charge high prices for new drugs for years after they hit the market. Competition during the life of the patent is usually limited, so profits and cash flows are huge. That's one reason Pfizer's average return on equity over the past decade has been greater than 30% and its net profit margins are currently north of 25% (compared with around 6% for the average S&P 500 company). That's also why it's been a great stock to own over the long haul. In fact, many of the major pharmaceutical players have outperformed the market over the past 10 years because of the economic moats inherent in this industry.

However, although patents and licenses can do a great job of keeping competitors at bay and maintaining high profit margins, they can also be ephemeral. If you're investigating a firm whose economic moat depends solely on a single patent or other regulatory approval, don't forget to investigate the likelihood of that approval disappearing unexpectedly. This will likely involve a detailed reading of the legal proceedings section of the firm's 10-K filing. (You can find financial filings through most firms' Web sites, as well as directly from the SEC's Web site.)

A much more durable strategy for locking out competitors is to take advantage of the *network effect*. A strong network becomes more valuable as the number of users increases—much like a telephone network, which wouldn't be worth much if you could call only a dozen people, but which has immense value given the enormous number of users. Companies that have a network protecting their competitive positions often have very wide economic moats.

In general, markets tend to have strong network effects—the more buyers and sellers that transact in a particular market, the greater the value of that market to participants. As a publicly listed auction market, eBay is the purest example of this idea: The firm has held its own against much larger companies, and it seems unlikely that another competitor will emerge soon.

It should be easy to see why eBay has a near-monopoly in online auctions in most of the world. Because eBay was the first major firm to connect individual buyers and sellers over the Internet in an auction format, the number of buyers and sellers grew very quickly. As more rare baseball cards and vintage posters came up for auction on eBay, more buyers were attracted to the site to bid on those items. Those extra bidders attracted still more sellers— the sellers wanted to go where the buyers were, and the buyers wanted to go where the sellers were.

By the time competitors such as Yahoo! and Amazon.com tried to get into the auction game, it was too late. There were already too many bidders on eBay for sellers to want to switch to a new, smaller auction service—they'd probably get a lower price for their wares because there were fewer bidders on each item. Meanwhile, the bidders weren't interested in going anywhere either because eBay had by far the most items for sale. Thus, eBay gained critical mass and, today, a near-monopoly position in the online-auction market.

Another great example is money-transfer concern Western Union, which is owned by First Data. With more than 170,000 locations worldwide, odds are pretty good that Western Union can get your money wherever you need it to go, and the value of the firm's agent network only grows larger as it adds locations. The central characteristic of a classic network effect is a virtuous circle—more users attract more users.

How Long Will It Last?

Our next topic is assessing the longevity of an economic moat, so we know how long a firm is likely to keep its competitors at bay.

Think about an economic moat in two dimensions. There's depth—how much money the firm can make—and there's width—how long the firm can sustain above-average profits. Technology firms often have very deep but very narrow moats, so they're incredibly profitable for a relatively short period of time until a competitor builds a better product. A niche firm such as WD-40 is just the opposite. It's never going to make an enormous amount of money in any one year by selling cans of household lubricant, but it has such a solid franchise that its excess returns are likely to persist for quite some time.

Estimating how long a moat will last is tough stuff, but you need to at least give it some thought, even if you can't come up with a precise answer. Just being able to separate firms into three buckets—a few years, several years, and many years—is very useful.

In general, any competitive advantage based on technological superiority—real product differentiation—is likely to be fairly short. Successful software firms, for example, can generate huge excess returns because they have high profit margins and they don't need to spend much money on fixed costs such as machinery. However, the duration of those returns is typically very short because of the rapid pace of technological change. In other words, today's leader can quickly become tomorrow's loser because the barriers to entry are so low and the potential rewards so high.

Cost leadership, brands (perceived product differentiation), customer lock-ins, and competitor lockouts can each confer competitive advantage periods of varying lengths—there's no good rule of thumb, unfortunately. To give you some guidance in what separates a wide moat from a narrow moat and what kinds of companies have no moat at all, I've listed 27 well-known large-cap companies in Figures 20.1, 20.2, and 20.3 and included an explanation as to

Dell	Classic low-cost producer: lean operating structure and direct Internet-based sales allow the company to run circles around its rivals.
eBay	Network effect: The more buyers and sellers the network has, the more attractive it becomes to prospective users and the tougher it becomes for competitors to contend with.
PepsiCo	By far the market share leader in salty snacks and sports drinks, the diversified food company boasts a stable full of strong brands, innovative new products, and an impressive distribution network.
Comcast	Controls roughly one-third of cable households in the U.S. This gives it unparalleled leverage with content providers and equipment suppliers.
Intel	Chipmaker's dominant position gives it significant economies of scale. Brand name and patents are also significant intangible assets.
H&R Block	Dominates the U.S. tax preparation market. One in every seven tax returns filed is prepared by Block.
Wal-Mart	Largest retail company in the world is also the preeminent low-cost provider. The firm flexes its muscles with suppliers in negotiating prices and passes the savings down to consumers.
United Technologies	Operates in a selection of concentrated industries. Buyers of elevators, cooling systems, and helicopters don't switch brands often.
Adobe	High customer switching costs: graphic designers are trained early in their careers to use the company's software and can't do their job without it.
Paychex	Vast sales network provides access to new accounts and scale gives it a cost advantage. Plus, it has pricing power over its diverse and unorganized client base.

Figure 20.1 Some examples of companies with wide economic moats. *Source:* Morningstar, Inc.

Federal Express	Sure, it practically invented overnight delivery, but behind the scenes, FedEx is a cargo airline, and airline margins are thin.
Nokia	Although the Nokia brand is strong, cell phones are becoming commodities.
Kraft	Despite a portfolio of familiar consumer brands, there isn't much breathing space between Kraft and its competitors, which has made it difficult for the firm to exert any pricing power.
Waste Management	Network of 300 landfills creates a wide-moat disposal business, but lack of brand loyalty in its collection business—where customers flock to the lowest price—earns this company a narrow moat.
Disney	Owns some of the most valuable intellectual property in the world, but increasing competition and an absence of creativity have eroded some of the brand's appeal.
ExxonMobil	Enjoys enormous economies of scale, but still operates in a commodity industry.
Target	"Cheap chic" strategy has helped it carve out a moat and differentiate itself from Wal-Mart. However, Target's strategy depends partially on accurately guessing fashion trends, which is more difficult than merely being the low-cost provider of everyday items.
Best Buy	Dominates home-electronics and entertainment-software retailing, but operates in a very economically sensitive industry.
AOL Time Warner	Still has some great media properties, but bungled attempts at formulating a successful broadband strategy have left the AOL business vulnerable.
SBC Communications	Former monopoly over local phone service is facing competition from wireless carriers, cable companies, and long-distance firms that can buy access to its local network.

Figure 20.2   Some examples of companies with narrow economic moats. *Source:* Morningstar, Inc.

General Motors	Operates in deeply cyclical industry. Legacy costs and reputation for mediocre quality puts it at a competitive disadvantage relative to most peers.
Micron	Memory chips are essentially commodities, which leads to product price volatility and lots of competition.
Circuit City	Main competitor Best Buy has higher profit margins, better inventory turnover, and twice the per-store sales numbers.
Staples	A saturated industry, lack of product differentiation, and intense price sensitivity prevent this company from digging a moat.
Maytag	Low-cost Asian producers have forced the company to focus on the premium appliance market, where competition is fierce and product differentiation is difficult to achieve.
Delta	Not the low-cost provider and doesn't offer a differentiated product. In a commodity industry where competition revolves largely around price, its business model is unsustainable.

Figure 20.3 Some examples of companies with no economic moats. *Source:* Morningstar, Inc.

why each firm's moat is wide, narrow, or does not exist. Having these examples will, I hope, help you analyze economic moats when doing your own research. I've also included at the end of the book a list of all the companies Morningstar follows that we consider to have wide economic moats.

Industry Analysis

Our last step is to investigate the industry in which the firm operates. Let's face it: It's just plain easier to make money in some industries than it is in others. (Ask the CEO of any airline company.) Although the attractiveness of an industry doesn't tell the whole story—after all, Southwest Airlines has made plenty of money for shareholders—it's important to have a feel for the competitive landscape.

First, get a rough sense of the industry so you can classify it. Are sales for firms in the industry generally increasing or shrinking? Are firms consistently profitable or does the industry go through periodic cycles when most firms lose money? Is the industry dominated by a few large players, or is it full of firms that are roughly the same size? How profitable is the average firm—are operating margins fairly high (more than 25%) or fairly low (less than 15%)? (An *operating margin* is income from operations as a percentage of sales. I discuss such financial ratios in more detail in Chapter 23.)

You can answer some of these questions by looking at aggregate statistics—average growth rates, average margins, and so on. However, averages can't tell you everything, so be sure that you examine a number of individual companies. An easy way to do this is to look at a list of companies in the industry you're researching sorted by sales or market cap, and examine a dozen or so to get a feel for the industry.

You don't need to do detailed analysis at this point—just glance over sales and earnings growth rates and margins. The most important thing is to look at a variety of firms over a reasonably long time frame—at least 5 years and, preferably, 10.

Investor's Checklist: Economic Moats

▶ Because success attracts competition as surely as night follows day, the most highly profitable companies tend to become less profitable over time. That's why economic moats are so important: They help great companies stay that way.

▶ For concrete evidence of an economic moat, look for firms that consistently earn high profits. Focus on free cash flow, net margins, return on equity, and return on assets.

▶ After you've looked at these specific measures, try to identify the source of the company's economic moat. Companies generally build sustainable competitive advantages through product differentiation (real or perceived), driving costs down, locking in customers with high switching costs, or locking out competitors through high barriers to entry.

▶ Think about economic moats in two dimensions: depth (how much money the company can make) and width (how long it can sustain above-average profits). In general, any economic moat based on technological innovation is likely to be short-lived.

▶ Although the attractiveness of an industry doesn't tell the whole story, it's important to get a feel for the competitive landscape. Some industries are just easier to make money in than others.

21

The Language of Investing

In the next three chapters, my goal is to help you understand how financial statements fit together and how you can use them to identify solid companies. First, we'll look at how the three main financial statements fit together by describing what's in them and by following a dollar through a business. Then, we'll build a hot dog stand to see how the operations of a very simple business are represented in financial statements.

In Chapter 22, we'll tour all three statements in detail by looking at the books of a real, complicated company. (Note to readers with some accounting background: You can skip to Chapter 23—Analyzing a Company—unless you want a review of the basics.) In Chapter 28, we'll apply our newfound accounting knowledge to the analytical process by looking at two real-world companies.

The Basics

As an investor, you're mainly going to be interested in the balance sheet, the income statement, and the statement of cash flows. These three tables are your windows into corporate performance, and they're the place to start when you're analyzing a company.

All three of these statements can be found in the three major types of financial filings: an annual report, a 10-K filing, and a 10-Q filing. You're probably familiar with annual reports—those glossy booklets with smiling employees that firms mail out every year—but to really understand a firm, you'll need to look up 10-Ks and 10-Qs. These are dense, detailed sets of financial information that companies file with the Securities and Exchange Commission (SEC) every year (the 10-K) and every quarter (the 10-Q). You can access these reports at http://www.sec.gov/edgar.shtml or http://www.freeedgar.com. The latter is a bit easier to use.

Think of the three statements like this: The balance sheet is like a company's credit report because it tells you how much the company owns (assets) relative to what it owes (liabilities) at a specific point in time. It tells you how strong the framework and foundation of the business is.

The income statement, meanwhile, tells how much the company made or lost in accounting profits during a year or a quarter. Unlike the balance sheet, which is a snapshot of the company's financial health at a precise moment, the income statement records revenues and expenses over a set period, such as a fiscal year.

Finally, there's the statement of cash flows, which records all the cash that comes into a company and all of the cash that goes out. The statement of cash flows ties the income statement and balance sheet together.

Right now, you're probably wondering why we need an income statement and a cash flow statement—after all, if a company makes money, it makes money, right? The difference lies in a confusing concept called *accrual accounting*. Here's how it works. Companies record sales (or revenue) when a service or a good is provided to the buyer, regardless of when the buyer pays. As long as the company is reasonably certain that the buyer will eventually pay the bill, the company can post the sale to its income statement.

The cash flow statement, on the other hand, is concerned only with when cash is received and when it goes out the door. I'll go over the cash flow statement in detail later in this chapter, but here's a quick example.

Let's say that Colgate sells a few cases of toothpaste to Joe's Corner Store for $1,000 on February 15 but gives Joe 60 days to pay because he's a regular customer and has a good track record of paying his bills on time. March 31 rolls around, Joe hasn't paid yet, and Colgate closes its books for the quarter.

Colgate shows $1,000 in sales on its income statement because it shipped the toothpaste to Joe—according to the income statement, the sale is complete, regardless of whether Colgate has received payment. But because Joe hasn't ponied up the grand yet, Colgate will post an entry on its balance sheet to show that Joe owes Colgate $1,000. (The entry goes into the accounts receivable line—more on this later in the chapter.)

As you can see, a company can show rip-roaring sales growth without receiving a cent of cash. In fact, if Colgate produces and sells toothpaste faster than its customers pay for the toothpaste, sales growth would look fantastic even though cash is flowing out the door—which is why we need a statement of cash flows.

Where the Money Goes

Figure 21.1 illustrates how money moves from investors, through the company, to consumers, and back to the company.

This isn't nearly as bad as it looks. Let's follow some money through the company to show you what I mean.

A group of investors and bondholders (1) provide capital to a firm, either by buying shares in the company (stockholders) or by buying the company's bonds (bondholders). The company takes the money and buys fixed assets (2) such as machinery and buildings—and uses those assets to produce inventory (3). Some of the inventory is sold for cash (4), and some is sold on credit (5).

The credit sales are posted to "accounts receivable"—a fancy name for IOU—until the customer pays the firm (6). Once the firm has cash in hand, it can spend it in all sorts of ways. Some of it goes back into production (7), which means buying replacement raw materials to create more inventory, and some of it goes into investment (8), which means buying more machinery or building another factory. (In accounting lingo, you'll usually see any investment that purchases a tangible long-term asset such as a building or factory called "capital expenditure," or simply "capex.")

Another chunk of cash goes to Uncle Sam as taxes (9), and some may flow out as dividends to stockholders if the firm pays a dividend or as interest to bondholders (10) if the firm has debt.

That's really all there is to it. Cash flows in, and (you hope) cash flows out. Let's walk through a simplified company—Mike's Hot Dog Stand—to

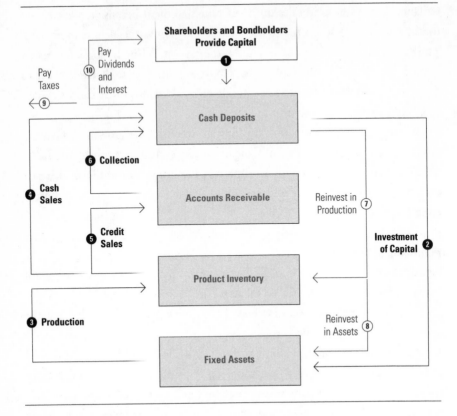

Figure 21.1 How money flows through a company. *Source:* Morningstar, Inc.

illustrate how all of this comes together. We'll use Mike's to introduce many of the specific line items in financial statements that tell us how well a company is doing its core job, which is investing shareholders' money to generate a solid return.

Practical Financials—The Statements in Use

It's the Fourth of July, and Mike thinks he can make a few bucks by setting up a hot dog stand near the parade route. Mike has $100 to start his hot dog–selling operation, with the money provided by the First National Bank of Mom.

I. Borrows $100 from First National Bank of Mom

ASSETS	Before	Change	After
Cash	0	+100	100

LIABILITIES			
Long-term debt	0	+100	100

Mike spends $70 for lumber, nails, and paint to assemble the stand as well as tongs for turning the dogs on the grill. (He's borrowing Dad's grill to cook the dogs.) Then he buys $20 worth of hot dogs, buns, ketchup, and mustard, and some charcoal and lighter fluid for the grill. He keeps the remaining $10 for making change and such.

II. Buys property, plant, and equipment (PP&E) and inventory

ASSETS	Before	Change	After
Cash	100	−90	10
Inventory	0	+20	20
PP&E	0	+70	70

He's spent $90 ($70 for the stand and $20 for ingredients), but that money hasn't disappeared—it's turned into assets and inventory. As shown in the chart, the $70 he spent on the hot dog stand and the tongs is "property, plant, and equipment," while the $20 in buns and such has become "inventory," and the $10 in cash is just that. Look at the simplified balance sheet in Figure 21.2 to see how this would look if Mike had to file an annual report. (Don't worry if you see an unfamiliar line item—we'll cover it later in the chapter.)

Mike opens for business while the crowd is gathering for the parade and sells 30 hot dogs at $1 apiece. By noon, half the hot dogs, buns, condiments, and charcoal are gone, so Mike's "cost of goods sold" is $10, or half of the $20 he spent to buy supplies. Seven people didn't have any cash on them, so Mike let them buy their dogs on credit—which means we need to record $7 in accounts receivable, which is the money that folks owe to Mike.

Assets	
Cash	10
+ Accounts receivable	0
+ Inventory	20
+ Net PP&E	70
= **Total Assets**	**100**

Liabilities	
Accounts payable	0
Long-term debt	100

Equity	
Retained earnings	0
Depreciation expense	0
Total Liabilities & Equity	**100**

Figure 21.2 Simple balance sheet for Mike's hot dog stand. *Source:* Morningstar, Inc.

III. Sells 30 hot dogs at $1 piece ($10 worth of inventory), with $7 worth being sold on credit (cash not received yet)

ASSETS	Before	Change	After
Cash	10	+23	33
Accounts receivable	0	+7	7
Inventory	20	−10	10

In the middle of the day, Mike runs out of buns, so he has to run over to the corner grocery store to buy more. But when he arrives, he realizes he left his money back at the stand, so he promises the grocer he'll come back with the money on Monday when the hot dog biz slows down. We post $5 to accounts payable, which is money that Mike owes to the grocery store for the buns. (Think of accounts payable like your credit card. If you buy a shirt or a stereo on your Visa, you can use it right away—but you still owe the credit card issuer some cash.)

IV. Buys $5 worth of buns on credit

ASSETS	Before	Change	After
Cash	33	0	33
Inventory	10	+5	15
LIABILITIES			
Accounts payable	0	+5	5

At the end of the second day, Mike realizes that his tongs aren't working as well as they used to, and it's taking him longer to grill each hot dog. The accounting name for this wear-and-tear is *depreciation,* which lets us record the fact that Mike's equipment isn't as productive as it used to be. (In the real world, depreciation isn't recorded at the moment something starts wearing out. It's actually a regular charge that assumes that an asset wears out over a set time period—as long as forty years for a building, and as short as three years for a computer.) Depreciation is a cost of doing business, just like buying hot dogs and buns, because Mike will eventually have to buy another set of tongs if he wants to stay in business. Because all costs have to be recorded—accounting is funny that way—we post $1 to depreciation.

V. Records wear and tear on tongs

ASSETS	Before	Change	After
Net PP&E	70	−1	69

After a long day of serving up delicious dogs to parade-goers, Mike's income statement is shown in Figure 21.3.

And his balance sheet is shown in Figure 21.4.

The eagle-eyed reader will notice that although Mike's net profit was $19, his cash account went up by $23—from $10 to $33—on his personal balance sheet. Why the difference? Let's find out by developing a statement of cash flows from the income statement and balance sheet information that we have available. By following this example, you'll see into the heart and soul of accounting.

To understand how much *cash* Mike's little business generated, we start with his $19 in net profits, which is the difference between what he paid for

Sales		30
− Cost of goods sold		10
− Depreciation		1
= **Net Profit**		**19**

Figure 21.3 Simple income statement for Mike's hot dog stand. *Source:* Morningstar, Inc.

the hot dogs, buns, and condiments, and what he received in payment for the hot dogs. But to arrive at the cash profits, we first need to add back the $1 in depreciation. You see, although we need to keep track of the expense that Mike incurred by partially wearing out his grilling tongs—remember, accounting is all about keeping score—Mike didn't have to pay out $1 in cash to cover the wear and tear. He'll have to replace the tongs eventually, but as yet, he still has his slightly worn-out pair, and he hasn't laid out any green to fix it.

This is *the* critical difference between accounting profits and cash profits—accounting profits match revenues (hot dogs sold) with expenses (a worn-out

Assets	Original	Final
Cash	10	33
+ Accounts receivable	0	7
+ Inventory	20	15
+ Net PP&E	70	69
= **Total Assets**	**100**	**124**

Liabilities	Original	Final
Accounts payable	0	5
Long-term debt	100	100

Equity	Original	Final
Retained earnings	0	20
Depreciation expense	0	-1
Total Liabilities & Equity	**100**	**124**

Figure 21.4 Balance sheet for Mike's hot dog stand. *Source:* Morningstar, Inc.

set of grilling tongs) as closely as possible, whereas cash profits measure only the actual dollar bills flowing into and out of a business.

Next, we need to take into account the fact that Mike used up half his original inventory of hot dogs and buns, as well as the fact that he went out and bought an additional $5 worth of buns. His inventory went from $20, to $10, and back to $15. This net decrease in inventory from $20 to $15 is a *source* of cash. In other words, Mike had $20 of capital tied up in inventory at the start of the weekend, but now he has only $15 of capital invested in inventory. As a result, he converted $5 in inventory to $5 in cash.

However, Mike also is owed $7 by hot dog eaters who haven't paid him yet. Because Mike had to pay to produce the dogs they ate and they haven't yet given him any cash, he's used up some money by letting those folks nosh on his tasty dogs on credit. In other words, Mike paid out cash to get the ingredients he needed to make the hot dogs, but he hasn't yet received any cash in return, so his decision to extend credit *used up* $7 in cash.

Finally, let's not forget that Mike himself is the beneficiary of credit because he still owes the grocer $5 for those extra buns he bought. Because Mike received something without paying out cash for it, his cash account *increases* by $5.

We can follow the trail from Mike's $19 in net profits to his $23 in cash flow with this simple table:

Net profits = $19
      + $1 depreciation
      + $10 inventory (hot dogs sold)
      − $5 inventory (extra buns purchased)
      − $7 accounts receivable (money owed *to* Mike)
      + $5 accounts payable (money owed *by* Mike)
   = $23 in operating cash flow

As you can see, the $23 in operating cash flow differs from the $19 in net income because of the choices Mike made in running his little business. For example, if Mike hadn't let anyone buy on credit, but had the same amount of sales, his cash flow would have been $30 ($23 plus $7). Conversely, if the grocer had forced Mike to pay cash for those extra buns, Mike's cash flow would have been $18 ($23 minus $5.) In both cases, however, Mike's net profits would have remained $19.

The key takeaway here is that the income statement and cash flow statement can tell different stories about a business because they're constructed using different sets of rules. The income statement strives to match revenues and expenses as closely as possible—that's why we had to deduct the $1 in depreciation from Mike's profits, and that's why Mike gets to record the $7 in sales that he made on credit. But the cash flow statement cares only about the dollar bills that go in and out the door, regardless of the timing of the actions that generated those dollar bills.

If you look only at the income statement without checking to see how much cash a company is creating, you won't be getting the whole story by a long shot. This simple concept—the difference between accounting profits and cash profits—is the key to understanding almost everything there is to know about how a business works, as well as how to separate great businesses from poor ones. In subsequent chapters, we'll move from our simple hot dog stand to real-world companies to learn how to analyze all three of the financial statements in detail.

Investor's Checklist: The Language of Investing

- ▶ The balance sheet is like a company's credit report because it tells you how much the company owns (assets) relative to what it owes (liabilities).
- ▶ The income statement shows how much the company made or lost in accounting profits during a year or a quarter. Unlike the balance sheet, which is a snapshot of the company's financial health at a precise moment, the income statement records revenues and expenses during a set period, such as a fiscal year.
- ▶ The third key financial statement—the statement of cash flows—records all the cash that comes into a company and all of the cash that goes out.
- ▶ Accrual accounting is a key concept for understanding financial statements. The income statement matches sales with the corresponding expenses when a service or a good is provided to the buyer, but the cash flow statement is concerned only with when cash is received and when it goes out the door.
- ▶ The income statement and cash flow statement can tell different stories about a business because they're constructed using different sets of rules. To get the most complete picture, be sure to look at both.

22

Financial Statements Explained

Now that you have a good idea of how businesses generate cash and how profits are recorded on financial statements, let's look at each of the three main financial statements in detail. Unfortunately, not all businesses are as simple as a hot dog stand, so we need to introduce some additional complexity if we want to analyze real companies. But fear not—as we walk through the balance sheet, income statement, and cash flow statement, we'll look at a few real-world companies to see what their financial statements can tell us about how their businesses are functioning.

Wherever possible, I'll refer to excerpts from the financial statements of Dell and Hewlett-Packard (H-P), taken from the two firms' 10-K filings with the SEC. (The Dell excerpts contain data through January 31, 2003, and the H-P excerpts contain data through October 31, 2002.) We'll start with the balance sheet, move on to the income statement, and finish with the statement of cash flows. At the start of each section, you'll see a financial statement from the originally named (and fictitious) "Acme Corporation" that will show you how each statement is organized.

Warning: This chapter may be tough going in parts, but it's possibly the most important chapter of the entire book, since reading financial statements is the foundation for analyzing companies. If you find yourself confused about a concept or getting tired, put down the book and take a break. There's no rush—it'll be here when you get back!

The Balance Sheet

The balance sheet (see Figure 22.1)—sometimes called a "statement of financial position"—tells you how much a company owns (its assets), how much it owes (its liabilities), and the difference between the two (its equity). Equity represents the value of the money that shareholders have invested in the firm, and if that sounds odd, think of it just like your mortgage—your equity in your home is the home's value minus the mortgage. Stockholders' equity in a firm is the value of the firm's assets minus its liabilities.

ACME Corporation: Balance Sheet

(In millions)	2002	2001
Assets		
Current assets:		
Cash and cash equivalents	$284	$205
Accounts receivable	842	827
Inventories	644	697
Other current assets	328	369
Total current assets	$2,098	$2,099
Investments	79	92
Property, plant, and equipment—net	1,874	1,872
Goodwill	633	337
Intangible assets	90	79
Other assets	415	390
Total assets	$5,188	$4,869

Figure 22.1   A balance sheet for the fictitious ACME Corporation. *Source:* Morningstar, Inc.

Liabilities and stockholders' equity		
Current liabilities:		
Short-term debt	412	458
Accounts payable	315	251
Payroll	137	180
Income taxes	173	199
Other current liabilities	449	416
Total current liabilities	$1,486	$1,503
Long-term debt	$ 713	$ 507
Other liabilities	913	830
Total liabilities	$3,112	$2,840
Stockholders' equity:		
Common stock	$ 2	$ 2
Additional paid-in capital	97	97
Retained earnings	4,249	3,971
Treasury stock	-1,589	-1,544
Accumulated other comprehensive income (loss)	-683	-497
Total stockholders' equity	$2,076	$2,029
Total liabilities and stockholders' equity	$5,188	$4,869

Figure 22.1 *(Continued)*.

The basic equation underlying a balance sheet is:

$$\text{Assets} - \text{Liabilities} = \text{Equity}$$

which can also be expressed as:

$$\text{Assets} = \text{Liabilities} + \text{Equity}$$

The key thing to understand about a balance sheet is simply that it must *balance* at all times, hence the name. An increase in liabilities—issuing a bond, for example—causes an increase in assets—the cash received from the sale of the bond. If a firm generates huge profits that drive an increase in assets, equity also increases. This makes sense because the value of shareholders' investment in the firm rises if that firm starts making a ton of money. Let's go through the balance sheet bit by bit to get a better grasp on how it's put together.

Asset Accounts: Current Assets

The accounting gods define *current assets* as those likely to be used up or converted into cash within one business cycle, usually defined as one year. The major portions of this category are cash and equivalents, short-term investments, accounts receivable, and inventories.

Cash and Equivalents and Short-Term Investments: These line items don't necessarily refer to actual greenbacks sitting around in a vault but to money in low-risk, fairly liquid investments. "Cash and equivalents" usually contains money market funds or anything that can be liquidated quickly and with minimal price risk, whereas "short-term investments" is similar to cash—usually, bonds that have less than a year to maturity and earn a higher rate of return than cash but would take a bit of effort to sell. In most cases, you can mentally lump this in with cash when considering how much a firm has on hand to meet an immediate need.

Dell Computer Corporation: Partial Balance Sheet		
Assets (millions)	2003	2002
Current assets		
Cash and cash equivalents	$4,232	$3,641
Short-term investments	406	273
Accounts receivable—net	2,586	2,269
Inventories	306	278
Other	1,394	1,416
Total current assets	$8,924	$7,877

Figure 22.2   Dell's current assets. *Source:* Dell SEC filings.

Accounts Receivable: As we saw in the hot dog example, accounts receivable are bills that the company hasn't yet collected but for which it expects to receive payment soon. Watch how this account changes relative to the company's sales—if accounts receivable are rising much faster than sales, the firm is booking a large amount of revenue for which it has not yet received payment. This can be a sign of trouble because it may mean that the firm is offering looser credit terms to increase sales—remember, a firm can record a sale as soon as it has shipped the product—but has less likelihood of ever receiving the cash it's owed.

In Figure 22.2, Dell looks like it was in fine shape on this front. Dell's accounts receivable rose about 14%, but sales increased by the same amount, as we'll see later when we look at the company's income statement.

However, H-P's accounts receivable (see Figure 22.3) took a huge jump from $4.488 billion to $8.456 billion, which was a 90% increase, whereas sales rose only about 25%. (Remember, comparing the growth rate of accounts receivable with the growth rate of sales is a good way to judge whether a company is doing a good job collecting the money that it's owed by customers.)

Hewlett-Packard Company and Subsidiaries: Partial Balance Sheet

Assets (millions)	2002	2001
Current assets		
Cash and cash equivalents	$11,192	$4,197
Short-term investments	237	139
Accounts receivable, net of allowance for doubtful accounts of $495 and $275 as of October 31, 2002 and 2001, respectively	8,456	4,488
Financing receivables, net of allowance for doubtful accounts of $184 and $68 as of October 31, 2002 and 2001, respectively	3,453	2,183
Inventory	5,797	5,204
Other current assets	6,940	5,094
Total current assets	$36,075	$21,305

Figure 22.3   Hewlett-Packard's assets. *Source:* Hewlett-Packard SEC filings.

Although H-P's results were somewhat distorted by its acquisition of Compaq during this time period, that's still a big discrepancy. At the time, H-P investors would have wanted to keep an eye on accounts receivable to make sure that the firm collected the cash that it was owed by customers.

You'll often see an "allowance for doubtful accounts" just after accounts receivable on the balance sheet. This is the company's estimate of how much money it's owed by deadbeat customers, and which it's consequently unlikely to collect. For example, on H-P's balance sheet, you can see that the firm was assuming that it wouldn't collect $495 million of the money that customers owed it as of October 2002.

Inventories: There are several types of inventories, including raw materials that have not yet been made into a finished product, partially finished products, and finished products that have not yet been sold. Inventories are especially important to watch in manufacturing and retail firms, and their value on the balance sheet should be taken with a grain of salt. Because of the way inventories are accounted for, their liquidation value may very well be a far cry from their value on the balance sheet. Use your common sense when judging this: Although a construction firm could probably get a decent price if it needed to sell off some extra steel girders it had lying around in inventory, a retailer that needed to sell last fall's teen fashions would likely have to take pennies on the dollar.

More importantly, inventories soak up capital—cash that's been converted into inventory sitting in a warehouse can't be used for anything else. The speed at which a company turns over its inventory can have a huge impact on profitability because the less time cash is tied up in inventory, the more time it's available for use elsewhere. You can calculate a metric called *inventory turnover* by dividing a company's cost of goods sold by its inventory level.

For example, Dell's cost of goods sold for 2002 was $25.6 billion (see Figure 22.4) and inventory was $278 million (see Figure 22.2), yielding an incredible inventory turnover rate of 92. In other words, Dell went through its entire inventory 92 times over the course of the year. Contrast this with H-P, which had a cost of goods sold of $34.5 billion (see Figure 22.5) and inventory of $5.8 billion for 2002, yielding much lower inventory turns of just 6. As you can see, H-P lets inventory sit around much longer than Dell, which is not a great idea when you consider how fast high-tech equipment loses its value.

Dell Computer Corporation: Partial Income Statement			
In millions Fiscal year ending	2003	2002	2001
Net revenue	$35,404	$31,168	$31,888
Cost of revenue	29,055	25,661	25,445

Figure 22.4   Dell's revenue and cost of revenue. *Source:* Dell SEC filings.

Asset Accounts: Noncurrent Assets

Noncurrent assets are assets that are not expected to be converted into cash or used up within the reporting period. The big parts of this section are property, plant, and equipment (PP&E); investments; and intangible assets.

Property, Plant, and Equipment: These are long-term assets that form the infrastructure of the company: land, buildings, factories, furniture, equipment, and so forth. Dell, for example, had about $913 million in PP&E at the end of 2002, whereas H-P had $6.9 billion.

If we compare these numbers to the firms' total assets (see Figures 22.6 and 22.7, we can get a feel for how capital-intensive the firms are—Dell's PP&E makes up about 6% of its total assets, whereas almost 10% of H-P's assets are in PP&E. Therefore, H-P is more capital-intensive than Dell.

Hewlett-Packard: Partial Consolidated Statement of Income			
For the following years ended October 31 In millions, except per share amounts	2002	2001	2000
Net revenue			
Products	$45,955	$38,005	$41,653
Costs and expenses			
Cost of products	$34,573	$28,863	$30,343

Figure 22.5   Hewlett-Packard's revenue breakdown. *Source:* Hewlett-Packard SEC filings.

Dell Computer Corporation: Partial Balance Sheet

Assets (millions)	2003	2002
Property, plant, and equipment, net	$ 913	$ 826
Investments	5,267	4,373
Other noncurrent assets	366	459
Total assets	$15,470	$13,535

Figure 22.6   Dell's assets. *Source:* Dell SEC filings.

Investments: This is money invested in either longer term bonds or in the stock of other companies, ranging from a token amount to a substantial stake. It's not nearly as liquid as cash and might be worth more or less on the market than the amount shown on the balance sheet. You'll need to dig around in the notes to the financial statements to see what exactly is in this account and with how much skepticism you should view its value. You can see in Figures 22.6 and 22.7 that H-P has no long-term investments, but Dell has a pretty sizeable amount—about $5.3 billion—sitting on its bal-

Hewlett-Packard Company and Subsidiaries: Partial Balance Sheet

Assets (millions)	2002	2001
Property, plant, and equipment, net of accumulated depreciation of $5,612 and $5,411 as of October 31, 2002 and 2001, respectively	$ 6,924	$ 4,397
Long-term financing receivables and other assets	7,760	6,126
Goodwill	15,089	667
Purchased intangible assets	4,862	89
Total assets	$70,710	$32,584

Figure 22.7   Hewlett-Packard's assets. *Source:* Hewlett-Packard SEC filings.

ance sheet. Because that's almost a third of Dell's total assets, it's definitely something you'd want to dig into. (Turns out that Dell's investments were mainly bonds, so you wouldn't need to worry too much about them—if they were equities or venture capital, you'd want to find out more about that $5.3 billion value.)

Intangible Assets: The most common form of intangible assets is goodwill, which arises when one company acquires another. Goodwill is the difference between the price the acquiring company pays and tangible value—or equity—of the target company. Essentially, goodwill represents the value of all of the other stuff that one company gets when it acquires another. For example, the majority of Coca-Cola's value is not in the firm's buildings and equipment; it's in the powerful brand that Coke has built up over the past several decades. If some firm were to buy Coke, it would have to pay far more than the *book* value of Coke's equity, and that extra amount is called goodwill.

You should view this account with extreme skepticism because most companies tend to overpay for their targets, which means the value of goodwill that shows up on the balance sheet is very often far more than the asset is actually worth. (In 2003, for example, AOL Time Warner reduced the value of the goodwill on its balance sheet by an amazing 40% with the stroke of a pen, essentially admitting that it had far overpaid for AOL when the two companies merged. If you'd been counting on this goodwill account as an asset that the company had at its disposal, you'd have been sorely disappointed.)

As you can see in Figure 22.7, H-P had more than $15 billion—or almost 20% of its total assets of $71 billion—in its goodwill account for 2002. Was Compaq really worth $15 billion more than the value of its cash, inventory, fixed assets, customer lists, and patents? Maybe it was—but if it's not, H-P will have to reduce the value of this account at some point in the future, which means the value of the firm's total assets will also drop.

Liability Accounts: Current Liabilities

Now that we know what the company owns, we can look at the other side of the coin—what it owes.

Current liabilities are the flip side of current assets: money the company expects to pay out within a year. You should focus on accounts payable and short-term borrowings or payables.

Accounts Payable: These are bills the company owes to somebody else and are due to be paid within a year, like Mike's IOU to the grocer for the extra hot dog buns. Large companies that have a lot of leverage over their suppliers can push out some of their payables, which means they hold on to the cash longer—and that's good for cash flow.

Short-Term Borrowings: This refers to money the company has borrowed for a term of less than a year, usually to meet short-term needs. It's often a line of bank credit that the firm has temporarily drawn down, though it might also be a portion of long-term debt that's due within the next year. This line item becomes especially important for companies in financial distress because the entire amount often has to be paid back quickly. H-P's notes payable and short-term borrowings (see Figure 22.8) were about $1.8 billion, which is fairly small relative to the size of the firm's assets, so no worries there.

Liability Accounts: Noncurrent Liabilities

Noncurrent liabilities are the flip side of noncurrent assets. They represent money the company owes one year or more in the future. Though you'll sometimes see a variety of line items under this heading, the most important one by far is long-term debt. This represents money the company has

Hewlett-Packard Company and Subsidiaries: Partial Balance Sheet

Liabilities and Stockholder's Equity (millions)	2002	2001
Current liabilities		
Notes payable and short-term borrowings	$1,793	$1,722

Figure 22.8 Hewlett-Packard's current liabilities. *Source:* Hewlett-Packard SEC filings.

borrowed—usually by issuing bonds, though sometimes from a bank—that doesn't need to be paid back for a few years.

Stockholders' Equity

Remember, shareholders' equity is equal to total assets minus total liabilities, and it represents the part of the company owned by shareholders. This can be the most confusing section of any firm's financial statements, because it's filled with many anachronistic line items that have little practical relevance.

The only account worth looking at is retained earnings, which basically records the amount of capital a company has generated over its lifetime—minus dividends and stock buybacks, which represent funds that have already been returned to shareholders. Retained earnings is a cumulative account; therefore, each year that the company makes a profit and doesn't pay it all out as dividends, retained earnings increase. Likewise, if a company has lost money over time, retained earnings can turn negative and is often renamed "accumulated deficit" on the balance sheet. Think of this account as a company's long-term track record at generating profits.

The Income Statement

Now that we know how much a company owns and how much it owes, we can move on to the good stuff—how much money it's making (or losing.) In a 10-K, you'll usually see the income statement labeled as the "consolidated statement of income" or the "consolidated statement of earnings" (see Figure 22.9).

Revenue

Sometimes labeled "sales," this is simply how much money the company has brought in during a quarter or a year. Larger companies sometimes break down revenues on the income statement according to business sector, geographic region, or products versus services.

Be sure to check the "revenue recognition policies" buried in the financial statements so you know what you're looking at—companies can record revenue at different times depending on the business that they're in. A software firm, for example, might record a big chunk of revenue when a product is

ACME Corporation: Income Statement

(In millions)	2002	2001	2000
Net sales	$5,444	$5,351	$5,566
Cost of goods sold	2,832	2,916	2,929
Gross profit	$2,612	$2,435	$2,637
Selling, general and administrative	$1,240	$1,345	$1,313
Research and development expenses	357	361	367
Other expenses (income)		-29	-62
Operating income	$1,015	$ 758	$1,019
Interest expense	$ 27	$ 41	$ 37
Interest and other income (loss)	13	12	9
Pretax income	$1,002	$ 729	$ 991
Provision for income taxes	$ 322	$ 234	$ 342
Net income	$ 680	$ 495	$ 650
Earnings per common share			
Basic	$ 2.78	$ 2.01	$ 2.63
Diluted	2.75	1.98	2.57
Weighted average shares outstanding			
Basic	244.2	246.7	246.7
Diluted	247.4	249.3	252.5

Figure 22.9   ACME Corporation's income statement. *Source:* Morningstar, Inc.

shipped to a customer, whereas a service firm might record revenue smoothly over the life of the service contract.

Cost of Sales

Also known as cost of goods sold, this number represents the expenses most directly involved in creating revenue, such as labor costs, raw materials (for manufacturers), or the wholesale price of goods (for retailers). Large companies that combine manufacturing with services (H-P, for example) sometimes break down this number into cost of goods sold and cost of services.

Gross Profit

This doesn't appear on all income statements, but it's simply revenue minus cost of sales. Once you have gross profit, you can calculate a gross margin, which is gross profit as a percentage of revenue. Essentially, this tells you how much a company is able to mark up its goods. As you can see in Figure 22.10, Dell has a gross margin of only 17.9% ($6.3 billion in gross profit divided by $35.4 billion in sales) because it sells commodity products. It's tough for Dell to charge much of a premium for the computers it sells.

H-P, meanwhile, sells higher end computer gear for which its customers are more willing to pay up. If you look at Figure 22.11, you can see this in its gross margin: Take product revenue of $45.9 billion, subtract product costs of $34.6 billion, and we have a gross profit of $11.4 billion. Divide that back into revenue, and we're left with a gross margin of 24.8%. As you can see, the more differentiated a company's products are, the more it can mark up its goods over what it costs to manufacture them. H-P also bundles proprietary software with a lot of the computers it sells, and software has very high gross margins.

Selling, General, and Administrative Expenses (SG&A)

This number, also known as operating expenses, includes items such as marketing, administrative salaries, and, sometimes, research and development.

Dell Computer Corporation: Partial Income Statement

In millions, except per share amounts Fiscal year ending	2003	2002	2001
Net sales	$35,404	$31,168	$31,888
Cost of goods sold	29,055	25,661	25,445
Gross profit	$ 6,349	$ 5,507	$ 6,443

Figure 22.10   Dell's partial income statement. *Source:* Dell SEC filings.

Hewlett-Packard Company and Subsidiaries: Partial Income Statement

For the following years ended October 31 In millions, except per share amounts	2002	2001	2000
Net revenue			
Products	$45,955	$38,005	$41,653
Services	10,178	6,819	6,848
Financing income	455	402	369
Total net revenue	$56,588	$45,226	$48,870
Costs and expenses			
Cost of products	$34,573	$28,863	$30,343
Cost of services	6,817	4,396	4,470

Figure 22.11 Hewlett-Packard's partial income statement. *Source:* Hewlett-Packard SEC filings.

(Research and development is usually broken out as a separate line item, as is marketing for firms that spend large amounts on advertising.) You'll often see a relationship between SG&A and gross margin—firms that are able to charge more for their goods (e.g., H-P) have to spend more on salespeople and marketing. You can get a feel for how efficient a firm is by looking at SG&A as a percentage of revenues—a lower percentage of operating expenses relative to sales generally means a tighter, more cost-effective firm.

H-P, for example (see Figure 22.12), spent about 16%—or $9 billion—of its $56.5 billion in revenue on SG&A, whereas Dell spent only 8.9% of revenue on these types of costs.

Some of the difference results from the fact that Dell sells direct to customers and H-P has to pay salespeople to sell big-ticket computers to large corporations, but it still looks as though Dell runs a leaner shop than H-P.

Unfortunately, it's tough to give any hard-and-fast rules as to just how much a company should be spending on SG&A. Your best bet is to compare a company with its closest competitors to see which is able to do more with less and to look at SG&A as a percentage of sales over time. (If it's rising fast, watch out—the firm is spending more on overhead without reaping the benefit of higher sales.)

Dell Computer Corporation: Partial Income Statement			
(In millions)	2003	2002	2001
Selling, general, and administrative	$3,050	$2,784	$3,193

Hewlett-Packard Company and Subsidiaries: Partial Income Statement			
(In millions)	2002	2001	2000
Selling, general, and administrative	$9,033	$6,950	$6,984

Figure 22.12   Dell and Hewlett-Packard's partial income statements. *Source:* Dell/Hewlett-Packard SEC filings.

Depreciation and Amortization

When a company buys an asset intended to last a long time, such as a new building or a piece of machinery, it charges off a portion of the cost of that asset on its income statement over a series of years. (Think back to Mike's grilling tongs.) This number is occasionally broken out separately on the income statement, but it's usually rolled into operating expenses. It's always included in the cash flow statement, though, so you can look there to see how much a company's net income was affected by noncash charges such as depreciation.

Nonrecurring Charges/Gains

This is the catch-all area where companies put all the one-time charges or gains that aren't part of their regular, ongoing operations, such as the cost of closing a factory or the gain from selling a division. Ideally, you'd want to see this area of the income statement blank most of the time.

You should view one-time expenses with a great deal of skepticism. Companies have gotten into the habit of rolling many costs that really are part of doing business into charges, and firms that are *serial chargers*—meaning that they seem to take some kind of hit every year—are much more difficult to analyze because all kinds of expenses can be buried in one-time charges. The reasons behind these charges are always detailed in the notes section of a firm's financial statements, which you should certainly read to understand what caused the charges.

As you can see in Figure 22.13, H-P took a $1.8 billion charge in 2002 for restructuring, a $793 million charge for "in process research and development," and another $700 million in other assorted charges related to its merger with Compaq. Although a merger of this size doesn't occur every day, which means we can cut H-P some slack, we can also see that H-P had a good-sized restructuring charge of $384 million in 2001. If I owned H-P, I'd want to look very carefully at all of those charges to make sure they really were nonrecurring because serial charging is a sign of bad faith on management's part.

Operating Income

This number is equal to revenues minus cost of sales and all operating expenses. Theoretically, it represents the profit the company made from its actual operations, as opposed to interest income, one-time gains, and so forth. In practice, companies often include nonrecurring expenses (such as write-offs) in figuring operating income, and you have to add back one-time charges (or subtract one-time gains) yourself.

Operating income is as close to a solid bottom-line number as you're going to get for most firms. Because it excludes most one-time items, as well as income from nonoperational sources such as investments, you can use it to calculate an *operating margin,* which is fairly comparable across firms and across industries.

Hewlett-Packard Company and Subsidiaries: Partial Income Statement			
For the following years ended October 31 In millions, except per share amounts	2002	2001	2000
Restructuring charges	$1,780	$384	$102
In-process research and development charges	793	35	—
Acquisition-related charges	701	25	—

Figure 22.13 Hewlett-Packard's partial income statement. *Source:* Hewlett-Packard SEC filings.

Interest Income/Expense

Sometimes interest income and interest expense are listed separately, and sometimes they are combined into net interest income (or expense, as the case may be). In either case, this number represents interest the company has paid on bonds it has issued or received on bonds or cash that it owns. You can get some insight into the financial health of a firm by looking at its earnings before interest and taxes relative to its interest expense, which is called an *interest coverage ratio*. This tells you the extent to which a firm's profits can cover needed interest payments. I talk more about such financial-health measures in the next chapter.

Taxes

Uncle Sam has to get paid, and tax information is usually the last expense listed before net income. Unfortunately, corporate taxation is an extremely complex topic because companies submit a completely separate set of financial statements to the IRS for tax purposes than the ones you and I see filed with the SEC. (There are a whole host of reasons for this—the biggest cause is different depreciation schedules—but it's not something you need to worry about.)

In general, the tax rate for U.S. corporations is around 35%. If the tax rate for a company you're analyzing is much lower than this, find out why, and find out whether that tax advantage is likely to be permanent or temporary. Some firms get tax breaks because they're located outside the United States, even if the bulk of their sales are made here in the States.

In addition, look at the tax rate of the firm you're analyzing over time. If it bounces around from year to year, the firm may be generating earnings by playing with tax loopholes rather than selling more goods or services. Tax advantages are nice to have, but politicians have a bad habit of taking them away at inopportune times, so it's not money you want to necessarily count on.

Net Income

This number represents (at least theoretically) the company's profit after all expenses have been paid, and it's the number most companies highlight in their quarterly earnings releases. As we saw in the Mike's hot dog example, net income may or may not be a good representation of the amount of cash the company has generated. For that, we'll need to look at the statement of cash flows. Although net income is the number you'll most often see companies tout in their press releases, don't forget that it can be wildly distorted by one-time charges and/or investment income.

Number of Shares (Basic and Diluted)

This figure represents the number of shares used in calculating earnings per share; it represents the average number of shares outstanding during the reporting period (a quarter or a year). Basic shares include only actual shares of stock, and you should pretty much ignore it—the fact that it's still recorded in financial statements is more of a historical legacy than anything else.

Diluted shares, however, include securities that could potentially be converted into shares of stock, such as stock options and convertible bonds. Given the amount of egregious granting of stock options that has occurred over the past several years, it's the diluted number that you'll want to look at, because you

Dell Computer Corporation: Partial Income Statement			
(In millions)	2003	2002	2001
Weighted average shares outstanding			
Basic	$2,584	$2,602	$2,582
Diluted	2,644	2,726	2,746

Hewlett-Packard Company and Subsidiaries: Partial Income Statement			
(In millions)	2002	2001	2000
Weighted average shares used to compute net (loss) earnings per share			
Basic	$2,499	$1,936	$1,979
Diluted	2,499	1,974	2,077

Figure 22.14   Dell and Hewlett-Packard's partial income statements. *Source:* Dell/Hewlett-Packard SEC filings.

want to know the degree to which your stake in the firm could potentially be shrunk (or diluted) if all those option-holders convert their options into shares.

You can see in Figure 22.14 that H-P's basic and diluted shares are the same but that Dell has about 2% more diluted shares. Because diluted shares can be as much as 5% or more higher than basic shares, that's not a huge amount of dilution.

Earnings per Share (Basic and Diluted)

This number, which represents net income divided by number of shares, usually gets the most attention when a company reports its quarterly or annual results. It's not the end-all, be-all of corporate financial performance, though—in fact, without looking at cash flow and many other factors, it's mostly meaningless. So when you read in the paper that a firm "beat" or "missed" earnings per share estimates, don't get excited. Find out *why* instead.

The Statement of Cash Flows

This statement is the true touchstone for corporate value creation because it shows how much cash a company is generating from year to year—and cash is what counts (see Figure 22.15). In fact, I would almost recommend that you look at the statement of cash flows first when evaluating a company to see how much cash it's throwing off, then look at the balance sheet to test the firmness of its financial foundation, and only then look at the income statement to check out margins and such.

The cash flow statement strips away all the abstract, noncash items such as depreciation that you see on the income statement and tells you how much actual cash the company has generated. Many of the items on this statement are also found on either the income statement or the balance sheet, but here they're rearranged to highlight the cash generated and how it relates to reported earnings. The cash flow statement is divided into three parts: cash flows from operating activities, from investing activities, and from financing activities.

The "cash flows from operating activities" section comes first and it tells you how much cash the company generated from its business. This is the area to focus most of your attention on because it's the cash-generating power of

ACME Corporation: Cash Flow Statement

(In millions)	2002	2001	2000
Cash flows from operating activities			
Net income	$ 680	$ 495	$ 650
Adjustments to reconcile net income to net cash provided by operating activities			
Depreciation and amortization	318	363	342
Deferred income tax provision	193	0	30
Pension contribution	-362	-52	-50
Changes in assets and liabilities			
Accounts receivable	-15	115	-57
Inventories	53	65	-87
Other current assets	41	-32	-23
Other assets	-25	36	-6
Accounts payable and other current liabilities	97	50	51
Other liabilities	83	5	-18
Net cash provided by operating activities	$1,063	$1,044	$ 831
Cash flows from investing activities			
(Capital expenditures)	$ -254	$ -327	$-372
(Acquisitions)	-419	-73	-157
Asset sales	28	38	35
Other investing cash flows	4	12	36
Net cash used in investing activities	$ -642	$ -350	$-458

Figure 22.15   ACME Corporation's cash flow statement. *Source:* Morningstar, Inc.

the business that we're most interested in. Dell's statement of cash flows is on page 298 so you can follow along (see Figure 22.16).

Net Income
This figure is simply taken from the income statement. All the items below it are added to or subtracted from net income to get the end result, "net cash

Cash flows from financing activities			
Purchase and retirement of short-term debt	$ -45	$ -7	$ -79
Purchases and retirement of long-term debt	207	43	157
Purchase or sale of stock	-140	-287	-130
Dividends paid to stockholders	-323	-316	-306
Other financing cash flows	-26	-6	-20
Net cash used in financing activities	$ -327	$ -572	$-377
Effect of exchange rate change on cash	$ -14	$ 1	$ 31
Increase (decrease) in cash and cash equivalents	$ 79	$ 123	$ 27
Cash and cash equivalents at beginning of period	$ 205	$ 82	$ 55
Cash and cash equivalents at end of period	284	205	82

Figure 22.15 *(Continued).*

provided by operating activities." In Dell's case, we start with the same $2.1 billion that was reported on the income statement.

Depreciation and Amortization

This is not a cash charge—remember, Mike didn't have to pay anyone just because his grilling tongs started to wear out—so we need to add it back to net income. In Dell's case, we add back $211 million.

Tax Benefit from Employee Stock Plans

When an employee exercises stock options, the employer gets to deduct the gain received by the employee against its corporate income. (Employee compensation is generally tax deductible.) Because the result is a lower tax bill, we need to add back the tax benefit to the already-taxed net income. Be wary of this line item—if it's large relative to total operating cash flow and the company's stock has been zooming upwards, you shouldn't count on this cash being around in the future. When the shares sink, fewer employees will exercise their options, and the company will receive a smaller cash tax benefit. As you can see, Dell's tax benefit from stock option exercises dropped in half between 2001 and 2002

Dell Computer Corporation: Partial Statement of Cash Flows

In millions Fiscal year ending	January 31, 2003	February 1, 2002	February 2, 2001
Cash flows from operating activities			
Net income	$2,122	$1,246	$2,177
Adjustments to reconcile net income to *net cash provided by operating activities*			
Depreciation and amortization	211	239	240
Tax benefits of employee stock plans	260	487	929
Special charges	—	742	105
(Gains)/losses on investments	(67)	17	(307)
Other, primarily effects of exchange rate changes on monetary assets and liabilities denominated in foreign currencies	(410)	178	135
Changes in			
Operating working capital	$1,210	$ 826	$ 642
Noncurrent assets and liabilities	212	62	274
Net cash provided by operating activities	$3,538	$3,797	$4,195

Figure 22.16 Dell's partial cash flow statement. *Source:* Dell SEC filings.

and sunk again in 2003. Over the same time period, Dell's stock wasn't such a hot performer—and that's not a coincidence.

Changes in Working Capital

Remember when Mike let some folks buy hot dogs on credit and owed money to the grocer for those extra buns? Both of those actions affected working capital, and they'd be accounted for here. If a company is owed more money by customers this year than it was last year, accounts receivable increase and cash flow decreases; if it owes more money to suppliers, accounts payable increase and so does cash flow. Finally, if a firm pumps more money into inventory that doesn't sell, cash flow decreases. Remember, inventory ties up capital.

In Dell's case, we need to go back to the balance sheet to see where the $1.2 billion entry for the line item came from (see Figure 22.17).

As you can see, accounts receivable increased from $2.269 billion to $2.586 billion, which ate up $317 million ($2.586 minus $2.269) because Dell's customers owed it more money at the end of fiscal 2003 than they did at the end of fiscal 2002. In addition, inventory increased a bit from $278 million to $306 million, which also used up cash because Dell increased the amount of capital it had tied up in inventory.

Meanwhile, accounts payable increased from $5.075 billion to $5.989 billion, which means that Dell owed $914 million more to its suppliers at the end of 2003 than it did at the end of 2002—and that meant more cash in Dell's pocket (see Figure 22.18).

So, we have $914 million in cash generated by an increase in accounts payable, minus the $317 million increase in accounts receivable, minus the $28 million change in inventory, which gives us $569 million in cash flow. Add in the $500 million increase in "accrued and other"—mainly warranties and employee bonuses that Dell may have to pay out in the future—as well as some other odds and ends detailed on the bowels of the financial filings, and you wind up with the $1.220 billion in "changes in operating working capital" that you see on Dell's cash flow statement.

Dell Computer Corporation: Partial Balance Sheet

For the following years ended October 31 In millions, except per share amounts	2003	2002
Current assets		
Cash and cash equivalents	$4,232	$3,641
Short-term investments	406	273
Accounts receivable—net	2,586	2,269
Inventories	306	278
Other	1,394	1,416

Figure 22.17 Dell's current assets. *Source:* Dell SEC filings.

Dell Computer Corporation: Partial Balance Sheet

Liabilities and stockholder's equity	2003	2002
Current liabilities		
Accounts payable	$5,989	$5,075
Accrued and other	2,944	2,444

Figure 22.18 Dell's current liabilities. *Source:* Dell SEC filings.

You don't need to go through all of this every time you look at a statement of cash flows because everything gets neatly netted out for you in the "net cash provided by operating activities" line. But because the "changes in working capital" entry is often the biggest cause of differences between net income and operating cash flow, this is an area that you'll want to pay attention to—hence our detailed analysis.

One-Time Charges
Remember these? Dell didn't have any, but H-P did (see Figure 22.19). Because most of these charges were noncash charges—that is, H-P didn't write a check made out to someone named Restructuring—they need to be added back when figuring cash flow (similar to depreciation, which is also noncash).

Hewlett-Packard Company and Subsidiaries: Partial Statement of Cash Flows

For the following years ended October 31 In millions	2002	2001	2000
Restructuring charges	$1,780	$384	$102
Acquisition-related charges, including in-process research and development	1,494	60	—

Figure 22.19 Hewlett-Packard's partial cash flow statement. *Source:* Hewlett-Packard SEC filings.

Net Cash Provided by Operating Activities

This is your holy grail for figuring out whether a company is generating cash. Also known as *operating cash flow,* it's the result of adding or subtracting the previous items from net income. It doesn't replace net income, but if you don't look at it in addition to net income, you're not getting the full picture because the two can often tell very different stories.

Now we arrive at the second portion of the statement of cash flows, the "cash flow from investing activities" section. These are activities that involve acquiring or disposing of PP&E, corporate acquisitions, and any sales or purchases of investments.

Capital Expenditures

This figure represents money spent on items that last a long time, such as PP&E—basically, anything needed to keep the business running and growing at its current rate. Operating cash flow minus capital expenditures equals free cash flow, or the amount of cash the company generates after investing in its business. We can see in Figure 22.20 that Dell spent $305 million on capex.

Investment Proceeds

Companies often take some of their excess cash and invest it in bonds or stocks in an effort to get a better return than they could in a basic savings account. This

Dell Computer Corporation: Partial Statement of Cash Flows

In millions Fiscal year ending	January 31, 2003	February 1, 2002	February 2, 2001
Cash flows from investing activities			
Investments:			
Purchases	$(8,736)	$(5,382)	$(2,606)
Maturities and sales	7,660	3,425	2,331
Capital expenditures	(305)	(303)	(482)
Net cash used in investing activities	$(1,381)	$(2,260)	$ (757)

Figure 22.20 Dell's partial cash flow statement. *Source:* Dell SEC filings.

number tells us how much money the company has made (or lost) on such investments. As you can see in Figure 22.20, Dell invested $8.7 billion of its cash in securities of one sort or another (purchases) and received $7.7 billion from previous investments that either reached maturity or were sold (maturities and sales).

The final portion of the statement of cash flows is the "cash flow from financing activities" section. Financing activities include any transactions with the company's owners or creditors. Items that typically show up in this section are briefly described next.

Dividends Paid

Unlike many line items, this one is just what it sounds like. You can see that H-P paid a total of $801 million in dividends in 2002 (see Figure 22.21).

Issuance/Purchase of Common Stock

This is an important number to look at because it indicates how a company is financing its activities. Rapidly growing companies often issue large amounts of new stock, which can dilute the value of existing shares but which also give the company cash for expansion. Slower growing companies that generate a lot of free cash flow tend to buy back significant amounts of their own stock, though companies that issue many stock options to their employees also buy back stock to minimize dilution.

You can see this kind of buyback activity in Figure 22.22 of Dell's financial statements printed to the right. Under "purchase of common stock," note that Dell spent $2.3 billion repurchasing its own stock, and on the income statement, you can see that the number of diluted shares outstanding fell about 3%, from 2.726 billion to 2.644 billion. Although share repurchases

Hewlett-Packard Company and Subsidiaries: Partial Statement of Cash Flows			
For the following years ended October 31 In millions	2002	2001	2000
Dividends	$(801)	$(621)	$(638)

Figure 22.21 Hewlett-Packard's partial cash flow statement. *Source:* Hewlett-Packard SEC filings.

Dell Computer Corporation: Partial Statement of Cash Flows

In millions Fiscal year ending	January 31, 2003	February 1, 2002	February 2, 2001
Cash flows from financing activities			
Purchase of common stock	$(2,290)	$(3,000)	$(2,700)
Issuance of common stock under employee plans and other	265	298	395
Net cash used in financing activities	$(2,025)	$(2,702)	$(2,305)

Figure 22.22 Dell's partial cash flow statement. *Source:* Dell SEC filings.

are generally a shareholder-friendly use of excess cash—after all, the fewer shares outstanding, the larger the piece of the company that each shareholder owns—you have to view share buybacks with caution when they come from firms such as Dell that grant large numbers of stock options. Firms that grant their employees a ton of options and then spend corporate cash on repurchases are essentially selling shares to their employees at low prices and buying it back on the open market at much higher prices, which is not the best use of capital.

Issuance/Repayments of Debt

This number tells you whether the company has borrowed money or repaid money it previously borrowed. In Figure 22.23, you can see that H-P received $2.5 billion from bondholders in exchange for some long-term debt and paid off $2.4 billion in short-term debt. You can see these two entries on the lines labeled "issuance of long-term debt" and "(decrease) in notes payable and short-term borrowings."

Conclusion

Painful though it may have been, you've just gained something very valuable: You now know enough about financial statements to meaningfully analyze a company. Although you can (and should) spend much more time learning the nooks and crannies of financial reporting, understanding how a company generates cash

Hewlett-Packard Company and Subsidiaries: Partial Statement of Cash Flows

For the following years ended October 31 In millions	2002	2001	2000
Cash flows from financing activities			
(Decrease) increase in notes payable and short-term borrowings	$(2,402)	$303	$(1,297)
Issuance of long-term debt	2,529	904	1,936
Payment of long-term debt	(472)	(290)	(474)

Figure 22.23 Hewlett-Packard's partial cash flow statement. *Source:* Hewlett-Packard SEC filings.

is now within your grasp, and that's what really matters. The details aren't nearly as important as the basic concepts that we've just walked through. Now that you've made it through most of this chapter, you're already ahead of the pack.

To wrap things up, let's follow a dollar through Dell to see what happens to it. A customer—let's call him Steven, just for kicks—buys a computer for $1,000 from Dell. Dell turns around and uses $821 to pay manufacturing employees and parts suppliers (cost of goods sold). How do I know this? Look at Dell's income statement (Figure 22.24): The firm spent $29,055/$35,404, or 82.1%, of every dollar in sales paying for the cost of manufacturing the computer, and 82.1% of $1,000 is $821. So. Dell has $179 of the $1,000 it received for the computer left over after paying for the cost of making the computer.

Now, look at the rest of the income statement (Figure 22.25) to see what happens to the remaining $179. About $86 is spent on television ads and cor-

Dell Computer Corporation: Partial Income Statement

	2003
Net revenue	$35,404
Cost of revenue	29,055
Gross margin	6,349

Figure 22.24 Dell's revenue breakdown. *Source:* Dell SEC filings.

Dell Computer Corporation: Partial Income Statement	
	2003
Operating expenses	
Selling, general, and administrative	$3,050
Research, development, and engineering	455
Special charges	—
Total operating expenses	$3,505
Operating income	2,844
Investment and other income (loss)—net	183
Income before income taxes and cumulative effect of change in accounting principle	3,027
Provision for income taxes	905
Income before cumulative effect of change in accounting principle	2,122
Cumulative effect of change in accounting principle—net	—
Net income	$2,122

Figure 22.25 Dell's partial income statement. *Source:* Dell SEC filings.

porate overhead (selling, general, and administrative), $13 goes to research and development, and another $25.50 goes to Uncle Sam. After adding back a little bit of investment income generated by Dell's huge cash balance, we're left with about $60 in net profit from the $1,000 computer sale. That $60 can be reinvested in the business, used to buy back stock, or simply kept in a bank account until a good opportunity comes along. You can calculate every single one of these numbers yourself right from Dell's income statement—just divide the line item by total sales, and multiply the resulting percentage by $1,000.

What do we now know about Dell's business? For one thing, we know that the profit margins are pretty low—with only about $60 in net profits of every $1,000 in sales, we can see that most of Dell's revenue goes right back out the door to the folks who build the computers, supply the parts, and run the company.

We also know that Dell doesn't spend much on R&D or marketing, which makes sense because the company is striving to be the low-cost producer in a commodity market. If Dell were a pharmaceutical company and spent only

1.5% of revenue on research, we'd get mighty worried. But R&D isn't all that important to Dell, so we're not too concerned about it.

There's much more you can learn about a company than this, and that's exactly what we do in the next chapter—we take what we've learned about financial statements and use it to generate analytical insights into how a business is functioning.

But don't overlook the power of this simple test: If you can't understand how a dollar flows from a company's customers back through to shareholders, something's amiss. Either the company's business model is too confusing or you need to do more digging before committing any of your money.

Investor's Checklist: Financial Statements Explained

▶ The balance sheet tells you how much a company owns, how much it owes, and the difference between the two, which represents the value of the money that shareholders have invested in the firm. Shareholders' equity in a firm is the value of the firm's assets minus its liabilities.

▶ Because the balance sheet must balance at all times, any change in assets or liabilities will cause a corresponding change in equity. If a firm generates huge profits that drive an increase in assets, equity will also increase.

▶ Keep an eye on the trend in accounts receivable compared with sales. If the firm is booking a large amount of revenue that hasn't yet been paid for, this can be a sign of trouble.

▶ When you're evaluating a company's liabilities, remember that debt is a fixed cost. A big chunk of long-term debt can be risky for a company because the interest has to be paid no matter how business is doing.

▶ Be wary of companies that report "nonrecurring" charges, particularly if they make a habit of it. All kinds of expenses can be buried in "one-time" charges.

▶ The statement of cash flows is the true touchstone for corporate value creation because it shows how much cash a company is generating from year to year—and cash is what counts. Look at the cash flow statement first.

▶ When you're analyzing a company, make sure you can understand how a dollar flows through the business. If you can't do this, you probably don't understand the company well enough to buy the stock.

23

Analyzing a Company— The Basics

Now that we have the basic tools of financial statement analysis in hand, we can start tearing into companies. Because this can be a daunting task, I suggest that you break down the process into five areas:

1. *Growth:* How fast has the company grown, what are the sources of its growth, and how sustainable is that growth likely to be?
2. *Profitability:* What kind of a return does the company generate on the capital it invests?
3. *Financial health:* How solid is the firm's financial footing?
4. *Risks/bear case:* What are the risks to your investment case? There are excellent reasons *not* to invest in even the best-looking firms. Make sure you look at the full story and investigate the negatives as well as the positives.
5. *Management:* Who's running the show? Are they running the company for the benefit of shareholders or themselves? This is such a critical topic that I've devoted an entire chapter (Chapter 24) to it.

One word of caution: In this chapter and the next, we'll be concerned only with evaluating the quality of the *company*. However, this is only half the story because even the best companies are poor investments if purchased at too high a price. We'll cover how to evaluate *stocks* in Chapters 26 and 27, where I'll show you how to estimate the right price to pay for a company's shares.

Growth

The allure of strong growth has probably led more investors into temptation than anything else. High growth rates are heady stuff—a company that manages to increase its earnings at 15% for five years will double its profits, and who wouldn't want to do that? Unfortunately, a slew of academic research shows that strong earnings growth is not very persistent over a series of years; in other words, a track record of high earnings growth does not necessarily lead to high earnings growth in the future.

Why is this? Because the total economic pie is growing only so fast—after all, the long-run aggregate growth of corporate earnings has historically been slightly slower than the growth of the economy—strong and rapidly growing profits attract intense competition. Companies that are growing fast and piling up profits soon find other companies trying to get a piece of the action for themselves.

You can't just look at a series of past growth rates and assume that they'll predict the future—if investing were that easy, money managers would be paid much less, and this book would be much shorter. It's critical to investigate the *sources* of a company's growth rate and assess the *quality* of the growth. High-quality growth that comes from selling more goods and entering new markets is more sustainable than low-quality growth that's generated by cost-cutting or accounting tricks.

The Four Sources

In the long run, sales growth drives earnings growth. Although profit growth can outpace sales growth for a while if a company is able to do an excellent job cutting costs or fiddling with the financial statements, this kind of situation simply isn't sustainable over the long haul—there's a limit to how much costs can be cut, and there are only so many financial tricks that companies can use to boost the bottom line. In general, sales growth stems from one of four areas:

1. Selling more goods or services
2. Raising prices
3. Selling new goods or services
4. Buying another company

The easiest way to grow is to do whatever you're doing better than your competitors, sell more products than they do, and steal market share from them. Mobile-phone giant Nokia, for example, increased its share of the global mobile phone market from around 15% in the mid-1990s to around 35% today by simply doing a better job selling phones.

Raising prices can also be a great way for companies to boost their top lines, although it takes a strong brand or a captive market to be able to do it successfully for very long. Anheuser-Busch, for example, has historically been able to raise prices by 1% to 3% per year because it has a strong portfolio of popular brands such as Budweiser, Bud Lite, and Michelob.

Cable companies have also used pricing power to increase their top lines, though it's due more to monopoly power than strong brands. Throughout the 1990s, most markets had only one cable provider for any given consumer, so cable firms were able to push through annual price increases of 6% to 7%.

If there's not much more market share to be taken or your customers are very price-sensitive, you can do what Wal-Mart did and expand your market by selling products that you hadn't sold before. In the mid-1980s, founder and then-CEO Sam Walton saw that the firm's growth was likely to hit a wall at some point in the ensuing decade, so he began investigating new markets. After a trip to Europe, where European retailers had begun to build hypermarkets that sold everything from clothes to toys to ketchup under one roof, Walton figured that groceries could be Wal-Mart's next big market. Fifteen years later, Wal-Mart is the largest seller of groceries in the United States, and supercenters that include food sales account for an ever-larger percentage of its sales.

Remember, the goal of this type of analysis is simply to know why a company is growing. In Anheuser-Busch's case, you'd want to know how much growth is coming from price increases (more expensive beer), how much is coming from volume increases (more beer drinkers), and how much is coming from market share growth (more Budweiser drinkers). Once you're able to segment a firm's growth rate into its components, you'll have a much better handle on where that growth is likely to come from in the future—and when it may tap out.

The fourth source of sales growth—acquisitions—deserves special attention. Acquisitive firms are often darlings of Wall Street because they're major consumers of investment banking services. They're often looking to either raise capital for a new acquisition or find a new target, which means they constantly have folks in suits lining up at their door trying to pitch them on deals. It shouldn't come as any surprise, then, that the analysts that follow acquisition-hungry firms usually have nice things to say.

Unfortunately, the historical track record for acquisitions is mixed. Most acquisitions fail to produce positive gains for shareholders of the acquiring firm, and one study showed that even acquisitions of small, related businesses—which you'd think would have a good chance of working out well—succeeded only about half the time.[1]

There are a host of reasons for this. For one, acquisitive firms have to keep buying bigger and bigger firms to keep growing at the same rate— and the bigger a target firm is, the harder it is to check out thoroughly, which increases the risk of buying a pig in a poke. Even Warren Buffett found this out when Berkshire Hathaway bought GenRe, a huge reinsurance firm, in 1998. Buffett knows more about insurance than almost anyone alive, but the GenRe purchase turned out to be less than stellar. Buffett himself said some time after the deal that GenRe was in worse shape than he'd thought when he bought it. Not even the savviest of CEOs can know all the skeletons that may be lurking in a huge target firm.

Another reason to be skeptical of acquisitive firms is simply that buying other companies takes time and money. Targets have to be investigated, in-

---

[1] Mark L. Sirower, *The Synergy Trap* (New York: Free Press, 1997).

vestment bankers have to be paid, and acquired firms have to be integrated into the new owner, all of which steals resources away from running the core business. If executives are spending all of their energy looking for ways to make the firm bigger, rather than better, the wheels are sure to come off the cart eventually.

From the investor's perspective, however, the biggest reason to be leery of a growth-by-acquisition strategy is even simpler: It makes the company more difficult to understand. Acquisitive firms usually post many merger-related charges and often wind up restating their financial results, which means the results of the acquiring company can be obscured in all the merger-related confusion. As a result, two things can happen:

1. An unscrupulous management team can use the fog created by constant acquisitions to artificially juice results, and this financial tinkering can take a long time to come to light because it's buried in the necessary financial rejiggering that comes with any sizeable acquisition.
2. The true growth rate of the underlying business may be impossible to figure out, especially if management is evasive about giving out information on the firm's organic growth rate.

Bottom line: If you don't know how fast the company would have grown *without* acquisitions, don't buy the shares—because you never know when the acquisitions will stop. Remember, the goal of a successful investor is to buy great businesses, not successful merger and acquisition machines.

Questioning Quality

As you might have guessed, I generally view acquisitions as a very low-quality way of generating growth. Unfortunately, there are plenty of other ways of making growth look better than it really is, especially when we turn our attention to *earnings* growth rather than *sales* growth. (Sales growth is much more difficult to fake.) Although the list of tricks that companies can use to boost earnings growth even as sales growth falters is a long one, there are a few basic areas to watch out for: Changing tax rates, changing share counts, pension

IBM Growth Rates	1995	1996	1997	1998	1999	2000	2001	2002
Revenue %	12.3	5.6	3.4	4.0	7.2	1.0	-2.9	-5.5
Operating income %	51.7	13.2	5.8	0.7	30.2	-2.5	-20.1	-26.9
Earnings per share %	43.7	41.4	17.6	9.3	25.2	7.8	-2.0	-28.0

Figure 23.1   Annual growth rates for IBM.

gains, one-time gains (often from selling off businesses), and rampant cost cutting are among the most common. (I'll show you the full spectrum of earnings-management tricks in Chapter 25.)

In general, any time that earnings growth outstrips sales growth over a long period—for example, 5 to 10 years—you need to dig into the numbers to see how the company keeps squeezing out more profits from stagnant sales. A big difference between the growth rate of net income and operating income or cash flow from operations can also hint at something unsustainable.

IBM is a classic example of what I call "manufactured growth," because it used almost all of the previously mentioned techniques to pump up its bottom line during the 1990s. As shown in Figure 23.1, Big Blue's earnings per share growth looks pretty good since the Lou Gerstner-led turnaround began in the early 1990s—close to double digits most years, which is not bad for a company of this size.

But when we look at operating income, it looks as though the company was growing much slower, while sales growth was stuck around 5% on average. As a double-check, take a quick look at cash flow from operations—unfortunately, this also looks pretty stagnant from 1995 through the end of the decade (see Figure 23.2).

So what was driving those great earnings-per-share results that Gerstner's IBM kept turning like clockwork? A whole host of items: For one, the firm's tax rate plunged from 46% in 1995 to around 30% by the end of the decade.

IBM	95	96	97	98	99	00	01	02
Cash flow ($bil)	10.7	10.3	8.9	9.3	10.1	9.3	14.3	13.8

Figure 23.2   Annual cash flow from operations for IBM.

For another, the firm cut overhead spending substantially during the 1990s—a laudable accomplishment, given the bureaucratic nature of the firm.

Finally, IBM bought back about a quarter of its shares during the latter half of the 1990s—fewer shares outstanding meant more earnings per share—and benefited from an overfunded pension plan that boosted earnings. As you can see, a simple comparison of IBM's earnings per share relative to its operating income and cash flow raised many red flags—enough that any investor looking at the company in the late 1990s could have been skeptical about the quality of the firm's earnings growth. (Note: Low-quality growth doesn't imply that a company is cooking the books, merely that the growth rate isn't likely to be sustained over the long haul.)

You should also keep an eye out for one-time gains and losses that can distort a historical growth rate. A big gain from the sale of a division, for example, can make growth look better than it really was. Large losses can also affect growth rates—if a company's earnings were depressed in the first year of a three- or five-year period, the firm's growth rate will be overstated because growth will be calculated from a depressed base. So don't take the trailing three-year and five-year growth rates that you see as gospel—always check to see what's behind the numbers.

In general, any time you can't pinpoint the sources of a company's growth rate—or the reasons for a sharp divergence between the top and bottom lines, as was the case with Big Blue—you should be wary of the quality of that growth rate. Paying less taxes and buying back shares are good things for shareholders, no question, but they're short-term fixes rather than long-term sources of earnings growth.

A word on cost cutting: All things equal, I'd rather own a more efficient firm—one with lower overhead costs—than a less efficient firm. However, cost cuts are not a sustainable long-term source of earnings growth, and if you're looking at a firm that's been slashing costs, you should be aware that at some point there won't be any more costs to cut. Earnings growth will eventually slow unless sales growth speeds up.

At some point, a cost-cutting firm is going to find that it has become as efficient as possible, and sales and earnings growth will converge unless the firm manages to boost revenue growth. So when you see a firm with earnings gains being driven by cost cutting, make sure you think about the sustainability of those cost cuts because they won't be around forever.

Profitability

Now we come to the second—and, in many ways, most crucial—part of the analysis process: How much profit is the company generating relative to the amount of money invested in the business? This is the real key to separating great companies from average ones, because the job of any company is to take money from outside investors and invest it to generate a return. The higher that return, the more attractive the business.

I've already briefly discussed profit margins and the importance of understanding whether cost cuts or price hikes are driving an increase in profit margins. Comparing cash flow from operations to reported earnings per share is another good way to get a rough idea of a firm's profitability because cash flow from operations represents real profits.

But neither net margin nor cash flow from operations accounts for the amount of capital that's tied up in the business, and that's something we can't ignore. We need to know how much economic profit a firm is able to generate per *dollar of capital employed* because it will have more excess profits to reinvest, which will give it an advantage over less-efficient competitors.

Think about it this way—a company's management is similar to the manager of a mutual fund. A mutual fund manager takes investors' money and earns a return on it by investing in stocks and bonds. Wouldn't you rather put your money with an equity manager who has consistently generated returns of 12% per year than one who has returned an average of only 9% per year?

Companies aren't much different. They take shareholders' money and invest it in their own businesses to create wealth. By measuring the return that a company's management has achieved through this investment process, we know how good they are at efficiently transforming capital into profits. Just like a mutual fund, a company whose management is investing well enough to generate returns on capital of 12% is usually a more attractive investment than a company that returns only 9% on its capital.

Our two tools for assessing corporate profitability are return on capital and free cash flow. I start with return on assets (ROA) and return on equity

(ROE), which we first saw in Chapter 3 when we evaluated economic moats. Then I'll show you how to compare free cash flow to ROE and I'll finish up with a quick discussion of a sophisticated measure of profitability called return on invested capital (ROIC).

Return on Assets (ROA)

You already know the first component of ROA. It's simply net margin, or net income divided by sales, and it tells us how much of each dollar of sales a company keeps as earnings after paying all the costs of doing business. The second component is asset turnover, or sales divided by assets, which tells us roughly how efficient a firm is at generating revenue from each dollar of assets. Multiply these two together, and you have return on assets, which is simply the amount of profits that a company is able to generate per dollar of assets.

$$\frac{\text{Net income}}{\text{Sales}} = \text{Net margin}$$

$$\frac{\text{Sales}}{\text{Assets}} = \text{Asset turnover}$$

$$\text{Net margin} \times \text{Asset turnover} = \text{Return on assets}$$

Think of ROA as a measure of efficiency. Companies with high ROAs are better at translating assets into profits. We can see this easily when we compare a top-notch retailer such as Best Buy with a firm like Circuit City, which was struggling in the late 1990s and early 2000s. Since 1998, Circuit City's returns on assets have been around 4% to 5%, whereas Best Buy's improved from 5% to almost 10% (see Figures 23.3 and 23.4).

Circuit City Profitability	1998	1999	2000	2001	2002
Net margin (%)	1.4	1.6	1.9	1.4	2.0
Asset turnover (average)	2.6	3.0	3.2	3.0	2.5
Return on assets (%)	3.6	4.8	6.1	4.2	5.0

Figure 23.3 Annual profitability figures for Circuit City.

Best Buy Profitability	1998	1999	2000	2001	2002
Net margin (%)	1.1	2.2	2.8	2.6	2.9
Asset turnover (average)	4.4	4.4	4.5	3.9	3.2
Return on assets (%)	4.8	9.7	12.6	10.1	9.3

Figure 23.4 Annual profitability figures for Best Buy.

Higher profit margins—almost 3% for Best Buy and below 2% for Circuit City—are part of the picture, but higher asset turnover is a bigger differentiator between the two. In 2002, for example, each dollar that Circuit City had invested in property and inventory (the two biggest assets for most retailers) generated about $2.50 in sales, while the same dollar invested by Best Buy generated $3.20 in sales. Clearly, Best Buy was running a more efficient shop than Circuit City and was much better at transforming its assets into profits.

ROA helps us understand that there are two routes to excellent operational profitability: You can charge high prices for your products (high margins), or you can turn over your assets quickly. Often, you'll see companies with lower profit margins, such as grocery stores and discount retailers, emphasize high asset turnover as a way to achieve solid ROAs. For any business that can't charge a big premium for its goods, tight inventory management is critical because it keeps down the amount of capital tied up in assets, which helps pump up return on assets. On the flip side, companies that can mark up their goods in a big way—a luxury retailer such as Tiffany, for example—can afford to have more capital tied up in their assets because they make up for low asset turnover with high profit margins.

Just using ROA would be fine if all companies were big piles of assets, but many firms are at least partially financed with debt, which gives their returns a leverage component that we need to take into account. Our next measure of returns on capital, return on equity, lets us do this.

Return on Equity (ROE)
Return on equity is a great overall measure of a company's profitability because it measures the efficiency with which a company uses shareholders'

equity—in other words, it measures how good the company is at earning a decent return on the shareholder's money. Think of it as measuring profits per dollar of shareholders' capital.

To calculate ROE, multiply ROA by a firm's financial leverage ratio:

$$\text{Financial leverage} = \frac{\text{Assets}}{\text{Shareholders' equity}}$$

$$\text{Return on equity} = \text{Return on assets} \times \text{Financial leverage}$$

Because Return on assets = Net margin × Asset turnover, ROE in all its glory equals:

$$\text{Net margin} \times \text{Asset turnover} \times \text{Financial leverage}$$

You'll notice that we've introduced a new metric—financial leverage, which is essentially a measure of how much debt a company carries, relative to shareholders' equity. Unlike net margin and asset turnover—for which higher ratios are almost unequivocally better—financial leverage is something you need to watch carefully. As with any kind of debt, a judicious amount can boost returns, but too much can lead to disaster.

Look at the kind of business the firm is in. If it's fairly steady, a company can probably take on large amounts of debt without too much risk because there's only a small chance of the business falling off a cliff and the company being caught short when bondholders demand their interest payments. On the flip side, be very wary of a high financial leverage ratio if a company's business is cyclical or volatile. Because interest payments are fixed, the company has to pay them whether business is good or bad.

Therefore, we have three levers that can boost ROE—net margins, asset turnover, and financial leverage. For example, a firm could have only so-so margins and modest levels of financial leverage, but it could do a great job with asset turnover (e.g., a well-run discount retailer such as Wal-Mart). Companies with high asset turnover are extremely efficient at extracting more dollars of revenue for each dollar they have invested in hard assets. A firm could also excel at convincing customers to pay up for its products—

asset turns might be just middling, and the firm might not have much leverage, but it would have great profit margins (e.g., a luxury goods company such as Coach). Finally, a firm can boost its ROE to respectable territory by taking on good-size amounts of leverage (e.g., mature firms such as utilities).

Although it's tough to generalize, let me offer some rough benchmarks for evaluating firms' ROEs. In general, any nonfinancial firm that can generate consistent ROEs above 10% *without excessive leverage* is at least worth investigating. As of mid-2003, only about one-tenth of the nonfinancial firms in Morningstar's database were able to post an ROE above 10% for each of the past five years, so you can see how tough it is to post this kind of performance. And if you can find a company with the potential for consistent ROEs over 20%, there's a good chance you're really on to something.

Two caveats when you're using ROE to evaluate firms: First, banks always have enormous financial leverage ratios, so don't be scared off by a leverage ratio that looks high relative to a nonbank. In addition, because banks' leverage is always so high, you want to raise the bar for financial firms—look for consistent ROEs above 12% or so.

The second caveat concerns firms with ROEs that look too good to be true because they're usually just that. ROEs above 40% or so are often meaningless because they've probably been distorted by the firm's financial structure. Firms that have been recently spun off from parent firms, companies that have bought back many of their shares, and companies that have taken massive charges often have very skewed ROEs because their equity base is depressed. If you see an ROE over 40%, check to see if the company has any of these characteristics.

Free Cash Flow

In the previous chapter, I introduced you to cash flow from operations (CFO), which measures how much cash a company generates. As useful as CFO is, it doesn't take into account the money that a firm has to spend on maintaining and expanding its business. To do this, we need to subtract capital expenditures, which is money used to buy fixed assets. The result is free cash flow:

Free cash flow = Cash flow from operations − Capital spending

Thinking back to our hot dog stand example, suppose Mike was so successful that he decided to use the cash he'd generated to build a second hot dog stand. The cost of building that stand would be posted to "capital spending," and subtracted from free cash flow.

Why? We need to be able to separate out businesses that are net users of capital—ones that spend more than they take in—from businesses that are net producers of capital because it's only that excess cash that really belongs to us as shareholders. You may sometimes see free cash flow referred to as "owner earnings," because that's exactly what it is: the amount of money the owner of a company could withdraw from the treasury without harming the company's ongoing business.

A firm that generates a great deal of free cash flow can do all sorts of things with the money—save it for future investment opportunities, use it for acquisitions, buy back shares, and so forth. Free cash flow gives financial flexibility because the firm isn't relying on the capital markets to fund its expansion. Firms that have negative free cash flow have to take out loans or sell additional shares to keep things going, and that can become a risky proposition if the market becomes unsettled at a critical time for the company.

As with ROE, it's tough to generalize about how much free cash flow is enough. However, I think it's reasonable to say that any firm that's able to convert more than 5% of sales to free cash flow—just divide free cash flow by sales to get this percentage—is doing a solid job at generating excess cash.

Putting Return on Equity and Free Cash Flow Together

One good way to think about the returns a company is generating is to use the *profitability matrix,* which looks at a company's ROE relative to the amount of free cash flow it's generating. Figure 23.5 shows free cash flow along one side and ROE on the other side, and this matrix can tell you a great deal about the kind of company you're analyzing.

Companies such as Microsoft, Pfizer, and First Data all have very high ROEs. People write books about how to manage a business as well as these

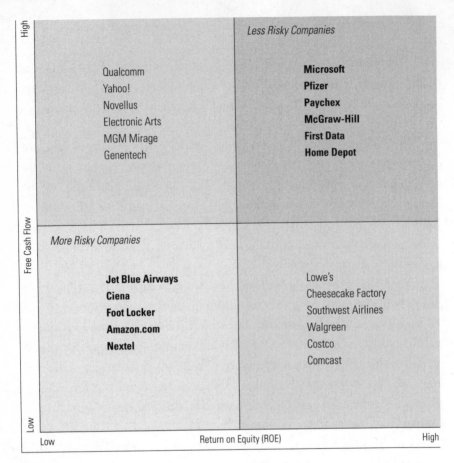

Figure 23.5   The Profitability Matrix: High ROEs and strong free cash flows are worth paying up for.
Source: Morningstar, Inc.

companies do, and it's easy to see why—they're all money machines. Investors pour new money into them, and large amounts of extra money get spit out. Their managements are very, very good at earning a high return on shareholders' money.

If you follow any of these companies at all, you'll notice they have another thing in common besides high ROEs—their stocks all had valuations that were high during the bull market of the 1990s. Again, it's easy to see why: A company that can earn a high return on its shareholders' money is worth more to those same shareholders.

Looking at the other axis, we see that these companies are also very good at generating free cash flow. Pfizer, for example, generated more than $8 billion in free cash flow in 2002. That's $8 billion Pfizer made *after* spending whatever it needed to invest in its business. Pfizer could have chosen to pay that $8 billion—which worked out to about $1.31 per share—out to shareholders. In fact, that's exactly what older, more mature companies often do with their free cash flow. Their businesses aren't growing very fast, and they figure that shareholders can earn a better return on the free cash flow than they can. So, they return it to shareholders in the form of dividends. (This is why slow-growth firms often have such high yields.)

Pfizer, on the other hand, thinks that it can figure out a way to invest that $8 billion more profitably than its shareholders. Because the company is in a relatively fast-growing area of the economy—health care—and has a solid track record of turning out profitable new drugs, it may very well be able to do so. However, if Pfizer started to pile up cash on its balance sheet the way Microsoft has over the past several years, we'd probably conclude that the company doesn't have many profitable avenues for reinvesting its excess profits. In this case, we'd want the firm to pay a dividend or buy back shares. Although Microsoft's dividend isn't very large at this writing, at least the company has one, which means that it has recognized that internal reinvestment opportunities are diminishing.

On the bottom half of the matrix, we have companies such as Amazon .com, JetBlue, Comcast, and Lowe's, which generate low or negative free cash flow. Companies like these aren't generating much free cash because they're using all the cash their businesses generate—and then some—to invest in expansion. They're investing heavily because they hope that those expansion efforts will pay off in the form of fat profits in the future. Amazon, for example, is spending heavily on building a brand and expanding its Web site, while JetBlue is spending heavily on new airplanes so that it can expand its service to new cities.

JetBlue and Amazon are like young entrepreneurs. They've taken out loans and maxed out their credit cards, and they're plowing every cent they have into building and expanding their businesses. Although they're not earning much in the way of profits right now, folks are investing in their businesses because they expect these companies to be very profitable sometime in the future, which is when investors will be rewarded. Pfizer, on the other hand, is more like a successful, middle-age businessman. He's already proven he can earn a good return on shareholders' money, so folks line up outside his door for the privilege of investing in his ventures.

You'd be taking a lot less risk investing with the older businessman than you would with the young entrepreneur—though that entrepreneur might just pay you back many, many times over. Just remember that for every Jeff Bezos or Steve Jobs, there are literally hundreds of entrepreneurs who never paid their investors a dime.

There's nothing wrong with investing in the entrepreneurs of the world, as long as you know what you're getting into. A profitability matrix can help you separate your long shots from your core holdings.

Think of the profitability matrix like this: That upper right-hand corner, where Pfizer sits, is the sweet spot—excess cash and the ability to earn a high return on it. Companies in this square tend to be the cream of the crop and have a low level of business risk. (They might be very risky *stocks,* though, if they're trading at high valuations.)

Moving down to the bottom right, where Lowe's is, you see companies that are reinvesting all of their cash in expansion but are still able to generate a high return on shareholders' money. If these firms still have profitable reinvestment opportunities, they *should* be spending all the cash they generate on expansion. For example, Starbucks and Home Depot posted high ROEs and negative free cash flow all through the 1990s because they were plowing every cent they earned into building more stores.

In the bottom left are young companies growing like weeds, but which haven't yet proven that they can earn a decent ROE—they're spending tons of money, but they're not yet making it pay off very well. This is where the most speculative companies hang out. These companies are generally long shots because it's still unclear whether all of that heavy investment will ever generate an attractive return.

Return on Invested Capital (ROIC)

Warning: The material in this box drifts dangerously close to finance-geek territory. If hard-core finance puts you to sleep, ignore this box and don't worry about the inner workings of ROIC and WACC.

The true operating performance of a firm is best measured by return on invested capital (ROIC), which measures the return on all capital invested in the firm regardless of the source of the capital. The formula for ROIC is deceptively simple:

$$\text{ROIC} = \frac{\text{Net operating profit after taxes (NOPAT)}}{\text{Invested capital}}$$

The numerator of this equation is easy: profits after taxes, but before interest costs. The denominator is a bit trickier, and although there are many different ways to calculate it, you'll do just fine if you use this version:

$$\begin{array}{c} \text{Invested} \\ \text{capital} \end{array} = \begin{array}{c} \text{Total} \\ \text{assets} \end{array} - \begin{array}{c} \text{Non-interest-bearing} \\ \text{current liabilities (usually} \\ \text{accounts payable and} \\ \text{other current assets)} \end{array} - \begin{array}{c} \text{Excess cash (cash} \\ \text{not needed for} \\ \text{day-to-day} \\ \text{business needs)} \end{array}$$

You may also want to subtract goodwill if it's a large percentage of assets.

Let's run through an example: At the end of fiscal 2002, Wal-Mart's total assets were worth $94.7 billion. Subtract accounts payable, accrued liabilities, and accrued income taxes, and $67.7 billion remains, which is Wal-Mart's invested capital. Looking at the firm's income statement, we see that operating profit was $13.6 billion. If we multiply this by the firm's 36% tax rate, we get a rough idea of what taxes would have been without any interest income or interest expense (remember, interest is tax deductible for corporations), and we find that NOPAT equals $13.6 - (\$13.6 \times 0.36) =$ $8.7 billion.

Next, divide NOPAT by invested capital, or $8.7 billion by $67.7 billion, and ROIC is 12.9%—pretty respectable for a firm as large and mature as Wal-Mart.

Return on Invested Capital (ROIC)

Return on invested capital is a sophisticated way of analyzing return on capital that adjusts for some peculiarities of ROA and ROE. Although you needn't worry about calculating it for yourself—it's pretty complicated—it's worth knowing how to interpret it because it's overall a better measure of profitability than ROA and ROE. (If you *are* interested in how to calculate it, see the ROIC box on page 323.)

Essentially, ROIC improves on ROA and ROE because it puts debt and equity financing on an equal footing: It removes the debt-related distortion that can make highly leveraged companies look very profitable when using ROE. It also uses a different definition of profits than ROE and ROA, both of which use net income. ROIC uses operating profits *after* taxes, but *before* interest expenses. Again, the goal is to remove any effects caused by a company's financing decisions—does it use debt or equity?—so that we can focus as closely as possible on the profitability of the core business.

What does all this mean to you if you hear someone talking about ROIC? Simply that you should interpret ROIC just as you would ROA and ROE—a higher return on invested capital is preferable to a lower one.

Financial Health

Once we've figured out how fast (and why) a company has grown and how profitable it is, we need to look at its financial health. Even the most beautiful home needs a solid foundation, after all.

The bottom line about financial health is that when a company increases its debt, it increases its fixed costs as a percentage of total costs. In years when business is good, a company with high fixed costs can be extremely profitable because once those costs are covered, any additional sales the company makes fall straight to the bottom line. When business is bad, however, the fixed costs of debt push earnings even lower.

Look at what debt does to the earnings volatility of the creatively named Acme (see Figure 23.6). With more debt, Acme's earnings fluctuate a lot: They're up more in good times and down more in bad times.

A common measure of leverage is simply the financial leverage ratio that we used in calculating ROE, equal to assets divided by equity. Think of fi-

Acme: Conservatively financed with a little debt.	2002
Sales	5,000
Gross profit	1,000
Less: Interest Expense	**200**
Earnings before taxes	800
Less: Taxes (35% rate)	280
Net income	520

2003 Hypothetical Scenarios: Good Year (Sales up 20%)	Bad Year (Sales down 20%)
6,000	4,000
1,200	800
200	**200**
1,000	600
350	210
650	390
Profits up 25%	**Profits down 25%**

Acme: Aggressively financed with a lot of debt.	2002
Sales	5,000
Gross profit	1,000
Less: Interest Expense	**600**
Earnings before taxes	400
Less: Taxes (35% rate)	140
Net income	260

2003 Hypothetical Scenarios: Good Year (Sales up 20%)	Bad Year (Sales down 20%)
6,000	4,000
1,200	800
600	**600**
600	200
210	70
390	130
Profits up 50%	**Profits down 50%**

Figure 23.6   The impact of financial leverage. *Source:* Morningstar, Inc.

nancial leverage like a mortgage—a homebuyer who puts $20,000 down on a $100,000 house has a financial leverage ratio of 5. For every dollar in equity, the buyer has $5 in assets.

The same holds true for companies. In 2002, home improvement retailer Lowe's had a financial leverage ratio of 2.1, meaning that for every dollar inequity, the firm had $2.10 in total assets. (It borrowed the other $1.10.) A financial leverage ratio of 2.1 is fairly conservative, even for a fast-growing retailer. It's when we see ratios of 4, 5, or more that companies start to get really risky.

In addition to financial leverage, make sure to examine a few other key metrics when assessing a company's financial health.

Debt to Equity

This is just what it sounds like—long-term debt divided by shareholder's equity. It's a little like the financial leverage ratio, except that it's more narrowly focused on how much long-term debt the firm has per dollar of equity.

Times Interest Earned

This one requires a little more work to calculate, but it's worth it. Look up pretax earnings, and add back interest expense—this gives earnings before interest and taxes (EBIT). Divide EBIT by interest expense, and you'll know how many times (hence the name) the company could have paid the interest expense on its debt. The more times that the company can pay its interest expense, the less likely that it will run into difficulty if earnings should fall unexpectedly.

For home improvement retailer Lowe's, for example, we add $182 million in interest expenses to $2.36 billion in pretax earnings to get $2.54 billion in EBIT, and we divide $2.54 million by the $182 million in interest expense to get times interest earned of 14. In other words, Lowe's earned enough money in 2003 to cover its interest obligation 14 times over, which is a pretty safe margin (see Figure 23.7).

It's tough to say precisely how low this metric can go before you should be concerned—but higher is *definitely* better. You want to see higher times interest earned for a company with a more volatile business than for a firm in a more stable industry. Be sure to look at the trend in times interest earned over time, as well. Calculate the ratio for the past five years, and you'll be able to see whether the company is becoming riskier—times interest earned is falling—or whether its financial health is improving.

Current and Quick Ratios

The current ratio (current assets divided by current liabilities) simply tells you how much liquidity a firm has—in other words, how much cash it could raise if it absolutely had to pay off its liabilities all at once. A low ratio means the company may not be able to source enough cash to meet near-term liabilities, which would force it to seek outside financing or to divert

Lowe's Companies: Partial Income Statement

Year ending January 31	2003
Net sales	$26,491
Cost of sales	18,465
Gross margin	8,026
Expenses:	
Selling, general, and administrative	4,730
Store opening costs	129
Depreciation	626
Interest	**182**
Total expenses	5,667
Pre-Tax Earnings	**2,359**
Income tax provision	888
Net earnings	$1,471

Figure 23.7   Lowe's Income Statement. *Source:* Lowe's SEC filings.

operating income to pay off those liabilities. As a *very* general rule, a current ratio of 1.5 or more means the firm should be able to meet operating needs without much trouble.

Unfortunately, some current assets—such as inventories—may be worth less than their value on the balance sheet. (Imagine trying to sell old PCs or last year's fashions to generate cash—you'd be unlikely to receive anything close to what you paid for them.) So there's an even more conservative test of a company's liquidity, the *quick ratio,* which is simply current assets less inventories divided by current liabilities. This ratio is especially useful for manufacturing firms and for retailers because both of these types of firms tend to have a lot of their cash tied up in inventories. In general, a quick ratio higher than 1.0 puts a company in fine shape, but always look at other firms in the same industry to be sure.

The Bear Case

After you've assessed growth, profitability, and financial health, your next task is to look at the bear case for the stock you're analyzing. Start by listing all of the potential negatives, from the most obvious to the least likely. What could go wrong with your investment thesis? Why might someone prefer to be a seller of the stock than a buyer? Constructing a convincing bear case is especially important for those who like to buy high-quality companies that have hit temporary speed bumps, because what looks like a speed bump may very well be a roadblock on closer inspection.

Equally important, your bear case will be a great reference point even if you do decide to buy the stock. You'll know in advance what signs of trouble to watch for, which will help you make better decisions when bad news comes down the pike in the future. Having already investigated the negatives, you'll have the confidence to hang on to the stock during a temporary rough patch as well as the savvy to know when the rough patch might really be a serious turn for the worse.

I'll admit to a painful example from my own history that shows the importance of developing a bear case before buying a stock. In the mid-1990s, I purchased some shares of a small firm called Ballantyne of Omaha, which was one of the world's largest manufacturer of motion picture projectors in the world at the time. (The big ones in movie theaters—not the ones your teacher used in elementary school.) The firm was growing at a decent clip, had few competitors, and management seemed to have their heads on straight. The stock was selling for what I thought was a pretty reasonable price, as well.

Unfortunately, the movie theater industry—Ballantyne's main customer—was in the midst of a huge debt-fueled building boom at the time. Remember all of those 10- and 20-screen suburban theaters that got thrown up during the 1990s? That's what was pumping up Ballantyne's sales, and the expansion wasn't sustainable. Many of the big theater chains had liquidity crunches, and a few even went belly up. Needless to say, this did not do wonders for movie-projector demand, and Ballantyne's financial results (and stock price) went into a fast slide.

The lesson? I should have constructed a convincing bear case for Ballantyne before I bought it. If I'd looked deeper into the financial health of Ballantyne's customers, I might have asked myself what would happen if the multiplex boom slowed down. I didn't and, as a result, I made a poor investment that could have been avoided.

Conclusion

To this point, we've investigated the financial performance of companies. We've assessed their competitive strengths by investigating their economic moats, and we've analyzed their financial statements.

In Chapter 24, I'll discuss how to assess the quality of management. In Chapter 25, I'll give you some tips on how to spot aggressive accounting, after which we'll turn to perhaps the toughest task faced by any serious investor: Deciding on a fair price for the stock. How can we avoid paying too much for excellent companies, while not being so cheap that we let wonderful opportunities pass us by? In Chapters 26 and 27, I'll show you how to value stocks.

Investor's Checklist: Analyzing a Company—The Basics

▶ When you're evaluating a company's growth rate, don't get swept away by heady historical growth. Make sure you understand where the growth is coming from and how it can be sustained over time.

▶ Be wary of companies that have relied on acquisitions to boost growth. Most acquisitions fail to produce positive returns for shareholders of the acquiring firm, and they make it tough to evaluate a company's true growth rate.

▶ If earnings growth outstrips sales growth over a long period, this might be a sign of *manufactured growth.* Make sure to dig into the numbers to see how the company keeps squeezing out more profits from stagnant sales.

▶ Return on assets measures the amount of profits that a company is able to generate per dollar of assets. Companies with high ROAs are better at translating assets into profits.

▶ ROE is a good measure of profitability because it measures how the company is at earning a return on shareholders' money. But because companies can boost their ROEs by taking on more debt, don't take it as gospel. For a nonfinancial company, look for an ROE of at least 10%, without excessive leverage.

▶ Free cash flow gives financial flexibility because the firm isn't relying on the capital markets to fund its expansion. Firms with negative free cash flow have to take out loans or sell additional shares to keep things going, and that can become a risky proposition if the market becomes unsettled at a critical time for the company.

▶ Be wary of companies with too much financial leverage. Because debt is a fixed cost, it magnifies earnings volatility and leads to more risk.

▶ Before you buy a stock, think through all the potential negatives. This can help you make better decisions if bad news does come down the pike.

24

Analyzing a Company— Management

Excellent management can make the difference between a mediocre business and an outstanding one, and poor management can run even a great business into the ground. Your goal is to find management teams that think like shareholders—executives that treat the business as if they owned a piece of it, rather than as hired hands. Unfortunately, managers like this are more rare than you might think.

People buy stocks all the time without checking out the folks in the executive suite, and the excuse I hear most often is that it's tough to assess management without meeting them face-to-face. Hogwash. There are many, many ways to get a feel for the folks running a company that have nothing to do with looking the CEO in the eye. No one can run a public company without leaving a trail of pretty strong objective evidence behind. My advice is to divide the management-assessment process into three parts: compensation, character, and operations.

Compensation

Compensation is the easiest of the three areas to assess because the bulk of the information is contained in a single document, usually called the *proxy statement*. This is the form that companies mail shareholders around the time of the annual meeting, and it details how much executives are paid and what perks they get. (You can find this form online at www.sec.gov or www.freeedgar.com. Look for form DEF14A.)

Here's what to look for in a company's compensation plan. First and most important, how much does management pay itself? (This is detailed in the aptly named "summary compensation table.") Generally, I prefer big bonuses to big base salaries and restricted stock grants to generous option packages. Bonuses mean that a good portion of the pay is at least theoretically at risk, and restricted stock means the executive loses money if the share price declines. That's just the tip of the iceberg, though.

First, look at the raw level of cash compensation to see if it's reasonable. There's not necessarily a strict limit here, though I personally think an $8 million cash bonus is silly no matter how well the company has done. (For reference, the average CEO of a large U.S. firm currently earns about 500 times as much as the average employee. Twenty years ago, this multiple was just 40.)

In any case, use your own judgment—if the amount that executives earn makes you cringe, it's probably too much. Also look at competing firms to see what their CEOs are paid, so you can see how the boss that you're investigating stacks up. In general, the larger the firm and the better its financial performance, the more an executive should be paid. But some executives think they have a license to print money just because they manage a huge company, no matter how poor a job they're doing, which is why you need to determine whether their pay is tied to the firm's operational performance. (Case in point: After retiring as chairman and co–CEO of Verizon, Charles Lee became a "consultant" to the firm at the exorbitant rate of $250,000 per *month*. To me, that's a cringe-worthy retirement package.)

Pay for Performance

What's even more important is whether executives' pay is truly tied to the company's performance. At many companies, so-called "performance targets" are set by a subcommittee of the board of directors, which can often rewrite the rules of the game if the CEO appears to be losing. In 2001, for example, Coca-Cola's board reduced CEO Douglas Daft's goal of 15% earnings growth over five years to 11%. Moving the goalposts like this can be justified in one sense—after all, if the performance target isn't achievable, it's hardly going to motivate the CEO—but you can also fault the board for not setting more realistic goals in the first place. In any case, I think it's a negative sign when the targets are changed but the potential reward stays the same, because it indicates that the board is unwilling to stand up to the CEO and punish him or her by slashing the bonus when performance slumps.

At least Coke's shareholders knew what the target was, though. According to the 2001 proxy, Walt Disney's compensation gurus decided that bonuses:

> may be based on one or more of the following business criteria, or on any combination thereof, on a consolidated basis: net income (or adjusted net income), return on equity (or adjusted return on equity), return on assets (or adjusted return on assets), earnings per share (diluted) (or adjusted earnings per share [diluted]).

In other words, Disney's CEO was going to get paid no matter what. To add insult to injury, the gang at Disney wrote that "[we believe] that the specific target constitutes confidential business information the disclosure of which could adversely affect the Company." More likely, it would have adversely affected Disney management because the board wouldn't have been able to move the goalposts in the middle of the game. This kind of nondisclosure on the compensation front is a bad sign when you're looking for good managers.

Another sign of poor compensation procedures is paying managers for actions that make the company bigger, but not better. In 2001, for example, Disney wrote the following in its proxy statement:

> As permitted by the plan, special bonuses were paid outside the plan to three executives . . . Peter Murphy, Thomas Staggs and Louis Meisinger—for extraordinary services to the Company unrelated to the plan's performance targets, including, in the case of Messrs. Murphy and Staggs, *services related to the Company's acquisition of Fox Family Worldwide, Inc.*

Rewarding management for consummating an acquisition is an absolutely terrible idea—paying big bonuses just for getting a deal done simply encourages executives to go out and do more dubious deals. A better idea, though not one I've ever seen implemented, would be to wait a couple of years and pay a bonus only if an acquisition has provided an adequate—and predetermined—return on the investment.

The bottom line is this: Executives' pay should rise and fall based on the performance of the company. So, after reviewing a company's historical financials, read the past few years' proxies to see whether this has truly been the case or whether some lackeys on the board of directors have cooked up justifications for big bonuses even in bad times. Firms with good corporate governance standards won't hesitate to pay managers less in bad times and more in good times, and that's the kind of pattern you want to see as a shareholder.

Other Red Flags

Aside from the big-picture question of whether executives' pay truly is linked to company performance, keep an eye out for the following issues when you're assessing executive compensation.

Were Executives Given "Loans" that Were Subsequently Forgiven? This was a common—and disgusting—practice before the Sarbanes-Oxley Act banned it in 2002. Companies would give loans to senior managers at below-market rates of interest and then often quietly forgive the loans a few years later. In my book, a loan that's not repaid is a bonus, and companies that tried to fudge executive pay in this fashion weren't treating shareholders with respect. If the executive needed a loan, he should have asked his bank, not his employer. Don't tolerate this kind of behavior from companies you're investigating—even though it's not legal any longer, companies that did this sort of thing in past should be viewed with skepticism. After all, would they have stopped unless they were forced to? (Loans of this sort are usually disclosed in the "other compensation" column of the executive compensation table in the footnotes.)

Do Executives Get Perks Paid for by the Company that They Should Really Be Paying for Themselves? It's a sure sign of corporate excess when execs get country club memberships and other frippery paid for by shareholders. After all, when you're paying someone several hundred thousand dollars per year, making shareholders foot the bill for their greens fees seems rather silly. More importantly, such behavior at the top sets a poor example for everyone else in the firm. Managers who enjoy ridiculous perks are acting like latter-day royalty rather than prudent custodians of shareholders' money. Conversely, thrifty CEOs are a plus: Managers who do things such as paying for their own parking and eschewing pricey perks set a good tone for the rest of the organization.

Does Management Hog Most of the Stock Options Granted in a Given Year, or Do Rank-and-File Employees Share in the Wealth? Generally, firms with more equitable distribution schemes perform better over the long run. Most firms break out the percentage of options granted to executives relative to the total granted in the proxy statement.

Does Management Use Stock Options Excessively? Even if they're distributed beyond the executive suite, giving out too many options dilutes existing shareholders' equity. If a company gives out more than 1% or 2% of the outstanding shares each year, they're giving away too much of the firm's equity every year. Conversely, it's a great sign if the firm issues restricted stock instead of options. Restricted stock has to be counted as an expense on the income statement (options don't, as of this writing), and restricted stock also forces the recipient to participate on the downside if the stock falls.

If a Founder or Large Owner Is Still Involved in the Company, Does He or She Also Get a Big Stock Option Grant Each Year? This makes me queasy. After all, it's hard to argue that, for example, CEO Larry Ellison of Oracle needs additional options to motivate him when he already owns 25% of the firm.

Do Executives Have Some Skin in the Game? That is, do they have substantial holdings of company stock, or do they tend to sell shares right after they exercise options? As a shareholder, I want management to have meaningful equity in the company. After all, selling shares in the name of "diversification" means not being exposed if the company goes downhill. Generally, I'm happier owning companies where executives own stock right alongside me because large unexercised option positions are cold comfort. You can find this information in the footnotes of the proxy. Companies indicate executives' percentage ownership *including* options prominently in a table labeled "security owner-ship of certain beneficial owners," but they declare only how many actual *shares* are owned in the footnotes. In PeopleSoft's 2003 proxy, for example, CEO Craig Conway was listed as owning 3.8 million shares, or 1.2% of the company. But if you looked at the footnote, you'd have seen that he owned only 626,000 shares, 625,000 of which weren't even vested yet.

Character

Compensation by itself is often a good litmus test for character—anecdotally, there's a pretty strong relationship between management teams that are in it for the money and management teams that treat shareholders poorly. How-ever, there are some other important questions you should ask to get a handle on whether a firm's management deserves your trust.

Does Management Use Its Position to Enrich Friends and Relatives?

In a company's annual 10-K filing, look for a section called "related-party transactions." If a friend or relative of a company officer has substantial busi-ness dealings with the firm, you'll read about it here. Often, this stuff is pretty innocuous—an ex-officer or director is paid some nominal amount each year for consulting services. As long as the firm isn't paying out hundreds of thou-sands of dollars, this kind of thing doesn't get my hackles up.

But when the firm pays substantial amounts of money to, for example, an interior-design firm run by the CEO's wife or to a law firm in which the CFO's son-in-law is a partner, I sit up and take notice. The key here is to make sure that (1) the firm isn't sending a great amount of business in the di-rection of related parties and (2) there's not an egregious pattern of abuse. One or two small related-party transactions aren't a big deal, but they do cause me to raise an eyebrow because they may be signs of a deeper problem. And if it looks as though virtually all family members of the company officers have their hands in the till, you have a big character issue.

Is the Board of Directors Stacked with Management's Family Members or Former Managers?

Look at the biographies of the board, which are also in the proxy statement. If many of them are closely related to top management—or are former managers themselves, it's a good bet the board isn't going to be as hard-nosed when questioning management's actions as it could be. And because the board is shareholders' last line of defense against a CEO running amok, that's hardly a good thing.

Is Management Candid about Its Mistakes?

Not even the smartest executives get everything right, and it's important that a management team be able to honestly discuss poor decisions and why they were made. CEOs who bury mistakes might be burying other things as well. Look for this type of candor in annual reports and in quarterly conference calls. I especially like to look at the letter to shareholders in the annual report. Is it a candid assessment of the past year's successes and failures or a fluff piece?

How Promotional Is Management?

Although a certain amount of rallying the troops is the job of a CEO, watch out for company officers who cross the line and begin blindly pumping up the stock or themselves. This is a red flag because management's job is to worry about running the company—if executives get that right, the stock price will take care of itself over time. Executives who complain about how undervalued their firm's shares are or who opine about its true worth are probably more concerned with the value of their options than with making solid, long-term business decisions. Self-promotional managers, meanwhile, are not likely to make decisions that are in the best interests of long-term shareholders. If you read a number of glowing media articles in which a CEO paints himself or herself as a latter-day savior, watch out. The cult of the CEO-as-hero is dangerous.

Can the CEO Retain High-Quality Talent?

This one is subtler, but it can tell you a great deal about the firm you're analyzing. Some firms judge the quality of managers by the turnover rate of their subordinates because turnover is seen as the ultimate acid test of the working environment and employees' views of a company's potential. Extend this view to the executive team: How often do officers turn over? What is the tenure of key officers? Is executive hiring done from the outside? (All of this can be uncovered by reviewing several years' worth of proxy statements.) Long tenure is a great signal of intrinsic motivation and confidence in the business, whereas a CEO who keeps forcing out immediate subordinates is likely spending too much time on internal power struggles and not enough on running the business.

Does Management Make Tough Decisions that Hurt Results but Give a More Honest Picture of the Company?

If a management team makes decisions that actually hurt reported results, you're in luck. Management teams that use restricted stock grants instead of options—because the former has to be expensed, while the latter doesn't—or who expense rather than capitalize items such as research and development or software costs are the kinds of folks who are more interested in running the business than playing numbers games. And those are precisely the kind of people you want running the companies you own.

Running the Business

In addition to managers who are paid reasonably and are honest, you also want folks who can run the business well.

Performance

The first stop is simply the financial performance of the company during the tenure of the current management team. Look for high and increasing ROEs and ROAs—but don't forget to check whether increasing ROE was driven by higher leverage, as opposed to improved profitability or asset efficiency.

Are there any big jumps in revenue? If so, the firm probably did an acquisition, and you should check to see whether management paid a reasonable price and whether the acquired firm wound up adding to shareholder value. Most acquisitions do not pay off, so digging into past merger and acquisition (M&A) activity is definitely worth your while.

Finally, look at the share count over a long period of time. If the number of shares outstanding has increased substantially because of aggressive options programs or frequent equity issuance, the firm is essentially giving away part of your stake without asking you. That's not a great recipe for long-term share performance.

Follow-Through

When management identifies a problem and promises a solution, does it actually implement the plan, or does it hope you forget about it? The same goes for any "new strategic initiatives" that are announced: Does the firm go ahead with a new plan once it's announced, or does every year see the firm announcing a grand new strategy that's never realized? One way to vet this is to look at past annual reports and see what new initiatives were discussed three to seven years ago. It's fine if they weren't all successful, but where are they now? Has management kept shareholders up to date on them, or do the initiatives just disappear from the radar screen? In the latter case, management is probably spending more time hiring consultants with grandiose plans than actually figuring out what's broken.

Candor

Does the firm provide enough information to properly analyze the business, or does it clam up about certain issues? Generally, management teams will talk ad nauseam about parts of the business that are hitting on all cylinders, but questions about a problem area are sometimes met with evasion or a straight, "We don't disclose that."

For example, Merck changed the way it reported its drug sales figures in 2001, but it wouldn't provide comparable data for past periods—which made it difficult to get a clear picture of what was going on. Lucent was another offender in this department because it grouped together high-growth and low-growth product lines when it broke out segment data. It's entirely proper for firms not to report certain things, but selective reticence about problem areas is never a good sign.

Self-Confidence

I generally applaud firms that do something markedly different from their peers or from conventional opinion. It's tough to take a pass on a hot consulting fad when all of your golfing buddies are singing its praises or to buy a beaten-down competitor when your industry is in the tank—but these are both moves that can pay off in spades. Maintaining research and development spending during an industry downturn is another good example of self-confidence that shows management is more concerned with beating competitors over the long haul than beating its quarterly earnings guidance.

Flexibility

Has management made decisions that will give the firm flexibility in the future? These include simple decisions such as not taking on too much debt and controlling fixed expenses (even in good years), as well as more strategic decisions such as issuing equity when the stock is high. Attaching call options to debt, retiring high-rate debt when the opportunity presents itself, and buying back stock only when the price is low are also good examples of capital allocation decisions that evidence a solid operational hand on the tiller.

Investor's Checklist: Analyzing a Company—Management

▶ Evaluating management is a critical component of analyzing a stock. Look for management teams that act like shareholders, rather than hired hands.

▶ Get compensation information from the proxy statement—SEC form DEF-14A. Check out how much management is paid and whether pay varies with the company's performance. If a pay package makes you cringe, it's too high.

▶ Avoid companies that give loans to executives, have many related-party transactions, or give out too many stock options. Look for executives that have substantial stock ownership positions.

▶ Make sure the company discloses enough information for you to properly analyze the business. "We don't disclose that" is often code for, "The news is bad, so we'd rather not say."

25

Avoiding Financial Fakery

As YOU'VE LIKELY figured out by now, picking great stocks is not a black-and-white process. Unfortunately, neither is accounting. There are literally dozens of techniques that are perfectly legal and aboveboard, but which have the effect of fooling an observer into thinking that a firm has posted true operational improvements when all it has really done is moved some numbers around. You need to know how to identify what's known as *aggressive accounting* so you can avoid the companies that practice it.

Even worse than aggressive accounting, of course, is outright fraud—the hucksters of the world are naturally attracted to the stock market because it's the perfect arena for profiting from the greed and carelessness of others. Knowing the signs of potential fraud can save you a lot of financial pain.

It's not that hard, either. Although you might need a CPA to understand *exactly* how an aggressive or fraudulent firm is exaggerating its results, you don't need to be an expert to recognize the warning signs of accounting chicanery. As long as you avoid the companies that bristle with red flags, you won't be caught owning them when the SEC starts investigating.

Six Red Flags

When you're giving a company the once-over, there are six major red flags to watch out for. Though some of these issues can pop up for innocent reasons, be sure you thoroughly investigate them before giving the firm a clean bill of health—or your money.

Declining Cash Flow

Even if accounting gobbledygook makes your head spin, there is one very simple thing you can do: Watch cash flow. Over time, increases in a company's cash flow from operations should roughly track increases in net income. If you see cash from operations decline even as net income keeps marching upward—or if cash from operations increases much more slowly than net income—watch out. This usually means that the company is generating sales without necessarily collecting the cash, and that's a very good recipe for a blowup down the road.

My favorite example of this is former high-flyer Lucent. Between 1997 and 1999, Lucent's net income soared from $449 million, to just over $1 billion, to almost $3.5 billion—an incredible growth rate for such a large company. At the same time, however, cash flow from operations was plunging precipitously, from $2.1 billion in 1997 to $1.9 billion in 1998, to *negative* $276 million in 1999. Why? It's a long and sordid story, but it boiled down to three big reasons:

1. Lucent was extending credit to anyone who could spell photon, which meant it was booking many sales without receiving the cash. (Think back to our hot dog stand example in Chapter 21—as long as a firm ships a product and has reasonable certainty that it will eventually collect the cash, it can post the sale.) Accounts receivable (A/R) ballooned from 20% of sales to 27% of sales between 1997 and 1999, a clear sign that the firm was having trouble collecting the money it was owed.
2. Lucent kept building more gear than it could ship, which sent inventories upward. (Remember, manufacturing something and then storing it in a warehouse uses cash.) This effect showed up in the "increase in inventories" line item in the firm's statement of cash flows.
3. Lucent's pension plan was pumping up net income with noncash gains.

If you do nothing else, watch cash flow like a hawk.

Serial Chargers

Be wary of firms that take frequent one-time charges and write-downs. This practice makes the historical financials muddier because every charge has a long explanation and usually has various components that affect different accounts—all of which need to be adjusted if you want to look at comparable year-to-year financial results.

More importantly, frequent charges are an open invitation to accounting hanky-panky because firms can bury bad decisions in a single restructuring charge. Usually, the rationale for a charge is pretty vague, which means there's a fair amount of leeway for management.

When a firm takes a big restructuring charge, it's essentially improving future results by pulling future expenses into the present. In other words, poor decisions that might need to be paid for in future quarters—an unsuccessful product that may need to be terminated or a bloated division that will need to pay severance payments to redundant employees—all get rolled into a single one-time charge in the current quarter, which improves future results.

If you run across a firm that has frequent restructuring charges, don't ignore them, despite the firm's blandishments about what earnings would be after excluding the charge. After all, if a firm dug itself into a deep enough hole that it needs quarter after quarter of charges to make things right, those charges are a normal cost of improving the business.

Serial Acquirers

As I mentioned earlier in the book, firms that make numerous acquisitions can be problematic—their financials have been restated and rejiggered so many times that it's tough to know which end is up. Aside from muddying the waters, acquisitions increase the risk that the firm will report a nasty surprise some time in the future, because acquisitive firms that want to beat their competitors to the punch often don't spend as much time checking out their targets as they should.

The Chief Financial Officer or Auditors Leave the Company

Quis custodiet ipsos custodes? is Latin for "who watches the watchmen?" And when it comes to financial reporting, those watchmen are the chief financial officer (CFO) and the corporate auditors. If a CFO leaves the company for reasons that seem at all strange—or inexplicable—you should be on your guard. It's normal for CFOs to move around just like other executives, but if you see a CFO leave a company that's already under suspicion for accounting issues, you should think very hard about whether there might be more going on than meets the eye. The same applies to corporate auditors. If a company changes auditors frequently or fires its auditors after some potentially damaging accounting issue has come to light, watch out. This one may not be a big deal by itself, but it's definitely something to watch with firms that have already displayed other warning signs.

The Bills Aren't Being Paid

There are few things Wall Street loves more than growth, and companies go to great lengths to keep their top line increasing as rapidly as possible. One of the sneakier ways for a company to pump up its growth rate is to loosen customers' credit terms, which induces them to buy more products or services. (Companies can also ship out more products than their customers ask for—known as "stuffing the channel"—but this is less common.)

The trick here is that even though the company has recorded a sale—which increases revenues—the customer has not yet paid for the product. If enough customers don't pay—and those looser credit terms are probably attracting financially shakier customers—the pumped-up growth rate will eventually come back to bite the company in the form of a nasty write-down or charge against earnings.

You should track how fast A/R are increasing relative to sales—the two should roughly track each other. But if sales increase by, for example, 15%, while A/R increases 25%, the company is booking sales faster than it's receiving cash from its customers. (Remember, A/R measures goods that are sold, but not yet paid for.) As a general rule, it's simply not possible for A/R to increase faster than sales for a long time—the company is paying out more money (as finished goods) than it's taking in (through cash payments).

On the credit front, watch the "allowance for doubtful accounts," which is essentially the company's estimate of how much money it won't be able to collect from deadbeat customers. If this amount doesn't move up in sync with A/R, the company may be artificially boosting its results by being overly optimistic about how many of its new customers will pay their bills.

Changes in Credit Terms and Accounts Receivable

Finally, check the company's 10-Q filing for any mentions of changes in credit terms for customers, as well as for any explanation by management as to why A/R has jumped. (Look in the management's discussion and analysis section for the latter and in the accounting footnotes for the former.)

Seven Other Pitfalls to Watch Out For

Watching for these six warning signs will help you avoid maybe two-thirds of potential accounting-related blowups. Unfortunately, though, there are many other ways that firms can embellish their financial results. When you're reading a 10-K or annual report, watch for the following pitfalls.

Gains from Investments

It's reasonably common for large firms—especially in the technology sector—to make small investments in other companies. Occasionally, these investments work out well, the owner sells some of the shares, and records the capital gain as income. This is no different from the way you or I would report a capital gain as income when we're doing our taxes every year, and it's perfectly legal and aboveboard.

An honest company breaks out these sales, however, and reports them below the "operating income" line on its income statement. The problem arises when companies try to boost their operating results—in other words, the performance of their core business—by shoehorning investment income into other parts of their financial statements.

The most blatant means of using investment income to boost results is to include it as part of revenue, though this isn't very common. Companies can also record the income "above the line" so that it is included as part of operating income and thus boosts their operating margins. This is manifestly a no-no because accounting rules require any piece of one-time income to be separated from income that comes from normal operations. Finally, companies can hide investment gains in their expense accounts by using them to reduce operating expenses, which makes the firm look more efficient than it really is.

If the firm you're analyzing is using investment gains or asset sales to boost operating income or reduce expenses, you know you're dealing with a company that might be less than forthcoming in other areas as well.

Pension Pitfalls

Pensions can be a big ball-and-chain for companies with many retirees because if the assets in the pension plan don't increase quickly enough, the firm has to divert profits to prop up the pension. To fund pension payments to future retirees, companies shovel money into pension plans that then are invested in stocks, bonds, real estate, and so forth. If a company winds up with fewer pension assets than pension liabilities, it has an *underfunded* plan, and if the company has more than enough pension assets to meet its projected obligations to retirees, it has an *overfunded* plan. (More on overfunded plans in the next section of this chapter.)

To see whether the company has an over- or underfunded pension plan, go to the footnotes of a 10-K filing and look for the note labeled "pension and other postretirement benefits," "employee retirement benefits," or some variation. Then look at the line labeled "projected benefit obligation." This is the first key number. It's the estimated amount the company will owe to employees after they retire, and it's based on assumptions about how long retirees will live, the rate that salary levels at the company will grow over time, and the interest rate that the company uses to discount its future obligations to their present value. Compare this with the line labeled "fair value of plan assets at end of year," which is the second key number.

If the benefit obligation exceeds the plan assets, the company has an underfunded pension plan and is likely to have to shovel in more money in the future, reducing profits. This can be a huge number for a large company with many retirees—General Motors, for example, had pension obligations of $80 billion at year-end 2002 versus pension assets of $61 billion. One way or another, GM will need to make up the $19 billion difference. (As recently as 2000, GM had a $1.7 billion *surplus* in its pension plan. When Wall Street goes south, so do pension plans—but the obligation keeps growing as employees earn benefits.)

What did this mean for GM? In 2002, the firm chucked in a whopping $4.9 billion to the plan. (You can see this in the pension footnote under "employer contributions.") That's almost $5 billion in cold, hard cash that an unwary shareholder might have been expecting to increase the firm's value, but which actually went straight to GM retirees.

So, always check out the pension footnote. There's a lot of accounting gobbledygook there, but you can also find out whether the firm you're looking at is going to wind up owing its retirees more money than it actually has. And if that's the case, they'll get the money before you will as a shareholder.

Pension Padding

Pensions can be a boon as well as a burden. When stocks and bonds do really well, as they did in the 1990s, pension plans go gangbusters. And if those annual returns exceed the annual pension costs, the excess can be counted as profit. Flowing gains from an overfunded pension plan through the income statement is a perfectly legal practice that pumped up earnings at General Electric for years and boosted earnings at many defense companies by 30% to 40% during the 1990s.

However, this pension-related income is a strange kind of profit. It's not available to pay out to shareholders—it belongs to the pension plan. And the only way to unlock that excess is to terminate the plan, which is highly unusual. But the excess does benefit shareholders: It should mean the company will have to contribute less to the pension plan in the future to keep it solvent. As a shareholder, you'd much rather have an overfunded pension plan than an underfunded one. But this income is completely dependent on the stock market, so it's not money you want to rely on in the future. You should subtract it from net income when trying to figure out just how profitable a company really is.

To find out how much profits decreased because of pension costs or increased because of pension gains, go to the line in the pension footnote labeled either "net pension/postretirement expense," "net pension credit/loss," "net periodic pension cost," or some variation. Companies usually break out the contribution of pension costs to profits for the trailing three years; therefore, you can see not only the absolute level of pension profit or loss, but also the trend. You won't see these numbers in the income statement—they get lumped in with other categories there.

Vanishing Cash Flow

There's one important caveat to the general rule that cash flow is a number to be trusted: You can't count on cash flow generated by employees exercising options. I mentioned this wrinkle in Chapter 22—the amount is labeled "tax benefits from employee stock plans," or "tax benefit of stock options exercised" on the statement of cash flows. Here's why you don't want to count on this cash flow.

When employees exercise their stock options, the amount of cash taxes that their employer has to pay declines. Let's say your employer gives you 100 options with an exercise price of $10. A few years later, the stock is trading for $30, and you decide to cash in. You pay taxes on the $2,000 difference (the $30 market price less the $10 exercise price), and your employer gets to take a tax deduction of $2,000 against its corporate income because taxable employee compensation is tax deductible for employers. In other words, your employer reduced its tax bill by $700—assuming a 35% tax rate—just because you exercised your 100 options.

As long as the firm's stock keeps going up and it keeps giving out options, this process continues. More options are exercised, tax deductions are taken, and the firm saves cash by lowering its tax bill. But what happens if the stock takes a tumble? Many people's options will be worthless—their exercise prices will be higher than the market price—and, consequently, fewer options will be exercised. Fewer options are now exercised, the company's tax deduction gets smaller, and it has to pay more taxes than before, which means lower cash flow.

Therefore, when the stock price declines, the firm generates less cash than it did when the stock was flying. Sun Microsystems, for example, reported about $2.1 billion in cash flow from operations in fiscal 2001, $816 million of which resulted from this lovely tax benefit. In other words, Sun would have generated 40% less cash in 2001 if its employees hadn't exercised tons of options. But the next year, when Sun's shares plunged to below $5, this portion of cash flow dried up very fast as fewer options were exercised. In 2002, Sun's option-related tax benefits dropped by almost 90%, to only $98 million.

If you're analyzing a company with great cash flow that also has a high-flying stock, check to see how much of that cash flow growth is coming from options-related tax benefits. Unless you think you can predict the stock market, that's not cash you want to count on in years to come.

Overstuffed Warehouses

When inventories rise faster than sales, there's likely to be trouble on the horizon. Sometimes the buildup is just temporary as a company prepares for a new product launch, but that's usually more the exception than the rule.

When a company produces more than it's selling, either demand has dried up or the company has been overly ambitious in forecasting demand. In any case, the unsold goods will have to get sold eventually—probably at a discount—or written off, which would result in a big charge to earnings.

This is what happened in late 2000 to virtually every company selling communications-related gear—inventories started to balloon as demand from telecom carriers started to slow. At the time, many analysts (including, I'm humbled to say, me) thought that the gear-makers had simply overestimated demand temporarily and that the situation would correct itself once telecom carriers used up the gear they'd already ordered. But it turned out that demand was not just pausing—it was falling off a cliff. Therefore, inventories continued to pile up until sales started to slow as well, and companies such as Cisco had to write off billions in unsold goods.

Change Is Bad

Another way firms can make themselves look better is by changing any one of a number of assumptions in their financial statements. As a very general rule, you should look skeptically on any optional change—some accounting changes are mandated by rule makers—that improves reported results. Odds are good that the motivation for making the change wasn't altruistic.

One item that can be altered is a firm's depreciation expense. If a firm is assuming that an asset—such as a building or factory—will wear out in 10 years, it subtracts (or depreciates) one-tenth of the building's value from its earnings each year. As you can imagine, the longer the depreciation period, the smaller the annual hit to earnings. Therefore, if a firm suddenly decides that an asset has a longer useful life and stretches out the depreciation period, it's essentially pushing costs out into the future and inflating current earnings.

Firms can also change their *allowance for doubtful accounts.* If the allowance for doubtful accounts doesn't increase at the same rate as accounts receivable, a firm is essentially saying that its new customers are much more creditworthy than the previous ones—which is pretty unlikely. If the allowance actually *declines* as accounts receivable rise, the company is stretching the truth even further. In either case, if more customers wind up not paying than the firm estimated, the firm will have to take a charge to earnings at some point in the future, which means current results are overstated.

Firms can also change things as basic as how expenses are recorded and when revenue is recognized (one of those gray accounting areas). You'll generally find this kind of information in the "summary of significant accounting policies" section of the 10-K—and if a firm chooses to make changes that materially reduce expenses or increase revenue, watch out. Unless these moves were required by the accounting rule makers, the firm is probably trying to cover up deteriorating results.

To Expense or Not to Expense

Companies can also fiddle with their costs by capitalizing them. As I discussed in Chapter 21, the basis of accrual accounting is that benefits have to be matched with expenses on the income statement. Operating costs—such as office supplies, office rents, and so forth—are expensed because they produce a short-term benefit. (You pay the rent only one month or year at a time, and the benefit you receive expires at the end of that period unless you make another payment.) On the other hand, costs such as a new piece of machinery are *capitalized*—that is, their value is recorded as an asset that slowly declines in value over time—because they produce long-term benefits. (A machine that you buy today will still be cranking out products three years from now, just at a lower rate because of wear and tear.)

The tricky part is that certain types of costs, such as marketing and some kinds of software development, can be treated either way. As you can imagine, a company that wants to inflate profits can easily do so by capitalizing $100 in marketing costs and spreading the expense out over several years, rather than expensing the entire $100 in the current period. This is exactly what AOL did in the mid-1990s—the firm argued that the subscribers it was acquiring were likely to produce long-term benefits, so it should be allowed to capitalize its marketing costs. The SEC disagreed, and AOL had to reverse course.

Finding this kind of information will take some digging around in the footnotes of a company's 10-K form, but it's time well spent. Any time you see expenses being capitalized, ask some hard questions about just how long that "asset" will generate an economic benefit. Looking at the *useful life* assumption will generally do the trick—a building might be useful for 40 years, but a piece of office furniture or a chunk of software won't.

Investor's Checklist: Avoiding Financial Fakery

▶ The simplest way to detect aggressive accounting is to compare the trend of net income with the trend in cash flow from operations. If net income is growing quickly while cash flow is flat or declining, there's a good chance of trouble lurking.

▶ Companies that make numerous acquisitions or take many one-time charges are more likely to have aggressive accounting. Be wary if a firm's chief financial officer leaves or if the firm changes auditors.

▶ Watch the trend of accounts receivable relative to sales. If accounts receivable is growing much faster than sales, the company may be having trouble collecting cash from its customers.

▶ Pension income and gains from investments can boost reported net income, but don't confuse them with solid results from the company's core operations.

26

Valuation—The Basics

So far, we've spent all of our time analyzing companies. If the investment process were as simple as identifying great companies with shareholder-friendly management teams and wide economic moats, we'd be finished—and investing would be much easier. But even the most wonderful business is a poor investment if purchased for too high a price. To invest successfully means you need to buy great companies at attractive prices.

This is an idea that lost credence during the bull market of the 1990s and was thrown completely out the window during the tech bubble. Valuations mattered less and less because investors were always willing to pay more and more—in fact, one popular investment commentary service stated baldly that business quality was 100 times more important than valuation.

For a while, this strategy—relying on a greater fool to take an asset off your hands at a higher price—was lucrative and made many people rich, at least on paper. The trouble was that no one knew when the music would stop. When it did, investors who bought overpriced assets hoping to sell them at even more inflated prices were sorely disappointed.

This is the difference between investors and speculators. Investors purchase an asset for less than their estimate of its value and receive a return more or less in line with the financial performance of that asset. Speculators, by contrast, purchase an asset not because they believe it's actually worth more, but because they think another investor will pay more for it at some point. The return that investors receive on assets depends largely on the accuracy of their analysis, whereas a speculator's return depends on the gullibility of others.

Over time, the stock market's returns come from two key components: investment return and speculative return. As Vanguard founder John Bogle has pointed out, the investment return is the appreciation of a stock because of its dividend yield and subsequent earnings growth, whereas the speculative return comes from the impact of changes in the price-to-earnings (P/E) ratio. Over the entire twentieth century, Bogle found that the 10.4% average annual return of U.S. equities broke down into 5 percentage points from dividends, 4.8 percentage points from earnings growth, and just 0.6 percentage points from P/E changes. In other words, over a long time span, the impact of investment returns trump the impact of speculative returns.[1]

However, the picture is much different when we look at it over shorter time frames. From 1980 through 2000, for example, the market's approximately 17% annual return was composed of 4 percentage points dividends, 6 percentage points earnings growth—and a whopping 7 percentage points per year from the increase in the P/E ratio.

During the horrific bear market of the 1970s, the market's *investment* return was a solid 13.4% per year, but as the aftermath of the early-1970s Nifty Fifty craze dragged the market's P/E ratio down from 16 times to 7 times, the market's *speculative* return was a crushing −7.5 percentage points per year. The market returned an average of only 5.9% per year during the 1970s, not because earnings and dividends refused to cooperate, but because the average investor paid less for the average stock in 1980 than in 1970.

Paying Up Rarely Pays Off

What does all this have to do with picking solid stocks? By paying close attention to the price you pay for a stock, you minimize your speculative risk, which helps maximize your total return. No one knows what a stock's speculative

---

[1] John C. Bogle, "After the Fall: What Lies Ahead for Capitalism and the Financial Markets?" (address given at the University of Missouri, Columbia, October 22, 2002).

return will be over the next year—or even 10 years—but we can make some pretty good educated guesses about the investment return. If you find great companies, value them carefully, and purchase them only at a discount to a reasonable valuation estimate, you'll be fairly well insulated against the vicissitudes of market emotion.

For example, let's take a stock that trades for $30 per share, earns $1.50 per share, and pays a $1.00 annual dividend. Assume that earnings and dividends grow at 6% per year, and the initial P/E ratio of 20 doesn't change.

After five years, earnings will be $2.01, so our shares would theoretically trade for $2.01 × 20 = $40.20. We've also received $5.64 in dividends, which means we have $45.84 after five years. That works out to an annualized return of 8.8%, which is our investment return. Because the P/E remained at 20, we didn't receive any speculative return.

However, if earnings and dividends grow at the same rate, *but* the P/E ratio decreases from its starting point of 20 to 15, our returns change dramatically. Although we still have $2.01 in earnings after five years, our shares are worth only $2.01 × 15 = $30.15. Add in $5.64 in dividends, and annualized return shrinks to just 3.6%—our 8.8% investment return was damaged by a −5.2% speculative return. Conversely, a rise in the P/E ratio from 20 to 25 would yield a fat 13.3% annual return because the speculative return builds on our investment return.

Thus, a change in the market's mood can reduce our solid 8.8% return to a paltry 3.6% or boost it to a wonderful 13.3%. You can buy an excellent company that kicks out earnings and dividends like clockwork, but the negative effects of a sharp decline in the stock's valuation can wipe out even the most robust investment return—and a P/E decline from 20 to 15 is hardly a worst-case scenario. In fact, declines in valuation are usually coupled with deteriorating corporate fundamentals—slowing earnings growth or some similar setback. When this happens, the investor gets socked with a decline in the speculative return as the valuation shrinks and a decline in the investment return as earnings growth slows down.

Careful attention to valuation lessens the risk that something truly unknown—what other investors will pay for our asset in the future—will hurt the return of our portfolio. As investors, we can diligently work to identify wonderful businesses, but we can't predict how other market participants will value stocks, so we shouldn't try.

Being picky about valuation isn't fun. It means letting many pitches go by and watching many stocks run—stocks that never met your strict valuation criteria. But when it's done properly, disciplined valuation also greatly increases your batting average—the number of stocks you pick that do well versus the number that do poorly—and it also limits the odds of a real blow-up damaging your portfolio.

Using Price Multiples Wisely

Our first stop in learning how to value stocks is traditional measures such as the price-to-sales (P/S) or P/E ratios. Although these measures do have some advantages—for example, they're very easy to compute and use—they also have some significant pitfalls that can lead the unwary investor to fuzzy conclusions.

Price-to-Sales

The most basic ratio of all is the P/S ratio, which is the current price of the stock divided by sales per share. The nice thing about the P/S ratio is that sales are typically cleaner than reported earnings because companies that use accounting tricks usually seek to boost earnings. (Firms can use accounting tricks to boost sales, but it's much less frequent and it's easier to catch.) In addition, sales are not as volatile as earnings—one-time charges can depress earnings temporarily, and the bottom line of economically cyclical companies can vary significantly from year to year.

This relative smoothness of sales makes the P/S ratio useful for quickly valuing companies with highly variable earnings, by comparing the current P/S ratio with historical P/S ratios. Motorola, for example, takes special charges so often that they're no longer very special, and, as a result, it had negative net income in three of the five years between 1998 and 2002. With such spotty earnings, a P/E ratio isn't going to help us very much. But over that same time period, sales haven't jumped around nearly as much, which makes the P/S ratio useful. In mid-2003, Motorola's P/S ratio was about 1.0, close to a five-year low, which made the stock look relatively inexpensive compared with where it traded in the past (see Figure 26.1).

Motorola	1998	1999	2000	2001	2002
Price/Earnings	NA	119.7	34.9	NA	NA
Price/Sales	1.3	3.2	1.2	1.1	0.7

NA = Earnings are negative, therefore, P/E ratios cannot be calculated.

Figure 26.1   When earnings are negative, price/sales can be a useful metric.

However, the P/S ratio has one big flaw: Sales may be worth a little or a lot, depending on a company's profitability. If a company is posting billions in sales, but it's losing money on every transaction, we'd have a hard time pinning an appropriate P/S ratio on the shares because we have no idea what level (if any) profits the company will generate. We can see the drawbacks of using sales as a proxy for value in the marketplace every day.

Retailers, which typically have very low net margins—that is, they convert a relatively small percentage of every dollar of sales into profits—tend to have very low P/S ratios. The average grocery store, for example, had a P/S ratio of 0.4 in mid-2003, whereas the average medical device firm had a P/S of around 4.3. The reason for this huge difference isn't that grocery stores happened to be dirt cheap—it was that the average grocery store had a net margin of 2.5%, whereas the average medical device firm had a net margin of 11%. A grocer with a P/S of just 1.0 would look ridiculously overvalued, but a medical device manufacturer with the same P/S ratio would be an absolute steal.

Therefore, although the P/S ratio might be useful if you're looking at a firm with highly variable earnings—because you can compare today's P/S with a historical P/S ratio—it's not something you want to rely on very much. In particular, don't compare companies in different industries on a price-to-sales basis, unless the two industries have very similar levels of profitability.

Price-to-Book

Another common valuation measure is price-to-book (P/B), which compares a stock's market value with the book value (also known as shareholder's equity or net worth) on the company's most recent balance sheet. The idea here is that future earnings or cash flows are ephemeral, and all we can really count on is the net value of a firm's tangible assets in the here-and-now. Legendary value investor Benjamin Graham, one of Warren Buffett's mentors, was a big advocate of book value and P/B in valuing stocks.

Although P/B still has some utility today, the world has changed since Ben Graham's day. When the market was dominated by capital-intensive firms that owned factories, land, rail track, and inventory—all of which had some objective tangible worth—it made sense to value firms based on their accounting book value. After all, not only would those hard assets have value in a liquidation, but also they were the source of many firms' cash flow. But now, many companies are creating wealth through intangible assets such as processes, brand names, and databases, most of which are not directly included in book value.

For service firms, in particular, P/B has little meaning. If you used P/B to value eBay, for example, you wouldn't be according a shred of worth to the firm's dominant market position, which is the single biggest factor that has made the firm so successful. Price-to-book can also lead you astray for a manufacturing firm such as 3M, which derives much of its value from its brand name and innovative products, not from the size of its factories or the quantity of its inventory.

Another item to be wary of when using P/B to value stocks is goodwill, which can inflate book value to the point that even the most expensive firm looks like a value. When one company buys another, the difference between the target firm's tangible book value and the purchase price is called *goodwill*, and it's supposed to represent the value of all the intangible assets—smart employees, strong customer relationships, efficient internal processes—that made the target firm worth buying.

Unfortunately, goodwill often represents little else but the desperation of the acquiring firm to buy the target before someone else did, because acquiring firms often overpay for target companies. Be highly skeptical of firms for which goodwill makes up a sizable portion of their book value. The P/B may be low, but the bulk of the B could disappear in a hurry if the firm declares the goodwill as "impaired" (in other words, the firm admits that it grossly overpaid for a past acquisition) and writes down its value.

Price-to-book is also tied to return on equity (equal to net income divided by book value) in the same way that price-to-sales is tied to net margin (equal to net income divided by sales). Given two companies that are otherwise equal, the one with a higher ROE will have a higher P/B ratio. For example, over the past five years, Nokia's P/B ratio has averaged about 14, whereas rival mobile-phone giant Motorola's has averaged 3.1. One major reason for this difference is that Nokia's average ROE of 29% over the same period left Motorola's average ROE of 3% in the dust. The reason is clear—a firm that can compound book equity at a much higher rate is worth far more because book value will increase more quickly.

Therefore, when you're looking at P/B, make sure you relate it to ROE. A firm with a low P/B relative to its peers or to the market and a high ROE might be a potential bargain, but you'll want to do some digging before making that assessment based solely on the P/B.

A caveat: Although P/B isn't terribly useful for service firms, it's very good for valuing financial services firms because most financial firms have considerable liquid assets on their balance sheets. The nice thing about financial firms is that many of the assets included in their book value are marked-to-market—in other words, they're revalued every quarter to reflect shifts in the marketplace, which means that book value is reasonably current. (A factory or piece of land, by contrast, is recorded on the balance sheet at whatever value the firm paid for it, which is often very different from the asset's current value.)

As long as you make sure that the firm doesn't have a large number of bad loans on its books P/B can be a solid way to screen for undervalued financial firms. Just remember that financial firms trading below book value (a P/B lower than 1.0) are often experiencing some kind of trouble, so you'll want to investigate just how solid that book value is before investing.

Price-to-Earnings: The Benefits

Now we come to the most popular valuation ratio, which can take you pretty far as long as you're aware of its limitations. The nice thing about P/E is that accounting earnings are a much better proxy for cash flow than sales, and they're more up-to-date than book value. Moreover, earnings per share results and estimates are easily available from just about any financial data source imaginable, so it's an easy ratio to calculate.

The easiest way to use a P/E ratio is to compare it to a benchmark, such as another company in the same industry, the entire market, or the same company at a different point in time. Each of these approaches has some value, as long as you know the limitations. A company that's trading at a lower P/E than its industry peers could be a good value, but remember that even firms in the same industry can have very different capital structures, risk levels, and growth rates, all of which affect the P/E ratio. All else equal, it makes sense to pay a higher P/E for a firm that's growing faster, has less debt, and has lower capital reinvestment needs.

You can also compare a stock's P/E to the average P/E of the entire market. However, the same limitations of industry comparisons apply to this process as well. The stock you're investigating might be growing faster (or slower) than the average stock, or it might be riskier (or less risky). In general, comparing a company's P/E with industry peers or with the market has some value, but these aren't approaches that you should rely on to make a final buy or sell decision.

However, comparing a stock's current P/E with its historical P/E ratios can be useful, especially for stable firms that haven't undergone major shifts in their business. If you see a solid company that's growing at roughly the same rate with roughly the same business prospects as in the past, but it's trading at a lower P/E than its long-term average, you should start getting interested. It's entirely possible that the company's risk level or business outlook has changed, in which case a lower P/E is warranted, but it's also possible that the market is simply pricing the shares at an irrationally low level.

This method generally works better with more stable, established firms than with young companies with more uncertain business prospects. Firms that are growing rapidly are changing a great deal from year to year, which means their current P/Es are less comparable to their historical P/Es.

Price-to-Earnings: The Drawbacks

Relative P/Es have one huge drawback: A P/E of 12, for example, is neither good nor bad in a vacuum. Using P/E ratios only on a relative basis means that your analysis can be skewed by the benchmark you're using.

So, let's try to look at the P/E ratio on an absolute level. What factors would cause a firm to deserve a higher P/E ratio? Because risk, growth, and capital needs are all fundamental determinants of a stock's P/E ratio, higher growth firms should have *higher* P/E ratios, higher risk firms should have *lower* P/E ratios, and firms with higher capital needs should have *lower* P/E ratios.

We can see why this is true intuitively, without breaking out any equations, by thinking about the basics of valuation—the three big factors that affect value are the amount, timing, and riskiness of a firm's future cash flows.

Firms that have to shovel in large amounts of capital to generate their earnings run the risk of needing to tap additional funding, either through debt (which increases the risk level of the company) or through additional equity offerings (which may dilute the value of current shareholders' stake). Either way, it's rational to pay less for firms with high reinvestment needs because each dollar of earnings requires more of shareholders' capital to produce it.

Meanwhile, a firm that's expected to grow quickly will likely have a larger stream of future cash flows than one that's growing slowly, so all else equal, it's rational to pay more for the shares (thus, the higher P/E ratio). On the flip side, a firm that's riskier—maybe it has high debt, maybe it's highly cyclical, or maybe it's still developing its first product—has a good chance of having lower future cash flows than we originally expected, so it's rational to pay less for the stock.

When you're using the P/E ratio, remember that firms with an abundance of free cash flow are likely to have low reinvestment needs, which means that a reasonable P/E ratio will be somewhat higher than for a run-of-the-mill company. The same goes for firms with higher growth rates, as long as that growth isn't being generated using too much risk.

A few other things can distort a P/E ratio. Keep these questions in the back of your mind when looking at P/E ratios, and you'll be less likely to misuse them.

Has the Firm Sold a Business or an Asset Recently? When you're looking at a P/E ratio, you must be sure that the E makes sense. If a firm has recently sold off a business or perhaps a stake in another firm, it's going to have an artificially inflated E, and thus a lower P/E. Because you don't want to value the firm based on one-time gains such as this, you need to strip out the proceeds from the sale before calculating the P/E. In late 2000, it looked as though Oracle had a ridiculously low P/E based on the past four quarters' earnings—until you dug into the numbers and saw that the company had booked a $7 billion gain by selling part of its stake in Oracle Japan. Based on operating earnings, the stock wasn't all that cheap.

Has the Firm Taken a Big Charge Recently? If a firm is restructuring or closing down plants, earnings could be artificially depressed, which would push the P/E up. For valuation purposes, it's useful to add back the charge to get a sense of the firm's normalized P/E.

Is the Firm Cyclical? Firms that go through boom and bust cycles—semiconductor companies and auto manufacturers are good examples—require a bit more care. Although you'd typically think of a firm with a very low trailing P/E as cheap, this is precisely the wrong time to buy a cyclical firm because it means earnings have been very high in the recent past, which in turn means they're likely to fall off soon. For cyclical stocks, your best bet is to look at the most recent cyclical peak, make a judgment whether the next peak is likely to be lower or higher than the last one, and calculate a P/E based on the current price relative to what you think earnings per share will be at the next peak.

Does the Firm Capitalize or Expense Its Cash Flow-Generating Assets? A firm that makes money by building factories and making products gets to spread the expense of those factories over many years by depreciating them bit by bit. On the other hand, a firm that makes money by inventing new products—drug firms are the classic example—has to expense all of its spending on research and development every year. Arguably, it's that spending on R&D that's really creating value for shareholders. Therefore, the firm that expenses assets will have lower earnings—and thus a higher P/E—in any given year than a firm that capitalizes assets.

Is the E Real or Imagined? There are two kinds of P/Es—a *trailing P/E,* which uses the past four quarters' worth of earnings to calculate the ratio, and a *forward P/E,* which uses analysts' estimates of next year's earnings to calculate the ratio. Because most companies are increasing earnings from year to year, the forward P/E is almost always lower than the trailing P/E, sometimes markedly so for firms that are increasing earnings at a very rapid clip. Unfortunately, estimates of future earnings by Wall Street analysts—the *consensus* numbers that you often read about—are consistently too optimistic. As a result, buying a stock because its forward P/E is low means counting on that future *E* to materialize in its entirety, and that's usually not the case.

Price-to-Earnings Growth (PEG)

The PEG is an offshoot of the P/E ratio that's calculated by dividing a company's P/E by its growth rate. The PEG is extremely popular with some investors because it seeks to relate the P/E to a piece of fundamental information—a company's growth rate. On the surface, this makes sense because a firm that's growing faster will be worth more in the future, all else equal.

The problem is that risk and growth often go hand in glove—fast-growing firms tend to be riskier than average. This conflation of risk and growth is why the PEG is so frequently misused. When you use a PEG ratio, you're assuming that all growth is equal, generated with the same amount of capital and the same amount of risk.

But firms that are able to generate growth with less capital should be more valuable, as should firms that take less risk. If you look at a stock that's expected to grow at 15% trading at 15 times earnings and another one that's expected to grow at 15% trading at 25 times earnings, don't just plunk your money down on the one with the lower PEG ratio. Look at the capital that needs to be invested to generate the expected growth, as well as the likelihood that those expectations will actually materialize, and you may very well wind up making a very different decision.

Say Yes to Yield

In addition to multiple-based measures, you can also use yield-based measures to value stocks. For example, if we invert the P/E and divide a firm's earnings per share by its market price, we get an earnings yield. If a stock sells for $20 per share and has $1 in earnings, it has a P/E of 20 ($\frac{20}{1}$) but an earnings yield of 5% ($\frac{1}{20}$). The nice thing about yields, as opposed to P/Es, is that we can compare them with alternative investments, such as bonds, to see what kind of a return we can expect from each investment. (The difference is that earnings generally grow over time, whereas bond payments are fixed.)

In late-2003, for example, I could get a risk-free return from Uncle Sam of about 4.5% by buying a 10-year treasury bond. Therefore, I'd want to demand a higher rate of return from my stocks because they're riskier than treasuries. A stock with a P/E of 20 would have an earnings yield of 5%, which is a bit better than treasuries, but not much considering the additional risk I'm taking. A stock with a P/E of 12, however, would have an earnings yield of 8.3% ($\frac{1}{12}$), which is much better than those poky treasuries. Thus, I might be induced to take the additional risk.

The best yield-based valuation measure is a relatively little-known metric called *cash return.* In many ways, it's actually a more useful tool than the P/E.

To calculate a cash return, divide free cash flow by enterprise value. (Enterprise value is simply a stock's market capitalization plus its long-term debt minus its cash.) The goal of the cash return is to measure how efficiently the business is using its capital—both equity and debt—to generate free cash flow.

Essentially, cash return tells you how much free cash flow a company generates as a percentage of how much it would cost an investor to buy the whole shebang, including the debt burden. An investor buying the whole company would not only need to buy all the shares at market value, but also would be taking on the burden of any debt (net of cash) the company has.

Let's use household-products giant Clorox as an example of how to use cash return to find reasonably valued investments. In late 2003, Clorox had a market cap of about $9.8 billion and carried $495 million in long-term debt and $172 million in cash on its balance sheet. Its enterprise value was $9,800 + $495 − $172, or $10.1 billion. That's half of our ratio.

The other half is free cash flow. Figure 26.2 shows Clorox's free cash flow over the past decade; the firm generated about $600 million in free cash flow in 2003. So, our cash return on Clorox will be $600 million/$10,100 million, or 5.9%.

With 10-year treasuries yielding just 4.5% in late 2003 and corporate bonds yielding a higher (but still relatively paltry) 4.9%, that 5.9% cash return from Clorox looks pretty good. Throw in the fact that Clorox's free cash flow is likely to grow over time, whereas those bond payments are fixed, and Clorox starts to look like a pretty solid value.

Cash return is a great first step to finding cash cows trading at reasonable prices, but don't use cash return for financials or foreign stocks. Cash flow isn't terribly meaningful for banks and other firms that earn money via their balance sheets. And because definitions of cash flow can vary widely in other

Free Cash Flow ($mil)	94	95	96	97	98	99	00	01	02	03
Cash operations ($mil)	266.8	290.9	406.7	362.1	312.7	588.0	658.0	747.0	876.0	803.0
Cap expenses ($mil)	-56.6	-62.9	-84.8	-95.2	-99.0	-176.0	-158.0	-192.0	-177.0	-205.0
Free cash flow ($mil)	**210.2**	**228.0**	**321.9**	**266.9**	**213.7**	**412.0**	**500.0**	**555.0**	**699.0**	**598.0**

Figure 26.2 Annual cash flows for Clorox.

countries, a foreign stock that looks cheap based on its cash return may simply be defining cash flow more liberally.

Investor's Checklist: Valuation—The Basics

▶ Be picky about valuation. You'll do well over the long haul by buying companies that are undervalued relative to their earnings potential.

▶ Don't rely on any single valuation metric because no individual ratio tells the whole story. Apply a number of different valuation tools when you're assessing a stock.

▶ If the firm is cyclical or has a spotty earnings history, use the price-to-sales ratio. Companies with P/S ratios lower than their historical average can sometimes be bargains.

▶ The price-to-book ratio is most useful for financial firms and firms with numerous tangible assets, and it's least useful for service-oriented firms. In addition, firms with higher ROEs will typically be worth a higher P/B ratio.

▶ You can compare a company's P/E with the market, with a similar firm, or with the company's historical P/E. In each case, you'll want the company's P/E to be lower than the benchmark, but make sure you're aware of any differences in risk or growth rates between the company you're valuing and the benchmark. The most reliable benchmark is likely to be the company's own historical valuations, assuming the company hasn't changed very much over time.

▶ Use the PEG with caution because fast-growing firms also tend to be riskier. Don't overpay for expected growth that may never materialize.

▶ The lowest P/E isn't always the best. Firms with high growth, low risk, and low capital reinvestment needs should have higher P/E ratios. You'll likely be better off in the long run paying more for a low-risk firm that's generating large amounts of cash than paying less for a cyclical company that's very capital intensive.

▶ Check the earnings yield and cash return, and compare them with the rates available on bonds. An earnings yield or cash return above current bond rates can indicate an undervalued stock.

27

Valuation—Intrinsic Value

THE BIG DRAWBACK of the ratios we discussed in the previous chapter is that they're all based on *price*—they compare what investors are currently paying for one stock to what they're paying for another stock. Ratios do not, however, tell you anything about *value,* which is what a stock is actually worth.

Without knowing what a stock is worth, how can you know how much you should pay for it? At Morningstar, we're firm believers that stocks should be purchased because they're trading at some discount to their intrinsic value, not simply because they're priced at a higher or lower point than similar companies. Comparing ratios across companies and across time can help us understand whether our valuation estimate is close to or far from the mark, but estimating the intrinsic value of a company gives us a better target.

Having an intrinsic value estimate keeps you focused on the value of the business, rather than the price of the stock—and that's what you want because, as an investor, you're buying a small piece of a business. Intrinsic valuation also forces you to think about the cash flows that a business is generating today and the cash it could generate in the future, as well as the returns on capital that the firm creates. It makes you ask yourself: If I could buy the whole company, what would I pay?

Second, having an intrinsic value gives you a stronger basis for making investment decisions. Without looking at the true determinants of value, such as cash flow and return on capital, we have no way of assessing whether a P/E of, for example, 15 or 20 is too low, too high, or right on target. After all, the company with the P/E of 20 might have much lower capital needs and a less risky business than the company with the P/E of 15, in which case it might actually be the better investment.

In this chapter, I'm going to walk you through a simplified version of how we estimate intrinsic values at Morningstar. Even if you choose not to go through the entire exercise yourself for every stock you think about buying—and you very well may not—knowing the basic principles will help you make better investment decisions.

A warning: This can be some difficult stuff, so don't be discouraged if you're a bit confused. It does get easier with practice, though—I promise!

Cash Flow, Present Value, and Discount Rates

Our first step is answering a basic question—what's a stock worth? Luckily, we can stand on the shoulders of giants such as economists Irving Fisher and John Burr Williams, who answered this question for us more than 60 years ago: The value of a stock is equal to the present value of its future cash flows. No more and no less.

Let's take this idea apart carefully, because understanding it is crucial to properly valuing stocks. Companies create economic value by investing capital and generating a return. Some of that return pays operating expenses, some gets reinvested in the business, and the rest is free cash flow.

Remember, we care about free cash flow because that's the amount of money that could be taken out of the business each year without harming its operations. A firm can use free cash flow to benefit shareholders in a number of ways. It can pay a dividend, which essentially converts a portion of each investor's interest in the firm to cash. It can buy back stock, which reduces the number of shares outstanding and thus increases the percentage ownership of each shareholder. Or, the firm can retain the free cash flow and reinvest it in the business.

These free cash flows are what give the firm its investment value. A *present value* calculation simply adjusts those future cash flows to reflect the fact that money we plan to receive in the future is worth less than money we receive today.

Why are future cash flows worth less than current ones? First, money that we receive today can be invested to generate some kind of return, whereas we can't invest future cash flows until we receive them. This is the *time value of money*. Second, there's a chance we may never receive those future cash flows, and we need to be compensated for that risk, called the "risk premium."

The time value of money is essentially the opportunity cost of receiving money in the future versus receiving it today, and it's often represented by the interest rates being paid on government bonds. It's pretty certain that the U.S. government will be around to pay us our interest in a few years.

Of course, not many cash flows are as certain as those from the feds, so we need to tack on an additional premium to compensate us for the risk that we may never receive the money that we've been promised. Add the government bond rate to the risk premium, and you have what's known as a *discount rate*.

The oddly named discount rate makes more sense when you think about it in these terms: What rate of return would you need to make you indifferent between receiving some quantity of money right now versus at some time in the future? The old saying that a bird in the hand is worth two in the bush expresses the same concept in a different way: We know we have the bird in the hand, so we need two birds in the bush to make us indifferent between the two options. In a similar vein, money to be received in the future is worth less to us because we don't know if we'll get it, and if we get it today, we could invest it to earn a return.

For example, if you were about to take a one-week vacation, but your boss asked you at the last minute to postpone it for a year, you might ask your boss for an extra day off to compensate for the delay. In other words, six days off next year is equivalent to five days off right now, because you'd rather take the trip now and because something else could crop up over the next year that would force you to delay the trip again.

So, your mental discount rate for vacation time is 20%. That's the rate at which five days becomes six days in a year (6 days − 5 days/5 days). And if you thought your boss might get fired—which would make it less certain that her promise of an extra day would be honored—you might ask for two extra days off next year. In that case, your mental discount rate would be

40%, which is the rate at which five days becomes seven days in a year (7 days − 5 days/5 days).

Now you can start to see why stocks with stable, predictable earnings often have such high valuations—investors discount their future cash flows at a lower rate, because they believe that there's a lower risk attached to the likelihood that those future cash flows will actually show up. Conversely, a business with an extremely uncertain future should logically have a lower valuation because there's a substantial risk that the potential future cash flows will never materialize.

You can see why a rational investor should be willing to pay more for a company that's profitable now relative to one that promises profitability only at some point in the future. Not only does the latter carry higher risk (and thus a higher discount rate), but the promised cash flows won't arrive until some years in the future, diminishing their value still further.

This can be a tough concept, so let's look at an example with some real numbers. Figure 27.1 illustrates the difference that changing discount rates and

	StableCorp		CycliCorp		RiskCorp	
Year	Free Cash Flow ($)	Discounted at 9%	Free Cash Flow ($)	Discounted at 12%	Free Cash Flow ($)	Discounted at 15%
2003	2,000	2,000	2,000	2,000	0	0
2004	2,200	2,018	2,200	1,964	0	0
2005	2,420	2,037	1,980	1,578	0	0
2006	2,662	2,056	2,376	1,691	2,000	1,315
2007	2,928	2,074	2,851	1,812	2,540	1,452
2008	3,221	2,093	3,421	1,941	3,226	1,604
2009	3,543	2,113	3,207	1,625	4,097	1,771
2010	3,953	2,162	3,900	1,764	5,203	1,956
2011	4,327	2,172	4,681	1,891	6,608	2,160
2012	4,746	2,185	5,383	1,941	8,325	2,366
Sum	32,000	**20,910**	31,999	**18,207**	31,999	**12,624**

Figure 27.1   Timing and uncertainty have a big effect on present value. The longer you have to wait to receive a set of cash flows and the less certain you are that you'll eventually receive them, the less they're worth to you today. *Source:* Morningstar, Inc.

the timing of cash flows can have on present value. In all three examples—StableCorp, CycliCorp, and RiskCorp—the sum of the *undiscounted* cash flows is about $32,000.

However, the value of the *discounted* cash flows is quite different from company to company. In present value terms, CycliCorp is worth about $2,700 less than StableCorp. That's because StableCorp is more predictable, which means that investors' discount rate isn't as high. CycliCorp's cash flow increases by 20% some years and shrinks in some years, so investors perceive it as a riskier investment and use a higher discount rate when they're valuing its shares. As a result, the *present value* of the *discounted* cash flows is lower.

The difference in the present value of the cash flows is even more acute when you look at RiskCorp, which is worth almost $8,300 less than StableCorp. Not only are the bulk of RiskCorp's cash flows far off in the future, but also, we're less certain that they'll come to pass, so we assign an even higher discount rate.

Believe it or not, you now know the basic principles behind a discounted cash flow model. Value is determined by the *amount, timing,* and *riskiness* of a firm's future cash flows, and these are the three items you should always be thinking about when deciding how much to pay for a stock. That's all it really boils down to.

Calculating Present Value

Now that you know the theory behind an intrinsic value calculation, here's how you can do it in practice. To find the present value of a $100 future cash flow, divide that future cash flow by 1.0 plus the discount rate. Using a 10% discount rate, for example, a cash flow of $100 one year in the future is worth $100/1.10, or $90.91. A $100 cash flow two years in the future is worth $100/(1.10)^2$, or $82.64. In other words, $82.64 invested at 10% becomes $90.91 in a year and $100 in two years. Discount rates are really just interest rates that go backwards through time instead of forwards.

Generalizing the previous formula, if we represent the discount rate as R, the present value of a future cash flow in year N equals $CF_n/(1 + R)^n$. Suppose, for example, that we have a $500 cash flow two years in the future with a 7% discount rate. The present value of that cash flow is:

$$\frac{\$500}{\left(1.07\right)^{2}} = \frac{\$500}{1.1449} = \$436.72$$

That same cash flow three years in the future is worth $408.16 today:

$$\frac{\$500}{\left(1.07\right)^{3}} = \frac{\$500}{1.225} = \$408.16$$

Looking three years into the future and changing our discount rate back to 10%, our present value is $375.66 today:

$$\frac{\$500}{\left(1.10\right)^{3}}$$

(If you want to do this in a spreadsheet program such as Excel, remember to use the carat [^] symbol to insert an exponent. Thus, 1.10^{4} would be written as 1.10^4 in an Excel formula.)

Fun with Discount Rates

Now that we have the formula down, we need to figure out what factors determine discount rates. How do we know whether to use 7% or 10%? From our previous example of the delayed vacation, we know that opportunity cost—or time value—is one factor and that the other big determinant of our discount rate is risk.

Unfortunately, there is no precise way to calculate the exact discount rate that you should use in a discounted cash flow (DCF) model, and academics have filled entire journal issues with nothing but discussions about the right way to estimate discount rates—but trust me, it's not a discussion in which you want to be involved.

Here's what you need to know for practical purposes: As interest rates increase, so will discount rates. As a firm's risk level increases, so will its discount rate. Let's put these two together. For interest rates, you can use a long-term average of Treasury rates as a reasonable proxy. (Remember, we use the interest rate on treasuries to represent opportunity costs because we're pretty certain that the government will pay us our promised interest.) In mid-2003, the average yield of the 10-year bond over the past decade was about 5.5%, so we'll use that. Because this isn't an exact science, you may want to use 5% or 6%.

Now for risk, which is an even less exact factor to measure. According to standard finance theorists, risk is the same thing as volatility, and the risk level of a company can be estimated simply by looking at how much its shares have bounced around relative to how much the market has bounced around. Thus, if a firm's shares suddenly drop from $30 to $20, this theory holds that the stock has just become much riskier.

We're not big fans of this definition of risk at Morningstar because we think stocks that are cheap are generally less risky than stocks with high price tags. (This assumes that nothing dramatic has changed with the underlying business, which isn't always the case when a stock drops.) We think it's better to assess risk by looking at the company, rather than by looking at the stock, and that a firm's riskiness is determined by the likelihood that it will or won't generate the cash flows that we're forecasting.

Why? Because what the share price has done in the *past* may have little bearing on what cash flows the company generates in the future. We think it makes more sense to define risk as the chance of permanent capital impairment—in other words, the likelihood that our investment will be worth much less when we go to sell it than it is today. Here are some factors we think should be taken into account when estimating discount rates.

Size

Smaller firms are generally riskier than larger firms because they're more vulnerable to adverse events. They also usually have less diversified product lines and customer bases.

Financial Leverage

Firms with more debt are generally riskier than firms with less debt because they have a higher proportion of fixed expenses (debt payments) relative to other expenses. Earnings will be better in good times, but worse in bad times, with an increased risk of financial distress. (Financial distress means that the firm is having trouble paying its debts.) Look at a firm's debt-to-equity ratio, interest coverage, and a few other factors to determine the degree of a company's risk from financial leverage.

Cyclicality

Is the firm in a cyclical industry (such as appliances or semiconductors) or a stable industry (such as breakfast cereal or beer)? Because the cash flows of cyclical firms are much tougher to forecast than stable firms, their level of risk increases.

Management/Corporate Governance

This factor boils down to a simple question: How much do you trust the folks running the shop? Although it's rarely black or white, firms with promotional managers, managers who draw egregious salaries, or who exhibit any of the other red flags covered in Chapter 7 are definitely riskier than companies with managers who don't display these traits.

Economic Moat

Does the firm have a wide moat, a narrow moat, or no economic moat? The stronger a firm's competitive advantage—that is, the wider its moat—the more likely it will be able to keep competitors at bay and generate a reliable stream of cash flows.

Complexity

The essence of risk is uncertainty, and it's tough to value what you can't see. Firms with extremely complex businesses or financial structures are riskier than simple, easy-to-understand firms because there's a greater chance that something unpleasant is hiding in a footnote that you missed. Even if you think management is as honest as the day is long and that the firm does a great job running its operations, it's wise to incorporate a *complexity discount* into your mental assessment of risk—unless you really want to memorize all 700 pages of the last 10-K filing.

How should you incorporate all of these risk factors into a discount rate? As I said earlier, there's no *right* answer. At Morningstar, we use 10.5% as the discount rate for an average company based on the factors in the preceding list, and we create a distribution of discount rates based on whether firms are riskier or less risky than the average. As of mid-2003, firms such as Johnson & Johnson, Colgate, and Wal-Mart fall at the bottom of the range, at around 9%, whereas riskier firms—such as Micron Technology, JetBlue Airways, and E*Trade—top out at 13% to 15%.

The key is to pick a discount rate you're comfortable with. Don't worry about being exact—just think about whether the company you're evaluating is riskier or less risky than the average firm, along with how much riskier or less risky it is, and you'll be fine. In addition, remember that assigning discount rates is an inexact science—there is no "right" discount rate for a company.

Calculating Perpetuity Values

We're almost there—we have cash flow estimates, and we have a discount rate. We need only one more element, called a *perpetuity value,* and we're ready to put the whole thing together. We need a perpetuity because it's not feasible to project a company's future cash flows out to infinity, year-by-year, and because companies have theoretically infinite lives.

The most common way to calculate a perpetuity is to take the last cash flow (*CF*) that you estimate, increase it by the rate at which you expect cash flows to grow over the very long term (*g*), and divide the result by the discount rate (*R*) minus the expected long-term growth rate. In formula terms, this equals:

$$\frac{CF_n(1+g)}{(R-g)}$$

The result of this calculation then must be discounted back to the present, using the method I discussed previously. Let's run through an example to show you what I mean.

For example, suppose we're using a 10-year DCF model for a company with an 11% discount rate. We estimate that the company's cash flow in year 10 will be $1 billion and its cash flows will grow at a steady 3% annual rate after that. (Three percent is generally a good number to use as your long-run growth rate because it's roughly the average rate of U.S. gross domestic product [GDP] growth. If you're valuing a firm in a declining industry, you might use 2%.)

First, multiply $1 billion by 1.03 to get an estimated $1.03 billion cash flow in year 11.

$$\$1 \text{ billion} \times 1.03 = \$1.03 \text{ billion}$$

Divide $1.03 billion by 0.08 (our 11% discount rate minus 3% long-run growth rate) to get $12.88 billion in estimated cash flows from year 11 onward.

$$\frac{\$1.03 \text{ billion}}{0.11 - 0.03} = \$12.88 \text{ billion}$$

To get the present value of these cash flows, we need to discount them using the formula we saw earlier: $CF_n/(1 + R)^n$, where n is the number of years in the future, CF_n is the cash flow in year n, and R is the discount rate. Plugging in the numbers:

$$N = 10$$
$$CF_n = \$12.88 \text{ billion}$$
$$R = 0.11$$
$$\frac{\$12.88}{(1.11)^{10}} = \frac{\$1288}{2.839} = \$4.536 \text{ billion}$$

Now, all we need to do is add this discounted perpetuity value to the discounted value of our estimated cash flows in years 1 through 10, and divide by the number of shares outstanding (see Figure 27.2).

I'll go through a couple of detailed examples in the next chapter, but here's a brief outline of the process. I'll use Clorox as an example again. You can follow along by matching the following steps to Figure 27.3:

1. Estimate free cash flows for the next four quarters. This amount will depend on all of the factors we discussed earlier in the book—how fast the

Simple 10-Year Valuation Model

Step 1	Forecast free cash flow (FCF) for the next 10 years.
Step 2	Discount these FCFs to reflect the present value:
	▸ Discounted FCF = FCF for that year ÷ $(1 + R)^N$
	(where R = discount rate and N = year being discounted)
Step 3	Calculate the perpetuity value and discount it to the present:
	▸ Perpetuity Value = $FCF_{10} \times (1 + g) \div (R - g)$
	▸ Discounted Perpetuity Value = Perpetuity Value $\div (1 + R)^{10}$
Step 4	Calculate total equity value by adding the discounted perpetuity value to the sum of the 10 discounted cash flows (calculated in step 2):
	▸ Total Equity Value = Discounted Perpetuity Value + 10 Discounted Cash Flows
Step 5	Calculate per share value by dividing total equity value by shares outstanding:
	▸ Per Share Value = Total Equity Value ÷ Shares Outstanding

Figure 27.2   A step-by-step discounted cash flow model for calculating the equity value of a company.
Source: Morningstar, Inc.

company is growing, the strength of its competitors, its capital needs, and so on. (We get into more detail on estimating cash flows in the next chapter when we analyze and value two firms top to bottom.) For Clorox, our first step is to see how fast free cash flow has grown over the past decade, which turns out to be about 9% when you do the math. We could just increase the $600 million in free cash flow that Clorox generated in 2003 by 9%, but that would assume that the future will be as rosy as the past. During the 1990s, the rise of mega-retailers like Wal-Mart—which now accounts for almost a quarter of Clorox's sales—has hurt the bargaining power of consumer-products firms. So, let's be conservative and assume free cash flow increases by only 5% over last year, which would work out to $630 million.

2. Estimate how fast you think free cash flow will grow over the next 5 to 10 years. Remember, only firms with very strong competitive advantages and low capital needs are able to sustain above-average growth rates for very long. If the firm is cyclical, don't forget to throw in some bad years. We won't do this for Clorox because selling bleach and Glad bags is a very stable business. We will, however, be conservative on our growth rate

Assumptions for Clorox

Current stock price:	$45.00
Shares outstanding (mil)	221.0
Next year's free cash flow (mil)	$630.00
Perpetuity growth rate (g)	3.0%
Discount rate (R)	9.0%

10-Year Valuation Model for Clorox

Step 1: Forecast free cash flow (FCF) for the next 10 years.
Assumes constant 5% growth rate, free cash flows in $ millions.

	Yr 1	Yr 2	Yr 3	Yr 4	Yr 5	Yr 6	Yr 7	Yr 8	Yr 9	Yr 10
Free cash flow →	630.0	661.5	694.6	729.3	765.8	804.1	844.3	886.5	930.8	977.3

Step 2: Discount these free cash flows to reflect the present value.
Discount Factor = $(1 + R)^N$ (where R = discount rate and N = year being discounted)

	Yr 1	Yr 2	Yr 3	Yr 4	Yr 5	Yr 6	Yr 7	Yr 8	Yr 9	Yr 10
Free cash flow	630.0	661.5	694.6	729.3	765.8	804.1	844.3	886.5	930.8	977.3
÷ Discount factor	1.09^1	1.09^2	1.09^3	1.09^4	1.09^5	1.09^6	1.09^7	1.09^8	1.09^9	1.09^{10}
= Discounted FCF →	577.9	556.8	536.3	516.7	497.7	479.4	461.8	444.9	428.6	412.8

Step 3: Calculate the perpetuity value and discount it to the present.
Perpetuity Value = Yr 10 FCF $\times$ (1 + g) ÷ (R − g) (where g = perpetuity growth rate and R = discount rate)

Perpetuity value	→	$(977.3 \times 1.03) ÷ (.09 - .03) = \$16{,}776.98$
Discounted	→	$\$16{,}776.98 ÷ 1.09^{10} = \$7{,}086.78$

Step 4: Calculate total equity value.
Add the discounted perpetuity value (see above) to the sum of the 10 discounted cash flows (see step 2).

Total equity value	→	$\$7{,}087.05 + \$4{,}913.01 = \$12{,}000.06$

Step 5: Calculate per share value.
Divide total equity value by shares outstanding.

Per share value	→	$\$12{,}000.06 ÷ 221.00 = \$54.30$

Figure 27.3   Valuing Clorox using discounted cash flow. *Source:* Morningstar, Inc.

because of the "Wal-Mart factor," and we'll assume free cash flow increases at 5% annually over the next decade.

3. Estimate a discount rate. Financially, Clorox is rock-solid, with little debt, tons of free cash flow, and a noncyclical business. So, we'll use 9% for our discount rate, which is meaningfully lower than the 10.5% average we discussed earlier. Clorox is a pretty predictable company, after all.

4. Estimate a long-run growth rate. Because I think people will still need bleach and trash bags in the future, and it's a good bet that Clorox will continue to get a piece of that market, I use the long-run GDP average of 3%.

5. That's it! We discount the first 10 years of cash flows, add that value to the present value of the perpetuity, and divide by shares outstanding.

This is a very simple DCF model—the one we use at Morningstar has about a dozen Excel tabs, adjusts for complicated items such as pensions and operating leases, and explicitly models competitive advantage periods, among many other things. But a model doesn't need to be super complex to get you most of the way there and help you clarify your thinking. For example, our valuation of Clorox—which pegs the value of the stock at about 15% higher than the stock price in late 2003—has the company generating free cash flow of about $800 million per year 10 years from now.

How realistic is this? As of late 2003, only 125 companies in Morningstar's database of more than 6,500 firms were able to accomplish such a feat, so it's certainly a high hurdle. However, given Clorox's portfolio of strong brands and solid track record of product innovation it's not unreasonable. Moreover, our 5% estimated annual growth rate in free cash flow is a good deal lower than the firm's past growth rate, which makes the model somewhat conservative. After all, Clorox has so many strong brands—including the eponymous bleach, Pine-Sol, and Formula 409—that it may be able to hold the line when it negotiates with big retailers like Wal-Mart.

The important thing is that we forced ourselves to think through these kinds of issues, which we wouldn't have if we'd just looked at Clorox's stock chart or if we'd just said, "Sixteen times earnings seems reasonable." By thinking about the business, we arrived at a better valuation in which we have more confidence.

Margin of Safety

We've analyzed a company, we've valued it—now we need to know when to buy it. If you really want to succeed as an investor, you should seek to buy companies at a discount to your estimate of their intrinsic value. Any valuation and any analysis is subject to error, and we can minimize the effect of these errors by buying stocks only at a significant discount to our estimated intrinsic value. This discount is called the *margin of safety,* a term first popularized by investing great Benjamin Graham.

Here's how it works. Let's say we think Clorox is worth $54, and the stock is trading at $45. If we buy the stock and we're exactly right about our analysis, the return we receive should be the difference between $45 and $54 (20%) plus the discount rate of about 9%. (The discount rate for a stock is sometimes called the *required return* for precisely this reason.) That would be 29%, which is a pretty darn good return, all things considered.

But what if we're wrong? What if Clorox grows even more slowly than we'd anticipated—maybe a competitor takes market share—or the firm's pricing power erodes faster than we'd thought? If that's the case, then Clorox's fair value might actually be $40, which means we would have overpaid for the stock by buying it at $45.

Having a margin of safety is like an insurance policy that helps prevent us from overpaying—it mitigates the damage caused by overoptimistic estimates. If, for example, we'd required a margin of safety of 20% before buying Clorox, we wouldn't have purchased the stock until it fell to $43. In that case, even if our initial analysis had been wrong and the fair value had really been $40, the damage to our portfolio wouldn't have been as severe.

Because all stocks aren't created equal, not all margins of safety should be the same. It's much easier to forecast the cash flows of, for example, Anheuser-Busch over the next five years than the cash flows of Boeing. One company has tons of pricing power, dominant market share, and relatively stable demand, whereas the other has relatively little pricing power, equal market share, and highly cyclical demand. Because I'm less confident about my forecasts for Boeing, I'll want a larger margin of safety before I buy the shares. There's simply a greater chance that something might go wrong and that my forecasts will be too optimistic.

Paying more for better businesses makes sense, within reason. The price you pay for a stock should be closely tied to the quality of the company, and great businesses are worth buying at smaller discounts to fair value. Why? Because high-quality businesses—those that have wide economic moats—are more likely to increase in value over time, and it's better to pay a fair price for a great business than a great price for a fair business.

How large should your margin of safety be? At Morningstar, it ranges all the way from just 20% for very stable firms with wide economic moats to 60% for high-risk stocks with no competitive advantages. On average, we require a 30% to 40% margin of safety for most firms.

Having a margin of safety is critical to being a disciplined investor because it acknowledges that as humans, we're flawed. Simply investing in the stock market requires some degree of optimism about the future, which is one of the biggest reasons that buyers of stocks are too optimistic far more often than they're too pessimistic. Once we know this, we can correct for it by requiring a margin of safety for all of our share purchases.

Conclusion

Every approach to equity investing has its own warts. Being disciplined about valuation may mean that you'll miss out on some great opportunities because some companies wind up performing better for longer periods of time than almost anyone would have anticipated. Companies such as Microsoft and Starbucks, for example, looked very pricey back in their heyday, and it's unlikely that many investors who were very strict about valuation would have bought them early in their corporate lives. Why? Because both firms managed to fend off their competitors for very long periods of time—much longer than a conservative estimate would have given them credit for.

Being disciplined about valuation would have meant missing these opportunities, but it also would have kept you out of many investments that were priced like the next Microsoft, but which wound up disappointing investors in a big way. Think about how many software firms have fallen by the wayside over the past decade, for example, or when bagel stocks were priced as if they were going to all become the next McDonald's back in the early 1990s. Although we acknowledge that some high-potential companies are worth a leap of faith and a high valuation, on balance, we think it's better to miss a solid investment because you're too cautious in your initial valuation than it is to buy stocks at prices that turn out to be too high.

After all, the *real* cost of losing money is much worse than the *opportunity* cost of missing out on gains. That's why the price you pay is just as important as the company you buy.

Investor's Checklist: Valuation—Intrinsic Value

▶ Estimating an intrinsic value keeps you focused on the value of the business, rather than on the price of the stock.

▶ Stocks are worth the present value of their future cash flows, and that value is determined by the amount, timing, and riskiness of the cash flows.

▶ A discount rate is equal to the time value of money plus a risk premium.

▶ The risk premium is tied to factors like the size, financial health, cyclicality, and competitive position of the firm you're evaluating.

▶ To calculate an intrinsic value, follow these five steps: Estimate cash flows for the next year, forecast a growth rate, estimate a discount rate, estimate a long-run growth rate, and add the discounted cash flows to the perpetuity value.

Putting It All Together

Now, IT'S TIME for the fun part. You now have an investment philosophy, you know what economic moats are, and you know how to read financial statements and evaluate companies. Let's put all this knowledge to work by analyzing two real-world companies: chipmaker Advanced Micro Devices (AMD) and Biomet, a medical device firm.

(Note: All of the financial data in this chapter is available free on Morningstar.com in the same format that you see it here.)

Advanced Micro Devices

At first, AMD might look like an attractive investment. It's one of only two companies that manufacture microprocessors—the brains in a PC or server—and computers are pretty ubiquitous devices. AMD also makes flash memory chips that are used in a variety of devices that should have solid long-term demand, such as mobile phones and network routers. In the microprocessor market, AMD has caught up to archrival Intel on the technological front over the past several years, and for a brief spell in the late 1990s, the firm was selling chips that were arguably faster and better than those being sold by Intel. In addition, AMD has been working on a powerful next-generation chip that may be better than anything Intel has to offer.

This is the AMD story that you might know if you followed the news a bit and casually flipped through the company's Web site and its recent annual reports. However, it's not enough information to make a sound investment decision, so let's approach the firm systematically to see just how solid an investment AMD really is.

Economic Moat

First, look for evidence of an economic moat. As we discussed in Chapter 3, we can do this by examining how profitable AMD has been in the past by analyzing free cash flow, margins, return on equity, and return on assets (see Figure 28.1).

It looks like AMD has had a pretty spotty history of generating free cash flow. After a few good years in the early 1990s, free cash flow turned negative as the firm heavily increased capital spending, and AMD didn't throw off any free cash again until the technology boom in 2000. That's not a good sign that the firm has much of an economic moat. However, some rapidly growing firms spend years plowing all of their money back into capital spending, which means their free cash flow is negative because they're still building their economic moat. (Starbucks was a great example of this during the 1990s.) Even these kinds of firms should have solid profits, however, so let's turn to AMD's margins and returns on capital (see Figure 28.2).

Looking at operating and net margins, we see that although AMD scores better on this front than it does on free cash flow, it still lost money for 6 of the past 10 years. The trend doesn't indicate that these were simply cyclical losses—the firm lost money for four straight years between 1996 and 1999, even though the U.S. economy was going gangbusters.

ROE and ROA tell a similar story. After some salad days in the early 1990s—ROEs in the high teens are pretty good—AMD's performance went

Free Cash Flow ($mil)	93	94	95	96	97	98	99	00	01	02
Cash operations ($mil)	456.2	573.2	611.9	73.2	398.8	144.4	259.9	1,205.6	167.7	-88.9
Cap expenses ($mil)	-323.7	-548.7	-620.8	-485.0	-685.1	-996.2	-619.8	-805.5	-678.9	-705.2
Free Cash Flow ($mil)	**132.5**	**24.5**	**-8.9**	**-411.8**	**-286.3**	**-851.8**	**-359.9**	**400.1**	**-511.2**	**-794.1**
FCF/Sales (%)	**8.0**	**1.1**	**-0.4**	**-21.1**	**-12.2**	**-33.5**	**-12.6**	**8.6**	**-13.1**	**-29.4**

Figure 28.1   AMD's free cash flow.

AMD Profitability	93	94	95	96	97	98	99	00	01	02
Operating margin (%)	18.5	24.0	14.3	-13.0	-3.8	-6.4	-11.2	19.1	-1.5	-45.4
Net margin (%)	13.3	13.8	12.4	-3.5	-0.9	-4.1	-3.1	21.2	-1.6	-48.3
Asset turnover (avg)	1.0	1.0	0.9	0.6	0.7	0.7	0.7	0.9	0.7	0.5
Return on Assets (%)	**13.3**	**13.8**	**11.2**	**-2.1**	**-0.6**	**-2.9**	**-2.2**	**19.1**	**-1.1**	**-24.2**
Financial leverage (avg)	1.4	1.4	1.4	1.5	1.6	1.9	2.2	2.0	1.7	1.9
Return on Equity (%)	**18.6**	**19.3**	**15.7**	**-3.2**	**-1.0**	**-5.5**	**-4.8**	**38.2**	**-1.9**	**-46.0**

Figure 28.2 AMD's profitability numbers.

into a big slump until the tech boom in 2000. We can also see that asset turnover has declined, which means that AMD has become less efficient and financial leverage has gradually edged upward, indicating that AMD has probably taken on more debt.

AMD has had one great year recently—ROE, free cash flow, and margins were all excellent in 2000—and it's worth our time to find out why so we can determine whether it was an aberration or a sign of better times to come. After reading through some recent annual reports, we find that AMD made money in 2000 the old-fashioned way: It rolled out a chip that was faster and cheaper than anything Intel had at the moment. This made the company a ton of money until 2001, when the demand for PCs slowed down and Intel rolled out a competing chip.

So, AMD's one big recent success was due to a product with superior technology, which we know from Chapter 20 is the least sustainable source of an economic moat. It shouldn't come as a surprise to us that Intel quickly used its superior size and cash hoard to accelerate the rollout of a competing chip and regain the market share it briefly lost to AMD.

Overall, there's not much evidence of a sustainable economic moat in AMD's historical financials. It's not difficult to understand why: Intel dominates the microprocessor market, and AMD's market share has typically been around 15% for the past several years. Intel's size lets it spend four times as much on research and development as AMD does, which is a big advantage when you consider how fast semiconductor technology changes. Intel's size has also allowed it to attain much greater economies of scale, because it can spread the fixed costs of its manufacturing plants across a much larger volume of chips.

AMD Revenue Growth	93	94	95	96	97	98	99	00	01	02
Year over year (%)	8.8	29.5	13.8	-19.6	20.7	7.9	12.4	62.5	-16.2	-30.7
3-Year average (%)	—	—	17.1	5.8	3.3	1.5	13.5	25.4	15.3	-1.9
10-Year average (%)	—	—	—	—	—	—	—	—	—	5.9

Figure 28.3 AMD's revenue growth.

AMD's lack of an economic moat means we'd want a big margin of safety if we wanted to buy the stock, but even no-moat companies can sometimes be decent investments if the fundamentals aren't too shaky and the stock is cheap enough. Let's complete our analysis by looking at the five areas I discussed in Chapter 6—growth, profitability, financial health, risks, and management—and then by doing a rough valuation of the stock.

Growth

Figure 28.3 shows that revenue growth has been somewhat volatile for AMD over the past decade. Overall, it's not been terrible, but a 6% average annual growth rate over a decade when PC demand was pretty hot is nothing to crow about.

It's tough to say much that's meaningful about growth in profits because AMD had so many money-losing years during the 1990s. About the best we can do is note that AMD made a lot more money in its most recent profitable year (2000) than it did in the previous profitable year (1995), but it also lost much more money in 2002 than it ever had before—a spotty track record, at best (see Figure 28.4).

Profitability

We looked at free cash flow and returns on capital when we were assessing whether AMD had an economic moat, and the verdict was pretty negative.

	93	94	95	96	97	98	99	00	01	02
Net income ($mil)	218.4	294.9	300.5	-69.0	-21.1	-104.0	-88.9	983.0	-60.6	-1,303.0

Figure 28.4 AMD's net income.

Let's dig a bit deeper to see what else we can understand about how AMD makes (and loses) money. Look at Figure 28.5, which is a *common size* income statement. Common size statements are great tools for evaluating companies because they put every line item in context by looking at each of them as a percentage of sales.

These numbers show some disturbing trends. In the early 1990s, gross margins were around 50%, and they've steadily slid to between 20% and 30% in 2001 and 2002. Spending on overhead (SG&A) has been pretty steady at 16% to 19% of sales, while R&D spending has increased dramatically. The big increase in R&D spending helps support our previous intuition that chip companies need to spend large amounts on R&D to stay competitive. It also correlates with the big increase in capital spending we saw on the statement of cash flows—AMD was spending boatloads of money on expanding its manufacturing capabilities.

Overall, we have a company making less money per chip, not becoming much more efficient in terms of overhead spending, and having to increase research spending in a big way. Couple these trends with highly variable sales—see the revenue growth line in Figure 28.3—and you have a pretty dismal profitability picture.

Financial Health

Unfortunately, things don't look much better when we examine AMD's financial health.

AMD	93	94	95	96	97	98	99	00	01	02
Revenue (%)	100.0	100.0	100.0	100.0	100.0	100.0	100.0	100.0	100.0	100.0
COGS (%)	47.9	46.0	53.5	73.8	67.0	67.6	68.7	54.1	66.5	78.1
Gross Margin (%)	**52.1**	**54.0**	**46.5**	**26.2**	**33.0**	**32.4**	**31.3**	**45.9**	**33.5**	**21.9**
SG&A (%)	17.6	16.8	15.8	18.7	17.0	16.5	18.9	12.9	15.9	24.8
R&D (%)	15.9	13.1	16.4	20.5	19.9	22.3	22.2	13.8	16.7	30.3
Other (%)	0.0	0.0	0.0	0.0	0.0	0.0	1.3	0.0	2.3	12.3
Operating Margin (%)	**18.5**	**24.0**	**14.3**	**-13.0**	**-3.8**	**-6.4**	**-11.2**	**19.1**	**-1.5**	**-45.4**

Figure 28.5   AMD's common size income statement, representing each line item as a percent of revenue.

At the end of 2002, the firm had $1.9 billion in debt and $2.5 billion in shareholders' equity. The resulting debt-to-equity ratio of 0.7 isn't terribly high relative to the market, but it's not great for a firm that has as much trouble generating profits as AMD does. AMD's current ratio—which, remember, is simply current assets divided by current liabilities—was about 1.5. Again, not terrible, but not comforting either, given AMD's second-tier industry position and spotty history of profitability.

Finally, we learn by digging into AMD's 10-K filing that the firm has some big loans outstanding with banks in Germany, relating to a large manufacturing facility that the firm is building there. Adding these loans to other contractual obligations, we see that AMD will need to pay out more than $950 million to various parties between 2004 and 2006. That's a huge amount of money for a company that has generated only $250 million in net operating income since 1993 and has bled about $2.7 billion in free cash flow over the same period.

(You can calculate the cumulative operating income and free cash flow amounts yourself from the previous figures.) I'd say AMD doesn't score very well on the financial health front.

The Bear Case

Although I normally recommend developing a strong bear case for any company you analyze, we've uncovered many more negatives than positives about AMD so far, so let's move on.

Management

Let's look at some of AMD's proxy statements to see what we can find out about management. For one thing, they're paid pretty well: Outgoing CEO Jerry Sanders pulled in about $1 million in salary every year between 1997 and 2002, an additional $400,000 in "deferred retirement compensation" for each of those years, and bonuses ranging from zero to $5.1 million. He also received a good-sized amount of additional "in-kind" compensation from use of company vehicles and the company plane. In 2002, for example, he received about $184,000 worth of company-provided vehicle services. That's either an expensive car or a well-paid chauffeur.

Other top executives also did well in 2002, with the top five individuals receiving salaries of between $450,000 and $900,000, and three of the five receiving hefty bonuses despite AMD's $1.2 billion loss that year. Incoming CEO Hector Ruiz didn't get a cash bonus, but don't feel too sorry for him—he received 1.2 million options (about 10% of the total granted that year) instead. Depending on the assumptions used, Ruiz's options will be worth between $12 and $30 million over the next decade.

Speaking of options, it looks to me as though AMD has been giving away the store to its employees and diluting shareholder value as a result. From 2000 through 2003, AMD issued about 46 million stock options to its employees and officers, increasing the number of shares outstanding by 15%. (You can find the total number of options granted each year in that year's proxy statement.) Therefore, anyone who bought AMD shares in 2000 and held them through 2003 saw their stake in the company shrink meaningfully after three years, simply because the firm gave away so many options to its employees. This kind of egregious options granting tells me that management cares little for outside shareholders.

Overall, I'd say that AMD's management is overpaid, and they are not the type of folks to whom I'd entrust my money.

Valuation

Valuation is tough, because AMD has lost money for the past two years. On a price-to-sales basis, AMD was trading at about 1.5 times sales in September, 2003, which was much cheaper than the seven times sales valuation of the chip industry average and in line with AMD's own 1.6 times sales average valuation over the past five years—not too bad.

We can't use a P/E because AMD was forecasted to lose about $0.30 per share in 2004. In any event, it would be tough to have much confidence in earnings estimates for a company that's been as volatile as AMD—for example, 2004 earnings estimates for AMD ranged from a low of −$0.85 per share to a high of $0.20 per share in September, 2003. In other words, no one has the faintest clue how much money AMD will be making (if any) in the near future, which tells us that we should demand a big margin of safety from our valuation we arrive at.

Because AMD is highly cyclical, we could also attempt to predict its earnings at the peak of the next cycle and value the company based on the resulting P/E ratio. Figure 28.6 shows that AMD's last peak earnings per share was almost $3 in 2000. However, we'd be wise to take this figure with a grain of salt because the earnings occurred during a technology boom that's unlikely

AMD Net Income	93	94	95	96	97	98	99	00	01	02
Net income ($mil)	218.4	294.9	300.5	-69.0	-21.1	-104.0	-88.9	983.0	-60.6	-1,303.0
Basic EPS ($)	1.15	1.51	1.42	-0.25	-0.08	-0.36	-0.30	3.18	-0.18	-3.81
Total shares	190.2	195	211.2	271.4	280.9	287.3	294.1	309.3	332.4	342.3

Figure 28.6   AMD's net income and shares outstanding.

to repeat and during a rare time when AMD was able to catch Intel napping. Still, even if we assume that AMD will earn only $1 per share during its next cyclical peak, the stock doesn't look too expensive—it was trading at $12 in September 2003, which is 12 times peak earnings.

The problem is that we have no idea when (or if) AMD's next cyclical peak will arrive. After all, the company has a weak competitive position and a troublesome balance sheet. Thus, I don't think valuing it on peak earnings makes much sense.

Finally, we can attempt to forecast cash flows and use a DCF approach. This is also tough because AMD has generated positive annual free cash flow only three times in the past decade. Let's give it a whirl, though.

If we conservatively estimate that AMD returns to positive free cash flow in 2005, generates $200 million that year, and increases free cash flow at 5% annually for the next 10 years, it will generate about $2.2 billion in free cash over the next decade. Discounted back to the present at 14%, that's about $1.0 billion. (I used 14% because AMD had a poor track record of profitability, had considerable balance sheet risk, and operated from a weak competitive position in a cyclical industry.) Add in our perpetuity value of $750 million, and AMD is worth about $1.8 billion, or about $5 per share (see Figure 28.7).

With the stock trading at $12 as of this writing, I'd take a pass. With such an uncertain future, this is a stock that I would buy only at a big discount to a conservative estimate of intrinsic value—and perhaps not even then, given how many strikes the firm has against it. The intrinsic value could be much lower if AMD fails to generate free cash flow in the near future or runs into liquidity troubles, or it could be much higher if AMD gains some kind of competitive edge against Intel. In particular, the next-generation "Hammer" family of chips AMD has rolled out could give the firm a boost. Given the firm's poor

Assumptions for AMD

Current stock price	$7.00
Shares outstanding (mil)	342.0
Next year's free cash flow (mil)	—
Perpetuity growth rate (g)	3.0%
Discount rate (R)	14.0%

10-Year Valuation Model for AMD

Step 1: Forecast free cash flow (FCF) for the next 10 years.
Assumes constant 5% growth rate, free cash flows in $ millions.

	Yr 1	Yr 2	Yr 3	Yr 4	Yr 5	Yr 6	Yr 7	Yr 8	Yr 9	Yr 10
Free cash flow $\rightarrow$	—	200.0	210.0	220.5	231.5	243.1	255.3	268.0	281.4	295.5

Step 2: Discount these free cash flows to reflect the present value.
Discount Factor = $(1 + R)^N$ (where R = discount rate and N = year being discounted)

	Yr 1	Yr 2	Yr 3	Yr 4	Yr 5	Yr 6	Yr 7	Yr 8	Yr 9	Yr 10
Free cash flow	—	200.0	210.0	220.5	231.5	243.1	255.3	268.0	281.4	295.5
÷ Discount factor	—	1.14^2	1.14^3	1.14^4	1.14^5	1.14^6	1.14^7	1.14^8	1.14^9	1.14^{10}
= Discounted FCF $\rightarrow$	—	153.9	141.7	130.6	120.3	110.8	102.0	94.0	86.5	79.7

Step 3: Calculate the perpetuity value and discount it to the present.
Perpetuity Value = Yr 10 FCF $\times$ $(1 + g) \div (R - g)$ (where g = perpetuity growth rate and R = discount rate)

Perpetuity value $\rightarrow$ $(295.5 \times 1.03) \div (.14 - .03) = \$2,766.86$

Discounted $\rightarrow$ $\$2,766.86 \div 1.14^{10} = \$746.34$

Step 4: Calculate total equity value.
Add the discounted perpetuity value (above) to the sum of the 10 discounted cash flows (see step 2).

Total equity value $\rightarrow$ $\$1,019.40 + \$746.34 = \$1,765.74$

Step 5: Calculate per share value.
Divide total equity value by shares outstanding.

Per share value $\rightarrow$ $\$1,765.74 \div 342 = \$5.16$

Figure 28.7 Valuing AMD using discounted cash flow. *Source:* Morningstar, Inc.

track record of holding its own against Intel, though, that's not a bet I'd want to make. The stock could move higher if the market gets enthusiastic about AMD's prospects—it tends to be pretty volatile—but it seems like a poor long-term investment.

Biomet

Medical-device firm Biomet, which will hopefully be more promising than AMD, makes artificial joints—mainly hips and knees—as well as a variety of other products used in orthopedic surgery, such as pins and screws for setting broken bones. The firm has been around for about 25 years, is still run by one of the founders, and competes with a relatively small group of firms. (The top five firms in Biomet's main market control about 85% of sales.)

The orthopedic device industry is pretty attractive. Developed-country populations are aging, and better health care means that people are staying active longer—which increases the demand for artificial joints. Moreover, artificial joints became a mass-market product only during the 1980s and 1990s. Because joints typically have a 10- to 12-year life span, the number of revision procedures, which replace or repair a worn-out artificial joint, is just now starting to climb. Add these revisions to the demand for first-time procedures, and the market is growing at 7% to 10%. And because annual price hikes of 3% to 4% are pretty usual in the orthopedic industry, sales growth of 10% to 14% looks pretty doable for the average orthopedic device company. Companies that gradually gain market share or compete in the high-end segment of the market might be able to grow a touch faster, as well.

Margins are fat because the industry has high barriers to entry and high switching costs. Surgeons prefer products with long clinical track records, which means it would be tough for an upstart to quickly gain market share. In addition, this is a heavily research-dependent business, so having decades of product development experience and expertise helps keep incumbents ahead of potential new entrants. Finally, each company's products are slightly different, which means that orthopedic surgeons develop product preferences and are reluctant to take time off from surgery to get retrained on a competitor's product unless it offers a large potential benefit. Because artificial joint innovations tend to be incremental, rather than revolutionary, this isn't terribly likely, so market share in the industry stays fairly stable.

You can learn all of this information by reading Biomet's 10-K and those of a few of its competitors, as well as surfing a few industry-oriented Web sites. Let's see if the financials bear out what seems to be an attractive company.

Economic Moat

First, we need to look for evidence that the firm has an economic moat—what sounds good in words may not always show up in the numbers. As with AMD earlier in the chapter, we can do this by examining the trends in Biomet's free cash flow, margins, return on equity, and return on assets (see Figure 28.8).

These are the kinds of consistently excellent financial results that serious stock investors dream about—consistent and constantly increasing free cash flow, a free cash-to-sales ratio well above 5% (and usually above 10%), and very consistent operating and net margins. There's little to quibble with here—any company that can convert more than 10% of sales into free cash flow for a decade is doing something right.

Trends in ROA and ROE also look stellar, with high margins, decent asset turns, and modest financial leverage (see Figure 28.9). Asset efficiency has declined a bit since the early 1990s, but not to an alarming degree. The only black spot is 1999, when net margin suddenly dipped from 19% to about 15%. Even though it recovered promptly the next year, this is something we should investigate.

A quick glance at the financial results in Figure 28.10 shows that the lower margins in 1999 were likely due to the $55 million in "other" expenses that the company recorded that year. After digging into the footnotes of the 1999 10-K filing, we find that the $55 million was a charge related to a legal dispute with a competitor, which claimed that Biomet competed with it unfairly. Although this is not a great development, the medical device industry is a litigious one,

Free Cash Flow	93	94	95	96	97	98	99	00	01	02
Cash operations ($mil)	43.8	65.7	52.6	68.5	123.0	121.8	148.5	131.6	190.5	184.2
Cap expenses ($mil)	-14.9	-6.6	-28.9	-14.1	-21.4	-44.1	-51.1	-43.1	-35.3	-62.3
Free Cash Flow ($mil)	**28.9**	**59.1**	**23.7**	**54.4**	**101.6**	**77.7**	**97.4**	**88.5**	**155.2**	**121.9**
FCF/Sales (%)	**8.6**	**15.9**	**5.2**	**10.2**	**17.5**	**11.9**	**12.9**	**9.6**	**15.1**	**10.2**

Figure 28.8 Biomet's historical free cash flow.

Profitability	93	94	95	96	97	98	99	00	01	02
Operating margin (%)	27.0	27.3	26.3	25.7	26.3	27.6	22.7	28.6	28.2	31.1
Net margin (%)	19.1	18.7	17.5	17.6	18.3	19.1	15.4	18.9	19.2	20.1
Asset turnover (avg)	1.1	1.0	1.0	0.9	1.0	0.9	0.8	0.8	0.8	0.8
Return on Assets (%)	**21.0**	**18.7**	**17.5**	**15.8**	**18.3**	**17.2**	**12.3**	**15.1**	**15.4**	**16.1**
Financial leverage (avg)	1.2	1.2	1.2	1.2	1.1	1.3	1.3	1.3	1.3	1.3
Return on Equity (%)	**25.2**	**22.4**	**21.0**	**19.0**	**20.1**	**22.4**	**16.0**	**19.6**	**20.0**	**20.9**

Figure 28.9   Biomet's profitability numbers.

and adverse legal charges are a fact of life from time to time. Because this is the only sizeable problem during the past several years—and none of the legal disputes discussed in Biomet's 2002 10-K sound particularly worrisome—it's not something I'm going to worry about too much. We should, however, make a mental note to pay extra-special attention to Biomet's balance sheet to make sure it has the resources to pay any more judgments that might come along.

Overall, it looks as though Biomet has a pretty sizeable economic moat. Returns on capital and free cash flow are consistently high, and there's not much year-to-year variation. Although we'll want to make sure we dig further into Biomet's competition—to make sure that these solid financial results are likely to persist in the future—Biomet has the financial hallmarks of a solid investment so far.

Growth

Figure 28.11 indicates that revenue growth has been a little volatile, ranging from 8% to 20%, but a sales growth rate in the mid teens is about average. That's pretty good, and it's right in line with the industry growth rates we ex-

Operating Expenses ($mil)	93	94	95	96	97	98	99	00	01	02
SG&A ($mil)	122.2	136.2	169.3	199.5	211.5	232.9	265.6	326.6	374.8	437.7
R&D ($mil)	18.0	20.5	21.8	24.1	23.2	36.1	35.5	40.2	43.0	50.8
Other ($mil)	0.0	0.0	0.0	0.0	0.0	0.0	55.0	11.7	26.1	0.0
Operating Income ($mil)	**90.5**	**101.8**	**119.0**	**137.3**	**159.8**	**180.1**	**171.7**	**263.7**	**290.7**	**370.7**

Figure 28.10   Biomet's historical operating expenses.

Revenue Growth	93	94	95	96	97	98	99	00	01	02
Year over year (%)	22.0	11.3	21.2	18.3	8.4	12.2	16.3	21.5	12.0	15.6
3-Year average (%)	—	21.2	18.1	16.9	15.9	12.9	12.3	16.6	16.5	16.3
10-Year average (%)	—	—	—	—	—	—	—	—	17.3	15.8

Figure 28.11 Biomet's historical revenue growth.

amined earlier in this section. That means Biomet is likely holding its own in terms of market share.

Now, let's see whether earnings growth is similarly solid (see Figure 28.12). Aside from 1999, which was affected by that $55 million legal charge that we mentioned earlier, earnings growth has been excellent. It's tough to increase the bottom line at 15% annually for a decade, but that's what Biomet has done. In addition, it looks as though long-term earnings growth of 15.7% is right in line with long-term sales growth of 15.8%, which means Biomet probably hasn't had to play any accounting games to generate such solid results. The firm increased earnings the way a great company should—by selling more products, year in and year out.

Profitability

We've already given very high marks to Biomet for its solid free cash flow and high returns on capital, but as we did with AMD, let's dig deeper to find out what was driving the firm's profitability. Again, we use a common size income statement as our tool (see Figure 28.13).

These are some very solid, steady results. Gross margins of 70% are high, and it looks as if they've been very gradually increasing over time, which means the firm has been able to maintain pricing power of the goods it sells and control costs of the materials used to make its products. Overhead (SG&A) costs have been very steady as a percentage of sales, which means Biomet isn't becoming

EPS Growth	93	94	95	96	97	98	99	00	01	02
Year over year (%)	21.7	8.9	13.1	18.9	14.6	18.1	-7.2	42.7	11.7	20.6
3-Year average (%)	—	20.4	14.5	13.6	15.5	17.2	7.9	16.1	14.0	24.3
10-Year average (%)	—	—	—	—	—	—	—	—	16.7	15.7

Figure 28.12 Biomet's historical EPS growth.

Biomet	93	94	95	96	97	98	99	00	01	02
Revenue (%)	100.0	100.0	100.0	100.0	100.0	100.0	100.0	100.0	100.0	100.0
COGS (%)	31.2	30.8	31.4	32.6	32.0	31.0	30.3	30.2	28.7	27.9
Gross Margin %	**68.8**	**69.2**	**68.6**	**67.4**	**68.0**	**69.0**	**69.7**	**69.8**	**71.3**	**72.1**
SG&A (%)	36.4	36.5	37.4	37.3	36.5	35.8	35.1	35.5	36.4	36.7
R&D (%)	5.4	5.5	4.8	4.5	4.0	5.5	4.7	4.4	4.2	4.3
Other (%)	0.0	0.0	0.0	0.0	0.0	0.0	7.3	1.3	2.5	0.0
Operating Margin (%)	**27.0**	**27.3**	**26.3**	**25.7**	**27.5**	**27.6**	**22.7**	**28.6**	**28.2**	**31.1**

Figure 28.13 Biomet's common size income statement, representing each line item as a percentage of revenue.

more efficient as it grows. This is all right, though, because a big chunk of those SG&A costs are Biomet's payments to its salesforce—when salespeople sell more, they get paid more, which is as it should be.

Finally, it looks as though research and development has been declining as a percentage of sales. Although this could be positive, because it means higher overall margins as Biomet spreads R&D costs over a larger sales base, we need to be sure that Biomet hasn't pared back too far on research. Innovation is the lifeblood of a company such as Biomet, so we want to do some digging to make sure the company has plenty of new products in the pipeline. We can probably determine this by going through the company's recent press releases and annual report, and we can also compare how much Biomet is spending on research with its competitors to make sure it's in line.

Overall, though, there are few quibbles here. Biomet passes the profitability test with flying colors, and the results are as clean as can be, with very few one-time charges. Most important, the charges that the company has taken truly were nonrecurring because they were the result of unpredictable legal disputes.

Financial Health

Biomet has no long-term debt, so that's one thing we won't have to worry about. The current ratio is around 4, which is high for a company with no debt to worry about, and the firm has consistently kept around 15% of total assets in cash.

One thing you want to watch with super-profitable companies such as Biomet is that they don't let too much cash pile up on the balance sheet. It's fine for a company to build a temporary war chest if it anticipates big investments sometime in the next few years, but cash that sits around on the balance sheet for a long time isn't being used efficiently. If you see cash as a percentage of total assets rising year after year for a firm that's already in fine financial health, try to find out why management isn't buying back stock, paying a dividend, or reinvesting it in the business. Any of the three are preferable to letting the cash account balloon.

The Bear Case

Creating a convincing bear case is especially crucial when evaluating companies like Biomet that score well on just about every front. Things that look too good to be true usually are, and every company has some warts that need to be taken into account.

First, we need to think about litigation risks. We mentioned earlier a recent $55 million charge related to an adverse legal settlement, and it's likely that the firm will be embroiled in other disputes from time to time. Therefore, we want to make sure that the firm has adequate insurance and that it's good about disclosing the status of whatever litigation it's party to. (The "commitments and contingencies" section of the 10-K will help us do this.) Legal risks are largely unpredictable, so we should be prepared for some potential headline risk from Biomet.

Another area of concern is that Biomet's foreign operations aren't in nearly as good a shape as its U.S. operations. If we look at the "segment data" section of Biomet's 2002 10-K, we find that the firm does about 25% of its sales outside the United States, but only 12% of the firm's operating income stems from its foreign units. Because the foreign segment is a big portion of the overall company and it's only half as profitable—and it's not growing as quickly—we want to find out what Biomet's plans are for its foreign operations. Why are they so much less profitable and growing so much slower? How does Biomet plan to fix them? If Biomet can't get its foreign operations on track, does it plan to exit them altogether, or is there some larger strategic reason that the firm needs an international presence? We want to try to get answers to these questions so we know just how big a risk the firm's foreign operations are likely to be.

Biomet's size is also an issue, because digging into the orthopedic devices industry reveals that Biomet is not as large as some of its competitors. Biomet has about 7% of the worldwide orthopedic market, whereas its competitor Stryker has 15% and the DePuy division of Johnson & Johnson has about 14%. Firms with more market share can sometimes gain greater economies of scale—which would allow them to price their products lower—and may also be able to outmuscle smaller competitors by offering customers a more diverse product lineup. Because Biomet has been growing nicely for some time and there's no evidence yet of margin pressure, it looks as though the firm is holding its own against its larger peers. However, we want to keep in mind the risk that a larger competitor will try to squeeze Biomet.

Finally, we want to look into some big-picture industry risks. Biomet's large gross margins suggest that the firm has been able to charge premium prices for its products, and highly profitable health care industries tend to attract political pressure from time to time—just ask the large drug firms. A change in the rules for Medicare reimbursements or some other arcane regulatory issue could have a big impact on the whole orthopedic device industry. Like legal risks, regulatory changes are tough to predict, so we want to mentally prepare ourselves for a potentially unpleasant shock.

Management

As with AMD, Biomet's proxy statement—which details executives' compensation—is a good first stop in assessing management. They're paid pretty reasonably: President and CEO Dane Miller pulled in less than $500,000 in salary *and* bonus, and other members of the executive team are in roughly the same range. One vice president even had a higher base salary than Miller in 2002. Salaries and bonuses have been moving up steadily over the past few years, but so have Biomet's profits. Finally, there's none of the "other compensation" frippery that executives at so many firms receive—no mention of loans, company cars, life insurance policies, special deferred retire-like-a-king accounts, and so on. Management is paid a healthy cash salary, some receive modest stock option grants, and that's that.

On the stock option front, neither Miller nor Chairman of the Board Niles Noblitt has received any stock options over the past three years, and some further digging into the proxy reveals that Miller has never received a stock option from the firm. Because Miller owns 3% of the outstanding shares and Noblitt owns 1.8%, this is entirely appropriate—both already have substantial ownership stakes that motivate them to act in shareholders' interests, and they see no need for greater ownership stakes. (Contrast this behavior with executives such as Larry Ellison of Oracle or Steve Jobs of Apple, each of whom has received substantial options grants in recent years despite already-large ownership stakes.)

For those executives who did receive option grants, the amounts look reasonable—over the past few years, no executive has received more than 1% of the total options granted in a given year, which means options are likely being widely distributed throughout the firm. Moreover, the total amount being granted each year is rarely above 1% of the total number of shares outstanding, and the firm's total number of shares has barely budged over the past decade. That tells me Biomet is using options responsibly to motivate employees and executives without diluting shareholder value, which is exactly the kind of behavior you want to see in the management team of a firm.

Valuation

For a firm as high quality as Biomet, valuation is likely to be the Achilles' heel in the investment analysis process. Companies this good are rarely cheap, so we need to tread carefully as we decide what a reasonable value would be for Biomet's shares. Even though the firm's high growth rate and strong profitability mean that we should be willing to pay up for the shares, we can't pay too much, or we'll be unlikely to receive a decent return on our investment.

Starting with the basic valuation multiples, we find that Biomet was trading at about 28 times the past year's earnings as of this writing. That's pricey—it's way above the market's price-to-earnings ratio of about 20—but it's substantially lower than the firm's average P/E of 38 over the past five years. Price-to-cash flow (P/CF) tells a similar story: The current P/CF ratio of 35 was higher than the market P/CF of 14, but lower than Biomet's historical average of 45.

Finally, Biomet's earnings yield and cash return of 3.0% and 2.1%, respectively, didn't exactly scream "undervalued." We could get better returns in risk-free treasuries, and given Biomet's higher risk than a T-bond, we should demand a *higher* cash return and earnings yield from its shares.

Assumptions for Biomet

Current stock price:	$29.00
Shares outstanding (mil)	258.0
Next year's free cash flow (mil)	$180.00
Perpetuity growth rate (g)	3.0%
Discount rate (R)	9.0%

10-Year Valuation Model for Biomet

Step 1: Forecast free cash flow (FCF) for the next 10 years.
Assumes 15% growth rate for years 1–5; 10% growth rate for years 6–10. Free cash flows in $ millions.

		Yr 1	Yr 2	Yr 3	Yr 4	Yr 5	Yr 6	Yr 7	Yr 8	Yr 9	Yr 10
Free cash flow	→	180.0	207.0	238.1	273.8	314.8	362.0	398.3	438.1	460.0	483.0

Step 2: Discount these free cash flows to reflect the present value.
Discount Factor = $(1 + R)^N$ (where R = discount rate and N = year being discounted)

		Yr 1	Yr 2	Yr 3	Yr 4	Yr 5	Yr 6	Yr 7	Yr 8	Yr 9	Yr 10
Free cash flow		180.0	207.0	238.1	273.8	314.8	362.0	398.3	438.1	460.0	483.0
÷ Discount factor		1.09^1	1.09^2	1.09^3	1.09^4	1.09^5	1.09^6	1.09^7	1.09^8	1.09^9	1.09^{10}
= Discounted FCF	→	165.1	174.2	183.8	193.9	204.6	215.9	217.9	219.9	211.8	204.0

Step 3: Calculate the perpetuity value and discount it to the present.
Perpetuity Value = Yr 10 FCF × $(1 + g)$ ÷ $(R - g)$ (where g = perpetuity growth rate and R = discount rate)

Perpetuity value → $(483.0 \times 1.03) \div (.09 - .03) = \$8,291.16$

Discounted → $\$8,291.16 \div 1.09^{10} = \$3,502.27$

Step 4: Calculate total equity value.
Add the discounted perpetuity value (above) to the sum of the 10 discounted cash flows (see step 2).

Total equity value → $\$1,991.13 + \$3,502.27 = \$5,493.40$

Step 5: Calculate per share value.
Divide total equity value by shares outstanding.

Per share value → $\$5,493.40 \div 258 = \$21.29$

Figure 28.14 Valuing Biomet using discounted cash flow. *Source:* Morningstar, Inc.

However, bond payments are fixed, whereas Biomet's earnings and cash flow should grow substantially over time. Moreover, Biomet's business has been consistent over the past several years, which means we can forecast the firm's future with more confidence than we could, for example, AMD's future. Sounds to me like Biomet is a perfect candidate for a discounted cash flow analysis.

Biomet's free cash flow has increased pretty steadily over the past several years, so let's use $180 million as our estimated amount for 2004. (Biomet's historical free cash flows are shown in Figure 28.8.)

If we increase free cash flow at 15% over the next five years and conservatively assume that Biomet starts to lose market share and grow more slowly after five years, we see that the present value of the free cash that Biomet will generate over the next 10 years is about $2 billion. (I used a relatively low discount rate of 9%—versus a market average of 10.5%—because Biomet is a very financially stable company.) Add in our perpetuity value of about $3.5 billion, and Biomet is worth $5.5 billion, or about $21 per share (Figure 28.14 runs through these calculations for you).

With the stock trading at about $28 as of this writing, Biomet doesn't look like much of a value under this set of assumptions. However, maybe we're being *too* conservative by forecasting that a competitor will start eating Biomet's lunch in just five years. Moreover, it might not be reasonable to assume that a firm in an industry as young and robust as orthopedic devices will be growing at just 3% after a decade. That's a really low growth rate—in line with the overall economy—and it's entirely possible that Biomet will still be growing at an above-average rate in 10 years' time. Therefore, let's try another scenario. We'll assume Biomet can grow faster starting in year six, and we'll push our forecast horizon out to 15 years, at which time we assume that Biomet's growth rate declines to a steady state of 3% (see Figure 28.15).

Biomet	Yr 6	Yr 7	Yr 8	Yr 9	Yr 10	Yr 11	Yr 12	Yr 13	Yr 14	Yr 15
Free cash flow ($mil)	362	406	454	509	570	638	702	772	849	934
Growth rate (%)	12	12	12	12	12	10	10	10	10	10
Present value ($mil)	216	222	228	234	241	247	250	252	254	257

Figure 28.15   Biomet's free cash flow estimates from year 6 onward.

This set of assumptions results in an estimated intrinsic value per share of about $30, which is right around where the shares are trading as of this writing. Assuming this is a reasonable scenario, I'd start getting interested in the stock at around $24, which would be a 20% discount to my estimated intrinsic value. I'm not looking for much of a margin of safety because Biomet's strong balance sheet, excellent industry prospects, and solid profitability all make it less likely that something will go horribly wrong with my assumptions.

However, this process has taught us something very important: For us to believe that Biomet's shares are worth $30, rather than $20, we have to believe that the firm can hold off its competition and grow at an above-average rate for a long period of time. Companies that can increase free cash flow at an average annual rate of 12% for a lengthy period of time—which is what our second scenario assumes—are few and far between, after all.

This is the key benefit of a discounted cash flow approach to valuation. Having thought through a couple of possible scenarios for Biomet, we now know exactly what assumptions are incorporated in our estimated intrinsic value of $30 per share. Armed with that knowledge, we can make a more informed investment decision—we wouldn't know as much about the assumptions needed to believe that the stock is reasonably valued if we'd just looked at the current P/E relative to the historical average P/E. For example, we should probably pay very close attention to Biomet's competitive position relative to other firms in the industry, as well as to any signs that the long-term demand for orthopedic devices might be slowing, because those two factors are what moved our value estimate from $20 to $30.

Conclusion

There you have it—real-world application of the tools of fundamental analysis, in a simplified form, is exactly what we do at Morningstar every day.

This is some pretty painstaking stuff, and it's not reasonable to do a super-thorough analysis of every single company you investigate. In the real world, time is short, so even the pros use shortcuts to help separate the companies that really are worth a great deal of analytical time from the ones that are unlikely to be good investments. In the next chapter, I show you exactly how to separate the wheat from the chaff when you're trying to narrow down a list of investment candidates to the ones that are really worth a thorough investigation.

29

The 10-Minute Test

WITH LITERALLY THOUSANDS of companies available to invest in, one of the toughest challenges for any investor is figuring out which ones are worth detailed examination and which ones aren't. Now that you know the tools of in-depth fundamental analysis, I want to give you some tips on narrowing down the field. Apply the following tests to any stock that you think might be a worthwhile investment, and you should be able to decide in 10 minutes whether it warrants much of your time.

In fact, I'll bet that asking the questions in this chapter will allow you to eliminate at least half—if not more—of the stocks you run across from consideration. Throwing out less-promising stocks early in the process will leave you more time to investigate and value the ones that really might be great investments.

Two caveats before we start: First, these rules of thumb are starting points, no more and no less. There are exceptions to every guideline I list in this chapter. These shortcuts aren't designed to cover every possible situation—but if you apply them, they will eliminate poor investments more often than not.

Second, although the following list of questions might seem daunting at first, you can answer all of them using a compilation of 10 years' worth of financial data that's available on Morningstar.com.

Does the Firm Pass a Minimum Quality Hurdle?

Avoiding the junk that litters the investment landscape is the first step in our 10-minute test. Companies with miniscule market capitalizations and firms that trade on the bulletin boards (or pink sheets) are the first ones to rule out. Also avoid foreign firms that don't file regular financials with the SEC—even some large foreign firms issue only brief press releases each quarter and publish full financials only once per year.

Finally, recent initial public offerings (IPOs) are usually not worth your time. Companies sell shares to the public only when they think they're getting a high price, so IPOs are rarely bargains. Moreover, most IPOs are young, unseasoned firms with short track records. The big exception to this rule is firms that are spun off from larger parent companies. Spinoffs are often solid companies with long operating histories that the larger firm no longer wants to manage, and the stocks can often be attractively valued as well.

Has the Company Ever Made an Operating Profit?

This test sounds simple, but it'll keep you out of a lot of trouble. Very often, companies that are still in the money-losing stage sound the most exciting—they're investigating a novel treatment for some rare disease, or they're about to offer some exciting new product or service, the likes of which the world has never seen.

Unfortunately, stocks like this will also blow up your portfolio more often than not. They usually have only a single product or service in the pipeline, and the eventual viability of the product or service will make or break the company. (Going by the statistics of how many start-ups fail, *break* is a more likely occurrence than *make*.) Unless you're looking for an alternative to lottery tickets, take a pass on any firm that hasn't yet proven it can earn a buck.

Does the Company Generate Consistent Cash Flow from Operations?

Fast-growing firms can sometimes report profits before they generate cash—but every company has to generate cash eventually. Companies with negative cash flow from operations will eventually have to seek additional financing by selling bonds or issuing more shares. The former will likely increase the riskiness of the firm, whereas the latter will dilute your ownership stake as a shareholder.

Are Returns on Equity Consistently above 10%, with Reasonable Leverage?

Use 10% as a minimum hurdle. If a nonfinancial firm can't post ROEs over 10% for four years out of every five, for example, odds are good that it's not worth your time. For financial firms, raise your ROE bar to 12%. Don't forget to check leverage to make sure that it's in line with industry norms. A 15% ROE generated with minimal leverage is a much higher quality result than one generated using lots of leverage.

One exception is that cyclical firms—companies whose results vary strongly with the general economy—may have wildly varying results from year to year. However, the best will make money and post decent ROEs even when times are tough.

Is Earnings Growth Consistent or Erratic?

The best companies post reasonably consistent growth rates. If a firm's earnings bounce all over the place, it's either in an extremely volatile industry or it's regularly getting shellacked by competitors. The former is not necessarily bad as long as the long-term industry outlook is good and the shares are cheap, but the latter is potentially a big problem.

How Clean Is the Balance Sheet?

Firms with a lot of debt require extra care because their capital structures are often very complicated. If a nonbank firm has a financial leverage ratio above about 4—or a debt-to-equity ratio over 1.0—ask yourself the following questions:

- ▶ *Is the firm in a stable business?* Firms in industries such as consumer products and food can withstand more leverage than economically sensitive firms with volatile earnings.
- ▶ *Has debt been going down or up as a percentage of total assets?* One thing you don't want to see in a highly leveraged firm is even more debt.

▶ *Do you understand the debt?* If a quick glance at the 10-K reveals questionable debt and quasi-debt instruments that you can't wrap your head around, move on. There are many fine companies out there with simpler capital structures.

Does the Firm Generate Free Cash Flow?

As we know, free cash flow is the holy grail—cash generated after capital expenditures that truly increases the value of the firm. Generally, you should prefer firms that create free cash to ones that don't and firms that create more free cash to ones that create less. As I discussed in Chapter 23, divide free cash flow by sales, and use 5% as a rough benchmark.

The one exception—and it's a big one—is that it's fine for a firm to be generating negative free cash flow *if* it's investing that cash wisely in projects that are likely to pay off well in the future. For example, neither Starbucks nor Home Depot generated meaningful free cash flow until 2001—yet there's no question that they had been creating economic value (and shareholder wealth) for many years before 2001. That's because they were plowing every cent they earned right back into their businesses because their management teams believed that they still had many high-return investment opportunities for the cash they were generating.

So don't automatically write off firms with negative free cash flow if they have solid ROEs and pass the other tests in this chapter. Just be sure you believe that the firm really is reinvesting the cash wisely.

How Much "Other" Is There?

Companies can hide many bad decisions in supposedly one-time charges, so if a firm is already questionable on some other front and has a history of taking big charges, take a pass. Not only are charge-happy firms more difficult to analyze because of their complicated financials, but numerous charges hint at a management team that may be trying to burnish poor results.

Has the Number of Shares Outstanding Increased Markedly over the Past Several Years?

If so, the firm is either issuing new shares to buy other companies or granting numerous options to employees and executives. The former is a red flag because most acquisitions fail, and the latter is not something you want to see because it means that your ownership stake in the firm is slowly shrinking as employees exercise their options. If shares outstanding are consistently increasing by more than around 2% per year—assuming no big acquisitions—think long and hard before investing in the firm.

However, if the number of shares is actually *shrinking,* the company potentially gets a big gold star. Firms that buy back many shares are returning excess cash to shareholders, which is generally a responsible thing to do. Just be careful that the company isn't going hog-wild with share repurchases even as their shares keep zooming ever upward because stock repurchases are a good use of capital only when the company's shares are trading for a reasonable valuation. You don't want to see a company buying its own overvalued stock any more than you want to invest in overvalued shares yourself.

Beyond the 10 Minutes

If the firm does pass these tests and it looks as though it's worth a detailed examination, here's how to proceed. This research process will take much longer than 10 minutes, but it's worth the effort for an idea that passes the initial hurdles:

► Look over the 10-year summary balance sheet, income statement, and statement of cash flows on Morningstar.com or another Web site. Look for trends, and make notes of anything that raises an eyebrow and deserves further investigation. This process should give you an initial road map for investigation.

► Read the most recent 10-K filing front to back. Pay special attention to the sections that describe the company and its industry, the sections about risks and competition, any mention of legal issues (sometimes labeled "commitments and contingencies"), and the "management's discussion and analysis" section. The latter is where the firm explains, in reasonably plain English, why the most recent year's financial results were what they were. Write down anything you don't understand or which you want to investigate further. You don't necessarily need to read every page of the 10-K—sometimes firms include scores of pages of mind-numbing detail about leases, for example—but you should at least skim every page to make sure there's nothing buried in the text that you do need to know. Be on the watch for any sections that describe loans, guarantees, contractual obligations, or the like. If the firm is going to owe someone a large amount of money in a few years, you need to know about it.

▶ Read the two most recent proxies (form DEF-14A, in the SEC's jargon). Look for reasonable compensation that varies with corporate financial performance and a reasonable options-granting policy. Check to make sure the board of directors isn't packed with individuals with close ties to management.

▶ Read the most recent annual report, as well as the past two years' reports, if possible, to get a feel for the company. Is the letter to shareholders candid and frank, or does management gloss over problems with jargon? Ignoring problems won't make them go away, after all. In addition, does the firm present industry information to give you context for evaluating it? Does the report look as though the firm spent way too much money on it?

▶ Look at the two most recent quarterly earnings reports and 10-Q filings to see whether anything has changed recently. Look for signs that business is getting better—or worse—as well as for anything major that has changed since the last 10-K. If it's still available, listen to the most recent quarterly conference call. (Companies often archive these on their Web sites for some time after the quarter is over.) Does management get defensive or evasive when analysts ask tough questions, or does it respond with straightforward answers?

▶ Start valuing the stock. Look at the stock's valuation multiples relative to the market, the industry, and the stock's historical valuation ranges. If the firm has low reinvestment needs, low risk, high returns on capital, or a high growth rate, be prepared to accept a higher price-to-earnings ratio. Do at least a very rough discounted cash flow valuation—think about how much free cash flow the firm is likely to generate next year, how fast it will grow, and add the discounted value of these cash flows to a perpetuity value. If your estimated intrinsic value is very different from the market price, check your assumptions. Are you being too pessimistic or too optimistic? If you recheck your assumptions, the stock still looks undervalued, and your multiple-based analysis didn't scream "sell," you might just have uncovered a great investment.

30
_____

A Guided Tour of the Market

IN THE PREVIOUS chapter, I discussed easy ways to home in on companies that will be worth your while. In the next section of the book, we'll focus on tools for understanding different areas of the market.

As I said in Chapter 20, it's easier for companies to make money in some industries than in others. Moreover, some industries lend themselves to the creation of economic moats more so than others, and these are the industries where you'll want to spend most of your time. Although we don't advocate a *top-down* investment strategy—in which you select areas of the market that you think will perform better than others and invest heavily in your top-rated industries—the economics of some industries are superior to others. Hence, you should spend more time learning about attractive industries than unattractive ones.

Every industry has its own unique dynamics and set of jargon—and some industries (such as financial services) even have financial statements that look very different from the ones we discussed in Chapter 22. I asked Morningstar's staff of 30 equity analysts to put together a series of criteria covering just about every corner of the market. These criteria should help you wade through the different economics of each industry and understand how companies in each industry can create economic moats—which strategies work and how you can identify companies pursuing those strategies.

Where to Look

Because you're likely as pressed for time as every other person with a day job who also manages his or her own investments, let me try to briefly steer you toward some areas of the market that are definitely worth more of your time.

Banks and Financial Services

In general, most financial services firms are in excellent economic positions as middlemen for money. Banks in particular enjoy the enviable position of paying very little to hold on to depositors' money (when you consider the low rates on checking accounts and all of the fee income that such accounts generate), which they then turn around and lend out at substantially higher interest rates than they're paying to depositors. In fact, some banks do so well at levying fees and cross-selling financial products that depositors literally pay the bank to hold their money. Moreover, because banks have somewhat confusing financial statements, many investors simply pass them by or look at only the biggest and most well-known firms. By learning what makes banks and other financial services firms tick, you'll be ahead of most investors, and because this ground is less picked-over, you'll likely find some solid investment ideas as well.

Business Services

This is the ultimate catchall area of the market, so many investors pass it by. That's a shame because it contains some very attractive firms. In addition to larger industries such as data processing—which is boring but profitable as can be—business services is packed with niche firms that dominate their corner of the economy. Cintas, for example, has generated an enormous amount of shareholder wealth by convincing companies that it can design and maintain employee uniforms better than employers can. Who would have thought that renting uniforms could be so profitable? Moody's (which rates bonds) and Equifax (which maintains a credit-scoring database) are other examples of highly profitable but not-so-well-known firms with strong positions in niche industries.

Business services firms often fly beneath the market's radar because they don't fit neatly into the industry-oriented coverage lists of Wall Street analysts—there are usually only a few public companies in any one niche, so the industry specialists on Wall Street tend to pass them by. As a result, the stocks don't get hyped as much to institutional investors. (The other reason companies in this area tend to get less attention from Wall Street is that they're usually self-funding, which means they don't need many investment banking services.) Less attention from Wall Street can mean more opportunity for smart investors, so don't ignore business services.

Health Care

This area of the market is similar to financial services because the long-term demand outlook is very strong, and companies tend to be highly profitable. As our Biomet analysis in Chapter 28 showed, even smaller firms can build lasting economic moats. Tread carefully with biotechs and some managed-care firms, though. Most biotechs are single-product lottery tickets, and most managed-care firms are affected by truly arcane regulatory issues—seemingly minor changes in Medicare rules can have a huge impact.

Media

Finally, spend some time getting to know the media business. Many media companies build moats around themselves through natural oligopolies or monopolies—there's little demand for more than a couple of daily newspapers in any one city, for example. Moreover, media is one of the few industries in which product vendors are paid before they have to deliver anything, because a large amount of media is sold via subscription. Can you imagine getting paid on January 1 for the coming year's work? That's how many media firms make money.

Conclusion

These aren't the only four areas of the market with worthwhile investments—I've highlighted these because they contain so many wide-moat companies. There are great firms in even the least likely areas of the stock market.

A few essential questions: How do companies make money? How can they create economic moats? What quirks does an industry have that an investor should know about? How can you separate successful from unsuccessful firms in each industry? What pitfalls should you watch out for?

Over the long haul, a big part of successful investing is building a mental database of companies and industries on which you can draw as the need arises. That database lets you jumpstart the selection process, making you a more successful, more profitable investor.

Appendixes

Appendix 1

1. How Does the Morningstar Rating for Mutual Funds Work?

THE MORNINGSTAR RATING (often known as the "star rating") guides investors to funds that have provided shareholders with superior risk-adjusted returns. Although investors should not buy or sell funds on the basis of the star rating alone, it is a quick and easy way to identify funds worthy of further research.

The Morningstar Rating for funds is a measure of a fund's risk-adjusted past performance relative to similar funds as classified within each of Morningstar's 50 categories. Funds are rated from one to five stars, with the best performers receiving five stars and the worst performers receiving a single star. We grade on a curve so that there are as many five-star funds as one-star funds in each category. The major goal is to provide a quick snapshot of past performance that includes both returns and the level of volatility shareholders had to endure to get those returns.

Although our star-rating calculation was formulated by finance PhDs, you don't need to go back to school to use it as a guide for selecting superior mutual funds. The star rating helps investors determine which funds have best compensated shareholders for the risks the managers have taken. It is calculated by subtracting a risk penalty from each fund's total return, after accounting for all loads, sales charges, and redemption fees. The risk penalty is determined by looking at the variation in the fund's monthly returns, with emphasis on downward variation. (In other words, when a fund has big losses versus its category, they have a greater impact on the calculation of a fund's risk penalty than do strong gains versus its peers.) The greater the variation, the larger the penalty. This rewards consistent performance and reduces the possibility of strong short-term performance masking the inherent risk of a fund.

Once we calculate the risk-adjusted return for all funds in a category, we rank them according to the results. Funds with scores in the top 10% earn five stars; the next 22.5%, four stars; the middle 35%, three stars; the next 22.5%, two stars; and the bottom 10%, one star.

Only funds that have a 3-year record receive a star rating. Funds are rated for up to three periods, the trailing 3-, 5-, and 10-year periods, and ratings are recalculated each month. For funds that remain in the same Morningstar category for the entire evaluation period, the following weights are used to calculate an overall rating:

Age of Fund	*Overall Rating*
At least 3 years, but less than 5	100% 3-year rating
At least 5 years, but less than 10	60% 5-year rating
	40% 3-year rating
At least 10 years	50% 10-year rating
	30% 5-year rating
	20% 3-year rating

If a fund changes Morningstar categories, its long-term historical performance is given less weight in the calculation, based on the magnitude of the change. For example, a change from a mid-cap category to large-cap category is considered less significant than a change from small-cap to large-cap. Giving less weight to a fund's previous record with a different style ensures the fairest comparisons and discourages fund companies from changing a fund's style and shifting to another Morningstar category in an attempt to receive a better rating.

Important Things to Remember When Using the Rating

▶ The star rating is a strictly quantitative measure—a high rating doesn't imply the approval or endorsement of a fund by a Morningstar analyst.

▶ The rating is based on the fund's historical performance. Not only does the boilerplate warning about past performance not guaranteeing future returns apply here, but a highly rated fund may no longer have the same portfolio manager or employ the same strategy responsible for that performance.

▶ Because funds are rated within their respective categories, not all five-star funds are equally good. A five-star sector fund, for example, might have the best risk-adjusted return within its specific category, but it's probably far more risky than a highly rated diversified fund.

▶ The star rating is time sensitive and a fund's star rating is updated each month. (See the response to Question 2 for more information on this subject.)

Instead of selecting funds based solely on their ratings, investors should use the ratings as an initial screen to identify funds worthy of further research.

2. What Should I Do When My Fund Loses a Star?

Sit down and take a deep breath. Above all, don't panic or immediately sell your shares in the fund.

Although the star-rating system is a quick way to analyze how a fund has balanced risk and reward, we recognize its limitations. It's not intended to provide investors with strict buy/sell recommendations for funds. It is merely a quantitative tool helpful in understanding a fund's past performance. Therefore, a fund's star rating should be used only as one step in a wider analysis of a fund.

When a fund's star rating slips, it implies that the fund's risk-adjusted returns relative to its category peers have declined. However, that may not actually be the case. And even if the fund's relative performance has declined, that may not warrant a decision to exit the fund.

A fund's star rating can fluctuate for a couple of reasons. A star rating is based on trailing risk-adjusted returns for a fund and its category, which are recalculated each month. (See the answer to Question 1 for more information.) As an exceptionally strong or weak month of performance for a fund enters into the calculation or is excluded from it, risk-adjusted trailing returns can vary greatly. If the other funds in the category did not experience as much change due to the new time period, the fund's rank within the category could change and so, too, could its star rating. Because we adhere to strict cutoffs for a fund's relative ranking, the fund's star rating can change even if its relative ranking has only changed slightly. For example, if a fund's ranking fell from the top 9% to the top 12% of its category, the fund's star rating would decline from five to four stars. Such a change probably doesn't merit raising a red flag.

Similarly, a fund with a 4-year 11-month record will establish a 5-year record the following month and the calculation for its star rating will change from a calculation based on its 3-year record to one based on its 5-year record as well as its 3-year record. This change could potentially have even more dramatic consequences for the fund's star rating than the simple changes attributable to monthly recalculations described previously. If the fund had a terrible record during its first two years, that legacy suddenly appears in the calculation of its star rating. In such a case, the fund's star rating may very well decline, but it may not reflect the strength of more recent performance.

It may turn out, however, that your fund didn't lose a star simply because of a technicality, but instead has shown markedly weaker performance lately. If that's the case, you'll want to take a closer look at what's hindering your fund. The easiest way to get the scoop on significant changes in a fund is to read the Morningstar Analyst Report. Our reports regularly discuss what has been driving both a fund's long- and short-term returns. We often highlight stock or sector bets that have done notably well or badly, and you can also check the fund's top holdings for names that have been in trouble lately. Good shareholder reports also address what has been hindering performance as well as what has been working. Most funds post the reports on their Web sites, and some post basic shareholder letters every month or quarter.

Even if that analysis raises a red flag about your fund, you must still think carefully about whether to sell it. Look into the fundamental issues we discussed in Chapter 15, such as whether the fund has recently undergone a management or strategy change. You'll also want to consider the available alternatives. Sure, there are more highly rated funds, but are you comfortable with the strategies the managers of the outperforming funds have used to garner these superior results? And speaking of managers, are the track records for the managers of the outperforming funds strong enough to earn your trust that they can continue to outpace the field? Also analyze the fund shops of the higher-rated funds. Do they have stronger or weaker reputations than the fund family whose fund you are considering selling? Are their track records longer or shorter? Finally, don't forget to consider the tax consequences of selling your fund.

3. How Does Morningstar's Style Box Work?

The style box is a tool that represents the characteristics of a security in a graphical format. For stocks and stock funds, two pieces of data determine where the security falls within the style box. One is market capitalization: how large or small a company is. Large companies show up in the top row of the style box, middle-size companies show up in the middle row, and small companies show up in the bottom row.

The other factor that determines a security's placement in the style box is its investment style. Investment style is based on a growth score and a value score. Half of a stock's growth score is based on its long-term projected earnings growth relative to other stocks in its market-cap range. The remainder of the growth score is based on a combination of historical earnings growth, sales growth, cash-flow growth, and book-value growth relative to the stocks in its market-cap range. The resulting score ranges from 0 to 100. Half of a stock's value score is based on its price-to-projected earnings relative to other stocks in its market-cap range. The remainder of the value score is based on a combination of price/book, price/sales, and price/cash-flow ratios, as well as its dividend yield relative to the stocks in its market-cap range. This score also ranges from 0 to 100.

Morningstar arrives at a stock's investment style by subtracting its value score from its growth score. A stock with a strongly negative score is assigned to the value column of the style box and one with a strongly positive score is assigned to the growth column. Those in between land in the core column of the style box (for funds, this is known as the blend column). The breakpoints can vary over time but, on average, each style will account for one third of the stocks in each market-cap range.

A stock mutual fund's style-box position is based on all the stocks in its portfolio. The portfolio's market cap is based on the geometric mean of the portfolio. That calculation takes into account the market cap of each stock and its weighting in the portfolio to come up with a number that best represents how the fund is positioned. The portfolio's overall stock style is based on the weighted average of the style scores for all its stocks (the weighting is based on the percentage of the portfolio each stock takes up). Funds with averages on the low side land in the value column, those on the high side land in growth, and those in between are blend.

The Fixed-Income Style Box

The fixed-income style box is a nine-square box that considers the two key determinants of bond-fund performance: credit quality and duration. The style box allows investors to quickly gauge the risk exposure of their bond fund. The horizontal axis of the fixed-income style box displays a fund's interest-rate sensitivity, as measured by the average duration of all the bonds in its portfolio. Morningstar breaks interest-rate sensitivity into three groups: short, intermediate, and long. Short-term bond funds are the least affected by interest-rate movements and thus the least volatile. Long-term bond funds are the most volatile. Taxable-bond funds (as opposed to municipal-bond funds, which are protected from taxes) with average durations of less than 3.5 years fall in the short-term column; those with average durations longer than 6 years fall in the long-term column. Everything else is intermediate. (The cutoffs for municipal-bond funds are slightly different, but not appreciably so.)

The vertical axis of the style box indicates credit quality. It is also divided into three groups: high, medium, and low. We determine a fund's placement by looking at the average credit quality of all the bonds in its portfolio. Funds with high credit quality tend to own either U.S. Treasury bonds or corporate bonds whose credit quality is just slightly below that of Treasuries. Conversely, funds with low credit quality own a lot of high-yield, or junk, bonds. Funds that have an average credit rating of AAA or AA are categorized as high quality, and those with an average credit rating lower than BBB are classified as low quality. Medium-quality funds fall between the two extremes.

The bond style box can make it far easier for investors to find appropriate funds. Say you need a fund that offers slightly more yield than a money market fund but you don't want it to be much riskier. Just look for funds that fall within the short-term, high-quality square of the style box. Or perhaps you want a rich income stream but you aren't comfortable buying junk bonds. A fund that falls within the long-term, medium-quality square might be the answer.

4. How Do I Buy My First Fund?

As a go-it-alone investor, you can buy funds directly from fund companies such as Fidelity, Vanguard, and T. Rowe Price. Many fund companies offer both load and no-load versions of the same fund, so be sure to specify that you are interested in the no-load version.

If you are thinking of buying more than one fund—and most fund investors do own multiple funds—you might want to work with one of these larger fund families. They offer stock and bond funds, U.S. and international funds, and large- and small-company funds. You can build a well-diversified portfolio of funds without venturing outside the family. By investing with one of the major fund families, you can easily transfer assets from one fund to another. You'll also consolidate paperwork, getting one statement for all of your funds instead of a separate one for each fund you own.

Another way to diversify is to invest with a series of fund-family boutiques that do one thing particularly well. You could buy a large-cap growth fund from Marsico, a small-company value fund from Royce Funds, a bond fund from Metropolitan West, a foreign-stock fund from Tweedy, Browne, and so on.

You could also consider buying your fund through a so-called supermarket. By using a fund supermarket, you can buy funds from a number of different fund families. (For more on fund supermarkets, see Question 13.)

Making the Purchase

If you're buying a fund on your own (without the help of a broker or planner), you need to contact the fund family or supermarket you have chosen. That means calling to request a prospectus and an application, going to the Web site to request that they be mailed to you, or downloading them from the site. Once you have filled out the application, mail it back with a check or money order to open your account. Many funds and supermarkets also allow you to open an account online without having to go through the process of mailing back the application.

When you fill out the application, don't worry about how many shares you're buying. Focus on the dollar amount you want to invest. Unlike stock shares, you can own partial amounts of fund shares. If you invest $1,500 in a fund with a share price, or NAV, of $122.50, you'll get 12.245 shares of the fund.

The application contains a number of options for buying the specific fund you want. The key ones are whether to reinvest dividends and other distributions and whether to invest a lump sum or a smaller amount each month.

Reinvesting Distributions

Unless you're planning to use the fund for income, be sure to reinvest distributions. Instead of getting a check in the mail whenever the fund makes an income or capital-gains distribution, you get more shares of the fund. Reinvesting makes a big difference for your long-term returns—studies have shown that 20% or more of the money shareholders make from a fund comes from such reinvestment. Keep in mind that the total-return numbers you see for a fund assume that you do reinvest distributions. You can't pocket the distributions and expect to get comparably good returns.

Lump Sum or Automatic Investing

The choice of whether to invest a lump sum all at once or set up what is known as an automatic investment plan can depend in part on whether you're buying a no-load fund or investing with a planner or broker. For no-load investors, the automatic investment plan is a terrific option. Under such plans, the fund company automatically deducts a set amount from your checking account every month. It's easy and you can invest small amounts at a time, allowing you to invest without having to lay out a large sum of money all at once. This may sound familiar—if you participate in a retirement plan at work, you're in an automatic investment plan. The process is also known as dollar-cost averaging, because your purchase prices average out over time.

If you're buying a load fund, however, the more you can invest at once, the better. Load funds usually have breakpoints above which the front-end sales charge drops. The charge declines further for larger investments. Most load fund families, however, also give you the option of a letter of intent, or statement of intention. This agreement gives you 13 months to invest a specified amount; if that total qualifies you for a breakpoint, all of your purchases will be invested after that smaller sales charge is levied.

Tracking Your Purchases

Whether you invest a lump sum or dollar-cost average or use some combination of the two, be sure to keep copies of the fund statements recording your share purchases. These are vital for keeping track of the fund shares you own. If you own the fund in a taxable account, knowing exactly when you bought shares and how much you paid for them can be a big help. When you redeem, or cash in, shares, you can minimize your taxable gains by paying attention to the share price and how long you held the shares.

Gains in shares that you have owned for at least 12 months are taxed at a lower rate than those you have held for less than a year, which are taxed at your income tax rate. And by selling shares priced close to the current price, you'll minimize gains. If the current share price is $20 per share and you sell the shares you bought 15 months ago at $17 per share, your taxable gain will be much less than if you had sold the shares you bought 20 months ago for $13. When selling, be sure to tell the fund company that you want to sell designated shares and which shares you want to sell.

Great First Funds

Most first-time fund investors want to find a fund that doesn't require a high initial investment. Unfortunately, one of the best "first fund" choices, Vanguard's Total Stock Market Index, requires at least $3,000 up front. (We like total stock market funds as first funds because they own a mix of value and growth and in-between stocks, they give investors exposure to many stocks in a variety of sectors, and they hold mostly large-cap stocks while offering diversification into mid- and small caps.)

You can pay a smaller minimum initial investment to get into a fund if you agree to commit to an automatic investment plan. If you agree to have your investment automatically taken out of your checking account every month, you can often buy into a fund for just $50 or $100. Vanguard still wants $3,000 up front, even if you set up an automatic investment plan, but families such as T. Rowe Price, Fidelity, and TIAA-CREF offer total stock market index funds that allow you to set up automatic investment plans with considerably less money.

If you don't want to set up an automatic investment plan, there are two other options for getting into funds that have minimum initial investments beyond your reach. One is to set up an Individual Retirement Account. Even funds with steep minimums will often cut it to as little as $1,000 for an IRA. You can't draw on an IRA until retirement, however, so that isn't a good option if you're hoping to use the money before then. Fund supermarkets may

First Funds to Consider	Minimum Initial Purchase
Conservative Funds	
Fidelity Asset Manager	$2,500
T. Rowe Price Personal Strategy Income	$2,500
Vanguard STAR	$1,000
Vanguard Target Maturity 2025	$3,000
Moderate Funds	
TIAA-CREF Equity Index	$2,500
Vanguard Total Stock Market Index	$3,000
Selected American	$3,000
T. Rowe Price Equity-Income	$2,500
Aggressive Funds	
Marsico Growth	$2,500
Fidelity Capital Appreciation	$2,500
Harbor Capital Appreciation	$2,500

FAQ Figure 1.1   Here are a few funds to get you started, grouped by risk level.

also allow you to buy into a given fund with a lower minimum than you would have to pay if you bought directly through the fund company. FAQ Figure 1.1 lists some of our favorite first funds.

5. What Should I Do When My Fund Manager Leaves?

An excellent question. Fortunately, we have an excellent answer: Wait and
see. Bold, no? But we're serious. Investors shouldn't rashly sell a fund when
the jury is still out about the new manager. There's no set period for passing judgment, either. But there are four questions to ask when your fund
manager quits.

1. *Is this fund in a taxable or nontaxable account?* If your fund is in a taxable account, you don't want to hightail it out of there without good reason,
especially if you've owned the fund awhile. Selling could mean a sizable
realized gain, which in turn would mean writing a sizable check to the IRS.
However, if you own the fund in a tax-deferred account, such as an IRA or a
401(k), selling won't have the same tax ramifications.

2. *Will the strategy change?* If the new manager brings a new strategy, the
fund may no longer play the same role in your portfolio that you bought it to
fulfill, and that's a valid reason to sell. For example, a small-company fund that
has turned into a large-cap offering clearly won't fill the same slot for you. Even
if the new manager vows to the stay the course, check in on the fund more regularly than you did before, just to make sure. New managers usually say things
will stay the same, but most do at least some tinkering once they arrive.

As soon as you hear about a manager change, keep a close eye on its portfolio and performance. You can use Morningstar.com's individual-fund reports to get a summary of all the essential facts on the fund. Make sure to
print out the report to make it easier to track changes. Revisit the fund's
Morningstar page every few months to confirm that the essential strategy is
still in place. How can you tell? First, make sure the fund's style-box position
remains the same. Also monitor turnover. Because turnover represents how
frequently a fund's holdings change, a surge could indicate that the manager
is ditching his predecessor's stocks in favor of a new strategy.

3. *Who is the new manager?* Fund companies don't want to gamble with
funds that have solid track records. In these cases, new managers are often
known factors: Either they've been hired away from competing funds, they
run other funds in the family, or they're high-profile analysts.

Use Morningstar's individual-fund reports to check out the performance records for any funds the new manager has previously been in charge of. Read what the Morningstar analyst has to say about the new manager's skill, too.

4. *How is the rest of the family?* If your fund is the only one in the family, a manager change definitely deserves close watch: There isn't apt to be the same type of backup staff to pick up the slack. Big fund families, such as Fidelity or T. Rowe Price, have deep research and management resources and can therefore absorb manager changes better than one-fund shops.

6. Should I Buy a Rookie Fund?

To figure this out, ask yourself the following five questions.

1. *What is the manager's record?* Just because the fund is a rookie doesn't mean the manager is. See how successful the manager has been at other funds. Check the new fund's prospectus or the fund company's Web site to find out what other funds the manager has run and when; then look up the Morningstar.com reports for each of the manager's former charges. When Morningstar analysts cover rookie funds, they'll tell you how the manager has done in the past.

2. *What is the fund family's record?* If the manager is a rookie, too, then you should at the very least have a lot of confidence in the family before buying in. Consider whether the rookie's parent company has several good funds. If the family is full of mediocre funds, or worse, what makes you think this one is going to be any different?

3. *What does the fund do?* Knowing the fund's strategy gives you an idea of what the fund is likely to own. That tells you the level of returns and risk you can expect from it. Say the fund will focus on fast-growing small companies. That indicates that you could score high long-term returns, but you're likely to endure a rough ride along the way.

4. *What will it cost?* The annual expense ratio is one of the more predictable things about any fund, rookie or veteran. You don't know how much money your funds will make next year, but you do know what percentage of your investment they're going to charge you.

Rookie funds tend not to be particularly cheap. Low expenses often result from the economies of scale that come with growth in a fund's asset base, and a rookie may not be big enough to pass savings along to shareholders. So investigate the family's other funds. Do they have modest expenses compared with their category peers?

Check with the fund company to find out whether the new fund's expenses have been temporarily capped. Many rookie funds will charge a set expense ratio for a year or so but might charge significantly more after that.

5. *Does the fund offer any extras?* Favor rookie funds that vow to close to new investors before assets can hinder their performance. As we discussed

in Chapter 15, small-company and focused funds are particularly likely to suffer if they bloat. Fast-trading funds (those with high turnover) may also be vulnerable.

If you're going to hold the fund in a taxable account, determine whether the fund is committed to minimizing taxes. Even if the fund holds out the prospect of great returns, that means little if you have to surrender large sums to the IRS.

7. Should I Buy a Fund That's Closing?

Groucho Marx once remarked, "I don't care to belong to any club that will have me as a member." That joke reflects something of the peculiar allure of closed funds. If they aren't letting people in, there must be something pretty cool going on in there, right?

Sometimes there is, often there isn't. Closing is a sign of success, but it often comes after the real glory days have passed.

Why Funds Close

There's only one reason to close a mutual fund: to preserve the manager's strategy. For example, if fund managers rapidly trade a small number of small-company stocks and are successful, investors will likely take notice and throw money at those funds. Faced with a growing asset base, these managers may have to increase their number of holdings, slow their trading pace, invest in larger companies, or take all of these steps. That creates a tension between the manager who takes pride in crushing the competition and the fund company, which makes more money when assets increase. (Although many fund companies are de-emphasizing asset growth when it comes to portfolio-manager compensation, fund firms sometimes get managers to share their interests by compensating them according to the amount of money they manage, not just by how well they perform. Many fund managers also own stakes in the management company, so when a fund grows large, they benefit, too.)

It's no wonder, then, that funds often close when the damage is already done. Morningstar conducted a study on just this issue and discovered that closed funds on average went from performing in the top 20% of their categories in the three years before closing to just average performance for the three years following closing.

Moreover, for every fund that saw its relative performance improve after closing, three more suffered a decline in the three years after they closed. On average, closed funds' returns relative to their peer groups fell from the top 20% to slightly below average and the median performance was a dismal 62nd percentile.

Does that mean closing a fund actually does damage? No. In fact, the performance slump probably has little to do with closing. The explanation is simply that hot funds usually cool off. While a fund may get steady inflows over most of its life, it usually closes at the point when inflows become a torrent. And that almost always happens when a fund's strategy or asset class is generating abnormally high returns. Pick any strategy that's producing big returns for a stretch and it's a good bet that performance will slide back to average or worse over the following period.

Another reason closed funds produce sluggish performance is that fund companies wait too long, failing to close until performance hits the skids or assets are gargantuan. By then, it's too late. If performance is already slumping, it may be a sign that it should have closed billions of dollars ago. Closing off new investment won't slim a fund down to its playing weight from its glory days.

Performance isn't the only factor that erodes the returns of closed funds. Their tax efficiency slumps, too. Unlike the dropoff in performance, however, this factor *is* attributable to being closed. While inflows can have negative effects on trading costs, they have a positive effect on tax efficiency. They reduce the tax burden on all shareholders because the fund distributes capital gains to more people. Morningstar found that, on average, funds' tax efficiency fell five percentage points after their closing dates.

When Closing Works

There is some good news in all this. Closing can work, if it's planned in advance. That's because the fund company gives some thought to how much money the fund can handle, then commits to closing it at that point. Most of the funds in our study, meanwhile, closed only after the company finally woke up to size problems.

If you're shopping for a fund, especially one with a concentrated portfolio, a fast-trading strategy, or a small-cap focus, look for a fund that has promised it will close when assets hit a certain predetermined level.

8. Should I Buy a Fund That's Doing Really Well?

Most investors can't help but notice funds that are up 30%, 40%, or 50% in a six-month period. Who wouldn't? But many do more than just look. They give in to temptation and buy these funds, chasing their attractive returns. Temptation like that can be hard to resist.

Buying hot funds is a bad idea. Because styles, market caps, sectors, and industries tend to move in and out of favor in the marketplace, some funds are bound to soar for short periods if the manager's style happens to be in the sweet spot. In the late 1990s, technology and large-cap growth funds skyrocketed, drawing the attention of many investors whose portfolios were tepid compared with these sizzling funds. For the past five years, small-value funds and energy and real estate offerings have been "the place to be." So is now the time to increase your portfolio's allocation of small-value funds or pick up an energy sector fund?

Not if your motivation is simply because they're hot. Here's why:

A fund that blazes in one market environment usually is as cold as ice in others. Furthermore, what's hot now has to cool off at some point. And many investors have the uncanny ability to notice what's hot right before it's ready to cool down. That's because they treat strong near-term returns as evidence that a fund is good. "Where there's smoke, there's fire," they reason. But by the time investors see enough smoke, the fire's fuel is often almost spent.

Need more proof? Morningstar studies have found that investors across all fund types—both stocks and bonds—have paid a price for buying hot funds. The damage is greater on the stock side, especially with aggressive funds, where volatility and temptation are highest. It's not surprising that in the small-growth category one Morningstar study found that investors had surrendered 1.8 percentage points of return annually over one five-year period by chasing performance instead of simply investing a little each month (dollar-cost averaging).

Look for Consistency

It's easy to get caught up in the excitement of exceptional returns. Try not to. What should you do instead? Emphasize consistent performers in your portfolio. Such funds rarely shoot out the lights, and they don't get nearly as much attention as their more volatile counterparts. What they do offer, however, is reliability and comfort. They make it easier for you to stay committed, and that often translates into good long-term returns.

A consistent fund lands in the top half to top third of its Morningstar category from one year to the next. Few funds will do that all the time, of course. But when a normally top-half fund lags, it usually isn't by very much—unlike a fund that is top of the heap one year and buried under the pile the next.

With a consistent fund, you can feel confident that no matter how its category does for a given period, your fund will be competitive. And because you'll be more comfortable with the fund, you'll be more likely to stick with it for the long haul. Investors who get caught up in chasing hot funds dump them when they turn cold.

In 1998, Morningstar did a study comparing a very consistent fund, William Blair Growth, with Delaware Trend, a more volatile but also higher-returning fund. Delaware Trend had higher 10-year returns, but when we adjusted for cash flows to reflect the typical investor's experience, William Blair Growth was superior. That's because investors found it hard to stick with Delaware Trend during the down periods; it lost as much as 43% in just three months, whereas William Blair Growth fell 25%. By missing the early stages of Delaware Trend's rebounds, investors cost themselves about three percentage points per year in returns. If you had invested $10,000, those three percentage points would have translated into $3,400 less in your pocket after 10 years.

Investors who chase hot funds usually get burned. They buy after a fund has generated big gains and sell when the fund loses steam. If you aren't the sort of investor who is thrown by a fund's gyrations, you're a rarity. Go for reliable consistency and you're likely to be more successful.

9. Should I Buy a Fund That's in the Dumps?

Astute readers may have noticed that this is a trick question. The answer depends on whether you're talking about absolute or relative performance. Though our response to the preceding question discussed how to approach funds that have generated high absolute returns, here we provide a more nuanced answer.

It depends. (How's that for nuance?)

Funds that are in the dumps in absolute terms may very well be good investments. We know that's counterintuitive, but playing against the crowd may let you catch a future trend today. Fund investors, as a group, have lousy timing. Most investors buy high and sell low, instead of the other way around. Opportunists can therefore make a bundle by buying what everyone else is selling. Morningstar's annual "Unloved Funds" study bears this out. With the "Unloved" strategy, investors buy one fund from each of the fund categories that have seen the biggest redemptions (in percentage terms) over the preceding year. We've found that these unpopular offerings outperform the S&P 500 more than 70% of the time in the ensuing three years, and these unpopular fund groups beat the three most popular fund categories 90% of the time.

If you are thinking about purchasing a fund because its category in general is lagging most others, looking for funds that are doing relatively well within that category is a good place to start your search. That said, you shouldn't necessarily exclude from your search those funds that are doing worse than their peers when the group is down. Although it's a harder call to justify purchasing such a fund, assess whether the fund does better than its peers when its style is in favor. For example, Scudder Dreman High Return Equity badly lagged its large-value peers in 1999, when large-value funds in general were being trounced by large-growth funds. However, manager David Dreman had a proven record of besting his rivals when value investing was strong, and the fund's long-term relative record was superior. Although it would have been a tough call to make at the time, investors who bought the fund in the middle of 1999 would have been handsomely compensated for signing on, since it has crushed its peers and the broader large-cap market since then.

It makes the most sense to buy a fund with sorry-looking returns when its style is not represented in your portfolio. When a fund's style, sector, or asset class is out of favor, it may provide you an opportunity to diversify your portfolio at an opportune time.

10. What Should I Do If My Fund Owns a Stock That Creates Headlines?

Wait a minute—aren't the professional managers running my money supposed to spot these problems ahead of time? That's the question many fund investors were asking during the bear market, when a number of funds were caught holding stocks of companies that imploded due to deceptive accounting or management misdeeds. Even the best managers got caught holding the stocks of headline-grabbing basket cases, from Enron to Worldcom to Healthsouth.

When one of your funds makes a big mistake with one or more of its holdings, you should ask the following three questions to figure out if it's an isolated problem or a sign that the manager just isn't doing his homework.

1. *Did the investment fit with the fund's stated strategy?* Third Avenue Value manager Marty Whitman lost some money on WorldCom debt in 2002, but there could be little doubt that the bonds fit with Whitman's strategy. He makes his living by buying stocks or bonds of companies that the market hates. He knows the ins and outs of bankruptcy laws so he can make sure he's first in line to get paid when a company goes bankrupt. He creates worst-case scenarios and will generally buy only if he thinks he won't lose money in a close-to-worst-case scenario. He bought WorldCom debt rather than stock because he figured bankruptcy was a real possibility. While Third Avenue's WorldCom investment passes this test, others don't. For example, some funds that are supposed to pay attention to valuations bought Enron near its peak when it was trading at extreme valuations. That should have been a red flag, and the fact that the company was engaging in fraudulent accounting just made matters worse.

2. *Was this an isolated incident or was the portfolio chock-full of mistakes?* Every investor makes mistakes. However, if you find a fund full of companies that were more focused on hype than building a business, you have good reason to question management's research abilities.

3. *How badly did it hurt the fund?* After you've looked at the details of a fund's mistakes, step back and get some perspective. Most funds own a good number of stocks, and a single bad investment is hardly a disaster. However, if the manager made a big bet on a stock without fully researching it, that's cause for more concern. Look at the fund's long-term record to see if the good investments outweigh the bad ones.

11. How Can I Pay Less in Taxes?

WE HAVE GOOD news and bad news. Let's start with the bad news. Even if you don't sell any shares of a fund you own during a given year, you can still end up owing Uncle Sam come April 15. By law, the fund has to distribute income and realized capital gains (gains are realized when your fund manager sells a stock at a profit) to its shareholders. Otherwise, the fund itself has to pay the taxes, and you know that isn't going to happen. (Even if it did, the money would come out of the fund's assets, so you'd still be hit.)

"But," you counter, "I elected to reinvest all my distributions. It isn't like the fund cuts me a check whenever it makes a distribution."

That doesn't matter. If you reinvest, you're getting more shares of the fund just as if the fund sent you a check and you used the money to buy those additional shares.

Don't hang your head, though. Here's the good news: There are ways to minimize the tax bite. Consider the following strategies.

Focus on Tax-Friendly Funds

If you're concerned with minimizing the taxes you pay on your investments, you'll want to avoid funds that pay out a lot of income, which is taxed at the highest rate (your ordinary-income tax rate). If you're investing in bonds and you want to minimize the taxes you pay, you should consider opting for a municipal-bond fund. Municipal-bond income is free from federal taxes, and if the bond is issued in the state where you pay taxes, it's likely free from state taxes as well.

Whether the fund pays out capital gains is another matter. Some funds have consistently minimized taxable gains, allowing investors to keep most of their pretax returns. But even funds that historically have limited taxes occasionally sell their winners. Longleaf Partners and Legg Mason Value both have good records of avoiding the tax collector, but in 1999, both funds wound up selling stocks after strong runups, leading to taxable events for shareholders.

The most reliable way to identify taxpayer-friendly funds is to look for ones with the words "tax-managed" in their names. Managers of tax-managed funds avoid income and capital-gains distributions. A lot of fund companies have introduced such funds in recent years, as investors realized that a 30% gain isn't so great if tax bills leave you with just two thirds of it in hand. Vanguard offers a variety of tax-managed choices covering different investment styles. Fidelity, American Century, Eaton Vance, and T. Rowe Price are a few of the other fund families with tax-managed offerings.

Sell Specific Shares

When you sell shares in a fund, your taxable gain is determined by subtracting the price you paid for your fund shares (your cost basis) from the sale price. Say you dollar-cost averaged into a fund, thereby picking up shares at different prices. What's your cost basis when you sell? For most fund companies, the default cost basis is the average price you paid for your shares. (The IRS' default cost basis is the price you paid for your first shares—not surprising, given that that method usually results in the highest taxable gain!)

Many investors can save on taxes by identifying which specific shares they'd like to sell. Suppose that your average cost basis in a fund is $10, but you recently purchased individual shares with a cost basis of $16. If your fund now sells for $20 per share, you'd have a much lower taxable gain by selling the shares with the $16 cost basis than by using the default $10 cost basis.

The specific-shares method involves a lot more record keeping and hassle than the default average-cost method, but the tax savings may be worth it. You can apply this rule only to funds on which you've never sold shares using the average-cost method because once you use that method on a fund, the IRS requires that you continue to use it.

Sell Purposefully

Suppose you own a fund that's been a longtime loser. In fact, it has underperformed to the extent that you have a loss on your investment. Think about using that loss to your advantage. Sometimes we hang on to funds that we don't particularly like and that aren't performing well because we want to break even on our investment. Instead, consider selling the clunker and using the loss to offset gains elsewhere in your taxable portfolio.

Shelter Like Crazy

Take full advantage of all the tax-deferral options available to you, whether they are 401(k)s, 403(b)s, or IRAs. Once you've contributed the maximum amount to those accounts, you should consider a tax-managed fund. And if you buy individual stocks, your taxable account is a good place to hold them. When you put together a stock portfolio, you have complete control over when to sell a holding. That's a key advantage over mutual funds, which pay out capital gains regardless of whether you've sold a single share. Exchange-traded funds are also generally more tax efficient than conventional mutual funds. That's because ETFs trade on an exchange, meaning that the ETF fund manager doesn't have to sell shares (potentially realizing taxable capital gains) to meet investor redemptions.

12. How Can I Determine Whether a Fund Is Best for a Taxable Account or a Tax-Sheltered Account?

Between 1999 and 2001, the typical investor with a mutual fund in a taxable account kept only $77.50 of every $100 he or she earned in returns: The rest went to taxes. And that figure is based just on the income and capital gains distributions that funds made; it doesn't factor in any additional damage investors might have done by realizing gains themselves.

As we noted in the answer to Question 11, it usually makes sense to stash funds that pay a lot of income in your tax-sheltered accounts. But even that principle doesn't apply in every situation—instead, it depends on who you are and how close you are to drawing on your money.

To help determine what types of funds investors should hold in what types of accounts, the tax experts at T. Rowe Price looked at three varieties of funds: growth, growth and income, and taxable bond. They assumed $10,000 investments in each fund, with holding periods of 10, 15, and 20 years. They also assumed that the accounts were cashed in at the end of the period. The tax specialists ran the numbers for all income-tax rates. The study showed that your holding period, your expected tax rate when you cash in the account, and whether the account is tax deferred (i.e., a traditional IRA) or allows tax-free withdrawals (i.e., the Roth IRA) are the key determinants of where tax sheltering will work best for you.

Guidelines

The conclusions from T. Rowe Price's study can be boiled down to three essential rules for the kinds of investments that should have tax protection.

1. The closer you are to retirement and the higher your tax rate will be in retirement, the better off you'll be putting your bond funds in tax-protected accounts and your stock funds in taxable accounts. There are two subsections to this rule:
    a. If you have 15 years or more until retirement and expect to be in a lower tax bracket then, protect your stock funds from taxes and keep your bond funds in taxable accounts.

b. If your retirement is fewer than 15 years off and you expect to be in a higher tax bracket in retirement than you are now, seek tax protection for your bond funds and store the stock funds in taxable accounts.

2. Because the Roth IRA permits tax-free withdrawals, put your stock funds in a Roth account, no matter what your time horizon and expected tax bracket are. Stock funds should make significantly higher long-term gains than bond funds, and a Roth ensures that you won't be taxed on those big gains.

3. If you are investing in a tax-deferred account such as a traditional IRA instead of a Roth, tax-managed and other tax-efficient stock funds should go into taxable accounts. Such funds avoid capital-gains distributions. If you hold them in a traditional IRA, your withdrawals will be taxed at your income-tax level, which will always be higher than the capital-gains rate you would pay when cashing in a taxable stock fund.

13. How Can I Find the Best Fund Supermarket?

In your grandparents' day, they had to visit the butcher, the baker, the green-grocer, and maybe even the druggist and the bootlegger to get everything they needed. Now we can get all those things—and a lot more—in a supermarket. Fund supermarkets share one of the best features of real supermarkets—they offer all kinds of stuff in one place.

What a Supermarket Is

A fund supermarket offers investors a one-stop shop for buying funds, with thousands of different funds typically available. Charles Schwab was one of the first brokers to offer a supermarket service, and now Fidelity, Vanguard, numerous other fund companies, and most major brokers offer their own versions. Typically, you'll find two kinds of funds in a supermarket: those for which there is no load and no transaction fee (NTF is the fund industry's shorthand) and those for which there is a load or transaction fee (or both).

The Advantages of Supermarkets

The main appeal of the fund supermarket is its convenience. Setting up a no-load mutual-fund account isn't very difficult to do, but if you buy your funds from several different fund companies, you have to go through the same steps multiple times. If you use a supermarket, you only have to set up one account. Moreover, it's generally simpler to switch funds within the same supermarket than it is to move your money among different fund companies.

Not only does a supermarket allow you to buy your funds in one location, but you also get consolidated reports on them. That's a huge plus, especially at tax time. Totaling up short-term and long-term gains from six different funds is a hassle. All fund companies have to report the same information on their 1099 forms (which show you the amount of income and capital gains you've earned from your investments), yet no two forms are laid out in the same way. You have to scrutinize them carefully to make sure you enter the right information on your tax forms.

Even if you don't care much about convenience, you might still find that a supermarket has something for you. Say you're interested in a particular fund but can't begin to meet the minimum investment requirement. Supermarkets will often let you into that fund for a much lower minimum because their investors' assets, pooled together, can easily meet that fund's minimum.

The Big Catch

So what's the catch? The real drawback to any fund supermarket is that funds have to pay for shelf space—they have to pay for the exposure they get from being part of the supermarket's lineup of funds. That adds to a fund's annual expenses, and those expenses come out of the returns on your money. You might think of that fee as the price you pay for convenience.

What's really annoying, though, is that investors pay for the convenience no matter how they buy the fund. If a fund is among Schwab's NTF funds, for example, you pay the supermarket fee even if you buy the fund directly from the fund company. Now that's irritating. To its credit, Davis/Selected Advisers, one of Morningstar's favorite fund shops, recently rolled out a non-supermarket share class of Selected American Shares that's far cheaper than the supermarket share class. In so doing, it enabled investors who buy directly from Davis/Selected to circumvent the supermarket fee. The firm didn't spark a trend, though: Nearly every other fund shop that sells its funds through a supermarket charges a fee to all shareholders, not just the supermarket shoppers.

In addition, most supermarkets offer online trading, and with so many funds from so many families that invest in so many different things, the temptation is great. But trading too much can hurt your portfolio's overall performance.

So Where Should I Shop?

Generally speaking, bigger is better. Beyond the convenience of consolidated statements and one-stop shopping, savvy investors want choices, and in particular, they want the greatest possible number of offerings that don't carry transaction fees (so-called NTF funds). There's no sense signing up for an account with a fund supermarket if it doesn't offer that fund you plan to use as the centerpiece of your portfolio, for example.

So sample the wares to decide which supermarket is right for you. Once you have a grip on what a supermarket with lots of breadth and depth looks like, you'll be in a better position to assess the competition.

14. How Do I Read a Fund's Prospectus?

Be warned: These documents aren't light reading. They can be packed with legal jargon, convoluted sentences, and boilerplate information to fulfill the Securities and Exchange Commission's disclosure requirements and to protect fund companies from legal liabilities. But if you're thinking about buying a fund, the prospectus is an important document. Reading it should help you understand a fund's investment policy, the amount of investment flexibility it has, what it owns, who runs it, and how it has performed.

The prospectus tells you how to open an account (including the minimum amount of money you'll need to open one), how to buy and sell shares, and how to contact shareholder services. But more important, you'll find the six things you absolutely need to know about a fund before you decide to buy shares in the first place.

Investment Objective

The investment objective is the mutual fund's purpose in life. Is the fund seeking to make money over the long term? Or is it trying to provide its shareholders regular income each month? If you're investing for a young child's education, you'll want the former. If you're retired and looking for a monthly dividend check, you'll want the latter. But investment objectives can be notoriously vague. Therefore, check out the next section.

Strategy

The prospectus also describes the types of stocks, bonds, or other securities in which the fund plans to invest. (It does not list the exact stocks that the fund owns, though. You'll find that list in the shareholder report.) Stock funds spell out the kinds of companies they look for, such as small, fast-growing firms or big, well-established corporations. Bond funds specify what sorts of bonds they generally hold, such as Treasury or corporate bonds. If the fund can invest in foreign securities, the prospectus says so. Most (but not all) restrictions on what the fund can invest in are also mentioned. Morningstar analysts value this section because it gives them a sense of what constraints the fund manager has and can expose the possibility of unexpected investments, such as shorting stocks, down the road.

Be warned, though. It's not unusual for funds to give a laundry list in the prospectus of all the possible things they could invest in. You shouldn't assume that the fund invests in all the types of securities mentioned. Prospectuses are written very broadly, so they don't always give you a specific idea of how the fund typically invests.

Risks

This section may be the most important one in the prospectus. Every investment has risks associated with it and a prospectus must explain these risks. A prospectus for a fund that invests in emerging markets reveals that the fund is likely to be riskier than a fund that invests in developed countries. Bond-fund prospectuses typically discuss the credit quality of the bonds in the fund's portfolio, as well as how a change in interest rates might affect the value of its holdings. A fund should spell out all the potential risks of its strategy, even if it has a solid track record.

Expenses

It costs money to invest in a mutual fund, and different funds have different fees. A table at the front of every prospectus makes it easy to compare the cost of one fund with another. Here, you'll find the sales commission the fund charges, if any, for buying or selling shares. The prospectus also tells you, in percentage terms, the amount deducted from the fund's assets each year to pay for management fees and operational costs. It even shows the estimated cost of owning the fund over projected 1-, 3-, 5-, and 10-year periods. Those dollar amounts assume that you invested $10,000 at the beginning of the year, that the fund's underlying fee structure stays the same, and that the fund returns 5% per year. The Financial Highlights section of the prospectus—usually found toward the end—also gives you historical expense data for the past five years.

Note: A fund's actual expenses might be lower than the numbers in the prospectus, particularly if its asset base is growing. If there is a shareholder report with a more recent date than the prospectus, be sure to check it for the most current picture (look for the Financial Highlights section, toward the end of the report). Conversely, funds sometimes issue prospectus supplements that change their fee levels going forward. Such supplements should give you the most accurate picture of a fund's future expense ratio.

Past Performance

As fund companies always point out in their ads, "Past performance cannot guarantee future results." But it can suggest how consistent a fund's returns have been. A chart known as the Financial Highlights or Per Share Data Table, provides the fund's total return for each of the past 10 years, along with some other useful information. It also breaks out the fund's income distributions, expense ratios, and turnover ratios, and provides year-end NAVs.

For funds with more than one year of performance history, prospectuses are required to include a bar chart depicting returns for each of the last 10 calendar years. If the fund has been around less than 10 years, the bar chart will cover the life of the fund. This chart can give you a handle on the magnitude of a fund's ups and downs over time. Below the chart, the fund must disclose its highest and lowest quarterly return during the period covered by the chart. The prospectus may also use a graph showing how $10,000 invested in a fund would have grown over time (also known as a mountain graph, because the peaks and valleys resemble a mountain range) or a table comparing the fund's performance to indexes or other benchmarks to present return information. Finally, the fund's average annual returns over the past 1, 5, and 10 years will be displayed in a table following the chart(s). (Unless otherwise stated, total-return numbers do not take sales charges into account.)

Be wary of comparisons between the fund and a self-selected benchmark. A fund company is motivated to present its offerings in the best possible light. There are guidelines to prevent the fund company from grossly misleading investors, but there's no guarantee that the fund will pick the most appropriate peer group against which to compare returns. Use an independent third party like Morningstar to ensure that you get appropriate comparisons.

Fund prospectuses are also required to provide tax-adjusted return information. This information can be found in the table of returns following the bar chart just discussed. It deserves your attention if you're going to hold the fund in a taxable account. You will see returns labeled Return before Taxes, Return after Taxes on Distributions, and Return after Taxes on Distribution and Sale of Fund Shares for 1-, 5-, and 10-year periods.

The first set of returns is just the total return, not adjusted for taxes. The next set shows what investors keep after paying taxes on any income or capital-gains distributions that the fund made. If a fund earns income from bonds or dividend-paying stocks that it owns, or sells a security at a profit, it is required to distribute that money to shareholders. Most shareholders choose to reinvest and get more shares instead of a check, but they still have to pay taxes on the distribution. The last set of returns is what investors would have kept after selling their shares of the fund and paying taxes on any gains they made from the fund. These calculations all assume that the investor is taxed at the highest federal rate, and they don't take state taxes into account.

Management

The Management section provides details about the folks who will be putting your money to work. Until very recently, funds were able to get away with not telling you who was actually running your fund. Instead, they could simply list "management team." No more. Prospectuses filed on or after February 28, 2005, must disclose the name, title, length of service, and business experience of the persons responsible for the day-to-day management of the fund. The disclosure only applies to the five team members with the most responsibility, but this should easily cover the entire management team of most funds.

Be sure to check how long the current manager has been running the fund. If much of the fund's past record was achieved under someone else, the fund's past performance may not tell you anything about the current manager's abilities or style. Find out whether the manager has run other funds in the past. A peek at those funds could give you some clues about the manager's investment style and past success.

15. What Do I Need to Know About the Statement of Additional Information?

While the prospectus is packed with important information, it shouldn't be your sole source of data on a fund. A fund's Statement of Additional Information (SAI) contains more useful tidbits about the fund's inner workings. Be sure to ask for this document specifically when you call for information on a fund: Fund companies routinely send out prospectuses and annual reports, but they don't treat SAIs as comparably important documents. Some fund companies are now making their funds' SAIs available on their Web sites.

If fund families think SAIs are secondary, why bother requesting one? For starters, the SAI often provides far more detail than the prospectus about what the fund can and cannot invest in. For another, this document is usually the place where you can find out who represents your interests on the fund's board of directors, how much you pay them, the number of funds they oversee (fewer is better), and whether they invest in the funds they're responsible for (if they don't, it's a red flag).

Since early 2005, SAIs have also been required to include key information about how the fund's manager(s) are compensated. They will tell you, for example, whether managers are paid based on short-term returns (usually bad), long-term returns (usually good), and/or asset growth (bad). It will also tell you how much money the managers run in other accounts and whether those accounts have performance-based fees—a potential conflict of interest. Finally, it will disclose how much money each manager has invested in the fund that he or she runs, within preset dollar ranges (again, if a manager has little money invested in the fund he or she runs, it could be cause for concern).

Finally, you can find more details about your fund's expenses here. Shareholders in Brandywine Fund would not know they shelled out $31 million in brokerage fees in 2004 unless they had read the fund's SAIs. (Brokerage fees are the cost a fund incurs to buy and sell securities, and they're not included as part of the expense ratio.) SAIs also break down where 12b-1 fees go, if the fund charges them. (These are fees that the fund can use for marketing, rewarding brokers, and attracting more investors.)

16. How Do I Read a Fund's Shareholder Report?

A mutual fund's shareholder report is part biography, part blueprint, and part ledger book.

A good shareholder report is like a biography in that it sets out what happened to the fund over the past quarter, six months, or year, and why. It's like a blueprint because it sets before you all the investments—stocks, bonds, and other securities—that the fund has made. And it's like a ledger book because it discloses a fund's costs, profits, and many other financial facts. Mutual funds are required to release a shareholder report at least twice a year, although some fund families publish them quarterly. Starting in late 2004, mutual funds have also been required to file their complete portfolio with the SEC on a quarterly basis.

Not all the items discussed here are required by law to appear in a mutual fund's report. The SEC allows some of the information to be included in other documents, such as a fund's prospectus or Statement of Additional Information. However, a good report will contain all of the following elements.

Letter from the President

Usually, the first item you'll find in a shareholder report is the letter from the president of the company that advises, or runs, your fund. The best letters will contain straightforward, useful discussions of the economic trends that have affected the markets during the past 6 or 12 months. This discussion provides some context for evaluating your fund. If you own a fund run by a big firm, however, you shouldn't expect to see much detail about your own individual fund in this section.

Letter from the Portfolio Manager

Similar to the president's letter, this letter is much more specific to the fund, and therefore much more important to you as a shareholder. Because the Sarbanes-Oxley Act may make fund managers criminally liable for any misstatements in the shareholder report, many fund shops now include only a bare-bones letter in the report, but send a separate letter to shareholders that is more detailed, though not technically a part of the report. These letters are also often available on fund company Web sites.

Well-written shareholder letters discuss individual stocks that the fund owns and industries to which it is exposed. Third Avenue Value manager Marty

Whitman writes exemplary shareholder letters every three months. In these letters, he describes which stocks he has sold, bought, or left alone, and why.

A good manager letter will also explain what fueled or hindered your fund's performance. The Weitz Funds' shareholder letters are noteworthy in this regard. The June 2002 semiannual report for Weitz Value bluntly stated: "After bucking the downtrend in the market for the past two years, we 'participated' (all too fully) in the decline in the second quarter of 2002." The letter goes on to explain that Adelphia's accounting fraud cost the fund about 3% of its assets. The fund also lost about 5% due to its investment in Qwest Communications.

Finally, a good shareholder letter should indicate what you can expect from the fund in the future, given the manager's strategy.

Performance Information

After reading your manager's comments, look to see how the fund has performed. A good report will compare your fund's performance to a benchmark, such as the S&P 500 index (the standard benchmark for large-company funds) or the Russell 2000 index (for small-company funds), as well as to the average performance of funds with similar investment strategies.

When evaluating your fund's performance, make sure that the benchmark the fund has chosen is appropriate for its style. A technology fund should not compare itself to the S&P 500 and nothing else; it should measure its performance against a technology benchmark.

In addition to comparing your fund's performance to a relevant yardstick's, a good report should give you an idea of how the fund has performed over various time frames, both short and long term. If you hold the fund in a taxable account, be sure to check its tax-adjusted returns. While these may also appear in the prospectus, you'll get the latest numbers in the shareholder report.

Reviewing Portfolio Holdings

Fund shareholder reports often call attention to the portfolio's largest holdings and provide some information about what these companies do or why the manager owns them. Some reports will also indicate, in the form of a pie chart or table, how portfolio assets are distributed among market sectors. International funds usually break out the portfolio's country exposure, too.

This general overview is complemented in most cases by a complete list of the fund's portfolio holdings—including stocks, bonds, and cash—as of the date of the report. These holdings are usually itemized by industry. (Foreign funds may break down their holdings by country.) Even though you might not recognize all the names of the stocks in the portfolio, this listing is useful if you're wondering whether the fund is holding many names in a specific industry or is making a few selected bets. And if you can't recognize the companies in a given fund's portfolio, that tells you something, too—namely, that the fund isn't sticking exclusively to the stocks of household-name companies. Funds have recently been permitted to list only their top 50 holdings, plus any affiliated holdings that are more than 1% of the portfolio, in the shareholder report, but few firms seem to be going this route. In any case, all funds must file their complete holdings with the SEC every fiscal quarter. These are available at www.sec.gov. Look for forms N-CSR, N-CSRS, and N-Q.

Board of Directors and Advisory Contract Approval

The shareholder report includes a list of the fund's directors (the SAI, discussed previously, contains much more information about the board). All reports covering periods that end on or after March 31, 2005, will also have to include a detailed description of the factors the board considered in approving the fund's contract with its management company (if it was approved during the period covered by the report), and the conclusions the board drew with regard to each factor. Depending on the level of detail presented, this may help you decide if the board is looking out for your best interests.

Footnotes

Don't forget to read the fine print. In the footnotes, you can find out if the fund managers are practicing such strategies as shorting stocks or hedging currencies, which can significantly affect the fund's performance.

Footnotes can also provide insights into particular portfolio holdings. The footnotes of Baron Asset's, September 30, 2004, report revealed that the fund held large enough stakes in some stocks that they were deemed "affiliates," meaning that the fund had a special ownership relationship with those firms. Other stocks were noted as restricted securities, which means they're more difficult to trade than common stocks. Because it's harder for the manager to get rid of these stocks if something goes wrong, they can spell greater risk for the fund.

Financial Statements

A fund's annual report concludes with its financial statements. Brace yourself: There's considerable data here, and it's not usually placed within any kind of useful context. Morningstar gets a lot of its data from this part of the report.

If you want to dig into the raw numbers, here's what you should focus on. First, examine the Financial Highlights section of the report, which is usually the last page of actual information, located just before the legal discussion of accounting practices. Here you'll find the fund's NAVs, expense ratios, and portfolio turnover rates for each of the past five years (or more). Check to see whether the fund's expense ratio has gone down over time (this should happen if the fund's assets under management have been increasing) and whether its turnover rate has changed much over time (if so, you may want to find out why—did the manager change his or her strategy?).

Cost-conscious investors can check out the breakdown of a fund's expenses, including management fees, under the Statement of Operations. Finally, find out how much unrealized or undistributed capital gains a fund has in the Statement of Assets and Liabilities. These figures can be the key to a fund's future tax efficiency.

A gain is unrealized when a stock has gone up in price but the fund manager hasn't sold it. When the fund sells the stock, that's a realized gain, which has to be distributed to shareholders. This means that if a fund has a lot of unrealized or undistributed gains, you will get socked with the tax consequences when the fund realizes this gain. High unrealized capital gains don't necessarily spell trouble, though. Funds can accumulate unrealized gains precisely because the manager has been trying to limit taxable distributions. Do be cautious, however, if a fund with a big unrealized gain has recently had a manager change or strategy change or shareholders have been cashing in. A change of strategy or manager could mean the fund will begin dumping the existing holdings and realizing the gains, which could spell a big tax hit. Likewise, if shareholder redemptions are large enough, the manager may be forced to sell stocks to raise cash and incur taxable gains in the process.

What to Do

You can request a prospectus, SAI, or annual report by phone, by mail, and sometimes by e-mail. Most fund companies also make their fund literature available for download at their Web sites. All mutual funds have to file their prospectuses and reports (and a host of other documents) with the SEC. You can view these at the SEC's Web site: www.sec.gov.

Although we suggest that you begin your fund evaluation with these documents, don't stop there. Seek out third-party sources, such as Morningstar, to help put your fund into context. Compare it with other funds that do similar things. You need to see how its costs stack up, if its performance is competitive, and if it compensates for the risks it is taking on.

Appendix 2

AT MORNINGSTAR, WE'RE huge advocates of low-cost investing, which means trading infrequently. One of the best ways to find companies that can stay in your portfolio for a long time is to look for firms with strong competitive advantages, or wide economic moats. The list that follows contains all of the companies in Morningstar's coverage universe that we think fit this description—ones that are likely to keep competitors at bay for years to come. It's not an exhaustive list, of course, but it's a great starting point if you're looking for high-quality companies to put on your watchlist.

Sector	Wide Moat Company	TTM Sales ($Millions)
Health Care	Abbott Laboratories (ABT)	18,076
	Alcon (ACL)	3,009
	Amgen (AMGN)	5,523
	AstraZeneca PLC ADR (AZN)	17,841
	Biomet (BMET)	1,290
	Boston Scientific (BSX)	3,051
	Bristol-Myers Squibb (BMY)	18,169
	Eli Lilly & Company (LLY)	11,406
	Genentech (DNA)	2,901

(Continued)

Sector	Wide Moat Company	TTM Sales ($Millions)
Health Care (cont.)	GlaxoSmithKline PLC ADR (GSK)	29,541
	Guidant (GDT)	3,415
	Biogen IDEC	442
	Johnson & Johnson (JNJ)	37,376
	Medtronic (MDT)	7,309
	Merck (MRK)	53,009
	Novartis AG ADR (NVS)	18,933
	Pfizer (PFE)	33,151
	Sanofi-Synthelabo ADR (SNY)	5,785
	Schering-Plough (SGP)	10,381
	Stryker (SYK)	3,156
	UnitedHealth Group (UNH)	25,982
	Zimmer Holdings (ZMH)	1,443
Consumer Services	H&R Block (HRB)	3,742
	Home Depot (HD)	58,247
	Lowe's Companies (LOW)	26,491
	Sysco (SYY)	25,479
	Wal-Mart Stores (WMT)	246,525
	Walgreen (WAG)	30,564
	eBay (EBAY)	1,445
Business Services	Automatic Data Processing (ADP)	7,081
	Cintas (CTAS)	2,614
	Equifax (EFX)	1,152
	Expeditors International of WA (EXPD)	2,404
	First Data (FDC)	7,905
	Fiserv (FISV)	2,644
	Getty Images (GYI)	479
	IMS Health (RX)	1,452
	Moody's (MCO)	1,070
	Paychex (PAYX)	1,054
	Total System Services (TSS)	955
	United Parcel Service B (UPS)	31,708
Financial Services, Insurance/Asset Management	AFLAC (AFL)	10,693
	Alliance Capital Management Holding LP (AC)	167
	American Express (AXP)	24,071
	Berkshire Hathaway (BRK.B)	44,255
	Blackrock (BLK)	574
	Eaton Vance (EV)	512

(Continued)

Sector	Wide Moat Company	TTM Sales ($Millions)
Financial Services, Insurance/Asset Management (cont.)	Marsh & McLennan Companies (MMC)	10,440
	Progressive (PGR)	9,946
	SLM (SLM)	3,119
Financial Services, Banks/Finance	Bank of New York (BK)	5,697
	Capital One Financial (COF)	9,883
	Citigroup (C)	93,101
	Fannie Mae (FNM)	53,470
	Fifth Third Bancorp (FITB)	6,937
	Freddie Mac (FRE)	8,986
	Northern Trust (NTRS)	2,709
	State Street (STT)	5,383
	Wells Fargo (WFC)	28,881
Software	Adobe Systems (ADBE)	1,194
	Autodesk (ADSK)	825
	Intuit (INTU)	1,495
	Microsoft (MSFT)	31,375
Hardware	Applied Materials (AMAT)	5,116
	Cisco Systems (CSCO)	19,005
	Dell Computers (DELL)	35,404
	IBM (IBM)	83,221
	Intel (INTC)	26,734
	Linear Technology (LLTC)	582
	Maxim Integrated Products (MXIM)	1,138
	Qualcomm (QCOM)	3,785
Media	Comcast A (CMCSA)	12,460
	Dow Jones & Company (DJ)	1,525
	John Wiley & Sons A (JW.A)	840
	McGraw-Hill Companies (MHP)	4,804
	Washington Post (WPO)	2,584
Telecommunications	None	
Consumer Goods	Altria Group (MO)	79,224
	Anheuser-Busch Companies (BUD)	13,710
	Avon Products (AVP)	6,326
	Cedar Fair LP (FUN)	503
	Coca-Cola (KO)	19,983
	Colgate-Palmolive (CL)	9,448

(Continued)

Sector	Wide Moat Company	TTM Sales ($Millions)
Consumer Goods (cont.)	Gillette (G)	8,692
	Harley-Davidson (HDI)	4,517
	Hershey Foods (HSY)	4,085
	International Speedway A (ISCA)	556
	PepsiCo (PEP)	25,331
	Procter & Gamble (PG)	42,626
	Wm. Wrigley Jr. (WWY)	2,820
Industrial Materials	3M Company (MMM)	16,760
	General Dynamics (GD)	14,148
	Gentex (GNTX)	422
	Pitney Bowes (PBI)	4,451
	United Technologies (UTX)	28,540
Energy	Kinder Morgan (KMI)	1,081
	Kinder Morgan Energy Partners (KMP)	5,796
Utilities	None	

Wide moat companies within each sector. *Source:* Morningstar, Inc.

Recommended Readings

THESE ARE SOME of our favorite books on investing and mutual funds.

The Great Mutual Fund Trap: An Investment Recovery Plan, by Gregory Arthur Baer and Robert Gensler (Broadway, 2002). Authors assert—quite correctly—that many mutual fund investors are paying unnecessarily high fees.

Capital Ideas: The Improbable Origins of Modern Wall Street, by Peter Bernstein (Free Press, 1993). A lively look at the marriage of academic research and Wall Street.

The Intelligent Asset Allocator: How to Build Your Portfolio to Maximize Returns and Minimize Risk, by William J. Bernstein (McGraw-Hill, 2000). Using a commonsense style, Bernstein discusses the fundamentals of building a diversified portfolio without the aid of a financial advisor.

The Four Pillars of Investing: Lessons for Building a Winning Portfolio, by William J. Bernstein (McGraw-Hill, 2002). More practical advice on constructing a winning portfolio.

Common Sense on Mutual Funds: New Imperatives for the Intelligent Investor, by John C. Bogle (John Wiley & Sons, 2000). The best book on mutual funds, period.

Capital: The Story of Long-Term Investment Excellence, by Charles Ellis (John Wiley & Sons, 2004). A detailed history of Capital Research & Management, parent company to the American Funds.

Asset Allocation: Balancing Financial Risk, by Roger C. Gibson (McGraw-Hill Trade, 2000). An essential text that has influenced a whole generation of financial advisors.

The Intelligent Investor: The Definitive Book on Value Investing, Revised Edition, by Benjamin Graham and Jason Zweig (HarperBusiness, 2003). The wisdom in this book still resonates decades after its publication; in this edition, Jason Zweig provides insightful footnoted comments.

Security Analysis: The Classic 1940 Edition, by Benjamin Graham and David L. Dodd (McGraw-Hill, 2002). This book is considered the bible of investing by many top mutual fund managers.

The Interpretation of Financial Statements, by Benjamin Graham and Spencer Meredith (HarperBusiness, 1998). This slim volume neatly summarizes an often-confusing topic.

A Purely American Invention: The U.S. Open-End Mutual Fund Industry, by Lee Gremillion (National Investment Co. Service Association, 2000). A comprehensive behind-the-scenes look at the mutual fund industry.

Buffett: The Making of an American Capitalist, by Roger Lowenstein (Main Street Books, 1996). A great biography. You cannot call yourself a serious investor and not be a student of Buffett.

When Genius Failed: The Rise and Fall of Long-Term Capital Management, by Roger Lowenstein (Random House Trade, 2001). A history of Long-Term Capital Management, a hedge fund that almost single-handedly destabilized the stock market.

One Up on Wall Street: How to Use What You Already Know to Make Money in the Market, by Peter Lynch (Simon & Schuster, 2000). This classic is one of the most accessible books on picking individual stocks.

A Random Walk Down Wall Street: Completely Revised and Updated Eighth Edition, by Burton G. Malkiel (W.W. Norton & Company, 2004). Makes the case for indexing and shows how much of what we attribute as brilliance among managers may really be random chance.

The Wall Street Journal Guide to Understanding Money & Investing, Third Edition, by Kenneth M. Morris and Virginia B. Morris (Fireside, 2004). This easily skimmed, user-friendly guide provides novices with solid money and market information.

The New Commonsense Guide to Mutual Funds, by Mary Rowland (Bloomberg Press, 1998). Rowland's guide is the perfect choice if you would rather not spend a lot of time reading about funds—or want to read about them in short, digestible chunks.

The Money Game, by Adam Smith (Vintage, 1976). While the attitudes are dated, this remains a great history.

The Only Investment Guide You'll Ever Need, by Andrew Tobias (Harvest Books, 2005). A great introduction to thinking about the key trade-offs of personal finance.

The Money Masters, The New Money Masters, and Money Masters of Our Time, by John Train (HarperBusiness, 1994, 2003). Wonderful introductions to some of the best money managers ever.

Morningstar Resources

IN ADDITION TO this book, Morningstar publishes a number of products about mutual funds and stocks, with something for everyone, from newsletters to sourcebooks. Most can be found at your local library, or you can call Morningstar to start your own subscriptions (866-608-9570).

Fearless Investing Series: Mutual Funds Workbooks
This three-part workbook series coaches investors on the ins and outs of using mutual funds in their portfolios. The first workbook, Find the Right Mutual Funds, focuses on the key questions to ask when selecting a fund, while the second workbook, Diversify Your Fund Portfolio, discusses how you can maximize your portfolio's risk/reward profile by achieving adequate diversification. The third and final workbook in the series, Maximize Your Fund Returns, shows how to use more specialized funds in your portfolio and also tells how to prepare your portfolio for varying market conditions.

Morningstar® StockInvestor™
Monthly newsletter offers 32 pages of stock investing help—including two Morningstar stock portfolios for different investment styles, comprehensive

analysis of selected portfolio stocks, as well as the best thinking of Morningstar's 30 stock analysts on additional stock prospects, including what to buy or sell.

Morningstar® Buy/Sell Report

Morningstar's new eight-page newsletter tells readers which stocks to buy and which ones to sell—and most importantly, why. In addition, each month the editors recap their previous picks and any changes in their opinions or our analyses that investors need to know about.

Morningstar® Mutual Funds™

This twice-monthly report service features full-page financial reports and analysis of 1,600 funds specially selected for building and maintaining balanced portfolios. Our report service is favored by professionals and serious investors and carried in more than 4,000 libraries nationwide. Trial subscriptions are available. Christine Benz is the editor.

Morningstar® FundInvestor™

Monthly newsletter offers 48 pages of fund investing help, including cutting-edge research, analysis of funds, funds to avoid, the FundInvestor 500, and Morningstar Analyst Picks. Russel Kinnel is the editor.

Morningstar.com

Our Web site features investing information on funds, stocks, bonds, retirement planning, and more. In addition to powerful portfolio tools, you'll find daily articles by Morningstar analysts and editors, including Christine Benz and Pat Dorsey. Much information on the site is free, and there's a reasonably priced Premium Membership service for investors requiring more in-depth information and sophisticated analytical tools, which you can try for free for 14 days.

Morningstar® Stocks 500™

Annual book of full-page reports on 500 of the best and most popular stocks. The new edition appears in January of each year and includes complete year-end results of stocks covered, comprehensive financial data, and key data on industry performance.

Morningstar® Funds 500™
An annual book of full-page reports on 500 selected funds. The new edition appears in January of each year. It includes complete year-end results of funds covered, as well as general fund industry performance information. Christine Benz and Russel Kinnel are the editors.

The Five Rules for Successful Stock Investing: Morningstar's Guide to Building Wealth and Winning in the Market
In this hardcover book, released in 2004, Morningstar's director of stock analysis, Pat Dorsey, imparts advice for selecting winning stocks for your portfolio and avoiding the most common investment mistakes. The book includes a thorough discussion of how to invest well in a variety of industries, from banks to technology to consumer products.

Index

A

Abercrombie & Fitch, 235, 256
ABN AMRO/Montag & Caldwell
    Growth, 97, 99
Absolute-value funds, 90–92
Accounting, 341–351
    accrual, 268–269
    aggressive, 341
    capitalizing versus expensing costs,
        350
    cash flow problems, 342, 347–348
    change in credit terms and accounts
        receivable, 345
    change in practices, 349–350
    checklist, 351
    fraud, 341
    increase in accounts receivable, 344
    inventory increases, 348–349
    investment gains, 345
    pension plan problems, 346–347
    profits, 274–275
    resignation of key parties, 343–344
    serial acquirers, 343
    serial chargers, 343
Accounts payable, 286
Accounts receivable, 281–282, 344,
    345

Accrual accounting, 268–269
Acorn funds, 55–56. *See also* Wanger
    Asset Management
Acquisitions, 310–311, 333–334, 338,
    343
Actively versus passively managed funds,
    104–112. *See also* Index funds
    costs, 109
    exchange-traded funds, 109–112
    foreign funds, 106
    indexes that funds follow, 107–108
    large-cap funds, 105–106
    mid-cap funds, 106
    small-cap funds, 106
    tax effects, 108–109
Adelphia Communications, 87–88
Adobe, 263
Advanced Micro Devices (AMD), 258,
    381–390
    bear case, 386
    economic moat, 382–384
    financial health, 385–386
    growth, 384
    management, 386–387
    profitability, 383, 384–385
    valuation, 387–390
Aegis Value Fund, 9
Aetna, 89

10 Free Morningstar Analyst Reports

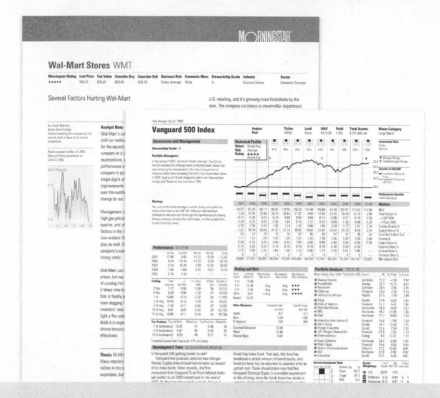

Choose from more than 3,000 Stocks and Funds

Morningstar Analyst Reports provide comprehensive investment analysis. Reports include Morningstar analysts' detailed written opinion. Information includes exclusive Morningstar tools, such as star ratings for stocks and funds, economic moat ratings for stocks, up to 12 years of financial data, and much more.

Normally reports sell for $10 each. But you can get 10 free reports—a $100 value—when you purchase this book!

To get your FREE Analyst Reports:

▶ Purchase this book

▶ Save your store receipt

▶ Go to this Web site and enter the information requested

http://www.morningstar.com/bookoffer

▶ Choose 10 stock or fund reports, or a combination of both